After Mao

The Harvard Contemporary China Series is designed to present new research that deals with present-day issues against the background of Chinese history and society. Books in this series will be published promptly enough to suit the timeliness of the subjects, and economically enough to be affordable. The focus will be on interdisciplinary research. The intention is to convey the significance of the rapidly changing Chinese scene.

Harvard East Asian Monographs, 115
Harvard Contemporary China Series: 1

edited by

JEFFREY C. KINKLEY

Published by
THE COUNCIL ON EAST ASIAN STUDIES / HARVARD UNIVERSITY
Distributed by The Harvard University Press
Cambridge (Massachusetts) and London 1990

After Mao

Chinese Literature and Society 1978-1981

The Council on East Asian Studies at Harvard University
publishes a monograph series and, through the Fairbank Center
for East Asian Research and the Japan Institute, administers
research projects designed to further scholarly understanding
of China, Japan, Korea, Vietnam, Inner Asia, and adjacent
areas. Publication of this volume has been assisted by a grant
from the Shell Companies Foundation.

Library of Congress Cataloguing in Publication Data
    Main entry under title:

    After Mao.

        (Harvard East Asian monographs ; 115)
        "Essays originally presented at St. John's University,
New York City, during an international research
conference convened under the auspices of the National
Endowment for the Humanities, 28–31 May 1982"—Pref.
        Includes index.
        1. Chinese literature—20th century—History and
criticism—Congresses.   I. Kinkley, Jeffrey C.,
1948–   .   II. National Endowment for the Humanities.
III. Series.
PL2303.A28   1984   895.1'5'09   84–23185
ISBN 0–674–00885–5

Designed by Adrianne Onderdonk Dudden

JEFFREY C. KINKLEY is Assistant Professor of Asian Studies at St. John's University, New York. He has published articles on modern author Shen Congwen and his works, and about Chinese literature as witness to history.

LEO OU-FAN LEE is Professor of Chinese Literature at the University of Chicago, and is the co-editor of two Chinese literature series for the Indiana University Press. Besides articles about Lu Xun and other modern Chinese authors, he has written *The Romantic Generation of Modern Chinese Writers,* edited a book of essays on modern Chinese literature by Jaroslav Průšek, and co-edited *Modern Chinese Stories and Novellas, 1919–1949.*

PERRY LINK is Associate Professor of Oriental Languages at UCLA. He has written about popular Chinese culture, from the contemporary art of comic dialogue (*xiangsheng*) to old-style popular romance, the subject of his book *Mandarin Ducks and Butterflies: Popular Fiction in Early Twentieth-Century Chinese Cities.* He is editor and co-translator of three recent anthologies of post-Mao literature, *Stubborn Weeds, Roses and Thorns*, and *People or Monsters?*.

KAM LOUIE is a Lecturer in the Department of Asian Languages and Literatures at Auckland University, New Zealand. Besides *Critiques of Confucius in Contemporary China*, he has published many articles on post-Mao fiction and several about contemporary Chinese education.

The brothers PAN YUAN and PAN JIE are graduate students at Indiana University. They graduated from junior high school in Beijing, were rusticated in the late 1960s, and went on to graduate from Beijing Teachers' College and Beijing Normal University, respectively, after passing China's 1977 college entrance examinations. Pan Jie has written poetry; his field is comparative literature. The brothers were friends of the major editors and writers of *Today* magazine, but were not themselves members of the group.

WILLIAM TAY is Associate Professor of Comparative Literature at the University of California, San Diego. The author of numerous articles about Western and Chinese literature, he is co-editor of *China and the West: Comparative Literature Studies*. In Chinese, he has written *Literary Theory and Comparative Literature*, edited a collection of stories by Luo Hong, and co-edited *Structuralism: Theory and Practice* and *Chinese-Western Comparative Literature: A Collection of Critical Essays*.

RUDOLF G. WAGNER is *Privatdozent* at the Free University of Berlin. His published works range from medieval Chinese intellectual history to *Reenacting the Heavenly Vision: The Role of Religion in the Taiping Rebellion*. Co-editor of *Essays in Modern Chinese Literature and Literary Criticism*, he has just edited a book about post-Mao writing, *Literatur und Politik in der Volksrepublik China*.

To those others who made this book possible

Bai Hua	Chen Ying-Chen
Huang Weizong	

Bi Hua (Kee Fuk Wah)	Peter Li
S. K. Chang	Liang Heng
Chang Sung-sheng	Julia Lin
Susan Chen	Lucien Miller
Chi Pang-yuan	Andrew H. Plaks
Ai-li S. Chin	Timothy Ross
Michael Duke	Benjamin I. Schwartz
Gilbert Fong	Helen Siu
Howard Goldblatt	Constantine Tung
Merle Goldman	Wang Meng
Edward Gunn	Wang Yaping
C. T. Hsia	Phil Williams
Huang Qiuyun	Wong Kam-ming
William J. F. Jenner	Wai-leung Wong
Anthony J. Kane	Wu Beiling
Wolfgang Kubin	Winston L. Y. Yang
Joseph S. M. Lau	Yen Yuan-Shu
Li-kou Lee	Yu Li-hua
Lee Yee	Yue Dai-yun
Bernadette Yu-ning Li	

The chapters of this book are essays originally presented at St. John's University, New York City, during an international research conference convened under the auspices of the National Endowment for the Humanities, 28–31 May 1982. The gathering was entitled "Contemporary Chinese Literature: New Forms of Realism?" Besides the major assistance from NEH and St. John's, a generous and unrestricted grant from the Pacific Cultural Foundation, Republic of China, gave the conference a boost—we used it to maximize participation by the foundation's countrymen. The Mellon fund of the Joint Committee on Contemporary China of the American Council of Learned Societies and Social Science Research Council brought a writer from the People's Republic of China (PRC) to New York. And timely assistance from the United Board for Christian Higher Education in Asia helped us bring other PRC guests to the conference.

The conference was convened in the spirit of a Hundred Flowers. It was open to any topic—literary, historical, social, or political—that any participant felt relevant to literature from either side of the Taiwan Straits (or Hong Kong) produced during the 1970s and 1980s. The flowers that bloomed had nary a "weed" among them, but the many species, coming from different climates, required different kinds of care. Some were accustomed to competing for sunlight in their struggle to survive, while others preferred shade. They were simply too diverse to form a homogeneous book. Just a few appear in this volume, those that fit together well and are not too exotic for general readers and undergraduates seeking background reading to go with the exciting new translations of Chinese literature now coming out from several different presses. I regret having been unable to think of a good arrangement that would blend the mainland and Taiwan literatures, setting off each to best effect. Nor was it possible to encompass all the schools of literary criticism represented at the conference. But the papers not included here are being published elsewhere; would that our thematic selectiveness could help obviate comparisons of other sorts—political, personal, disciplinary, or even of romanization systems.

For a broader view of what went on at the conference, please refer to Kam Louie's report in *The Australian Journal of Chinese Affairs* 9:99-113 (January 1983), and that of *Time* International reporter Oscar C. K. Chiang (Jiang Jingkuan) in *Zhongbao yuekan* or *Chung Pao Monthly* 33:72-76 (October 1982). Friends translated reports of mine into Chinese for publication in *Haineiwai* (At home and abroad; New York) 34:5-9 (March-April 1982), and *Qishi niandai* (The seventies) 150:25-32 (July 1982), "Beyond Realism." The latter, a summary of the proceedings, is accompanied by photographs and further synopses by the staff of *The Seventies*. Tape recordings were made and broadcast by the Voice of America. Presses from the two sides of the Straits printed brief, more ambivalent, and defensive retrospective references to our conference, penned by conference guests who assumed roles as official spokespersons during the proceedings. These accounts were printed in the *People's Daily*, 3 October 1982, and in some early June articles on the literary page of *The Times of China* (Taiwan). A more positive note is that learned scholars in the Institute of Literature, Chinese Academy of Social Sciences, have undertaken to translate some of the conference papers for internal-use publication in China. This work is not an officially authorized conference project, although it certainly is a welcome one, whose purpose evidently is to disseminate and clarify among Chinese readers the diverse views of Chinese literature that we have here abroad.

For help and suggestions in planning the conference, I wish to thank C. T. Hsia, Joseph S. M. Lau, Leo Ou-fan Lee, Perry Link, Jonathan Spence, Moss Roberts, Andrew Plaks, and many others, including friends on both sides of the Taiwan Straits. Special thanks are due Peter Nosco, Rev. John Colman, C. M., and Rev. Thomas Hoar, C.M., of St. John's, as well as our excellent staff and assistants, Sandra Esposito, Vicki Estevez, Joseph Jun-jie Mao, David Guang-mo Ho, Ruth Ditzel, and Raymond Schmeirer. I am also grateful to The National Committee on United States–China Relations, the Asia Society, and the China Institute in America, for arranging coordinate literary and scholarly activities for the St. John's conference guests. And, I should like to echo the thanks to my wife, Chuchu, already expressed by so many who came to us from afar. The whole enterprise would have been hard to manage without her continual help and spiritual uplift.

In the course of preparing this book, much encouragement and assistance came from Patrick Hanan and Yih-young Chen. William A. Lyell, Jr. provided quite invaluable advice, and Florence Trefethen, the benefit of her great editorial expertise. Problems remaining in the book, but not necessarily the literary works it surveys, ought to be laid at my door.

Above all, I am grateful to all those who contributed to the larger ferment of ideas at the St. John's conference. It is to them that the authors dedicate this book, beginning with the three who could not get permission to come meet with us. We wish the best to all of China's writers, and look forward with eager anticipation to the future products of their impressive talents.

Jeffrey C. Kinkley
Jamaica, New York

CONTENTS

After Mao

Introduction

JEFFREY C. KINKLEY

Most Chinese, like their counterparts in the West, read fiction in quest of new windows on the world: on society and its inner workings, a creative author's imagination, or the wisdom of the ages. In the West, critics may find such tastes old-fashioned, but hardly subliterary. Books by Dickens and Verne appear in our mall bookstores under "literature," although Michener and Puzo will be shelved with "fiction," still apart from books sold generically as "romance/gothic" or "science fiction." The variety of other reading experiences available under "literature" can bewilder browsers unaccustomed to works that analyze consciousness and the nature of literary art itself.

Only now are Chinese readers beginning to enjoy such choice. Even during the three decades when China faced West, prior to the founding of the People's Republic in 1949, China produced little experimental literature. Most writers preferred a conscientious but technically unadventuresome social realism, the better to criticize modern Chinese life. Authors more intent on self-expression developed yet another literature of conscience, a plaintive, sometimes hyperbolic romanticism. Serious writers of both types fancied themselves China's avant-garde, challenged less by impending decadence than by Philistine pulp literature or subliterature that appealed to the more traditional sensibilities of urbanites who had the old education. Leftists nevertheless stood on guard against experimental works, whose Western techniques and literary ambiguity seemed to put them beyond the reach of political criticism (like new poetry today, William Tay's chapter explains below). So modernist literary pieces were not published at all during the three subsequent Maoist decades, 1949–1976. But neither were love poems, romances, martial-arts novels, or works of critical realism. Literature of the 1950s had to follow literary policies codified by Mao Zedong during his Yan'an Talks of 1942. China's readers were left with rosy socialist realist formulas, leavened only by modified folk literary forms and dialect.

The Maoist literary scene "thawed" somewhat during the Hundred Flowers Movement of 1957 and again during the early 1960s. Yet, confessional works and popular entertainment genres failed to revive. Only the engagé literature of social realism reappeared, probably because it had been the tool of China's socialist writers during their years in opposition. Writers who criticized Communist society did so at their own peril, but the risk was somewhat less for Party members, for whom politics was a vocation.

China's new post-Mao literary climate has more than thawed, by comparison. Popular, romantic, and even a few modernist works have appeared, along with pieces of social criticism whose audacity has attracted much attention in the West. The contrast with the cultural desert years of the late 1960s and 1970s is particularly stark. Only a decade ago, "under the Gang of Four," one could not read Hugo, listen to Tchaikovsky, paint with ordinary black ink sticks (which made black "lines"), or depict an owl with its left eye closed.[1] Blinkers remain on Chinese literature, still keeping most works from venturing beyond the pre-twentieth-century realms of mimesis, self-expression, entertainment, and moral elevation. But Westerners as well as Chinese can take heart from the Chinese people's interest in letting literary works be windows on their society. It is a society searching for new ways out, where windows are as scarce as the doors.

In the heady aftermath of Sino-American normalization after 1978, when magazines could be published privately and official journals favored works by Singer, Bellow, Updike, and Cheever, China seemed to be turning West again, even "liberalizing."[2] There was a precedent for this in the May Fourth Movement of 1919, when Chinese intellectuals and students first mobilized themselves for national salvation. Westernization, individual self-determination, and self-expression were the goals in 1919; adversary publishing, to create new culture, new literature, and new thought, was the tool.[3]

Today, perhaps the most popular non-official literary journal of the post-Mao era, was particularly close to the spirit of May Fourth. This is clear from Pan Yuan's and Pan Jie's firsthand account of the magazine in this volume. The Pans' writer friends found the older socialist generation "behind the times" and saw "aspects of rottenness" in their own cultural inheritance. Calling for "new blood" and fresh ideas from abroad, the young people argued that politics was a symptom, not the cause, of China's "Ten Lost Years" under the Gang of Four. Like Chen Duxiu and Hu Shi sixty years earlier, the *Today* group even concluded that China needed a moratorium on politics, so that the national character could be remolded through a new humanistic literature.

In 1980–1981, the state clamped down again on radical departures from artistic and social conformity, which it called evidence of harmful "bourgeois liberalization."[4] Yet, the works most embarrassing to the authorities were penned by social critics of all generations and hardly "liberal" in inspiration. The chief offenders had taken aim at the socialist cadre system, ignoring the literary neophytes of *Today,* with their avant-garde tastes and political moratorium. Writers taking the Deng regime to task were dissident in the tradition not of China's liberals but of her old leftist writers—if "dissident" at all.

Most writers of note during the post-Mao thaw were of the generation between the old socialists and the angry youth. They had been apprenticed to the Maoist literary line, in the 1930s, 1940s, or 1950s. Some, including Wang Meng, Fang Ji, Qin Zhaoyang, and Liu Binyan, criticized socialist China during the Hundred Flowers Movement, but even then had remained a loyal opposition. Rudolf Wagner has demonstrated in another book that the accusatory pieces of this first thaw, like other Chinese literature of the 1950s, indeed like the post-Mao science fiction he analyzes in this volume, owed a great deal to trends in Soviet literature. One of those trends was critique of bureaucratism.[5]

Today, most writers' criticism is still on behalf of the whole people, or groups ill-used by the system, not on behalf of individuals presumed to have inalienable rights. When Liu Binyan and Wang Meng were rehabilitated and became prominent again for their outspokenness in the post-Mao thaw (as one may gather from Leo Lee's chapter in this volume), once again they pointed to the collective ideals that had been betrayed. Had our Communist writers not been exiled from the capital when Jiang Qing asked, uncomprehendingly, "Where is this artists' 'conscience' that you often talk about?"[6] they might have answered her in Mao's own rhetoric: "With the masses" rather than "Deep in the artist's soul." The idea of using literature to form a "bridge between souls," as *Today* writers put it, probably puzzles the middle-aged Communists. They wonder rather how the party of Mao could ever have strayed so far from the people, for the Party ought to be the bridge, directly apprehending the will of the masses. Even the humanistic social criticism of Bai Hua, who became a hero to many in China and the West when the state chose to make an example of him in 1981, may well be rooted in a less-than-liberal, still other-directed conception of dissent. In his formulation, "We must rely on our own conscience in writing, thinking all the time about the people, forever loyal to the people."[7]

Chinese literature has, in sum, developed within an intellectual hothouse, if not a desert, the last decade or three. The Western reader must be prepared to find most works "wonderfully naive," as one of Wagner's colleagues has characterized

Chinese science fiction. What is one to make of a post-thaw literature that celebrates the police and considers the writing of love stories and tales of female celibacy a breakthrough? Has China no cynics, even now?

We see the post-Mao literary revival as having at least three aspects. There arose, indeed, a literature of social criticism, even a muckraking fiction. There also appeared works of artistic excellence, many of them influenced by Western technique of the sort long politically suspect. Third, the roles and meanings of literature in China multiplied. This book will focus on that new multiplicity—not only on the remarkable works of exposure, which continued the Chinese linkage of literature with politics—but on China's new serious and popular works which instead took advantage of the national respite from politics (above all, from the atmosphere of revolutionary politics) in the years just after Mao's death.

Many of the most devastating pieces of social criticism are now available in English. One can re-experience the impact of their historic accusations and ponder whether or not the works are "liberal" as charged, through anthologies such as Perry Link's *Stubborn Weeds* and *People or Monsters?*, Helen Siu's and Zelda Stern's collection *Mao's Harvest*, Lee Yee's *The New Realism,* Mason Y. H. Wang's selections, and Edward Gunn's *Twentieth-Century Chinese Drama.* Bonnie McDougall's book of poems by Bei Dao, and Link's other anthology, *Roses and Thorns,* translate some of the new works that are more noteworthy for their artistic innovations.[8] We ask the reader to sample these unusual masterpieces of art and testaments to courage, as we proceed with a broader, more exploratory survey of the new intellectual and social significance of post-Mao Chinese literature at large.

THE COURSE OF EVENTS

This book treats the changing place of literature in post-Mao China topically, using both literary and sociological approaches. The literary history of the period has yet to be written, for society was in considerable upheaval during the late 1970s. Individual acts of literary bravado played no small part in the general ferment; quite political acts of authorship paved the way for literature to be less political. Briefly, the "thaw" occurred as follows.

The "Gang of Four" were arrested in October 1976, only a month after the death of Mao, but a relaxation in literary and art policies was more than a year in coming. It quickly accelerated when it arrived, reaching a climax, or arriving at the limits of the acceptable, in 1979–1980. At first, literary progressives merely skirmished against the Gang of Four's most recent polemics. Those in command, including Hua Guofeng (now deposed) as well as Deng Xiaoping, still had to cite the deceased elder statesmen, Mao Zedong as well as Zhou Enlai, as authorities in their attacks on the Gang's ultra-left interpretations of what was in truth a longstanding Maoist literary line. Drama, the focal point of Jiang Qing's cultural dictatorship, became a leading forum for reversing cultural policy.[9] Pre-Cultural Revolution dramas banned by the Gang were revived, as were traditional-style operas, including local genres. Audiences were quick to appreciate dramas about reversals of verdicts as allegories for the contemporary justice being meted out to the Gang and their followers.

In March 1978, a policy of letting a "Hundred Flowers" bloom was written into the state constitution. Deng Xiaoping was still strengthening his grip on the Party apparatus as the Third Plenum of the Eleventh Central Committee published a communiqué calling for "emancipation of thought" and the seeking of truth from "facts." Subsequently, intellectuals were welcomed back into the fold of the working class.

By then, much new ground had already been broken by actual literary works exposing the fallen "Lin Biao and the Gang of Four." Exposure of the dark side of socialist society had been explicitly forbidden by Mao in his Yan'an Talks, but criticism of the Gang synchronized well with Deng Xiaoping's continued fight against remnant leftism. Such fiction was christened "new wave literature," avoiding explicit characterization of it as "exposure literature." The trend-setting work was "The Homeroom Teacher" ("Banzhuren") by Liu Xinwu, published in November 1977. In that story, a juvenile delinquent appears and even acts as a foil for a wrongheaded member of the Communist Youth League. Lu Xinhua's "The Wound" ("Shanghen," August 1978), about a young girl who comes to regret having believed the Gang when they falsely capped her mother as a traitor, lent its title as a new name for this sort of literature in popular parlance. "Literature of the wounded" was mostly written by young people, such as Liu and Lu, who as a "wounded generation" were demoralized by China's loss of social and spiritual direction during the Cultural Revolution. After much debate, the right of such literature to exist was finally affirmed; it was important, though, that the literature pointed its finger at Lin and the Gang, not at the Cultural Revolution, for the latter had not yet been delegitimated.[10] Our contributor Kam Louie reminds us that Liu Xinwu had had a long and perfect record as an orthodox interpreter of Party policy in the literary medium; "The Homeroom Teacher," although at the leading edge of a policy still evolving, was not necessarily a departure from that record. Chinese writers' cultivated sensitivity to the political environment in which they function successfully masks—from us as well as their government—the ultimate motivations of exposure literature itself.[11]

Within a year, Mao and the Cultural Revolution were in fact taken down a notch; later, the Anti-Rightist Movement (1957) and Great Leap Forward (1958–1960) were deemed excessive too. One result was works like Gao Xiaosheng's acclaimed "Li Shunda Builds a House," about social wrongs that dated back to the 1950s.[12] Gao satirizes confiscatory and ever-reversing Party policies that continually thwart a peasant struggling to satisfy his basic need for shelter, making the collapse of post-Leap "collectivization" seem as inevitable as the failure of "individualism" in Lao She's pre-Liberation novel, *Camel Xiangzi (Rickshaw Boy)*. In both works, society finally allows the pathetic hero to succeed, by corrupting himself.

The direct social impact on China's intellectual class of debunking the Maoist legacy made further literary tumult inevitable. "Rightists" were released by the tens of thousands from the labor camps where they had toiled since the 1950s. Well-educated and vocal members of another generation thus joined youth among the "wounded." And, with this, the ex-Rightists' sons and daughters, young people like the former Red Guard

Liang Heng who had been objects of discrimination for two decades in the only society they had ever known, had their manifold grievances against society legitimated.[13]

Reflecting increasing social and economic realism, the press, in 1979, began to speak of serious *current* problems, including poverty, begging, ideological disillusionment, and lying by the press. Spontaneous mass movements seemed possible again; commemorations of Zhou Enlai on the anniversary of the Tian An Men Incident broke ground for other social protests. Young ex-Red Guards exiled to the countryside who believed that they, above all, had legitimate social claims against the regime came flooding back into the cities. All this occurred amid the rehabilitation of formerly denounced writers and increased intercourse with the West, through translated books and television images showing how developed the West really was. Ultimately, it became apparent that the state was looking the other way as privately sponsored publishing flourished.

In such an environment, radical, "liberal" ideas could indeed be advocated, such as the importance of one's private mental world, and transcendental social values beyond materialist collectivism. Into the breach stepped the young people back from rustication. They were too young to have Wang Meng's and Qin Zhaoyang's preconceived 1950s-style notions of controlled literary protest. Those who were young adults in the late 1970s had "made revolution" as Mao's Red Guards. They had experienced something quite foreign to the generations just before and after them, adolescent rebellion of the sort their grandparents had known during the May Fourth Movement. Like the May Fourth generation, young people again felt cultural and personal despair at living in a "backward" country, not the cultural self-confidence characteristic of China when she "stood up" in the 1950s, a feeling that seems to motivate Wang Meng's generation even now. Yet China's young radicals of the late 1970s lacked the educational advantages of their May Fourth predecessors. They were not an intellectual vanguard, but a downwardly mobile generation created by the baby boom and failed idealism of Mao's revolution. They could claim only the wisdom of the dispossessed, and were more often obsessed with the Cultural Revolution long past than with the stirring policy debates of the post-Mao moment itself.

Back in the realm of the older and middle-aged generations, public affirmations of literary freedom climaxed at the Fourth National Congress of Chinese Writers and Artists, which met in October and November 1979.[14] There came a new wave of literature exposing Party corruption, even of official malfeasance, that was felt to be continuing under Deng Xiaoping's rule. Yet, the moment of freedom was brief, and never completely fulfilled. A crackdown on the dissident movement and Democracy Wall, including the arrest of Wei Jingsheng, had begun in March 1979. Deng Xiaoping began 1980 with a call for strengthened Party leadership and an announcement that four kinds of freedom of expression would be deleted from the constitution. The negative "social effects" of pessimistic literature were discussed. Most non-official publications were closed down by the fall of 1980, all of them by the next spring. Finally, in 1981, Bai Hua became the target of a seemingly familiar sort of coordinated official criticism. Leo Lee has called it a "pseudo-campaign," one which, to amend the Chinese phrase, did not even have physically to harm "the chicken to warn the monkey" (warn the group by making an example of an individual).[15] The power of the state to disrupt literary creativity through patronage and other benign forms of intervention can be observed in its exhortations to produce a literature with heroes capable of realizing the Four Modernizations, its official literary competitions, promotion of "one-minute stories," and so forth.[16] Yet, as the keen literary observers Lee Yee, Bi Hua, and Yang Ling have noted,[17] interesting pieces of exposure continued to be produced through 1980. They declared these works "the new realism." Aesthetic innovations are continuing even now, with the blessing of moderates anxious to discard social engagement, such as Wang Meng, Leo Lee points out in his chapter.

NEW MEANINGS FOR LITERATURE IN CHINA

When we look at what Chinese writers are now producing, it becomes apparent that Chinese society and reader tastes kept right on evolving during the "Ten Lost Years" (1966–1976), however undefinably. Many of the changes in Chinese literature have little to do with the new "two-line struggle" to re-establish a place for realism and the politics of realism. Some Chinese authors now write and publish, for the first time since 1949, stories intended just to pass the time. True, these works exist only on sufferance; the detective interest, for example, was in 1982 already being deflected from domestic crime fiction back into more politically edifying tales about police who sleuth for treason, or went undercover decades ago to help found New China. Yet, untutored "popular" taste was served by hand-copied romances and thrillers that circulated underground even during the Cultural Revolution, Perry Link tells us. He explains why the official press, by contrast, is so helpless when it comes to satisfying the public. But since when have Chinese publishers catered to popular taste? It is strange to see them churning out large quantities of crime fiction by foreign authors, if not domestic ones, in pursuit of their new post-Mao goal of running a profit.

The state's concession to popular taste is even counterbalanced by a disdain for spy fiction, love stories, science fiction, and thrillers (including the historically edifying ones), by China's elite intellectuals. Many educated people plead innocence of such low-level stuff, although nearly all confess to having read some "a few years ago, when there was so little to read." This may presage a split between "high" and "popular" literatures, as in the West. Both would be creatures of urban mass culture. The old Maoist distinction between a "bourgeois" high literature and a "mass" literature for the peasants is not helpful. Perry Link points out that, although most of them now are able to, Chinese peasants do not read.

Because of these new developments in genre, as well as the many issues raised by the current freedom of Chinese literature to enter what were once "taboo areas," we devote much of our volume at the outset to "literary subject matter." Rudolf

Wagner, Kam Louie, and I, in succession, treat post-Mao science fiction, love stories, and crime fiction. Either sophistication of aesthetic conception (form) or seriousness of social-moral commentary (content) may elevate works from any of these basically popular genres onto the plateau of "high literature." But most Chinese readers and writers, not to mention critics, still attach more interest to content than form. Indeed, the three of us find the new distinctiveness of these stories, literature and pabulum alike, to lie in their subject matter. Moreover, in this relatively rich universe of social, moral, and scientific topics that literature now treats, it becomes the more obvious what subjects remain taboo in literature, and perhaps public discourse generally.

The more serious works must actually tread a finer line than pieces written just for entertainment. Science fiction enjoys more state sponsorship than the other genres, for it popularizes scientific knowledge and prepares the way for the privileged role scientists must play in the Four Modernizations. Yet, this turns out to be just one more burden for the literature, which must not antagonize non-scientists or seem to argue that scientists know best how to run society. Similarly, one can write a whodunit about an ordinary murder with some abandon, incorporating all sorts of theatrical "bourgeois" conventions, but a "serious" story that sleuths out cadre corruption and argues that China needs more "rule of law" must not only take a firmer political line; it must eschew techniques and Western stereotypes that might trivialize the moral significance of the crimes at issue.

Love stories, being relatively less formulaic, in China enjoy the advantage of being taken seriously, and the disadvantage of being taken too seriously. Critics object to the depiction of socially unconventional love relationships, even in fiction. Women, on the other hand, feel threatened when male authors use the avowedly progressive medium of literature to write again of virtuous "chaste" (non-remarrying) widows. With fiction itself shadowed by the social responsibility required of nonfiction, small wonder that even novels just for entertainment cannot wholly escape the demands made on "serious" literature.

For all the limits on science fiction, Wagner shows that it offers unique insights into Chinese scientists' vision of utopia.

And, while I find that China's "serious" detective stories argue as much for "rule by good men" as for "rule of law," it is interesting to see how such a closeted thing as a Chinese legal trial materializes in writers' imaginations. In China, law has much in common with literature; it must educate people in socialist morality rather than simply promote the "aesthetic" end of justice for its own sake.

Of the serious post-Mao works of literature that have no trouble differentiating themselves from "merely popular" genres, most remain "literature of purpose." Comparison with the equally didactic socialist realism of Mao's era can begin with a comparison of viewpoints. Society is still the subject. In the genre of "problem plays," solutions to social problems may be moot, but the definition of the problem is unlikely to be so. Muckraking works deliver their *j'accuse* with even less ambiguity. But, in these changing times, it can be problematic whether the author is giving voice to his or her conscience (itself divisible into the ego and the internalized socialist super-ego), to the thoughts of the Party, or to what he or she thinks—or hopes—the Party may be poised, or persuaded, to adopt. Literature may even represent group interests—not necessarily the homogenized interests of Mao's "worker-peasant-soldier" "vast majority," but of groups newly self-conscious in post-Mao society.

Notable among the latter is the wasted generation of "wounded" young people, who lost their chance for education and advancement because of the Cultural Revolution. Their generational outcry in literature, anthologized in English by Siu and Stern, has in turn encouraged the middle-aged to champion Chen Rong's "When You Get to Middle Age." The middle generation, who consider themselves the tossed-out dishrags of a revolution they founded with the energy of their own youth, see Chen Rong as "representing" their interests. Such a stance is not necessarily part of the story's inherent meaning as art, nor Chen Rong's intention. But Chinese readers have learned to appreciate a story, like anything else published in the official press, as significant in the first instance because its "viewpoint" must have been sufficiently in tune with current politics to get it published. And who can ignore a weather report?

Particularly intriguing is Wagner's hypothesis that a profession (scientists) has used literature (science fiction) to lobby for its own narrow interests. This may be an extreme example. It is guilt-ridden intellectuals rather than Mao's peasant poets who are writing about the countryside again, characteristically highlighting the hunger and backwardness of the peasants in ways sure to evoke sympathy and pity. But it gives one pause to see policemen now dabbling in detective stories, glorifying themselves more than the law. Even divorcees have taken up the pen in their own defense.

Our next topic is "literary art"; William Tay and Leo Ou-fan Lee assess the accomplishments of post-Mao poetry and fiction respectively, using comparative and other methods. Only in this section do we treat the rather select body of recent literature that might, in international perspective, be called experimental. Modernism offers a respite from politics that is clearly "serious" rather than simply diverting. It would appear subtly to undermine socialist realism, by tacitly challenging the latter's exclusive claim as a high literary end. This has led to a chilly reception, particularly for China's new experimental poetry, even though Tay finds the latter avant-garde only by 1920s standards. Paradoxically, poems seem to have even less freedom to stray from concrete "reality" than stories; unsympathetic critics charge much of China's new poetry with being harmfully "obscure." Moreover, a different group of poets who really want to comment on politics have, in fact, deliberately obscured their more concrete "messages," as a defensive measure. China's thirst for critical realism, still unquenched—even intensified by adversity—makes it that much harder for genuine ambiguity to be accepted as such.

In China, discussions of literary technique have yet to soar into the rarefied atmosphere of current international theory. They remain enmeshed in the concerns of utilitarian critics; Lee finds that it is "dissident" just to analyze the formal achievements of literary works on their own terms. Chinese readers as well as critics have in effect translated the techniques of the new literature into content, reintroducing much of the problematik of the section on literary subject matter.

Considerable experimentation has been tolerated in fiction,

though, presumably because modernistic stories so far seem politically innocuous. But what if authors should strike heroic poses as "dissidents" in aesthetic matters exclusively, the better to evade their responsibility as protectors of literary freedom to treat difficult subject matter? Might this not ultimately discredit modernism in the eyes of men and women of conscience, as seems to have happened in Taiwan? Lee, who takes up these questions, is the first to agree that form and content are related; he worries that their dissociation may be detrimental to both. As with poetry, China's century-long fixation on realism is part of the problem. Theories of realism have disembodied literary experimentation, making technical questions seem irrelevant to rather than characteristic of the most pressing dilemmas facing modern Chinese culture.

Our volume closes with "sociology of publishing and reading." The Pans' moving account of unofficial publishing by young people is historical affidavit as well as sociological exposition. Link analyzes the official presses, having enjoyed an unprecedented year of field work and interviews with publishers. He confesses, in a footnote, that once he even accidentally invaded a bookshop restricted to cadres, thanks to a friend's practical joke. In telling us what books people actually read, his chapter takes us full circle; it reminds us that socialist realism itself can have elements of popular appeal. But Link also shows how much contemporary Chinese literature remains in competition with literary classics and translations of foreign works. The Chinese state demands less social responsibility from novels about alien societies. Might not China's native literature even be laboring under a handicap in comparison to the foreign imports?

Now that Chinese literature is for once being imported our way, Western readers can make their own comparisons. Rather than second-guess the outcome as two aesthetic traditions come into contact and perhaps conflict, we proceed with the complex background on the Chinese side, confident that Western readers will at the very least find that this literature depicts Chinese life and social values more vividly than any other medium.

PART ONE

Literary Subject Matter

Lobby Literature: The Archeology and Present Functions of Science Fiction in China

RUDOLF G. WAGNER

In 1978, a long forgotten and never well developed form reappeared on the Chinese literary scene—science fiction. Statistics tell of well over 600 works that appeared before the end of 1981, when research for this study ended, ranging from novels and short stories to poems and comic dialogues (*xiangsheng*).[1] On both national and provincial levels, readers' polls have named science-fiction stories as among the best new literary works.[2] Bookstores stock some science-fiction collections,[3] while a variety of periodicals regularly publish the genre, ranging from *People's Literature* (*Renmin wenxue*) to the one journal exclusively devoted to this literature, *Science Belles-lettres* (*Kexue wenyi*), and the non-official *Beijing Spring* (*Beijing zhi chun*).[4] Some stories have inspired filmscripts and actual films.[5] Many foreign science-fiction works have come out in translation, including the script of *Star Wars*.[6] Occasionally, an article on the new Chinese science fiction is seen in the foreign press, in sources ranging from *China News Analysis* to *Asahi shimbun*.[7] Chinese stories have been translated into Japanese, French, and German.[8]

This exploratory sketch of Chinese science fiction will focus on two problems relevant to the new genre.

First, science fiction has played a role in the East European socialist camp, notably in the USSR, the German Democratic Republic (GDR), Rumania, and Poland. The Chinese Communist Party has thus inherited a socialist order of literary things in which science fiction has an allotted place. However, during the 1920s and after the thaw following the death of Stalin, science fiction in the Soviet bloc actually became a major form of literary expression beyond the confines of traditional socialist realism, thanks to Zamyatin, Efremov, and the Strugatski brothers in the Soviet Union, Lem in Poland, and the Brauns in East Germany.[9] Archeological unearthing of the structures of science fiction in the larger socialist world is an important preliminary step for throwing current Chinese practice into relief.

Second, science fiction reappeared in the PRC in the specific environment of 1978 and the years following. The archeological elements will have to be studied in the context of the specific function that this literature assumed during these years. That function has imposed new meanings on the inherited structures.

Science fiction can also be investigated as popular fiction, but that remains beyond the scope of this paper. So will such important topics as narrative technique in the genre, the relationship of the new PRC science fiction to Chinese literary tradition, and comparisons of PRC works with recent Taiwan and Hong Kong science fiction.

ARCHEOLOGICAL EXPLORATION

The Surface: The Chinese Category of
Science-Phantasy Fiction

The Chinese leadership rehabilitated science fiction in 1978. This was part of a "new deal" offered to the much-battered science community. The scientists would be the heroes of the new genre, their exploits would be eulogized, and the stories would serve to attract young people into the field. Together with improved material conditions, promises of a greater say in decision-making on scholarly subjects, and a greatly improved political status through the inclusion, in 1979, of the intellectuals into the category of "working-class" people, science fiction was designed to harness the scholarly community to the purpose of the Four Modernizations. However, there was nothing vague in the notion of the science fiction which was to come back. It was restored to a highly defined categorical place and function.

Since the late 1950s, the Chinese have called science fiction "science-phantasy fiction" (*kexue huanxiang xiaoshuo*), a subcategory of "science belles-lettres" (*kexue wenyi*). The latter includes all science propaganda by artistic means: writing, art, or the modern media. Science belles-lettres again is a subcategory of "science popularization" (*kexue puji,* or *kepu* for short). The flourishing of all these forms followed in good logic the refounding of the Chinese Association for the Popularization of Science (Zhongguo Kexue Puji Xiehui) in Shanghai in May 1978. Science belles-lettres remains institutionally bound up with this association and its provincial branches; the periodical *Science Belles-lettres* is published by the Association's Sichuan branch. Most other periodicals carrying science belles-lettres are also published by branches of the Association. Science fiction is controlled and administered by the Association's Committee for Science Belles-lettres (Kexue Wenyi Weiyuanhui), of which one science fiction author, Zheng Wenguang, was vice-chairman in 1980.[10]

Because science fiction is institutionally affiliated with science popularization, it is targeted for a young audience, divided into "children" (*ertong*) and "youths" (*qingnian*). The texts' action-oriented linear narrative, inclusion of children in the action, level of science information, and illustrations show how strongly the institutional determination of a target audience has influenced the stories. Many science-phantasy stories first appear in the specialized periodicals and publishing houses for children and young people.

The few science-phantasy-fiction writers who have been accepted as members of the Writers Union[11] all belong to the subgroup "Children's Literature." Wang Xiaoda received a prize for his story "Waves" in the Sichuan provincial competition under the same category. This does not mean that all science-phantasy stories still correspond to this pattern. Most of them are now clearly adult literature and might be considered some form of "literature" rather than science popularization. The categorical and institutional place of these works remains unchanged, however, offering certain advantages to the writers but also leading to tensions between the actual texts and their institutional position.

Among the various forms of science popularization, science belles-lettres is considered the most appropriate form for youth, because it conveys scientific knowledge with literary means adapted to the fancy of young people. This noble end justifies the utilization of otherwise suspicious elements, like phantasy (huanxiang) and suspense (jingxian), both of which have become elements constituting science-phantasy fiction.[12] Thus, it was in the framework of children's and youth literature that the specific elements of science-phantasy fiction originally found their legitimate place.

In all the stories of this genre published during the 1950s and 1960s, and in many that have come out recently, young readers find peers within the text—young science heroes with whom young folk can and are supposed to identify. Thus, in Tong Enzheng's "The Visitor from Fifty Thousand Years Ago" (1962),[13] a young boy on a school excursion discovers a strongly magnetic "floating stone" in a Guangdong swamp. He tries without success to determine its substance, then sends it to the Academy of Sciences. The stone turns out to be a fragment from an extraterrestrial spaceship which hovered about the earth before crashing in 1635, according to Chinese chronicles.

A professor from the Academy comes in a helicopter and accompanies the boy to the site for further exploration, giving much useful information along the way.

Zheng Wenguang's best-selling novel of 1979, *Flying Towards Sagittarius,*[14] similarly has a group of three young people accompany an engineer on a final inspection of a new Chinese spaceship, the *Eastern.* The envious "Polar Bear" (Russia) has sent two robots to abduct the spaceship. Only the robot programmed to enter the control room and start the ship succeeds; the young people, alone in the craft, keep the doors locked against the other. This begins their involuntary flight "towards Sagittarius," which is to last many years and confront them with numerous dangers. For the benefit of the reader, the youths educate themselves in all relevant knowledge, using the microfilm library on board. The story thus combines elements of science popularization for youth, science phantasy, suspense and, as might be expected in stories written at this time, romantic love.

The subsumption of science-phantasy fiction under science popularization strictly limits the leeway of phantasy. "Phantasy has to be based on science," says Ye Yonglie, the most productive science belles-lettres writer today, who has also written the quasi-official *Treatise on Science Belles-lettres.*[15] This means that phantasy elements must be based on known scientific facts or extrapolations from them. Phantasy differentiates science-phantasy fiction from both the "science story" (*kexue gushi*) and the "science tale" (*kexue tonghua*), which do little more than popularize known scientific facts with the help of a little plot and story, excluding science phantasy. To keep to its solid base, the phantasy must deal with the foreseeable future, looking ahead one or two decades. So far, Chinese stories have adhered to this rule of "near future phantasy."[16] The highly optimistic forecasts for China's development that prevailed in 1978 and again after the Twelfth Party Congress in 1982 have given writers somewhat greater latitude. But even as China builds her gigantic *Eastern,* revolutionaries of 1949 are still active. The phantasy will come true, the reader is told, within his or her lifetime.

Writers have, however, extended their allotted time span in

the other direction, the past. Besides the crashed spaceship of 1635, another story tells of a complete spacecraft that has been put on reserve long ago, in "Chi You's Cave," by benign messengers from another star who want to facilitate future communication. Tong Enzheng and Zheng Wenguang describe the discovery of proto-humans.[17] Chinese texts contain no small number of hints of the wisdom of earlier Chinese generations, who observed and recorded all these wonders. The most dramatic use of this device, however, has been made by Ye Yonglie in his "The Man Who Flies to Pluto." A Tibetan serf who has lain frozen for fifty years in a mountain snowdrift is revived. Originally, he had sought refuge from his persecutors on this mountain because he believed this to be the seat of a goddess who would let him fly to the heavenly paradise. Waking up in socialist Lhasa, and walking through a fully automated supermarket, he cannot help but believe that he really is in heaven. Thus, the present appears as the past's achieved utopia, and the possible critical potential of science-phantasy fiction as a description of how things could be better is turned into a eulogy on the "present" conditions.[18]

The category science-phantasy fiction takes science as its main topic—hard science. And, as Ye Yonglie puts it, "The main characters is science-phantasy stories are always scientists,"[19] to which one might want to add "young people aspiring to become scientists." This is most certainly not the case in most recent Western or even socialist-camp science fiction, but Chinese writers are most rigorous in keeping to the rule, both in theory and in practice. The original purpose of the categorical restrictions was to provide information about the hard ("more important") sciences, to set up models of behavior for aspiring scientists, and finally to advertise the interesting life of this group and attract young people to it.

The categorical subordination of science fiction to science popularization also fixes the attitude of the texts towards science. In the postface (November 1978) to his *Flying Towards Sagittarius,* Zheng Wenguang writes:

Our science-phantasy fiction stories are fundamentally different from the [Western anti-utopias]. We praise science, we praise the glorious future a highly developed science will give to the life of mankind, we sing the praises of all the beautiful things the laboring masses produce with the help of science, and we sing the praises of the thousands and tens of thousands of people who heroically struggle for the realization of the Four Modernizations.[20]

Such praise of science and its workers is indeed a common purpose of the Chinese texts. It is known and admitted in China, however, that negative and even disastrous consequences might result from a scientific discovery if it ends up in the hands of imperialistic powers. In these stories, which contain a good deal of "future international politics phantasy," China's "socialist system" and promise not to become a "hegemonic state" ensure that here science is free from such negative side effects. Thus, in Tong Enzheng's award-winning story, "Death Rays from Coral Island," the first science phantasy to be published in a prestigious literary journal (*People's Literature*) since 1949, the powerful laser beams generated from a handy nuclear battery—both inventions of Overseas Chinese professors in Southeast Asia—are dangerous only in the hands of a "certain superpower," whose representatives have Russian and German names. This superpower would use it as a deadly weapon to achieve world hegemony. But the two Overseas Chinese are patriotic enough to give their invention to their "socialist fatherland," where neither of them has ever been. There the invention is safe from misuse.[21]

Similarly, sharks used to patrol waters near the Xisha Islands in a story by Zheng Wenguang detect and explode intruding, typically Vietnamese or Russian nuclear submarines. Provisions are made for the submarines to blow up only at their home port, to prevent nuclear fallout in Chinese waters. But the sharks never intrude into other nations' waters. The Chinese amphibious aircraft-cum-underwater vessel in Sima Chunqiu's "The Sinking of the Giant Ship" (1979) is stationed in Southeast Asian international waters. But it is there only to protect the ships of the smaller nations of the region from the torpedoes of a "certain superpower." And "Waves" that create optical illusions in a story by Wang Xiadoa seem beyond misuse by the Chinese; they only trap sadly dull-witted Soviet spies.[22]

In fact, the misuse of science today appears to be the sole privilege of the Soviet Union. Americans are involved only in a story reprinted from 1963, which deals with things that went on before Liberation, when even in today's historiography the United States was an enemy.[23] Consequently, the "Polar Bear" appears as the archenemy in battles for the beneficial use of science. The difference between Chinese and Russian uses of science are spelled out by the chief engineer of the *Eastern*, following the craft's abduction (p. 8):

Indeed, the enemy is utterly perverse. While we want to build a park of flowers on earth, they want to erect camps and prisons; while we want to gallop through space to let the firmament of science stretch towards the depths of unbounded space, they only want to install laser cannon there, pointed towards the earth, to destroy the culture and knowledge of mankind. A bear truly is not a human being. His ambition and endeavor are to trample underfoot all beautiful things of other people, so that they will be afraid of him.

Some Chinese readers may, at a deeper level, be more pessimistic about the glories of science. The pessimism is articulated in two scenarios: an eventual takeover by robots, with Orwellian consequences; and a terminal nuclear World War III. Such doubts seem strong enough to have merited explicit rebuttal.

In "The Beta Secret" by Liu Zhaogui, a Chinese scientist returning from a conference abroad suddenly proclaims the theory of the eventual takeover of the world by robots, which was originally advanced by Norbert Wiener and Lord Ashby. His colleagues quickly smell a rat; he turns out to be a (presumably Soviet-made) bionic double of the Chinese original, programmed to turn the Chinese robots against their masters and spread this noxious doctrine in order to disarm the Chinese.[24]

Before being blown into space with the *Eastern*, the young Chinese of *Flying Towards Sagittarius* discuss among themselves whether another, final world war will come. One youth foresees the end of civilization. During the involuntary space trip, world war does occur. The USSR occupies Europe and attacks China. But mankind does not go under. Eventually, the "Polar Bear" suffers a "shameful defeat"; the surviving Chinese instantly rebuild their cities, "more beautiful than ever." The first message to reach the *Eastern,* beamed with a new communication device developed during the war, says that, despite the gloomy warnings of one of the youths aboard, World War III has not been the end of mankind (pp. 172–210).

The story also shows the function of science optimism. The young people start their trip into space literally as unconscious victims of a Russian plot. They have no control over their fate and lack the training to handle the spacecraft, which carries them away from home at 40,000 kilometers per second. But their optimism that they will escape their predicament, their patriotic desire to contribute to the science of their country, and their background as children of scientists enable them to overcome their passive position and become masters of the *Eastern.* It is not technology that saves them but their science optimism.

The confrontation of good and bad uses of science brings into relief the most prominent non-scholarly feature of the Chinese scientists (PRC citizens and Overseas Chinese alike), their patriotism. Even in the absence of advice or help, this patriotism is a reliable guide in discovering hidden enemies, and inevitably leads Chinese scientists to China, the only place where discoveries and inventions can be put to positive use. It is this unswerving patriotism and not the atomic battery in his pocket that keeps Professor Zhao's son-in-law swimming after his private plane has been shot down over the South China Sea by a ship of a "certain superpower." He reaches the coral island where a Professor Matai has his laboratories. Both Professor Zhao and Matai work for the Soviet Union; Matai's laboratory has even been built by this superpower.[25] But both are utterly ignorant of this, being devoted only to their scientific research for the benefit of mankind. They have to learn the hard lesson that it does indeed matter who controls an invention. Their patriotism eventually overcomes their lovable naiveté when they discover who is behind the innocuous-looking European firm through which the Soviets are operating.

In these texts, the Chinese Revolution is the final one, come what may, evidently, even World War III. Technical and scientific modernization of the Chinese fatherland is the battle cry, and so patriotism is the key virtue of the Chinese scientist, not revolutionary fervor.

The educational purpose of Chinese science phantasy is also reflected in its strong ethnocentrism. All important discoveries and inventions are made by ethnic "Chinese scholars," living in China or abroad. Foreign scholars congregate at Chinese research sites to admire Chinese achievements,[26] or are Soviet spies in disguise. There is no scholarly exchange with foreign non-Chinese scholars through literature, joint research, or travel.

Socialist literary theory by no means treats science-phantasy fiction as if it were a unicorn. Gorki demanded that socialist literature combine "active" romanticism with realism. After Mao Zedong's directive of 1958, Zhou Yang and Guo Moruo developed this into the Chinese version of socialist realism. Revolutionary romanticism is supposed to show the buds of the great future in the realities of today. Science-phantasy fiction is "realistic" with its science element, and shows "revolutionary romanticism" with its "phantasy" component. Within this framework, there are differences of opinion both in theory and literary practice. While Ye Yonglie stresses the "realistic" and "scientific" aspect and does not even use the term "romantic" in his *Treatise on Science Belles-lettres,* authors and critics like Zheng Wenguang, Lou Qi, and others use the category of "romanticism" to characterize science-phantasy fiction of both the Vernean past and the present.[27]

The Soviet Layer

The categorical roster above does not necessarily fit all works of Chinese phantasy fiction, but it does define their perception. It was not invented by the Chinese in 1978; each of the elements described is of Soviet origin.

The term *kexue wenyi* is itself a literal translation of the Soviet technical term *nauchno-khudozhestvennaya,* "science belles-lettres." The *Kratkaia Literaturnaia Enciklopedia* (1968) describes the latter as a form of science popularization originally mostly addressed to the young and characterized by its use of belles-lettres forms.[28] It seems to go back to Gorki's remarks on Il'in. Il'in's works have been translated into Chinese since the 1930s, when his *The Story of the Five-Year Plan* came out.[29] A nine-volume Chinese edition of his works appeared in 1953, including *The Story of the Five-Year Plan,* which portrays the Soviet Union in full communism. Chinese science-phantasy writers immediately associate Il'in's name with science belles-lettres.[30]

The second name in this lineage is Tsiolkovski (1857–1935),[31] a nineteenth-century Russian Christian philosopher who was, it seems, haunted by the thought of a crowded earth after the resurrection of the dead, which he thought imminent. Thereupon he devised spaceships to relieve the earth of some of this pressure. Both Il'in and Tsiolkovski wrote science stories, *kexue gushi,* and also science-phantasy fiction. The latter remained, however, a mere sub-category of *nauchno-khudozhest-vennaya.* The Chinese science-phantasy-fiction writers come from the same background; all of them have been writing science popularization and all of them have a background in the sciences or are working full time as scientists.[32]

The original Chinese term for science fiction was *kexue xiaoshuo,* science fiction or scientifiction, as Hugo Gernsback, the editor of the first American science-fiction journal, called it at the time. Lu Xun used the term in 1903 in his Verne translations, in accordance with Verne's *roman scientifique.* It remained the accepted term until at least 1957, when an article on U.S. science fiction published in the periodical *Literature in Translation (Yiwen)* still used the word.[33] The Soviet term for science fiction is *nauchno fantastika (rasskaz);* the present Chinese term translates this verbatim with "science-phantasy (fiction)." *Fantastika* corresponds to the English *phantasy,* which the *Oxford English Dictionary* defines as "imagination, visionary intuition," as opposed to *fantasy,* defined as "caprice, whim, fanciful invention." The Soviet encyclopedia stresses the "possibility or even plausibility of this phantasy becoming reality some time in the future."[34] Thus the term *phantasy* moves within narrow confines.

The intended readership of Soviet science-phantasy fiction was, at least originally, youth. Impressive statistics show that young people eagerly read this literature. Parnov writes in 1968 about a study showing that 60 percent of the Moscow undergraduate physics majors selected their specialty under the influence of science fiction. Forty percent of the young physicists, astronomers, and astrophysicists first considered taking up their specialties after having read Efremov's *Andromeda Nebula.* Heidtmann quotes East German studies to the effect that science fiction, comprising only 1 percent of all titles published in the GDR, is the fourth most popular reading material taken from public libraries, after adventure, thriller, and crime stories.[35] Gerhard Rausch, the only full-time science-phantasy writer in the GDR, writes for young people. The association of science belles-lettres with youth literature dates from the 1920s, when science popularization was organized; it is already evident in Alexei Tolstoi's *The Garin Death Ray* (1926–1927), wherein young readers find one of their peers among the leading characters.[36]

The restricted leeway of Chinese phantasy in terms of object and time again corresponds to the Soviet pattern of the 1930s, 1940s, and early 1950s. In 1950, Ivanov described in the most explicit terms the field to be covered by science phantasy. "Soviet science phantasy must reflect tomorrow, that is, that space of time separated from our days by one or two decades, or perhaps only years. Certain writers, however, themselves are reoriented and orient others toward the depiction of the distant future. Recently, at a meeting of the Soviet Writers' Union, L. Upenskij furiously attempted to prove the necessity of writing about that which will come to be a hundred or even two hundred years from now. In our opinion, this is not an accidental error. This is the stirring of an admirer of Western science fiction to direct our literature in the same direction." Even Jules Verne had been criticized in this vein as leading youth away from reality into fantasy. Ivanov recommended describing the realization of the gigantic projects envisaged in the so-called "Great Stalin Plan."[37] Thus, there is a tendency in Soviet science phantasy to explore beyond these narrow confines, as well as an established pattern of how to counter these efforts, both of which have recurred, quite independently, in China during recent years. The Strugatskis have amply used the technique of confronting more backward stages of humanity on earth and elsewhere with the "communism" realized in the USSR, presenting the latter as the achieved utopia of man's history. I have not found a reference to a Chinese translation of their works; thus, we might have an independent Chinese creation.

The Chinese emphasis on the natural sciences and on scientists again repeats a Soviet pattern established during the Stalinist period. Heller links the development of this restricted science phantasy to the deterioration of Soviet science during the 1930s. Most sciences controversial in the USSR at the time, such as genetics, molecular biology, anthropology, sociology, and psychoanalysis, remained outside the Soviet scholarly world and outside Soviet science phantasy of the time.[38] These categorical limits surround Chinese science phantasy today, as dead structures whose origins are long forgotten.

The science optimism promoted in the Chinese texts was decreed in the USSR early in the 1930s, as a measure against quite different trends. Writers like Majakovski, Platonov, Slonimski, and particularly Zamyatin, had become increasingly puzzled by both the technical and social perspectives of the new Soviet Union. In *The Bedbug*, Majakovski freezes a bureaucrat and a bedbug; after the advent of communism, they are inadvertently revived, only to infest the new Communist man with decadent habits. Bulgakov has a bureaucrat commit a planning error so that rays newly invented to enlarge everything a hundred times produce giant snakes against which all of mankind must wage a fierce battle; and Slonimski's hero in *The Emory Machine* writes in a last message before lodging a bullet in his own head: "Before, I regarded the present through the future and I had no pity for anything or anybody. But now, it is the future which I regard through the present, and I start having doubts. Are we right?"[39] Against these anti-utopian trends, prevalent among writers who did not see themselves as enemies of the new Soviet state and often were cultural leaders, the utopian optimism of Il'in and others became mandatory. Only thirty years later, in 1957, were Soviet writers able to link up with this buried critical tradition.[40] But by then the Sino-Soviet rift prevented this new wave from reaching China.

The battle for control of a technological gadget which lends suspense to Chinese texts is a well-established Soviet pattern. The model is A. Tolstoi's *The Garin Death Ray,* translated

into Chinese in the early 1950s.[41] Engineer Garin tries to subdue the world with his powerful beam, which can be either a
weapon or an instrument for mining. By drilling through the
earth's crust, he gets access to the gold of the "Olivine Belt."
With gold and arms in hand, he achieves his goal for a short
while until the denouement; the "death ray" ultimately comes
under the control of the young Soviet state, where it is, of
course, safe from misuse. "Death Rays from Coral Island" obviously is written in the tradition of this Russian piece.

Depending on the time of publication, Soviet science fiction
shows two different key virtues in its heroes. *The Garin Death
Ray* ends with world revolution, organized by a devoted Communist who enters Garin's services to get control of his invention. Soviet texts written during the 1930s and 1940s have not
been the subject of research, but patriotism was the main theme
of Soviet literature during these years; science phantasy probably
offered no exception. In Soviet works of the war years, world
revolution disappeared and defense of mother Russia by all
Soviet patriots of good will became the focus. Chinese science
phantasy clearly follows the pattern of the later Stalin years.

The strong ethnocentrism in Chinese texts also has its Soviet
precedent. Even the anti-Soviet, but Russian, villain Garin is a
hundred times more gifted than the American moneybags. In
1950, Ivanov bluntly stated that Soviet science phantasy should
portray the "previsions of Soviet geniuses."[42]

Soviet texts seem to lack one component of Chinese ethnocentrism. An inordinate amount of Chinese science phantasy
deals with the hidden wisdom of the Chinese ancestors, which is
preserved in written records, as of astronomical observations, or
in techniques like the *qigong* breathing exercises.[43]

Defining science phantasy in the context of socialist realism,
the Soviet author Britikov wrote in 1970: "Indeed, if one studies
the well-known characteristics of socialist realism—its fusion of
romanticism and realism, the representation of life in its revolutionary development, the active socialist ideal—one realizes
that, in principle, they present all the characteristics of a scientific vision of the future." He adds, "The realm of science phantasy . . . consists mainly in the fact that it elaborates within the
sphere of socialist realism itself, the instruments that will permit

a concrete artistic prevision." And Heller concludes that "the near-future science fiction [of the USSR] retains all the principal features, all the structural traits of socialist realist literature."[44]

As this archeological excursion has shown, the highly structured patterns of the past exert a strong and even decisive influence on the perception of the new Chinese texts. It was on this basis that science phantasy was readmitted into China. The layer on which the new science phantasy rests is that of the Soviet Union of the 1930s, 1940s, and early 1950s. Neither the voices of the 1920s nor those of Russia's post-thaw period, which took up these earlier strains, are heard in China. While the elements examined hitherto by and large seem quite compatible with the Leninist categorical universe, there remain a number of unassimilated elements within Chinese science phantasy that lead us briefly to probe into the deeper layer of Vernean traditions.

The Second Layer: Saint-Simonian Machinery and Sociology

Like most science-fiction technology, the gadgetry in Chinese stories is not operated by workers or related to production. In Yu Zhi's "Elephants sans Proboscis"[45] (1956), elephants walking—sans proboscis—down the streets of a newly built park-city in the middle of the Gobi Desert happen to be new giant pigs, bred by stimulation of their pituitaries. But this story has few if any successors. Chinese fiction has numerous videophones and robots, but I have not come across a single scene indicating the chief practical advantage of the videophone, its ability to display drawings and documents. Robots only appear as workers in laboratories, in the kitchen of a scholar, or in his defense. Even in their design, projects are not linked with any productive purpose; the giant spaceship *Eastern* is intended to establish a research station on Mars, but this appears as an end in itself. In "The Human from the Pacific," a whole mountain is repatriated into China for no other purpose than to return a mountain from space.[46] Eventually, a proto-human woman is found in a cave of the mountain, which makes it an indubitable scientific success, adding to China's respect in the scientific community, but hardly to the well-being of the populace, even broadly defined. This unexpected discovery rebuts narrow and practice-oriented conceptions of science. The great benefits of basic research cannot be anticipated.

Jean Chesneaux perceptively explains the presence of such machinery in the fiction of Jules Verne: "Verne's machines are designed for travel, communication, and comfort with the sole object of giving each man a greater control over nature, and of widening the natural and physical conditions governing human life. . . . His machines are not designed to serve the purposes of great captains of industry or large scale manufacturers. In other words, Verne's machines and mechanical arrangements do not produce surplus value. . . . For the machines in these stories do not generally require any human labour; they exploit the resources of nature, not the labour of men."[47] Verne's attitude toward his machinery corresponds well with his Saint-Simonian views, but the persistence of this pattern in China during the Four Modernizations will require further explanation.

Verne solves the problem of the financial costs involved in science by giving his heroes access to unlimited resources, like the Begum's fortune. His protagonists freely dispose of these resources and, as a rule, do not have to get approval for any project; this is different from Verne's later works, where bankers take over the financing of science for their own evil purposes (Stahlstadt), but among the positive heroes this remains unchanged. In Chinese texts, the same pattern is maintained. With huge spacecraft, labs, and the helicopters constantly flown by scientists, there is no question that the funds available to them are unlimited and that scientists alone may dispose of them. There are some stories in which, for minor problems, an "agreement of the higher-ups" is described as necessary, but it is never denied. Actual control by Party or government is patently absent. The costs involved are never discussed; the only limits come from insufficient scientific progress.[48]

Verne subscribed to the Saint-Simonian idea of a future world governed by scientists. As for the present, his hero-scientists leave their war- and money-ridden societies, going into the sea, space, wilderness, or to islands, where they establish communities with their peers. Captain Hatteras explains: "The sea is everything! ... There is perfect peace. Despots have no rights of property over the sea. On its surface they may still try to exercise their iniquitous power, to fight each other, to devour each other, to transport to sea all the horrors of the land; but thirty feet below the surface their dominion ends, their influence fades away. Oh, Sir, you should live in the sea! There alone is freedom! There I recognize no master! There I am free!"[49]

Verne's adventurer-scientists go so far as to establish their own Saint-Simonian utopian communities, like Franceville in Oregon, where they are free from interference by outside powers. The Chinese texts share this motif. Scholars live in scattered enclaves on islands and in research stations, or, ideally removed, in a spaceship, the pure community of scholars. Even in sensitive defense matters, which may require security personnel, as in Wang Xiaoda's "Waves" or Liu Zhaogui's "The Beta Secret," it is inevitably the scientists who achieve the solution. Even the Overseas Chinese professors manage alone against the "certain superpower." Thus, there seems to be a sprinkling of areas that are in a way controlled by Chinese scientists and where they are, in science phantasy, as free as Captain Hatteras 30 feet below the sea. This petrified Saint-Simonian ideal from Jules Verne again needs explanation as a trait in Chinese writing of the post-Mao period.[50]

Finally, Chinese scientists, like Verne's, are Renaissance men. Vernean heroes like Captain Nemo have freed themselves from the constraints of a society that frustrates their humanitarian impulses. These scientists are strong, defiant characters, a pattern maintained later, even in negative figures like Garin. During the 1930s, these protagonists were mostly watered down in the Soviet Union to become bland "positive heroes."[51] Chinese writers followed this later tradition. However, after Xu Chi's well-known portrayal of the mathematician Chen Jingrun (1979), new ways were opened up for the description of unusual and slightly bizarre intellectuals.[52] Although this freedom was explicitly granted, science-phantasy writers were reluctant to enter this field, even with Verne, elements of the Russian tradition, and a highly praised Chinese story as forerunners. Some traces can be seen in Matai, one of the Overseas Chinese professors. He lives and does research on a coral island with his robots and a mute Malayan servant. His colleague, Professor Zhao, is also slightly odd. When Matai recalls their last encounter in Malaysia, the following scene comes to his mind:

Ten years ago he had been in that room, in which Professor Zhao had now been killed. In front of the table there was a Christmas tree with silver shining bells and electric candles in different colors. Professor Zhao and his wife held their 10-year-old Minna and sang with soft voices, "Silent night, holy night." Matai softly opened the door and slipped in. He had a present in his hand and came up behind them; overawed by the family happiness of his friend, he joined them in singing the last verse. (p. 131)

While certainly different from Captain Nemo's heroic stance, this picture of a good and patriotic Chinese scientist living in Malaysia, calling his daughter Minna, and singing "Silent Night" under a Christmas tree, must be quite surprising to the Chinese reader.

We thus see two earlier layers operative below the present surface of Chinese science-phantasy fiction, each one having its own meaning and history. They have congealed, forming a petrified pattern in which the original elements are but dead matter, of which the causes and functions are long forgotten. This does not, however, prevent Chinese science-fiction writers from explicitly referring to these traditions.

Beneath these two layers lies the autochthonous Chinese tradition, in works like *Journey to the West, Enfeoffment of the Gods,* and even *Romance of the Three Kingdoms.*Traditional influences are strongly felt in the military phantasy, where "magical" tricks and technical delusions dominate, as in "Waves." The bionic obsession of the Chinese texts, their absence of energy-intensive battles and *Star Wars* weaponry, again follows traditions in Chinese military and technical thinking. However, the more recent structures are so dominant that older layers become discernible only after the most intensive study of the topmost strata. We continue with the latter.

The Straight Pedigree: A Chinese View
of the History of Chinese Science Fiction

In 1980, two tracts on the history and functions of science-phantasy fiction appeared in China, Ye Yonglie's *Treatise on Science Belles-lettres,* and Xiao Jianheng's article in the periodical *Science Belles-lettres,* "A Tentative Review of the Development of Chinese Science Phantasy Fiction."[53] Ye's draft had circulated widely, been read before various regional science popularization conferences, and received comments and criticism from about everyone officially concerned with science belles-lettres. "As there are practically no systematic studies on the theory of creating science belles-lettres, I could in no way shoulder this responsibility alone. The present book underwent four revisions and absorbed the precious advice of many comrades," writes Ye in his introduction, indicating the official character of his book (p. 1).

Xiao treats science-phantasy fiction separately and is thus less concerned with its integration into science popularization. He feels that, as a romantic literature within the doctrine of socialist realism, science-phantasy fiction claims the tradition of the "active romanticism" ascribed to popular classic Chinese narratives like *Journey to the West.* The Monkey King, in fact, figures prominently in illustrations for science belles-lettres. Ye Yonglie, too, stresses continuity between traditional space phantasies and present-day science-phantasy fiction through his own story, "The Man Who Flies to Pluto." The revived Tibetan serf in that piece finds both of his dreams about life in heaven realized in New China. The supermarket with its ample supply of goods, for which nobody has to pay (he believes), resembles his vision of the easy life in heaven. He finally joins the team flying to Pluto and thus realizes his second dream, to fly to heaven. Modern science phantasy is thus the contemporary version of this "active" romanticism.

This tradition, however, is not actually mentioned by the relatively orthodox Ye Yonglie. He finds two sources for science-phantasy fiction: Verne, who is primarily interested in science, and Wells, whose first interest is in the fictional aspect (p. 34). In Russia, Tsiolkovski and Il'in followed the first tradition, and A. Tolstoi, the other. Gorki had demanded that "in our literature there should be no sharp division between literary works and science popularization" (p. 1), and Il'in had proclaimed the dialectical unity of both strains by saying that science belles-lettres were "literature in full scientific armor" (p. 38). Ye finds the two currents persisting in China, where literary journals favor a more literary approach, while science popularization journals insist on scientific content. Ye and others describe the genre as ambivalent, like "light" (p. 3), the "bat" (with the fur of an animal but wings like a bird), or "pills for children"—bitter in content but sugar-coated.[54]

All writers trace Chinese phantasy fiction back to Lu Xun. The preface to his 1903 translation of Verne's *From the Earth to the Moon* is the *locus classicus* for the official definition of the potential of science fiction,[55] as proclaimed by the man Mao called the "commander-in-chief of China's cultural contingents":

When one describes science in detail, common people loathe it, and before they have read it to the end they have already fallen asleep. Even if you force them against their will, there is nothing you can do about it. Only the power of fiction (*xiaoshuo*) can, by clothing [science] in the [fabulous] garments of [someone like the ancient actor] You Meng, let [science] penetrate into the mind without evoking boredom, even when specific principles are dissected and one delves into [scientific] mysteries. . . . Therefore, if one avoids seriousness in explaining scientific principles and stays facetious, then the reader focuses his eye, concentrates his mind, and grasps [the scientific information] without effort. Thus it has such a power that without fail it gets the reader to reap, without even noticing it, quite a variety of scientific information, to abandon his traditional superstitions, to reform his thinking, and to make up for defects in his education. . . . To fill the *lacunae* in today's translations and lead the Chinese people towards progress, one has to start with science-fiction novels.

Writing over a decade before the May Fourth Movement, Lu Xun expressed the prevalent contemporary hope that China could be transformed through a revolution more technical and educational than political. His words can be dug out as authoritative dicta at any time when, as at present, technical and educational reform, rather than political revolution, is named the magic key for unlocking a prosperous future. With its explicit functionalization of science fiction as science popularization, the passage both corresponds to the present categorical place of this genre and to a widely shared opinion.

Inspired by Tao Xingzhi's 1930 call to "bring the sciences down to the workers and peasants," Lu Xun and Chen Wangdao in 1934 founded the periodical *Taibai*. It attempted to reach the public through radical use of the vernacular, and contained a specific Chinese contribution to science belles-lettres, the science sketch (*kexue xiaopin*). Politically, we are told, the magazine spread a scientific world view, as against Lin Yutang's "humor literature." The honor of having written the first Chinese science-fiction stories also goes to a writer of the left, Gu Junzheng. His "Dream of Peace" (1940) describes how the American people have been brainwashed by mysterious radio waves of Japanese origin into believing that these "Far Eastern Imperialists" are their best friends. Only after the secret broadcasting station is captured and a new program is broadcast to the Americans do they change their stance. An anti-imperialist position is also attributed to other science belles-lettres works appearing at the time, both in Kuomintang areas (Gao Shiqi, Zhou Jianren) and around Yan'an (Dong Chuncai); Gao Shiqi described white blood cells pointedly as "quiet heroes offering resistance to the enemy everywhere and anytime" (unlike the Kuomintang).[56]

Subsequent to the founding of the PRC, an initial sprinkling of science-fiction works appeared only after the Party's call to "March Forward to Science," on 16 September 1955. More classical and Soviet works came out in translation, while *Literature in Translation* printed an American article denouncing capitalist science fiction, although finding merit in Ray Bradbury.[57] More stories came out in the "second flowering" of 1962–1963. The current revival of science fiction is generally described as a consequence of the downfall of the Gang of Four. One author claims that the "Four" threw an "atomic bomb" on science fiction which contaminates the field down to the present.[58]

Science fiction thus has a straight and immaculate pedigree. It is linked with the policies that seem appropriate in today's light—pursuit of science, praise of scientists, and modern scientific education; with the proper names, Gorki, Il'in, Lu Xun, and Gao Shiqi; and the proper times, 1956–1957, 1962–1963, and following 1978. Ye Yonglie modestly sums it up thus: "According to the opinion of some, science-phantasy fiction is one of the barometers of the political climate. When emphasis is on 'letting a hundred flowers bloom and a hundred schools contend,' and on the role of science, works of science-phantasy fiction flourish."[59]

It is certainly not the purpose of the writers composing such a powerful and immaculate pedigree to give a balanced view of the actual history of the genre in China, but to establish its legitimacy. The historical precedents that have been left out are as significant as those included. They are briefly as follows.

Since the first decades of this century, most popular literary magazines in China have carried science fiction. The magazines grouped the articles they published according to category in their tables of contents; one heading was "science fiction" (*kexue xiaoshuo*),[60] the term used also by Lu Xun. Most of the works under this heading were translations, although some might have been written by Chinese and sold as translations to enhance their market value. The protagonists are hardly ever Chinese and the action takes place in other countries. This was still true for Gu Junzheng's stories in 1940. China as the site of a technological utopia seemed unimaginable.

But, apart from science fiction, there was another category, "utopian fiction" (*lixiang xiaoshuo*). It would correspond to what is today "social-science fiction." Its emphasis was not on the technical but the social aspect of modernization. Perhaps the first modern works of this kind were Kang Youwei's *Datong shu* (written around 1901–1902, published in 1935), and *The Future of the New China* (*Xin Zhongguo weilai ji*, 1903) by Liang Qichao, another translator of Verne. Both writers had been influenced in their thinking by Bellamy's *Looking Backward*, a tremendously popular socialist social-science fiction, which was available in Chinese by 1892.[61] The works by both Kang and Liang deal mostly with educational, social, and political changes. In Liang's piece, it is 2062 and China is a success story. A descendant of Confucius outlines the reasons for it, before an international assembly. (He can do this in Chinese, inasmuch as the Russian czar, American president, and British king have all learned this important language.) He mostly refers to tremendous political, administrative, and social changes. Similar narratives appeared later, like "Electric World" (1909). Finally, the anti-utopian texts, which were in fashion both in the West and the Soviet Union during the 1920s and which belong to this same category, found a Chinese counterpart in Lao She's *Cat Country,* a satire on China written in 1939 which, like Orwell's *Animal Farm,* uses the imagery of domestic animals without turning to Aesopian language.[62]

The official pedigree as made up by Ye and Xiao has a point in excluding the texts of this second category because they already figured under a different heading before the Revolution. In the 1930s, they would not have been included in science fiction in either the United States or the Soviet Union. On the other hand, there obviously is an inherent tendency in science fiction to move towards or to include social-science fiction, be it of the utopian or anti-utopian kind. Ye Yonglie even stresses this "ideological" (*sixiangxing*) aspect of the stories within the accepted pedigree (p. 59). Some of the recent Chinese works are also becoming "social-science fiction" by virtue of stronger emphasis on psychological factors rather than plot and suspense. Yan Jiaqi's "Religion, Reason, Practice" has a journalist move through time with Wells's machine. He arrives in Beijing in 1994. It has turned into an idyllic park-city populated by harmonious families; the last dark cloud in their memory is the Gang of Four. The vilification of this faction is also the purpose of Zheng Wenguang's "The 'White Ant' and the Perpetuum Mobile," which imputes to Jiang Qing the intention of overcoming the laws of nature by having a real perpetual-motion machine built. And there is Wei Yahua's "Dream of the Cosy Home," a witty, well-written and controversial story about a scholar's state-arranged marriage with a bionic woman robot. Her complete subservience to all whims of her "lord and master" eventually leads him to disaster. The story nicely satirizes the Chinese (male) scholar's ideal of the docile woman, one that strictly conforms to the behavior traditionally demanded of Chinese women. Thus, while pure social-science fiction remains excluded, science fiction with a social component is not anathema.[63]

More explicit social-science fiction was excluded from Ye's and Xiao's pedigree not for being political but politically "incorrect." Works in the genre receiving their approval had to offer evidence that science fiction was primarily a concern of progressive and "correct" authors. Therefore, stories written during the Great Leap Forward were excluded from the pedigree, although one play of that era had a portrait of Beijing two decades in the future, while Zhao Shuli was in 1955 already describing a big wall painting in *Sanliwan* where the glorious future, with electricity and all, could be seen. Science fiction owed its re-emergence to the so-called Second Great Leap Forward (1977–1978), with its gigantic projects and perspectives; but, after the Third Plenum in 1978, the Great Leap Forward was denounced as irresponsible voluntarism, so later writers did not enter upon this inheritance. It is evident why there was no mention of the restoration of science belles-lettres through the reprinting of Lu Xun's preface in 1973 and the resurgence of most scholarly fields in 1972; it would be at variance with the new past mapped out by the Party, which sees the turning point as 1976, or rather 1978.[64]

Moving into No Man's Land:
Science Phantasy and Literature

Actual Chinese stories quickly moved beyond the confines of genre and pedigree. First, children and youths disappeared from most works, indicating that science phantasy, as opposed to common science belles-lettres and science popularization in general, was now directed at an adult public.[65] Second, the element of science popularization was greatly reduced, while plot and character were emphasized ever more strongly. Already in 1978, the award-winning "Death Rays from Coral Island" had no young people in it, and gave no more than the vaguest idea about the functioning of its super-laser and little nuclear battery.

Third, while generally maintaining the framework of near-future science phantasy, there were signs that *huanxiang*, or phantasy, could encompass much more than simple extrapolations from present technologies. In 1939, Gu Junzheng had already written in the introduction to his "Under the North Pole,"

"Science fiction novels are not inferior to literary works in their capacity to deeply enter one's mind. As a consequence, can we not and should we not clothe some scientific point with a science-fiction story as one of the aids to science popularization? I think this can be done, and it should be tried." But, having seen the wings of phantasy clipped by the Soviet Union in the 1930s, he identified phantasy (*kongxiang*) as the most difficult element: "When I wrote this preface, I realized that this park of science fiction indeed can and must be opened up, but thistles cover the ground in this park and the labor is very demanding. It is indeed a very great problem not to misunderstand the part of phantasy in science fiction."[66]

Once the texts moved out of science popularization for children and became literature to be published in literary periodicals, they entered a categorical no man's land. Into literature, a field defined as "realist," they carried the contraband of phantasy, which did not feel bound by the definition of "rational induction" from present-day scientific knowledge.[67] However, for socialism as for nature, the rule is *vacuum obstat.* Undefined phenomena are seen as a threat in a universe where the political power of the Party is reflected in its complete definition of all recognized phenomena. The actual texts written since 1978 corresponded less and less to the established categories, while still claiming the old privileges. There were nervous reactions in some quarters. The new works were branded "escapist," as going "counter to the Four Modernizations," being "ghost-darts-from-the-cave literature," or, at best, like the prewar knight-errant novel *Jianghu qixia zhuan.*[68] Writers were criticized for "one-sidedly going after the narrative," and "not spending their time at the basic task, which is the popularization of scientific knowledge." Science phantasy, it was said, was "an organic part of science popularization" and the wrong tendencies of these texts "should be watched."[69] Ye Yonglie's description of two currents of science phantasy coexisting since Verne and Wells is thus not just a detached view of history; it is a carefully worded plea to permit a more literature-oriented science phantasy.

Fourth, apart from phantasy, the element of suspense (*jingxian*) had its legitimacy only as a sugar-coating around the bitter but healthful pills of science which were administered to youth. Ye Yonglie writes in his *Treatise on Science Belles-lettres* (pp. 101–103): "In my literary work I have made it so that some techniques of the thriller (*jingxian xiaoshuo*) can be grafted onto science-phantasy fiction. As an example, thrillers pay great attention to getting [the reader] involved. Many thrillers start with an alarming event." Reader enthusiasm for suspense is unabashedly cited as a good reason why such lowly "twigs" should be used for grafting. But, again, the reintroduction of popular forms needs the protective umbrella of science popularization to be acceptable. Once these features are carried over into straight literature, demands are heard to cut the paper supply for science phantasy.

Science-phantasy writers have made great efforts to get the best of both worlds, literature and science popularization. The editors of the periodical *Science Belles-lettres* are all professional writers.[70] Besides the science popularization journals, science phantasy is carried in literary periodicals from *People's Literature* to *Literary Works, Border Literature and Art,* and *Donghai.* Xiao Jianheng has gone furthest in demanding a change of science phantasy's "family name" from "Science" to "Literature," and in proposing to include biology, psychology, sociology, and political science in the term "science." Political, economic, religious, and ethical questions might also be taken up by science phantasy. The common demand of most writers, who have not yet received much support from their literary colleagues, is for a greater latitude for phantasy. In his introductory article to the first issue of *Science Belles-lettres,* the editor, Ma Shitu, writes in the euphoric vein of the summer of 1979: "Yes, we need phantasy. Lenin says, phantasy is 'most precious'; without phantasy one cannot create great works of art. . . . It is true, science needs phantasy, but phantasy needs freedom, and freedom needs democracy. . . . Without scientific freedom and scientific democracy, the scientific phantasy cannot be stimulated, and only when the flower of phantasy opens can a rich scientific harvest be gathered."[71]

Criticisms of the new wave of science phantasy have rarely been directed against specific works, but against a perceived tendency to establish science phantasy as literature. Criticisms have referred to the potential of science phantasy to leave its accepted categorical framework and establish a self-governing island in the realm of literary forms, which might develop into an instrument of innuendo or utopian social criticism, as it did in the West and, for some time during the 1960s, in the Soviet Union with the Strugatskis et al. The absence of a neatly defined theory of science-phantasy fiction, while seen by some as a proof that the genre lacks legitimacy, has been regarded by writers as a chance to explore the potential of science phantasy as part of a new popular literature.

THE NEW SCIENCE-PHANTASY FICTION
AS A LOBBY LITERATURE: A FUNCTIONAL ANALYSIS

The Hypothesis: Science Fiction as a Lobby Literature

Turning from surface, archeology, and pedigree to a functional analysis of science-fiction works under the present circumstances, it hardly needs to be stated that science phantasy was reinstalled in the context of a renewed emphasis on science in the modernization of the country and a concomitant rehabilitation of the social status of scientists. Science-fiction utopia, through the "estrangement" which Darko Suvin regards as the genre's main characteristic, always implies a critical view of the present, by presenting a different future. This does not have to be "dissident," as the Chinese government itself has mapped out a program to rapidly change and improve the present circumstances. Heller has described some of the specific techniques of this estranged reflection in his study, *De la science fiction soviétique.* Some of these techniques are used in the Chinese texts, while others might have to be added. Those applicable include the following.[72]

First, "extrapolation from the present." A Chinese example would be the description of improved standards in Chinese science as a consequence of current science policies. Second, "inversion." Example: Depiction in the science phantasy of unlimited resources for scientific activities, and lack of controls, even though tight financial limits and political controls are imposed on present-day science. Third, "negation." Example: The simple absence of a phenomenon in science phantasy, the presence of which is only too conspicuous today. Fourth, "exaggeration." Example: A modest promise made by government leaders by way of verbal concession is taken verbatim and blown up in its future effects far beyond the original intention.

Heller is dealing with texts that present an ensemble of the future society; this, however, is not true for the Chinese science phantasies. They are very adamant in presenting only that segment of future society which has to do with scientists and science. In no works do the government or the Party, the military or the "workers and peasants" play any role, although other intellectuals, like journalists, may occasionally be admitted. The stories do not indicate (as does Efremov) any assumption that Chinese society some decades hence will consist only of scientists. Scientists live among themselves, in their typically remote colonies, but these are only enclaves within a society where there are also those (never mentioned) who deal with the "class struggle" and "the struggle for production." [73] In Maoist thought, class struggle, struggle for production, and scientific experiment are the totality of man's struggle activities. While there is a rank order, the three activities are basically on the same level, as are the social groups engaging in them. Chinese literature since 1949 has eulogized China's cadres (political struggle) and workers and peasants (production), but never her scholar heroes, with their separate hopes and demands. I hypothesize that the new science fiction is such a literature, presenting scientists' group aspirations in the form of the phantasy future, and portraying how scientists would operate in the larger framework of society if their demands were met.

The intended readership would, if this were true, fall into two groups. First, the traditional intended reader would be the actual and potential scientific community. The texts would have to inform and reproduce the collective phantasy or demands of this group. The second group of readers might be called the "addressee," namely the authorities to whom these texts would be presented publicly in printing, as the collective demand and offer of compromise from the science community. Since the texts are published officially, within the state printing monopoly, all participants in the Chinese literary process—

writers, authorities, and readers—would conclude that there is basic official acceptance of both the demands and compromises. To present the collective demands of a social-interest group to the authorities, promising benefit to the public, and a willingness to compromise on other big issues of society (the political structure, national interests, and so forth) in reciprocation, is the function of a lobby. The hypothesis I shall try to verify is that the new adult science-phantasy fiction of the PRC operates as a lobby literature for the scientific community. The term *lobby literature* is intended as a functional concept, without derogatory connotations.

The Territory of the Science Republic

Chinese science phantasies carefully delineate the territory with which they deal. Scholars operate at their research sites, which tend to be in isolated, outlying places like Tibet, the forests of Guangdong, the Xisha Islands, or under a barren mountain in Heilongjiang close to the Soviet border. They may be complete science cities like the space center in Zheng Wenguang's *Flying Towards Sagittarius* or they may be institutes that somehow, like the Bionics Institute near the Vietnamese border in "The Beta Secret," do not seem to be surrounded by dense population. [74] Professor Matai from Malaysia, with his mute servant and robots running a complete research unit on a coral reef in the South China Sea, is the extreme case of the single-minded scholar. The spaceship and the space station are likewise the purest of all scientist communities.

The scholars are not tied down to a single site. They constantly move, but from research site to research institute, or from institute to conferences with other scholars in Beijing's Academy. They would normally have to move through territories not run by scientists, but I have not come across any description of it, except for Ye Yonglie's atypical work, "The Man Who Flies to Pluto," wherein the revived former serf leaves the institute and wanders through socialist Lhasa. Description of life outside the scholarly enclaves would allow, even necessitate, description of and commentary on the life of other segments of the population in the future. The lack of it means that science-fiction writers very explicitly do *not* articulate possible demands and criticisms from other sectors of the population, but it also implies that the writers refrain from comparing the relative social, economic, and moral status of their protagonists to that of "the others."

Communication between the scholars' islands is usually achieved through videophones; their purpose is not technical communication, but direct personal contact between the members of the science community across the nondescript territories of the "others." If the physical transposition of scholars to one of the other islands is necessary, as for a conference, or to go from the institute to the research site (in the case of archeology), the helicopter is in common use, allowing scientists to hop over the intervening *terra incognita*.[75] In rarer cases, a plane is used, but there seems to be no contact between scholars and "others" on the plane. Sometimes cars are used, as in *Flying Towards Sagittarius* and "The Beta Secret." But these cars only drive on highways going through wooded land, and the chauffeur is an automaton. While the scattered territory of this science republic obviously occupies only a small part of China, it is immeasurably enlarged by the whole of outer space. Space is, moreover, inhabited exclusively by scholars; beings met in interstellar encounters as a rule are scholars, too.

The "others" remain so undefined that we hear neither derogatory remarks about those who labor in production, nor romantic sighs about how nice it would be to lead a simple, industrious life on the land. The science community is good but no better or worse than any other, it just happens to be the exclusive focus of these texts. This would imply that all other literary works are similarly subsumed under an appropriate lobby literature; for the military, there would be the war novels, and numerous other writings for the workers, peasants, and cadres. In many cases, no intellectuals appear in those other works and, if they do, only as caricatures who have to learn from the common people and the Party. Science phantasy fills the gap, without denying the legitimacy of other social activities, the status of the territories in which they take place, or the literature describing them. Science territories do not expand, becoming the model for the others. Being located in out-of-the-way places, they do not even compete for land.

The works also offer a compromise through a strange feature they share with their Russian and East German counterparts. For all their freedom of movement, scientists never go to Japan, Switzerland, or Poland, even though international travel is a much-coveted status symbol among Chinese scholars in real life. Socialist science fiction excludes the right of foreign travel from its demands. The scientists' remarkable vertical (extra-terrestrial) mobility may compensate for the governmental restrictions on their horizontal (earthly) mobility.

The Members of the Science Republic

Membership in the science community is elaborated through elimination or replacement of people not belonging to it, and recruitment. The large body of workers and other personnel potentially present in scientific units, as well as in the private homes of scholars (cooks, cleaning women, chauffeurs) is com-pletely absent from Chinese science phantasy; either they are not necessary any more, as their work has become obsolete, or they have been replaced by robots, who cook in the kitchen, do the routine work of scientific research, and act as body-guards in security-related fields.

The higher forms of research are exclusively done by the genial scholars themselves. The robots are trained, as some Chinese authors state, according to Asimov's three criteria— not to hurt their masters, to be obedient to their masters, and to protect themselves without endangering man.[76] This marks the ironic "inversion" of the relationship between the scholar on the one hand and the "workers and cadres" on the other, as it was portrayed in texts published during the Cultural Revolu-tion. There, the scholar had to "learn" from the others, follow their guidance and direction, and submit to the "dictatorship of the proletariat" when he failed to do so. Science phantasy does not go so far as to portray workers as the docile servants of scholars. That would be politically unacceptable; letting robots fill the role makes the point clearly enough.

The eliminated "others," however, are not just "workers, peasants, and soldiers," but also the representatives of the government and Party, who exert considerable control over all aspects of science. By "exaggerating" the effects of recent Party concessions which allow scientists to participate in decision-making in science matters, the stories reduce the role of the politicans to zero. There are no derogatory or polemical statements about "the politicians"; they are simply omitted from the future science community. In some security-related stories, security personnel might even turn up as the narrators, as in "The Beta Secret," but care is taken to state that they have studied their respective scientific field and that they are learning from the scientists, not vice versa.[77] Even security problems are solved by scientists, not the Public Security Bureau.

Recruitment of new members into the science republic strongly emphasizes the self-perpetuation of the community. All the inmates of the *Eastern* on its way to Sagittarius are children of scientists. They educate themselves in the spaceship to become worthy successors to their parents. Professor Zhao's daughter in "Death Rays from Coral Island" is his scientific assistant. The woman geologist in "The Son-in-Law Who Didn't Sleep" is the daughter of a schoolteacher and is married to a scientist. In many cases, the genealogy is not given, but, if it is, scientists are the children of scientists. This implies criticism, via "negation," of the goal of producing an intelligentsia from children of the "working class." It also promotes the advantages of being the child of a scientist—having early initiation into the mysteries of science. Even when no family background is given, the actual features of the science heroes present the implied criteria for their qualification. These criteria are exclusively endogenous to the science community, which implies, via "negation," the rejection of externally imposed political criteria.

In one single case, a real outsider makes it into the science community, the Tibetan serf who can neither read nor write, in "The Man Who Flew to Pluto." But Ye Yonglie had to go to some lengths in this highly propagandistic piece to make this intrusion acceptable. The serf first enters the science community as a frozen object of research, not as a member. As it turns out, his involuntary fast-freezing offers the proof, otherwise difficult to come by, that humans can be frozen and revived after decades. He has unwittingly conducted a scientific experiment upon himself. His success is instrumental for the realization of China's plan to explore Pluto, which had been hampered by the human life span being too short for such a long flight. This repeats the pattern, encountered in other stories, of the attentive youth who hits upon an important find. Second, he shares with the scientists the "vision" of flying in heaven, although in an archaic, religious cloak. On the basis of this important contribution as well as his proto-scientific vision, which led him up the mountain braving wind and snow, he can be considered a likely candidate for the science community. He also shows a marked patriotism. Then, informed about the plans to go to Pluto, he wants to join, to fulfill his dream. He is willing to throw himself into an intensive course, from basic reading and writing of Tibetan, Chinese, and English, to astronomy, so that he can pass, within a year, the rigid examination for astronauts. Thus he has to leap impressive hurdles in order to be frozen in again, but now as a member of the scientific community on its way to Pluto. That is not all. Even his lineage contains a strong scientific endowment. The young woman researcher sitting at his hospital bed when he awakens from his cold sleep turns out to be his granddaughter. His wife, pregnant at the time of his separation and freezing, had borne a son, who grew up to become the director of the medical team that found the frozen man and restored him to life. Dreams, chance, and willingness are necessary but not sufficient conditions for membership in the science community.

The Social Life of the Science Republic

In the closed circle of scientists, spouses, too, are scientists, if mentioned at all. The wife of the "Son-in-Law Who Didn't Sleep" is a geologist, the chief engineer in *Flying Towards Sagittarius* is married to a scientist, and love affairs among the young people in this novel are all between young scientists. In "The Human from the Pacific," a woman astronomer falls in love with China's top astronaut. Professor Zhao's daughter in

Malaysia is married to another physicist, who is an assistant to her father.

Among the motives listed by Zheng Wenguang as driving scientists forward in Verne's *roman scientifique*, "helping friends in distress" precedes "the search for knowledge" and "struggle against nature."[78] Indeed the close family ties among scholars play an important role in the plots. Professor Zhao's son-in-law takes it upon himself to bring the laser to China after Zhao is assassinated, and he again is saved by his wife, who searches for him in the South China Sea. A compelling motive for the chief engineer in *Flying Towards Sagittarius* to accelerate the development of the next, still faster generation of spaceships is the fact that two of his children are on the *Eastern;* his other daughter joins the rescue crew to save her brother and sister, as well as her lover. Besides family relationships, the novel shows strong bonds between teacher and disciple, and among fellow students.

Closed social relationships are attributed to China's feudal past in such 1979 works as Liu Binyan's "Between Men and Monsters," Wang Meng's "The Barber's Tale," Ru Zhijuan's "Path through the Grasslands," and Sha Yexin's *What If I Really Were?*[79] In science phantasy the very same bonds that, in these other texts, hold an entire caste together in a mutual exchange of backdoor privileges, appear only in their purest terms. They motivate scholars towards their greatest and most selfless exploits. There is not a single case in science-phantasy fiction where these bonds are used for "irregular" purposes, for example, getting an unqualified person into an institute, pushing through an immature project to aggrandize oneself, or simply misusing the multiple gadgets available in the science territory for personal pleasure.

Even Ye Yonglie, whose exceptional story "Corrosion" ("Fushi," 1981) probes the darker aspects of a Chinese scientist's psychology, never imputes corruption or backdoor dealing to his character.[80] He contrasts a young scholar, whose dark skin, muscular build, uncouth manners, and ignorance of foreign languages betray a working-class background, with a white-skinned, delicately built and well-educated colleague who is considered to be the better scholar. An unknown type of corroding bacteria has invaded a returning Chinese spacecraft, killing the astronaut as well as the rescue team hurrying to the landing site in the Gobi Desert. The dark-skinned biologist accompanies his professor into the makeshift laboratory in the desert to analyze and tame these bacteria, which threaten them and mankind. The scientists succeed in isolating the corroding agent and transform it into a useful industrial product. The only material resisting corrosion is titanium, named after the Greek superhuman Titans. While the two scholars in the desert prove to be true "Titans," their white-skinned colleague is corroded by an academic bacterial agent, envy, because of their breakthrough. He jumps on the bandwagon, spending much energy wondering which of the authors' names will appear first at the top of their common paper. Together all three receive the Nobel Prize, but with the call from Stockholm comes another, saying that the desert station does not respond any more. Sent there with a rescue mission, the white-skinned survivor signals to the waiting helicopter to return without him. In a telegram from the laboratory he explains that the true Titans were his colleagues in the desert. Shamed but inspired by their example, he volunteers to stay there alone to finish the work they started.

Ye shows his familiarity with the workings of many a scholarly mind in his description of the maneuvers of the white-skinned scholar. But even he remains a good scholar throughout. What is more important, the science community depicted does not need "heart-to-heart talks" with Party cadres or criticism meetings to solve its internal problems. Models of pure scholarly devotion abound within the science community; their silent and modest presence suffices to cure the corrosive effects of academic envy. This self-regulatory capacity of the science community is in stark contrast to the bureaucracy as it is presented by writers like Liu Binyan or Wang Meng. In their stories, the stimulus for correction inevitably comes from "outside" the bureaucracy, from the common people.

The manifold social problems one might expect in any community either do not arise in the science republic or are quickly solved. In none of the texts is there a single squabble among the scientists. There is only the most perfect harmony, based on the values of the nuclear family, teacher-student loyalty, fellow-student friendship, and an unmitigated devotion to the motivations appearing at the end of Zheng Wenguang's list, such as thirst for knowledge and desire to subdue nature.

The social harmony prevailing within these territories and the floating islands in space does not show any trace of a fundamental change in social relations due to China's rapid technical development. The scholar has all the traditional virtues associated with his calling. In the most extreme case, *Flying Towards Sagittarius,* young scientists pass the decisive years of their youth under the extreme stress of imprisonment in space, but at no time is there any tension among them. The writer introduces, it is true, a certain social hierarchy within the spacecraft by letting three youths form a provisional cell of the Communist Youth League, complete with Secretary, but this is the only mention of any political structure or concern, and the Youth League Secretary does not derive any decision-making power from his role.

The complete absence of friction under stress in this "family of scientists" is reinforced by the devices employed by the authors to remove any taint from the pure values that dominate the scientists. Parents and children are reunited, lost spouses found again ("Death Rays from Coral Island"), small misunderstandings between the generations are cleared up ("The Son-in-Law Who Didn't Sleep"), and doubts about the motives of old friends are removed ("The Beta Secret," "Waves"). Again, Ye Yonglie provides an interesting example; the frozen Tibetan serf, shortly before taking off for Pluto, is reunited with his spouse. She had been taken away from him during the flight decades ago. But now her husband is flying off to Pluto and their happy reunion after fifty years seems about to end as abruptly as it came about. Ye soothes the reader's fears about an infringement of the marital happiness of scientists in his last scene; the spaceship has just taken off when the old lady appears on national television with a friendly smile, to reassure the public that she will now enter a freezing tube, patiently to await the return of her husband from Pluto.

The Chinese scientists' most important virtue is their pronounced and unquestionable patriotism. While not exclusive to scientists, this virtue is essential to them; their claim to autonomy rests on it. At harmony, the scholarly community is indeed innocent of the dark forces still rampant in the world. The extreme case is Mo Lilin's "Strange Course," wherein scholars from Sirius (who share their earthly colleagues' features and have even memorized Chinese poems) are overpowered by predatory astronauts from another star, because in the science community on Sirius human relations are, as one of the scholars explains, so "pure and honest" that the scholars have become "too muddleheaded." They "know cunning, greed, envy, and slaughter only from old records."[81]

The enemies of humanitarian science know about this naïveté of the scholar. In "Death Rays from Coral Island," "Waves," and "The Beta Secret," foreign agents try to use former fellow-student or teacher-disciple relationships to get access to Chinese inventions for their own evil purposes. For a moment, they manage to fool the Chinese scientist, which gets the story going, but inevitably the sensory power of Chinese patriotism smells them out, so that in no case are the spies able to do much damage. Not a single ethnically Chinese member of the science community is turned around by the forces of evil; those seeming members who switch allegiance are either imposters ("Waves"), non-Chinese (Hans of "Death Rays from Coral Island"), or robot-doubles ("The Beta Secret"). Thus, patriotism is stronger than any other motivation in the Chinese scientist. Even the chief engineer in *Flying Towards Sagittarius* makes it clear that his primary motive in rescuing the *Eastern* is to do something for China's glory, not to save his children (p. 192).

While the strong colors in which the patriotism of the Chinese scholar is presented most certainly have some factual basis, their emphasis serves another purpose as well. The science republic can be a self-contained social unit because its high moral standards and all-pervading Chinese patriotism guarantee against foreign intrigue. This patriotism, goes the argument, is so reliable that no further controls from the "outside" will ever be necessary. Thus, government, Party, and security personnel are never instrumental in the denouements of the plots, although the presence of these people on the fringes of the republic is tolerated. Given the current very strong control over Chinese scholars and their contacts at home and abroad, this depiction contains both a promise of virtuous and patriotic conduct, and a demand that there be no government interference.

Defining and Financing Scientific Projects

The theoretical postulate of the right of the science republic to govern itself finds practical expression in the description of the definition and financing of science projects. Chinese science-fiction writers solve this problem with the instrument of "negation." Scarcity and outside control of funds are not to be found in the stories. Never do the "authorities" rule out a project because funds are lacking. The problem gets more intricate, however, when we come to the definition of research content, which might reflect priorities of the "others."

The categories out of which the projects are developed are scientific interest, in the strictest sense, and feasibility. Neither practical use for the "others," nor potential other uses of the funds ever enter as criteria. "The Human from the Pacific," with its repatriation of a complete mountain from space, explicitly makes the point that one cannot predict the benefits of basic research. The work of the science republic is entirely self-centered and concerned with the "enlarged reproduction" of science. We do not know what the purpose of the station on Mars might be in *Sagittarius,* nor whether the military use of "Waves" was an explicit research end or a spinoff, like the wave-simulated "Mona Lisa" in the living room of the professor and "fence" around his house. Usually a study which seems to be without any further interest turns up unexpected scientific results. While this line of thought might be highly rewarding and comfortable for the members of the science community, it might be justly argued that it will not endear its members to the productive or administrative "others." What, then, does scientific research as presented in these stories have to offer the "others," since it promises no better machinery, plants, or ways to solve the problems of industrialization?

Two positive effects are described as resulting from the research. The first and constantly repeated one is prestige for China as a country of advanced science. This motif is already present in Liang Qichao's *The Future of the New China*. In current stories, foreigners flock to the Chinese science enclaves to see surprising feats like the *Eastern*. Chinese scientists routinely receive Nobel Prizes. They have topped the world's most advanced levels in astronautics, bionics, paleontology, and medicine, and have gone a step further through scientific adaptation of ancient wisdom from the ancestors, such as *qigong* breathing techniques.

The second contribution made by China's scholarship is defense against the Polar Bear. Examples already adduced include the "Waves," the shark patrol fish, the robot-double from the Bionics Institute, a communication device in *Flying Towards Sagittarius*, the amphibious aircraft/submarine, and the "Death Rays."

These virtues of science for international status and defense rather than for lifting living standards permit us to define the "addressee" of these stories. The works are not addressed to the participants in production, to the "workers and peasants," but to the government and Party leaders. However, benefits are only mentioned as the eventual outcome of scientific endeavor. They do not at any moment enter discussion of the selection of priorities and definition of goals. Writers are careful not to provide government and Party authorities an excuse for joining in the decision-making process.

Hence, the scientific community defines itself as capable of handling its social life, security problems, and research decisions quite independently of the "others," without in any way questioning the legitimacy of these "other" endeavors. It modestly demands unlimited funds and complete autonomy in setting its work goals, promising international prestige and military modernization as a spin-off for the government. The texts take the authorities as their main addressee; they try to present the common aspirations of the intended readers, the scientists. The inherited structures of science phantasy in China today do indeed take on surprisingly new meanings.

The Lifestyle of the Science Community

Read as a kind of lobby literature, the stories would have to give some idea of the lifestyle anticipated or demanded by the science community. Indeed, this is a major preoccupation of the works. Although futuristic gadgetry exclusively serves the scientists' personal comfort and the end of scientific research itself, scientists are presented as a devoted and hard-working group; I have never in any text found a single scientist who has become lazy, bored, or cynical, or who has started to question the wisdom of further research in certain areas (like nuclear energy). No external pressures are necessary to keep the scientist going. The problem is rather to prevent him from overworking, like the chief engineer in *Flying Towards Sagittarius,* who neglects his children—the only unfavorable comment I have been able to find (p. 6).

The gadgetry of scientific research, consisting of robots and computers, is legitimized by its direct service to professional activity. The stories, however, refuse to separate the scientists' work from their private sphere. The scholars work at home in a separate study (*Flying Towards Sagittarius*); they receive other scholars or journalists at home ("Waves," "The Man Who Flies to Pluto"); and, in one case, a scholar experiments on himself at home ("The Son-in-Law Who Didn't Sleep"). All the scientists constantly telephone from their homes by videophones. The spheres of home and work are unified by the single-minded activity of the scholar. Ideally they merge, as in spaceships and astronaut recreation camps (*Flying Towards Sagittarius,* "The Human from the Pacific"). As in Verne's Saint-Simonian utopian cities, and well in tune with the strong familism present in the Chinese genre, the ideal home of the scientist contains all the gadgetry from the institute; it is spacious, with a robot in the kitchen and a music room. Even when working underground, in a secret base in China's rough north, scientists do not have to miss the amenities of a comfortable, mechanized home. In "Waves," the mountain has been completely dug out from inside; in the gigantic cave which encloses the local science republic, a powerful lamp (straight from *Black Diamonds*) has been hung to act as the sun; there, the inventor of the "waves" lives in his well-appointed one-family house with lawn. The aircraft/submarine resting on the Pacific floor is equipped with "Chinese rugs and sofas."[82] Professor Zhao's large home in Malaysia has a vault housing his invention, and his private plane is used only to bring the invention to the "fatherland."

The indivisible activity of the scholars legitimizes the presence of supermodern and comfortable technology in their "private" sphere. They never use their helicopters, robots, or cars for pleasure. Thus, their living conditions may be described with loving care. Let me quote from two descriptions. They seem to express a deep longing.

When the young people enter the spaceship *Eastern* together with the engineer, before the Russian attack, they are pleased to see how the interior decoration of these spaceships has developed. A 15-year-old girl from Shanghai reacts thus:

She had the impression that she had not entered the capsule of a spaceship but a comfortable parlor. This was quite different from the narrow capsules of the spaceships she had seen in films! A row of light sofas. . . . Ai, the floor was covered with a rubber carpet, which was soft and resilient. And the walls? They were made of a darkish material. Xulai touched it with her hand; it was exceedingly hard. The room was quite bright, but there were no lamps. Xulai at first did not understand this, but Yabing pointed towards the ceiling, and she noticed that the entire ceiling radiated a mild light, so that it was as bright inside the craft as outside.

Indeed, this is "not a normal spaceship, but simply a space house, a 'house' in which one could live for a long time."[83] It is equipped with an automatic kitchen stuffed with a liberal amount of delicacies, automatic garbage recycling, and an entire roof that can eventually be rolled aside on simple command to open a window into space. This spaceship is 800 meters long and 100 meters in diameter!

These dimensions seem to reflect the plight of the often badly housed Chinese scientists (as described by Chen Rong in "When You Get to Middle Age") rather than to anticipate the real dimensions of future spaceships in this age of miniaturization. The image of the narrow capsule of the old spacecraft would nicely convey the former living conditions of scientists.

Thus, with the instrument of inversion, scientists' demands for private comfort are presented.

Here is an introductory scene from "The Human from the Pacific" by Zheng Wenguang:

> So clean and white was the sand of the beach at Sea Star Park, so green the softly rolling sea, like a piece of jadeite, like a piece of green velvet, that it radiated under the sun rays of the early summer with indescribable splendor and luster. . . . At dawn, the well-known astronaut Lu Jiajun came trotting out of the recreation center. He wore brown swimming trunks, which left the greater part of his muscular but exceedingly lissome body free. He was a man of medium size, just past his thirties. His entire attitude and expression showed that he was in the Golden Age of his astronautical career. He went to the sandy beach and started exercising, leaping up wildly and letting his body nimbly roll off in the soft sand. Then he slowly went towards the water. He bent and splashed the icy-cold water over his chest and back; easily, and with hardly a sound, he dived into the water and swam like a barracuda towards the deep. [84]

His swim however only lasts some pleasant minutes. Then a colleague gesticulates to him from shore, with a telegram calling him to his next assignment. The structure of scientists' work and their own motivation guarantee that they will not become lazy. The texts also refuse to put the life of the future scientist into comparative perspective. Thus, science phantasy does not demand special privileges for scientists, nor does it accept the argument that some compatibility should prevail between the lifestyle of this group and that of the "others." Like their scientific projects, the scientists' lifestyle should be exclusively determined by the internal conditions and necessities of their science republic.

The intellectual life of the science community is part of the same pattern. Scientists talk exclusively about science. The literary and artistic products they mention are mostly science-phantasy fiction and science-fiction films. [85] While this is in part a self-advertisement for this literature, showing that young people eagerly read and are "inspired" [86] by it, it also indicates that the science republic is culturally and ideologically self-contained. Apart from general patriotic statements and the foreign-policy projections in "The Man Who Flies to Pluto," the scientists never talk about politics or mention a political system or problem, nor do they ever read political works. The absence of political references is, via "negation," a comment about the system of political-study classes for scientists. At the same time, however, it contains the promise that scientists will keep out of politics and support the present government in its assumptions about international politics, especially with regard to the Soviet Union.

SCIENCE-PHANTASY FICTION
AS LOBBY LITERATURE

The intended readership of Chinese science phantasy is the potential and actual science community. Within the texts, science phantasy is read by scientists. The real writers of science fiction are, with rare exceptions, themselves scientists, active in science popularization. They are familiar with the interests and hopes of their peers. They have moved into science phantasy to express, develop, and mold the common phantasy of their community. From occasional remarks it can be gleaned that a science-fiction-fan community is developing in China. Quite apart from its official function as science popularization and "recruiting officer"[87] for the scientific community, science phantasy presents the common aspirations of this community.

To the authorities, their addressee, the texts present both demands and offers of compromise. The latter include tacit acceptance of the social system of the "other" China, explicit support for the government's view of international politics, the promise of perfectly moral and patriotic behavior, and of contributions to the international renown and defense of China. Offers of compromise even include the acceptance of government-imposed travel restrictions. In return, science fiction quite unequivocally demands a self-regulating science republic, with many improvements in the scientists' lives, such as in housing. However, none of the texts could have been published without some official "outside" approval. This informs the reading strategies with which the texts are approached, and these strategies again influence the leadership's deliberations as to whether or not to publish these works. As officially published pieces, they can claim a certain official approval for both the demands and offers of compromise. Changes in the patterns of the texts will be read as changes in government policies.

The most conspicuous feature of the stories is their exclusive treatment of the science community. Politically speaking, this implies that these communities are not a model for the "others." This leaves the Party monopoly in these realms intact. However, the introduction of a lobby literature dealing with a single interest group transforms other literature into lobby works for other social groups. A number of statements by Chinese writers concerned with science fiction indicate that they consciously see science-phantasy fiction as a lobby literature for the science community. Ai Wu, the writer of industrial novels who is also on the board of *Science Belles-lettres,* writes that biographies of "revolutionary heroes" and of "workers and peasants" have been written under socialism, but "at the same time we need literary descriptions of scientists."[88] In the postface to his *Flying Towards Sagittarius,* Zheng Wenguang explicitly states that science, as one of the three revolutionary activities (besides class struggle and struggle for production), needs its own literature.

There is some literary criticism dealing with the new science phantasies. The editors of the first collection of science-phantasy stories have written in their preface: "There is a prevalent problem. The depiction of the environment of the story does not fit the time background. There are even some quite good science phantasies that describe the environment as not transcending present levels, while the characters and the wonders they perform are futuristic."[89] Others explicitly demand that future social relations should become one of the themes of science phantasy. These criticisms, however, never question the exclusive depiction of scientists in these works. Their criticism does not ask for an enlargement of the constituency of the lobby or a description of its interaction with other segments of the population.

The near absence of social-science fiction does not seem to be due to the assumption that social relations within the community might not change, but is explained by the implied promise of good behavior. The fact that the self-regulation demanded for the science community is not extended to other communities implies acceptance of the official limits of discourse under the Four Modernizations. The latter include only technical modernizations, pointedly excluding democracy, the "fifth modernization." The link between the science community and the "others" is patriotism, not a common democratic pattern.

This is exactly the point where the only science-phantasy fiction I have found in the unofficial periodicals (*minban kanwu*) starts, "A Tragedy that May Yet Happen in the Year 2000," by Su Ming. It was published in May 1979, in the periodical *Beijing Spring*. The author concedes that China will have a very advanced science by the year 2000, especially in the field of defense. A gigantic military parade in that year shows a wealth of strategic missiles, ultra-secret arms, and bombers. The hero lives on the 47th floor of the "green city." But the story focuses on the consequences of rapid technological development unaccompanied by democratic changes. An important leader, presumably Deng Xiaoping, dies in 1998; shortly thereafter, in 2000, the Gang of Four are rehabilitated and, on 2 October 2000, a "big character poster" is hung on Democracy Wall carrying the title "A poster which was hung here 22 years ago." The story consists mostly of this poster. It begins: "Last month, in November 1978, Japanese friends asked Chinese leaders a question, to which they did not receive an answer: 'What Vice-Premier Deng Xiaoping has said is excellent, but might he not change his opinion next year?' The political situation in China changes so rapidly that the laws fixed today might already be obsolete a year later. China is a big country with many people; its economic development and the improvement of the living conditions of its people are both very slow. Only the hectic pace of its political changes is observed by all modern nations, with eyes aghast. . . . What is the reason for them? . . . The reason is that, under the high degree of centralization of power in this country, the security or instability of the state depends on some individuals and the fate of 900 million people is in the hands of a few leaders."

The author traces this system back to the war and to Stalinism and argues that, as long as this system continues, a sudden coup at the central level remains possible. His charge is that Deng's reforms in the social field have not gone far enough. "You have to give democracy and effective power to the people, and you should not give the people the honorary title of master of the house, as if painted bread could satisfy hunger." The poster, ending on these words, has been put up again because the author feels that, with the return of the Gang of Four, things have gone exactly as he predicted.

The author of this unique piece of near-future social-science fiction supports the program associated with Deng Xiaoping, but assumes that social progress has quite consciously been left out of the modernization program, and that this has indeed led to the danger of a state with a modern military technology but a very backward political system. Thus, the repetition in Chinese science phantasy of the Vernean pattern of idealized and unchanging social relations and attitudes portrayed amid a rapidly advancing technology, which might seem due to naiveté, in fact turns out to be a rather conscious political concession. Su Ming challenges this compromise as being dangerous for the country.

Love Stories: The Meaning of Love and Marriage in China

KAM LOUIE

After more than a decade of silence on the topic of love, the Chinese literary scene has, in the last four years, seen the emergence of hundreds of stories with love themes. While the absence of love as a topic in the official literature of the Cultural Revolution was artificially imposed and so may not have had a basis in reality,[1] the sudden appearance of so many love stories does mark a more liberal and individualistic trend that has typified Chinese thinking in recent years. This chapter is an examination of that trend as reflected in the treatment of love in short stories during the years 1978-1981.

The chapter focuses on love in the short story because, as a *People's Daily* commentary points out, that literary format has been the "most outstanding" one in Chinese literature these last four years.[2] Moreover, since a short story can be written and published quickly, it is often more sensitive to changes in social attitudes and behavior. This is not to say that stories have been the only literary works dealing with love. Indeed, poems, plays, and filmscripts have all been "flooded" with romance.[3] Love has become such an indispensable ingredient in creative writing that the authors have been criticized for using the formula, "A literary creation is equal to X [which may be any topic at all] + wounds + love."[4]

As love has been such a pervasive feature of creative writing in the last four years, only stories that have generated controversy or represent a certain type have been chosen for discussion here. They are taken from national as well as regional literary magazines. While there may be slight regional differences in orientation,[5] such variations are not significant enough to warrant special consideration.

The literature is surveyed roughly by chronology. This approach highlights the fact that the stories have moved from a prescriptive treatment of love, in 1978–1979, to a more descriptive one later. We first deal with changing views of the abstract idea of love itself, and then with more concrete problems that writers now perceive in society.

Although literature is no substitute for sociology, and writers sometimes act as spokesmen for official policies,[6] the conscious attempts by authors to write by "delving into life" (*ganyu shenghuo*) in the last few years do mean that they express, within acceptable political limits, what they perceive to be major concerns facing lovers at the time they were writing. Even Zhang Jie, whose story "Love Cannot Be Neglected" emphasizes love above all else,[7] says of her work that "it is not a love story, but one that investigates problems in sociology."[8]

The stories are thus treated not merely as literary pieces, but as social commentaries. As much as possible, the accuracy of the writers' perceptions of social problems will be tested against other accounts such as press reports and "readers' letters" published in newspapers and magazines.[9]

IN SEARCH OF A DEFINITION

Due to the dramatic upheavals that have occurred in China in the last few years, the treatment of love in literature has undergone radical changes. When the topic was first raised in literature in 1978, writers were most concerned with finding a suitable definition for love. This was understandable, not only because the political climate at the time still demanded a political definition, but because love had gone unmentioned in literature for more than ten years. The early writers thus felt it was their role to reassert love by defining it back into existence, as it were.

The first love story, by the award-winning Liu Xinwu, appeared in January 1978. As one critic pointed out, it was more an ideological treatise than a literary work.[10] With all its shortcomings, though, credit should still be given to "The Place of Love" for breaking the silence on this topic. The official publications had neglected any mention of love for so long that, at this stage, any information regarding love was eagerly sought, especially by the young. After the story appeared, Liu was besieged with letters by people both seeking advice and telling about their own romances.[11] The authorities must also have felt the need to advise the young on this, since many books and numerous columns in newspapers and magazines began to offer advice to young readers about love.

In 1978, how was this love prescribed? Love, according to the character Aunt Feng in "The Place of Love,"

should be built on a common revolutionary goal and purpose. It should be able to withstand the struggles of life, and continually develop over time and thus enrich and enhance itself.[12]

Personally, this fictional expert on love has had only one lover, and he has been dead for thirty years! Liu Xinwu's notion of love is based, one surmises, not on the actual but the ideal, not on experience but on faith.[13]

The ideal of falling in love because of a shared commitment to socialism has been standard in Communist literature since 1942,[14] and dominates most stories published in 1978. The model lover, as in the case of "The Unsatisfactory Brother-in-Law," is someone whose dedication to work is so intense that he

spends the days working in the fields and the nights guarding the seedlings. He works regardless of the weather, to the point of forgetting to sleep and eat.[15]

His attractiveness is increased, too, by his parents' having been cadres who suffered under the Gang of Four.[16] In the case of "The Unsatisfactory Brother-in-Law," the young couple also have to put up with opposition from the girl's family. But, after the Gang of Four falls, the families are reconciled and the boy's chances of getting into university greatly increase, with his mother resuming her post as Director of the City Transportation Department.

Such a happy ending is typical of many of the early stories, which describe lovers who oppose the Gang-of-Four line and who are willing to work for socialism. Many stories, such as "Fate" and "Baoyu Cliff," describe similar "reversals of verdicts" (*fan'an*) regarding cadres who once opposed the Gang of Four. The changed verdicts increase their sons' prospects for marrying daughters of "desirable" families.[17] Always, of course, the sons are hard-working and fervently support the new leadership. In cases where the woman rejects such a man and marries someone less politically reliable, as in "Lost Love,"[18] it is made clear that she will suffer a lifetime of regrets.[19] It is obvious that, in 1978, the political orientation of literature of the Gang-of-Four period and earlier continued to exert a strong influence.

Thus, except for the inclusion of love, the story "I Love This Kind of Work" could easily have been written under the Gang of Four.[20] The kind of work referred to in the title is that of an ordinary cook. While most young people want to work in factories or offices in the cities, the protagonist in this story decides to become a cook, and his girlfriend has to be "guided" into accepting this. Naturally, in a society where only a very small percentage of young people can go to university, stories such as "The Unsatisfactory Brother-in-Law" and "Fate" cannot be held up as models for everyone. "I Love This Kind of Work" is typical of scores of stories that encourage young people to be content with their jobs. The title of this story is, in fact, the heading of a regular column in the magazine *The Young Generation (Qingnian yidai)*.

The view that love is a feeling that not only concerns two people, but is strengthened by the love of work and society, is, of course, a rephrasing of the directive "Serve the people," so prevalent during the Cultural Revolution. These stories are reminiscent of the Cultural-Revolution period, too, in the contrived, facile solutions they suggest for complex conflicts.

IS THIS REALLY MY HUSBAND?

In trying to define love as a relationship between two people whose aim in life is to build socialism in China, many 1978 writers have simply dismissed from consideration those whose ideas of love differ from their own representation of "true love." In "Chinese Roses," the author, while acknowledging the possibility of couples having different philosophies of life, concludes that there is only one correct philosophy and that the misguided partner should be made to accept it. In the story, the wife wants to build an emotionally satisfying marriage and a comfortable home, while the husband works day and night to increase steel production and scientific knowledge in China. When the husband carelessly dirties the apartment which the wife has spent half a day cleaning,

she feels something she has never experienced before. She suddenly feels her husband, Mingyan, is becoming a stranger to her. Is this person who is sleeping in such a carefree manner in his work-clothes really her husband? [21]

In fact, the husband has not slept for several days because he is so involved with his work in the factory.

At the end of the story, the wife faces a dilemma. She feels ashamed that she does not have her husband's enthusiasm for work. For her, work is secondary to the house and the family. She is also alarmed at the sacrifices she would have to make in order to be as involved as her husband, especially in having to clean her apartment if her husband's students were to go there often in their dirty work-clothes. Although the author does not state this explicitly, it is obvious in the story that he approves of the husband's attitudes and thinks the wife is lagging behind in her political consciousness.

In almost all these early stories, the man is the model lover. He is described as being able to throw himself wholeheartedly into his work, neglecting mundane chores in life such as housework. The woman, by contrast, either adores the man and gives him moral support by doing his washing and cooking as in 'The Unsatisfactory Brother-in-Law," or, if, as in "Chinese Roses," she has different perceptions of love and life, appears petty and selfish. The women are usually beautiful and shun hard work. This may be partly explained by the fact that all these early writers were men. Their idealization of love reflects both their own attitudes and the political climate of the time.

Many of the writers were male intellectuals who tended to project their own image onto the main characters. Intellectuals were described during the Cultural Revolution as belonging to the "stinking ninth category" (choulaojiu) and so were unsuitable as lovers or husbands. Their social position rose dramatically after the Gang of Four fell. It must have been gratifying for the writers to be able to depict this historical change in their stories.

In 1978, this trend was neatly illustrated in the story "Glasses." As the title suggests, the hero wears glasses, and his girlfriend, although embarrassed by them in the beginning, gradually comes to see them as symbols of his status as an intellectual:

A university student is, after all, a university student, and an intellectual is, after all, an intellectual. He is so young, yet he wears a pair of glasses; and, when he talks, one wonders how he knows so many words.[22]

While there may be an element of irony here, there is no doubt that love is represented as the adoration of a man's educational and cultural achievements. In more lofty terms, it is a love of the mind and spirit rather than of one's personal appearance, although, at this stage, this lovable attribute seems to be mostly a male one. The man is deeply involved in his work and ideas, while the woman, impressed by this, does the loving. This view does not differ greatly from traditional ideas.

BREAKING INTO MORE FORBIDDEN AREAS

In 1978, then, love was seen in very simple terms. Because of this, it was almost possible to define love: It was when two people who wanted to build socialism decided to marry. Anything outside this narrow definition was simply not seen as "true love." By 1979, however, literature had begun to explore many more areas that had long been forbidden,[23] and a greater variety in love stories resulted. Kong Jiesheng, who had already written on more unorthodox aspects of love, such as marrying a returned Overseas Chinese,[24] in 1979 wrote "Because of Her." The man in this story loves a teenager who is eight years his junior. The age difference and the youthfulness of the girl are not typical of the stories that came before. Interestingly, what he finds attractive about her is that "she is so pure, so lovable. She is more beautiful than all the girls in the world, she is like Beauty personified!"[25] Although the girl is depicted also as hardworking, there is little doubt about just what she is most valued for.

If the theme of this story did not shock anybody, then Kong Jiesheng's "Across the River" certainly created some controversy.[26] The story is about a young man and a young woman who live across a river from each other in Hainan. Although the place where they now live is primitive and isolated, they are both from the city, and are naturally attracted to each other. One stormy night, they become lovers. They discover afterwards that they are brother and sister. Although, by the end of the story, this alarming discovery turns out to be false, there is no doubt that the possibility of incest has been admitted. Love is no longer seen as a simple matter of the union of two people for the benefit of industrial and agricultural production.

The complex problems that can be caused by love are given greater emphasis in the story "What Should I Do?" Here, a woman whose husband was in prison during the Cultural Revolution has been told that he committed suicide. After not hearing from him for three years, she marries someone else. Five years later, the first husband returns. So she has two husbands, both of whom she loves. There is no solution to her question, "What should I do,"[27] but the story certainly poses complexities in love which the ideal situations treated a year earlier had not recognized.

Of course, this is not to suggest that 1979 was a year for raising only unusual problems in love stories. Tales like "Across the River" and "What Should I Do?" were permissible because they denounced the Cultural Revolution. Many of them were supposedly based on fact, including "What Should I Do?" While they showed aspects of love that did not fit the 1978 definition, they could not be easily disqualified as "true love" because the characters were, after all, victims of the Cultural Revolution. However, while such stories stand out because of their unusual subject matter and the controversies they raised, the majority of love stories continued in 1979 to stress the theme of choosing the right person with the right political perspective.

Although the stories discussed so far broke new ground in talking about previously "taboo areas" (jinqu), they remained politically orthodox. To say that love was for the modernization of the country, or to suggest that unusual or tragic outcomes resulted from misguided political movements, accorded with the political climate of the day. Such views of love would not undermine the social fabric. Yet, love in any social setting involves feelings between people, and literature about love that does not describe these feelings must eventually become uninteresting. It was almost as if the writers had been talking about love without lovers. In 1979, two women writers overcame this reticence over talking about the humanistic element of love, and began to write more assertively about it.

LOVE FOR LOVE'S SAKE

The very title of Zhang Kangkang's story "The Right to Love" expresses a feeling that was to be repeated often in later writings. Love is seen as a fundamental human right, no longer a means to an end but an end in itself. The story is constructed around a musical family. The father, a professor of music, loves music so much that he names his daughter Shubei, after Beethoven, and his son, Shumo, after Mozart. He is imprisoned for two years in the Cultural Revolution for his love of Western music.

After his release, he dies of grief, his parting words being, "Shumo, do not learn the violin anymore and Shubei, when you marry, marry a worker; be ordinary people . . . do not get involved in politics . . . do not love."[28] Shubei takes down these words as her father's last testament and dares not play or enjoy music, even after the Gang of Four is overthrown. Shumo, however, cannot contain his love of music and takes up the violin again. When questioned by his distraught sister, he claims he loves it. He accuses her of "not daring to love, not daring to laugh, not daring to talk, and not daring to become angry."[29] Her fear has become so internalized that she lies to the man she loves, saying she already has a boyfriend, because this man is interested in politics and music. In the end, however, she is persuaded by her brother and boyfriend that she, like everyone else, has the right to love.

This story is, of course, a political statement in its affirmation of the fundamental right to love. From love of music to the love of another person, the message is clear: The political movements of the past terrified people so much that they lost the ability to love. After nearly two years of trying to justify love literature, this story at last paved the way for the treatment of love for its own sake rather than for politics or for production. By saying that a fear of love, whether for a person or for work, is a fear of life itself, Zhang Kangkang implicitly attacked those in authority and elsewhere who were afraid that love would interfere with work.

If one is afraid to love, one might as well be dead: This theme comes across even more strongly in Zhang Jie's controversial story "Love Cannot Be Neglected." It questions the traditional idea of love in several ways. A 30-year-old woman wonders whether or not she should accept a proposal of marriage. After much consideration, she concludes not by gladly accepting but by shouting to the world:

Don't meddle in other people's business. Let us wait patiently for the right person to awaken our feelings. Even if we wait in vain, we shouldn't marry without knowing what we are doing. Don't be afraid that a solitary existence is some kind of disaster. We should realize that this may be a manifestation of progress in different aspects of social life such as culture, education and taste.[30]

This conclusion is quite remarkable, because, to most people in China, a woman unmarried at 30 must be inadequate in some way. Zhang Jie's heroine remains single, in defiance of aspersions inevitably cast upon her desirability.

This story is the first of many dealing with "old spinsters."[31] When, in the Cultural Revolution, thousands of city youths were sent to the villages, many did not want to marry and settle there; they hoped some day to get back to the city. Now that some have returned, the women have reached an age at which they may be "old maids," whereas the men are still considered eligible bachelors. The Young Generation received in one "matchmaking" quest 2,354 letters from women.[32] In the same issue, a "reader's letter" was published urging people "not to put pressure on old maids" to get married.[33] It is quite clear that China has now a problem of an oversupply of returned "educated" women from the countryside. These stories therefore perform the function of justifying the decisions many of these girls have made, or of consoling them when the social system discriminates against them.

In the case of "Love Cannot Be Neglected," however, the reason given for the heroine's hesitation in getting married is a lot more ideological in its insistence on love before marriage. Zhang Jie makes a clear distinction between love and marriage, a distinction previously often blurred. After the appearance of this story, many others were written about the possibilities of extra-marital love. Marriage as a final and inevitable conclusion of love was therefore questioned. The popularity of this and other stories of this kind is perhaps an indication that, like many other countries, China has a lot of loveless marriages. The problem was acute enough for the Guangming Daily to publish articles on the moral responsibilites and social importance of marriage.[34]

While a loveless marriage can be tragic in any society, it is perhaps even more so in countries like China where divorce is still relatively difficult. Zhang Jie makes this point in her descriptions of the abnormal behavior of the narrator's mother, who stayed married despite being in love with someone else. Apparently, for over twenty years she compulsively read and reread *The Collected Works of Chekhov,* simply because it was a present from her "lover." Also, she is a committed Communist, but her dying words are: "I believe in materialism. Yet I long for the existence of heaven. If there really were a so-called heaven, I know you would be waiting for me. . . . Dearest, wait for me, I am coming.[35] This Keatsian romanticism is utopian and idealistic and unrelated to Communist materialism. It is often attacked as such.[36]

This description of love is very different from the early portrayals of lovers toiling in the fields and factories for socialist construction. Here, romance hinders the lovers' efficiency as professionals. They do not sublimate their energies productively; instead, they are pictured as gazing longingly at each other across crowded streets or retracing steps the other has frequently walked. For a marriage to create an effective social unit, Zhang Jie argues, it must first of all have love.

HOME IS WHERE YOU BELONG

As it happens, the authorities much prefer people to sacrifice their personal needs and desires to the stability of family and society. Local newspapers often receive letters from readers for advice on marital problems, and the advice inevitably is to preserve the family at all costs.[37] At magazines such as *China Youth* and *The Young Generation,* numerous letters are received describing situations remarkably similar to the tales told in literature. Triangular love affairs, wherein a husband falls in love with another woman, are a common complaint. In a typical case, for example, *The Young Generation* received a letter from a woman who had fallen in love with a married man. She claimed in her letter to have been influenced by the popular story "Open Love Letters," which was about a triangular love affair.[38] Whether this letter was authentic or not, it aroused a big response from readers, and the editors, after publishing some readers' letters, concluded the whole episode by confirming the sanctity of marriage.[39] Other popular magazines, like *Chinese Women,* also published accounts of husbands, especially intellectuals and cadres, who married before they entered university or officialdom and, after some years, felt they were too good for their wives.[40] Such accounts generally conclude by condemning the "guilty" husband or "the other woman."

In 1980, literary reflections of such social dramas and conservative attitudes are to be found in the writings of authors such as Liu Xinwu.[41] In the story "The Cuckoo Calls Homewards" by Chen Kexiong and Ma Ming, a young man from the countryside goes to the city to study, leaving his wife behind. While studying, he falls in love with a fellow student. But, for the sake of the wife and his marriage, the girlfriend urges him to return home, and he does. Love, at least in its capacity for self-abnegation, is seen here as a socially stabilizing force.

In comparing "The Cuckoo Calls Homewards" and "Love Cannot Be Neglected," some critics claim that "The Cuckoo Calls Homewards" is more realistic and thus the more successful of the two in its treatment of love.[42] While the story has highlighted the difficulties of love faced by the "educated youth," one is hard-pressed to find the girlfriend's altruism, or the wife's willingness to let her husband leave her, realistic. In fact, the story "Love Cannot be Neglected" seems to begin where "The Cuckoo Calls Homewards" ends, for, although the husband in the latter story goes back to his wife, he is really in love with someone else.

Whatever love is, if one partner in a relationship decides to love someone else, the pain caused to the injured party is considerable. It is perhaps for this reason that many people in China believe that the first love is the only true love and should not be broken. It is also one reason why, when "Echo of the First Love," which appeared in 1981, discussed this problem, it was condemned by many critics for providing a bad model for young people. In choosing one's first love, one is supposed to choose wisely, for that person is likely to remain with one for life. The contradiction here is, how is one to choose wisely if one has had no experience? Arranged marriages to a certain extent avoid this problem.

As one of the main characters in "Echo of the First Love" discovers, "all marriages, without exception, are arranged through 'introduction.'"[43] She, like the woman in "Love Cannot Be Neglected," tries to ignore the pressures for marriage and waits for the right person to come along. But, when she reaches 26 and still can find no one, she too has to rely on a go-between. In this case, the scientist she is introduced to is hard-working and decent. Unfortunately, he cannot get over his "first love," a married woman who has since died. Although the story ends happily, many critics attack it because it describes extra-marital love in a positive way. Calling the love for a married person "muddled love" (*aimei lian'ai*), one critic claims that such stories

> not only have no educational value, they would lead to skepticism about the correct moral attitudes towards marriage ... and, no matter how loftily you describe this kind of love, it is still immoral.[44]

To these critics, marriages should be preserved at all costs.

In one sense, such critics are justified in calling these love stories of 1980 and 1981 "muddled," for, although they show many manifestations of love, the concept of love remains vague. What is love? After the initial attempts of 1978 to predicate love on a joint commitment to communism, many of the later attempts remain outbursts offering no clarification. They continue to be prescriptive declarations on the supremacy of love or apologies for the status quo. Many stories at this time, however, have turned away from this approach and have begun to examine more ordinary problems confronting lovers.

LOVE AS A COMMERCIAL TRANSACTION

In the love stories discussed above, the writers have emphasized love's political and moral aspects in their attempts to define it. Increasingly, love is seen as something that has to be fought for, and the strongest message that comes across in all these stories is that, in spite of political repression, which hinders this kind of human activity, the pursuit of happiness in love and marriage is politically and morally worthwhile. No matter what this love may be, one has the right to seek it. Such sweeping and romantic aspirations, however, do not solve the everyday problems the ordinary person faces in a relationship.

It is one thing to be a storyteller and condemn the selfishness of the wife in "Chinese Roses" for expecting her husband home more often, rather than having him spend most of his time at his work place. It is quite another to be the housewife herself, who spends all day scrubbing and waxing the floor only to have her husband carelessly dirty it, and, at the same time, to be morally condemned for getting angry. Again, it is quite plausible in a story to have a man, like the scientist in "Echo of the First Love," eagerly seeking the child and mother of a dead woman that he did not even marry, while his fiancée is still prepared to love and marry him. But what would their economic burden be were they to marry, having an old woman and someone else's baby to support as well?

In a country that is still poor, where housework is still done by hand, and where the financial burden of an extra mouth to feed is enormous, it is interesting that the majority of love stories do not deal directly with economic problems.[45] Fortunately, with the growth of realistic literature over the last two years, there have been some good discussions of this. The controversial play, *What If I Really Were?*,[46] based on fact,[47] shows clearly the power of money and material goods. It depicts not only how money buys love, but also the fact that, without it, marriage is impossible, since the parents of a bride-to-be would oppose having a poor son-in-law.

One of the best stories to deal with this socio-economic problem is Ru Zhijuan's "The Love of Sons and Daughters." It tells of a dying mother's disapproval of her son's new lifestyle and his choice of a partner. The objection she has to the son's girlfriend is the latter's preoccupation with materialistic pleasures and fashion. But, as the girl explains, "Why do people exist? Is it not to enjoy one's food and dress well? It's not as if I do anything bad."[48] The girl in this story comes from Shanghai, the most sophisticated of all Chinese cities. Her concern with enjoying materially what this life has to offer, though different from that of the heroine in "Love Cannot be Neglected," is typical of stories that describe ordinary people. In another story, the boyfriend is so frustrated by his fiancée's demands that he exclaims to himself in a moment of anger: "What kind of love is this? It's really a commercial transaction!"[49] In the end, however, he marries her. In real life, the problem of girls demanding material things before marriage is documented in numerous press reports. It is also a popular subject in cartoons, comic dialogues (*xiangsheng*), and other forms of mass art.[50]

Even though public opinion and the arts frown on girls who are materialistic, they nevertheless recognize that there is a restricted supply of basic commodities. In Wang Meng's "Kites"[51] and Liu Xinwu's "Elevated Highway Bridge,"[52] for example, the lack of urban accommodations is explored as an obstacle to romance, although neither writer can be said to be antiestablishment generally. Even if shelter is taken care of, any girl with sense will realize that she will be the one responsible for cooking and housekeeping. It would be difficult to start married life without a kitchen or a wardrobe.

This state of affairs is reflected, though in a distorted way, in literature, where women are normally portrayed as being unreasonable and the men innocent victims. This is very neatly expressed in the negative character of the "lathe queen" in a story named after her. For an ideal match, she lays down three conditions:

1. An only son—it would be better still if both parents have passed away.
2. Someone famous and outstanding. If he's not known in the province or the city, then he should at least be known in his place of work. He must also be a Party member, because only by joining the Party is it possible to become a cadre. . . . 3. He must also be handsome.[53]

Such down-to-earth demands are very different from idealizations of the perfect husband in earlier stories. No mention of the word *love* is present in the three conditions and the only reference to the man is to his physical appearance, and that is listed last. If such an attitude is representative at all, love and marriage can only be commercial contracts. In the story, the "lathe queen" is punished for her "wrong attitudes" by losing an ideal "catch." But suppose she did not care about the social position of her suitor and married for love. What would become of such a union?

In the stories of 1978, moral and political rectitude were rewarded with happiness in marriage. By 1980–1981, however, many stories question this premise. In "Waiting—Shuqing's Manuscripts," the husband, who refuses to lower his own moral standards by trying to cultivate contacts with those in positions of power, discovers that his marriage is disintegrating precisely because he cannot provide the kind of life his wife wants. His wife, who tries to get him to seek help from the cadre who had once been his rival in courtship and who still pursues her, sighs:

> Do you really think I want to see you bow your head and beg? But you should open your eyes to reality. If you don't kowtow to those in positions of power and privilege, then you can't move an inch. You can't survive. I also want to be upright and dignified! But life forces me to become worldly and common. . . . For our sake, you must go and see him.[54]

When he refuses again and again to seek help, she loses hope, and transfers her affection to the cadre. Her disappointment in her husband is not, as she says, something she wants to feel, but righteousness cannot buy food.

The portrayal of the cadre in this story is similar to that in other stories critical of the social system. He is ruthless, vain, and cunning. He does not hesitate to use his social position to obtain whatever he desires, including love. This particular story, like many others of its type, is supposed to have taken place in 1975, just before the Gang of Four were overthrown. It does not take much imagination, however, to see that the author is "using the past to comment on the present." Economic hardships are not easy to overcome, especially if they are as huge as those in China. Of course, the case discussed in "Waiting—Shuqing's Manuscripts" is extreme. While marital disintegration is relatively rare in China, domestic tension caused by lack of material goods is certainly common. When this ordinary problem is reflected creatively rather than melodramatically, as it has been thus far, Chinese literature will have made more progress in the direction of social realism.

THE LOVE OF SONS AND DAUGHTERS

In the stories of 1978, the older generation's role in the romances of the young is very much a political or moral one. Right from the beginning, "The Place of Love" has the older revolutionary Aunt Feng giving a political and moral lecture on love. Other stories, such as "The Unsatisfactory Brother-in-Law" and "I Love This Kind of Work," also feature model old revolutionaries as parents. If the old figure in the stories at all, they are models, either positive or negative. Even in "The Right to Love" and "Love Cannot Be Neglected," where the parents are dead, their influence is still strongly felt. As the literature became more realistic, however, portraits of older people from the viewpoint of the young appeared.

Ru Zhijuan's "The Love of Sons and Daughters" has some of the best insights into generational differences. The mother in the story belongs to the older generation of revolutionaries who apparently forsook their own personal comfort and so disapprove of the dress and manners of Westernized youth. Ru Zhijuan does not stereotype the mother, but portrays her as having inconsistent expectations and desires. As her son remarks, "One minute she wants me to learn the violin, the next minute she wants me to learn mathematics, physics, and chemistry."[55] Regardless of her insistence on a proletarian lifestyle and pride in her past as a guerrilla leader, the mother yearns for a comfortable and bourgeois life, at least for her son. She wants to be rich but appear poor.

The son and his girlfriend are depicted as being a lot more realistic and honest in their approach to life. They try to dress as well as they can. However, this is not a lifestyle they have chosen, but one that is ironically forced on them by economic circumstances. While getting rid of his work clothes and putting on a fashionable Western-style suit to attend his girlfriend's brother's wedding, the son explains to his mother's friend that he has to look smart because his girlfriend's parents are not happy with him; at the reception they will try to pair her off with the son of a tenth-rank cadre.

The mother and her friend find the reasoning of the young people incomprehensible. One can, of course, analyze such stories psychologically and say that the mother's jealousy is derived from the fact that the girlfriend has replaced her in the son's affections: she deliberately calls the girl "bitch." In social terms, however, these psychological conflicts have an economic base. The Chinese press has in recent years reported cases of old parents being forced into the streets when they are no longer of use, as for looking after the grandchildren. In one particular case, the readers of *China Youth Daily* were so outraged that the children had to make a public apology to the mother and pledge to look after her.[56] Movies like *The In-Laws* (*Xiyingmen*), which take as their theme the problems of the old being rejected because of economic hardship, have proven to be extremely popular. In most stories that describe such a conflict, the daughter-in-law is shown to be unreasonable and grasping in her search for a better life. Stories such as "An Unhappy Wedding" dramatize the situation so much that the mother, even though on her deathbed, has to pawn her personal belongings to satisfy her son's girlfriend's demands.

Such stories, of course, highlight only part of reality. Often, it is the parents who are eager to have their children marry into the "right" families. Parental interference in love and marriage is again frequently discussed in popular magazines. In one particular instance, when a mother wrote to *China Youth* about her disapproval of her daughter's romantic relationship, over 6,000 letters were received commenting on the case.[57] Parental interference has always been a common theme in literature, and, in the recent love literature, it is also being discussed. The younger generation is thus not always perceived in the stories in a bad light. Indeed, in Bai Hua's "A Packet of Letters,"[58] it is the mother who, in a thoroughly traditional fashion, tries to force her daughter to marry into a family that matches hers in social standing. It seems, then, that, when differences arise between the two generations, they tend to be based again on economics.

GODDESSES IN AN ANCIENT CASTLE

In the early stories of 1978, when most of the authors were men, women were depicted in a subordinate position. They were described at best as lovable or beautiful, but never showing any signs of excelling their male partners. Their role as women was to serve their men, and, if they did not, they felt guilty and inadequate. After "The Right to Love" and "Love Cannot Be Neglected," this imbalance began to be righted.

Zhang Kangkang in 1981 produced another timely story, "Northern Lights," which describes a young woman's fleeting romances with three men.[59] The first, her fiancé, is a cadre's son who is interested only in material goods and in getting on in the world. She finds the relationship stifling and seeks the company of a university student, who in the end bores her with his cynicism about life and his cold and detached analyses of everything, including the wonderful colors of the Northern Lights. The last man is a worker, full of energy and life. He is not well off, but his masculinity and vitality are evident everywhere, symbolized by the badge he wears, that of a young buck. Although the story ends with the girl likely to choose the last "boyfriend," there is no guarantee of this. As if influenced by Zhang Jie's cry to wait patiently for the right man, she is indecisive. For this, some critics find her "self-centered" and "attempting to exceed the limits of social convention and morality."[60]

The implicit double standard against women is obvious in these criticisms, for "the limits of social convention and morality" dictate that women can not have a string of lovers. The case is different for men. Although, in stories like "The Cuckoo Calls Homewards," the man returns to his wife after an affair, it is seen as an act of compassion and supreme sacrifice, and the wife an object to be pitied, someone who could not survive on her own. This is what the wife says when her husband tells her that he wants to leave her:

You can go, I don't want to detain you. Seeing you walk away, my heart is breaking. I really want to die. . . . There is no need for you to think about me. Let's just say there is another Grandma Huo in the world now.[61]

Grandma Huo had gone mad because her husband deserted her. She died waiting for him.

In many stories, such as "Chinese Roses" and "The 'Great Soldier' of the Tianshan Mountains,"[62] the woman is seen as weak-willed and trying to prevent the man from carrying out his duties. The implications are that, under such circumstances, it is perfectly correct politically and morally to change or abandon one's wife or girlfriend. In no case is this considered even a realistic possibility for the woman. Right from the very first love story, "The Place of Love," the integrity of the woman depends on her faithfulness to her lover or husband, even if he is dead.

In most later stories, faithfulness and chastity continue to be the norms "nice" women adhere to. "Love Cannot Be Neglected" was criticized for even questioning this position. The influence of Confucian ethics certainly reigns supreme, at least among the literati.

However much it might have shocked progressive writers such as Lu Xun two generations earlier, the expectation that even widows should stay faithful to the memories of their husbands is a theme that is repeated in several stories. Unlike "The Place of Love," wherein this is supposed to bring prestige and satisfaction, some of the later stories do finally once again tell of the misery that women encounter because of it. In "The One Who Survived," published in 1981, such feelings are described in a most heart-rending manner by the widow of a high-level cadre:

When I was young, I was told of the bitterness endured by widows. In order to kill the feeling of emptiness and loneliness, a widow would every night scatter a hundred coins on the floor. She would then blow out the light and grope in the dark for each of the coins until they had all been found and placed in the bag. Only then, through utter exhaustion, could she go to sleep.[63]

Compare these perceptions to the story "Butterfly" by Wang Meng, where the cadre, after two wives and a lover, still considers himself morally upright. The double standard that operates against women is starkly revealed.[64]

Women have thus been portrayed as beautiful and helpful wives or sweet and naive girlfriends. Without their male partners, they become wretched and helpless. This medieval view is illustrated most vividly in "The Goddess in An Ancient Castle."[65] The goddess here is Venus, goddess of love. The artist in the story is pushed to suicide after being humiliated for having painted a semi-nude figure of Venus. She is also abandoned by her father and husband because of the painting. The story suggests quite unambiguously that women who seek love and beauty on their own will meet with nothing but doom and despair.

A CORNER FORGOTTEN BY LOVE

The love stories dealt with so far are mostly set in the cities, and most are about relationships between intellectuals. Yet, judging from the fact that many problems posed are a direct result of economics, and as the villages are a lot poorer than the cities, one would expect romantic problems there to be more widespread. Furthermore, as peasants comprise over 80 percent of the Chinese population, it is a pity that only a handful of stories deal with their love problems. One feels almost apologetic for devoting so little space to the peasants, treating this topic almost as an appendix. This is not a matter of choice, but rather a reflection of the paucity of material. As the title of the best and most influential of love stories set in the countryside suggests, the village is "a corner forgotten by love."[66] In this story, Zhang Xian discusses the romantic tragedies that can be caused by a conservative village morality, which in turn is shaped by economic factors.

A peasant woman wants to match her daughter with a distant cousin, who is richer than the boy to whom she is attracted. When she tells her daughter this, the daughter gets very angry and exclaims, "You want to sell your daughter like merchandise!"[67] The effect of this exclamation on the mother is stunning. She can only murmur to herself, "Retribution, retribution! This is what is called retribution!" For her daughter's words are the exact ones she herself had used against her own mother when she decided to marry a poor peasant. Her husband has remained a poor peasant. She married for love, yet has remained poor, and so had come to resent both her husband and her daughters:

She hates her bitter life. She hates this patch of land that she had once come to with youth and happiness. She hates this patch of land she has labored on for three-quarters of her life, and which has given her nothing but despair.[68]

As she says to her daughter, love is all very well, but, if you don't have enough to eat, it is all empty talk. The persistence of economic poverty in the villages and its effects on love are here dramatically portrayed.

In the official press of recent years, there have been reports of peasants having to "buy" brides. The literary works that discuss this are therefore not without a real basis. Even in "happy" stories, such as "The Marriage Meeting,"[69] the theme is still based on the problem of dowries. While, in stories set in the cities, girls may demand intangible objects such as the "conditions" of the "lathe queen," in "The Marriage Meeting," the transaction is a straight monetary one. The economic hardships peasants face are often reflected in literature in no uncertain terms.

Of the few stories that have appeared dealing with love in the village, nearly all recognize the importance of economics. Peasant women in particular are shown to marry for money, or a better life, as in "Oh, Man . . ."[70] In many cases, they are forced by starvation to marry anyone who can feed them, as illustrated in Li Jian's "Woman Bridge," wherein the young women of a famine-stricken village "marry" en masse into a wealthier village.[71] In the story "Net," a young girl is virtually sold to a drunkard because of starvation.[72]

To many writers, the villages are also very brutal and merciless places. Rape and sexual abuse occur in many of the stories. The victims are either driven out of a marriage, as in "Sister Changxiang,"[73] or to suicide, as in "Woman Bridge." In the case of "Net," the woman is also humiliated afterwards by the village cadre who raped her. Because she is caught stealing food to feed her daughter, he forces her to parade through the village, hitting a gong and calling out "I have stolen grain from the brigade, no one should follow my example."[74] When she suddenly changes her tune and tells the village that the cadre had openly taken huge quantities of public property, she is beaten, imprisoned, and dies.

The rigidity of village morality takes its toll even when sexual relations are a result of young love. In "A Corner Forgotten by Love," the older sister of the girl mentioned above is driven to suicide by drowning, because her affair with her boyfriend has been discovered. The boy is arrested for having "raped her, causing her death." The strength of his feelings can be gauged from the force with which he struggles to free himself from the policemen, runs to the grave of his lover, cries, and digs his fingers into the earth before being taken off to prison.

The descriptions of "love" in some of these stories are bestial in the extreme. For example, Li Jian describes the feelings of an "educated youth" married to a peasant as he makes love to her in the following way:

It is midnight when he comes home.
"Take your clothes off."
"No . . . I am tired."
"I don't care if you're tired, I cannot wait. . . ."
She boxes his ears. He savagely punches her twice. There is no more sound from her.
"Husband, husband, my husband. . . ."
She is again lying on the vegetable path.
A pig slowly comes up. . . .
That pig suddenly leaps up at her, forcing down on her body.
"Kiss me!"
The pig's snout is on her lips, causing her whole face to be covered with dirt. [75]

While all these descriptions may be a reaction to the glowing accounts of Chinese rural life given during the Cultural Revolution, they nevertheless provide an insight into one line of intellectual thought.

BENEATH THE WOUNDS: AN UNCHANGING CHINA

Love stories in the last four years have matured from a "literature of the wounded" that bitterly denounced the Cultural Revolution as the cause of all social problems into a more realistic appraisal of society. [76] While some issues raised before 1966, such as the choice of a partner with a different political ideology, continue to draw interest, [77] other pre-Cultural Revolution problems, such as prostitutes falling in love, are no longer seen as important enough to warrant discussion. [78] Of more significance perhaps are the descriptions of older, recurrent problems such as the deforming pressures exerted on lovers by economic hardship and traditional morality.

Many stories indicate that, after thirty years of Communist

rule, marriages are still often arranged by "introduction" on the basis of economic and social status. They also show the tragedies that can occur for those who try to resist this system. Young writers like Zhang Kangkang and Yu Luojin rebel against such a system in much the same way as the May Fourth writers. In many ways, their stories can be compared to those written by people like Lu Xun or Ba Jin some fifty years ago.

The short stories produced so far suggest that the influence of economic forces is even stronger in China than in the West. In China, it seems, marriage may not even be a possibility without basic commodities such as furniture, kitchen utensils, and a reputation for chastity. As Perry Link points out, however, literature is essentially written by the educated for the educated. It should be seen, then, as reflecting their concerns and values. The views on poverty of the educated class are illustrated most strongly when love among peasants is described. Peasants are often depicted as ignorant and crude, and their marriages without love. Peasants do not comment on this. Even readers' letters have been written mostly by people of urban background. In this, the current literature resembles both traditional and May Fourth literature; it remains the province of the educated.

While male and female roles are clearly differentiated, sex is left out altogether. Unlike Western love fiction, in which erotica are almost indispensable, discussion of the physical aspects of love in Chinese literature is still frowned on. Criticisms of authors like Li Jian, though always clothed in Marxist terminology, are in fact made from the Confucian viewpoint of an abhorrence of explicit descriptions of sex. And, when sexual desire is expressed, as in the stories "Ah, Man . . ." or "Miao Qing,"[79] it is expressed by such classes of people as landlords or former Kuomintang officers. Despite the breaking of so many taboos, then, sex remains a topic that cannot be elaborated. That erotica are not published does not, of course, mean they do no exist. Sexually evocative stories such as "A Young Girl's Heart" are banned, but apparently widely read. Again, comparisons can be made with traditional literature. Erotic classics from centuries past, such as *The Golden Lotus* and *The Prayer Mat of Flesh,* are widely read but never classed as part of the official, high literature. Moreover, with the revival of foreign literature in the last few years, there is no doubt that, even if Chinese writers do not publish on particular themes of love, they, and their readers, will be influenced by the ideas of love described in other countries.

CHAPTER THREE

Chinese Crime Fiction and Its Formulas at the Turn of the 1980s

JEFFREY C. KINKLEY

Chinese readers enjoy a good crime story as much as anyone. Their forebears half a millennium ago relished tales about bizarre murders and could attend dramas in which a wise and clever magistrate solved one or more ghastly and intriguing crimes simultaneously. A young Chinese reader today might have had a literate great-grandparent who read the complete adventures of Sherlock Holmes in translation, or an older cousin who read a Soviet "socialist" spy novel—prior to the Sino-Soviet rift in the 1960s.

Ever since 1949, though, the cousin would have had difficulty acquiring Western mysteries, or any contemporary literature about ordinary crimes committed by typical Chinese. Socialist realist fiction was supposed "realistically" to reflect the brightness of the future in the society of the present. Indeed, Maoist criminological thinking reductively attributed all wrongdoing to the politics of the perpetrators' bad class attitudes. Crime "as we know it," committed for individual and petty motives, was said to occur in bourgeois, not socialist, society. Hence, to post-Liberation authorities, Sherlock Holmes was a propagandist for "bourgeois morality"; "detective fiction" as a whole, despite its ancient roots in China, was linked to Holmes, his times, and his ideology. The genre was also classed as mostly "low-grade," "arousing base lust for sex and violence."[1]

China's Cultural Revolution surprised even the authorities when all of Holmes's Chinese counterparts, the "public security" (police), procuracy (state's attorney), and judiciary, became enemies to be "smashed" in the name of the proletariat. Chinese now shudder when remembering Mao Zedong's war on routinized crime-fighting; they yearn for nothing so much as law and order. Yet, no one looks forward to a visit from the police. Some readers, on encountering the new crop of stories about policemen and jailers unjustly sent to prison by the Gang of Four, may secretly savor the Gang's short-lived turning of the tables on China's disciplinarians.

For all this, China since the thaw in the late 1970s has seen a renaissance of writing about crime, and police procedure too. Popular taste has made a comeback. Unlike science fiction,[2] crime genres have no societies or magazines to promote them; the utility of detective stories to the Four Modernizations is not so obvious. The foreign mystery fiction China is now reprinting, by Conan Doyle, Dashiell Hammett, and Agatha Christie, seems especially lacking in evident "redeeming social value."

By the end of 1979, Chinese literature treating crime was showing such vitality that one can identify the beginnings of a "crime interest" in some works, a subtler attempt to sublimate the physical aspects of crime in others, and many admixtures. There were works of social exposure, about criminal negligence, graft, and rape, committed by those in authority.[3] Yet, in China, the very mention of rape was sensational enough to overshadow the implicit accusations being lodged against the Communist

Party. Certain "problem plays" and stories of "social investigation," by featuring young hoodlums, their lifestyle, and the
"black argot" they spoke, must have from the start attracted
audience interest through their more voyeuristic exposé of a
criminal social underworld.[4] Of still different impact, and potential, were stories of psychological depth that probed the
nature of guilt itself, as it applied even to those who overthrew
the Gang of Four.[5]

These more exceptional pieces were criticized as soon as they
were written; exposé literature in general came to be suspected
of propagating "bourgeois liberalization." More than current
legal theory in actual society,[6] criminological exploration in
Chinese literature is already back on the defensive. In this negative frame of mind, one could also observe that the great bulk
of China's new crime fiction seems from the start to have been
written according to formula. Yet, the new crime formulas are
at least as intriguing as those known to mystery fiction aficionados in the West; they are rooted in Chinese and Western traditions of writing about crime rather than anything so restrictive
as socialist realism. Without a "pedigree" such as the state has
conferred on science fiction, crime formulas lack both the protection of a license and the restraints of a leash law. We seek to
define the formulas and suggest how Chinese history and society might have channeled post-Mao crime literature into its
present forms.

"DETECTIVE FICTION," EAST AND WEST

Nearly all crime literature in China today either has a prepon-
derating detective interest, or delivers a strong message about
China's need for more "rule of law" and "legal system." The
stories whose appeal is simply detection are such direct imitations of Western and Japanese "classical detective stories" (in
the tradition of Poe, Conan Doyle, and Agatha Christie) that
nearly anything one can say about the "classics" and the reasons
for their popularity is likely to be true for the latter-day Chinese versions. In this genre, Chinese writers have once again
slighted their own "detective story" tradition in favor of Western
forms.[7]

Rather unique are Chinese stories that combine the detective and social interests. Classical detective writing was not quick to take that path in the West. Most theorists would even argue that successful "classical" plotting cannot bear the distractions introduced by "deeper meanings."[8]

Yet, when China's propagandists for "rule of law" construct their plots, they delay the triumph of justice through mystery and concealment as often as through obstacles thrown up by "social reality." Their justice in the end comes about through detection as well as legal probity. The stories seem anomalous in Western terms, but in China they already constitute a kind of formula unto themselves and have their own aficionados, who think of them as "the serious detective stories," implying that these, not the classical whodunits, are China's "real" detective stories.[9] A look at the stories indicates why. Far from being anomalous, the "serious" stories have detectives and methods of achieving justice that conform rather closely to China's own longstanding "detective" tradition. Let us define that tradition, in comparison to the West's.

China has known crime stories for a millennium, but what remains alive today, in operas, movies, and conversation, is the *gongan* or "criminal-case" tradition, in which a renowned wise judge (such as Bao, Di, or Peng) solves a difficult crime. The tradition originally developed in Yuan and Ming dramas, Ming and Qing fiction, and in Qing Peking operas. New heights of elaboration were reached in the eighteenth and nineteenth centuries.[10] Usually, the judge must prevail against ingenious obstructions of justice by iniquitous people in a seemingly corrupt society. He may even be called on to reverse an unjust verdict handed down by a corrupt predecessor. Many traditional plays and novels outside the *gongan* tradition also draw on the dramatic potential of the court of law, and likewise the motif of verdict reversal, or *pingfan*.[11] Fascination with *pingfan* is now greater than ever in China, since so many trumped-up verdicts "of the Gang of Four" have been reversed in real life.

Chinese *gongan* have some elements in common with the Western whodunit—enough, in fact, for the Sinologist Robert van Gulik to have created his own classical Western-style whodunits, using traditional Chinese heroes and plots.[12] There is, in the Chinese originals, a premeditated and concealed crime, typically murder, so terrible that settling the score is motivation enough for the plot. No reticence need surround the brutality of the crime. It may be bizarre, even "interesting"—like starving a person to death by imprisoning him under a giant bell in a monastery.[13] Detached contemplation of the elemental horror of the crime is likely to be fostered by its discovery in Chinese equivalents of the vicarage and serene English country estate— the monastery, or the boudoir of a scholar's wife.

The criminal is not a professional, a psychotic, or necessarily even a tyrant, only an ordinary person, though likely of the monied or examination classes, or their fringes. His or her criminality proceeds from a universal human failing, such as avarice or lust. Class-consciousness may play a part, as in schemes to avoid a socially unsuitable marriage.

At the center is a master detective, who is in China a wise magistrate like Judge Bao. Intelligent and upright, he cuts through all obfuscation with singleness of purpose. His process of discovering the criminal for himself is at least part of the plot, and it has a clear denouement.[14] Some of the discoveries may take place in the courtroom. The reader usually knows the identity of the criminal from the start, but such a plot structure, "the inverted tale," has long been developed and propounded within the Western classical tradition, too, beginning with R. Austin Freeman.[15] Local color is another element adding to the texture of both Chinese and Western tales. To some observers, it is part of what makes certain Western whodunits "classical"; once more bells figure as the classic example (Dorothy Sayers's excursion into Fen country campanology in *The Nine Tailors*), although again none too benignly—noise from the bells is used to kill a person.[16]

Western critics would probably stress the differences rather than the similarities between Chinese and Western detective stories. John Cawelti, having applied Northrop Frye's myth criticism to literature associated "with the times of relaxation, entertainment, and escape," characterizes the classical Western detective story as a formula; like a western or a horror story, to succeed it must fulfill conventional reader expectations both in its plot construction and in its treatment of stereotypical people and things appropriate to its limited universe.[17]

The archetypal plot in the classical Western whodunit is inquiry into a mystery. Chinese stories present rather a quest for justice. Their concern is as much with the commission of the crime in the beginning and restitution or retribution at the end, as with the middle process of detection which is all that matters in the West. Chinese stories must end only after the criminal has confessed; better still, he ought to have been punished, and the honest man he cuckolded happily remarried.

The Western reader moreover craves detection revolving around "clues" and other tidbits of information about how the world works; many stereotypical traits of the main protagonist (the detective) and the action follow in train. The Chinese Judge Bao tales diverge even farther in these particulars. What they narrate is no doubt a kind of formula, but not a "detective story," rather a melodrama, "a complex of actions in a world that is purportedly full of violence and tragedy we associate with the 'real world' but that in this case seems to be governed by some benevolent moral principle. It is not a tragic or naturalistic world because we can be confident that no matter how violent or meaningless it seems on the surface, the right things will ultimately happen" (Cawelti).[18]

At bottom, the Chinese and Western traditions inhabit different epistemological universes. Western whodunits take place in a positivist, nineteenth-century world that is the sum total of an immense but calculable number of phenomena waiting to be apprehended as clues. "[P]roofs for and against are everywhere—*in people, places, and things*," as Balzac said (his emphasis) of an actual murder investigation.[19] Jacques Barzun links the rise of the West's detective interest, "par excellence the romance of reason," directly to the capture of the "literary imagination of the first half of the nineteenth century" by "what it understood of method in the new sciences (especially fossil reconstruction in geology) and by its sympathy with the new criminology, which called for the accurate use of physical evidence."[20]

In Judge Bao's world, there are demons. Moral principles such as filial obligation take concrete expression as blood debts; revenge takes precedence over professional process in achieving justice. And spirits of the deceased solve cases by entering the dreams of the Judge, who was once himself reckoned the Stellar God of Literature.[21]

The detective hero varies according to the world he inhabits. Sherlock Holmes, in the classical detective story, prevails by using his wits, or "little grey cells" (Inspector Poirot, Christie). Philip Marlowe, in the godless, more random and violent world of the "hard-boiled detective story," survives by prowess. Judge Bao is a third type, a Solomon, distinguished by shrewdness and intuition rather than analytic powers (he can read faces as well as omens). The very technique of settling a child-custody dispute by proposing a compromise injurious to the child appears in the medieval play *The Chalk Circle;* its origin may be the same as the Biblical story's.[22] Bao excels at interrogation and trapping people into giving themselves away. He not only assumes disguises, which is only marginally admissible in the Western formula; he solves crimes with the aid of torture.[23] Above all, though, Judge Bao prevails through probity. His biggest challenge may be resisting the temptation to punish the poor devil closest at hand, or free the culprit who has good connections. And his mission is not just to identify a criminal, but to see that justice is actually carried out. In this, he is as alone as a hard-boiled dick; he has runners but no Watson to confide in, or even show off in front of. His runners may be corrupt.

On the other hand, Judge Bao, unlike Holmes, assumes in his person the majesty of the Emperor's law. He speaks for the conservative morality of the scholar class and defends that class's interests, says Y. W. Ma.[24] Western classical detectives, like Holmes, Inspector Maigret (Simenon), and any number of investigators called to do their sleuthing on a country estate, are likely to be men of the people, distinctly bourgeois, whether in their eccentricity (Holmes) or their domesticity (Maigret). It is with a certain ironic detachment that they sift through the peccadilloes as well as the criminality of the class above them, using their outsider's expert knowledge of that class's manners. Chesterton's Father Brown, a man of the cloth but of England's minority religion, views the classic aristocratic arena of crime with equal analytical understanding, achieved from as great a distance.

Explicit ideology, or social commentary, is excess baggage hardly ever found in classical Western detective stories. "[W]e are more interested in the form of the crime and the process of its solution than in the sinfulness of the criminal and his punishment," says Cawelti, who feels that the classical detective even "proves the social order is not responsible for the crime because it was the act of a particular individual with his own private motives."[25] Communist critics of the genre would quite agree, but think of this as a weakness. The stories naturally have an implicit ideology favorable to law and order, generally "conservative," Dennis Porter feels;[26] this is again to say that the stories' ideology does not attract attention.

As melodramas, the Chinese crime stories and dramas are charged with moral energy of a different order. They uphold the status quo still more strongly than the Western tales, and may be didactic, as when the judge sternly passes sentence. The traditional stories and plays cannot be considered an affirmation of the adjudication process, for readers are enjoined from seeking remedies in the courts, if they can help it. Of interest, too, are the negative opinions one might derive of Buddhist monks and women were one to read the Chinese works as realistic fiction. We will return to the melodramatics of Judge Bao as they reappear in China's "serious" detective stories, but first let us examine recent Chinese imitations of the Western formula, whose ideological reticence is by contrast so strong that one cannot help noticing it.

THE CLASSICAL DETECTIVE STORY
IN POST-MAO CHINA

An age of positivism, of faith in science such as invigorated classical detective fiction in the nineteenth-century West, may well be dawning only now among China's urban masses. The potential of the natural world especially fascinates the nation's multitudes of young people. Television serves as a demonstration, and a medium. It makes the wonders of lasers and space exploration materialize before the viewer, and broadcasts the state's positivist ideology: Modernization, through technology and a rational, production-oriented attitude toward life. Part of the latter is "system," including "legal system." By gratuitously sprinkling about bits of information concerning China's new legal codes, the new whodunits, as well as "serious" stories about rule of law, demonstrate token redeeming educational value. But whodunits are too entertaining for their "popularization of the law" to be taken very seriously. It is their emphasis on social order that may well earn the state's appreciation, as well as their positivist application of criminological "science" to every aspect of reality, which popularizes a "scientific" attitude toward life the way the state presumes science fiction does. Legal exhibits in Chinese museums, in paranoid 1970s style, thus direct the masses' attention to physical clues, urging them to remain vigilant for the pieces of evidence by which enemies of society give themselves away.[27] Such a simplistic rationale for tolerating whodunits in China today would, of course, be a joke on the state. Who can doubt that exposure to science itself, rather than propaganda, has made Chinese readers, like aficionados everywhere, actually enjoy becoming engrossed in social and physical details, so as to be led into suspense, or to satisfy their curiosity about "life"? It is presumably for the same kinds of gratification that Chinese readers like good science fiction (not just that written in China) and inevitably, like their counterparts in the West, combination SF/detective formulas, futuristic whodunits.

The detective story's plot is standard; it is, in the words of Frye, "a ritual drama around a corpse in which a wavering finger of social condemnation passes over a group of 'suspects' and finally settles on one."[28] Wang Hejun's "The Murder Happened Late on a Saturday Night" is a lengthy and well-developed example, complete with a large- and a small-scale map of the scene of the crime, à la Christie.[29] The story opens with the discovery of a corpse—that of a young man, Liu Zhi. Good police work turns up a murder weapon nearby; but more important, a master detective, Gao Si ("Lao Gao"), reasons that the body has been assaulted by two weapons, a hammer as well as a knife. In procedural fashion, the story follows Lao Gao and his subordinates as they interview the decedent's circle of acquaintances, piece together his whereabouts the night of the crime, and begin tracing the history of the murder weapons, one of which has been verified in the lab, while the other is still hypothetical. Gradually one learns about Liu Zhi. He was quite an ordinary person, a worker about to be married—to the ex-sweetheart of a local hoodlum.

According to the usual contract between author and reader, it is understood that a person, not society, will be found unambiguously responsible for the crime. He or she will be revealed at the end and prove to be well known to the reader, although the culprit will be "least likely," able ultimately to delight the reader with his ingenious but plausible unguessability. For instance, while it was once unthinkable in fiction for a crime to be committed by a cadre, power-holders have become such common villains in recent exposure literature that a suspicious cadre in a whodunit looks like a red herring. Yet, that is to say that he is once more "least likely"—good material for a perpetrator. By the same reverse reasoning, social dropouts and people with overseas connections make good perpetrators in truly devious classical whodunits, because conventional wisdom finds them so suspect.

In "Saturday Night," the "finger" of suspicion hovers over both a hoodlum and a son of a cadre, in succession—in fact, back and forth. Yang Huting, the hoodlum, is implicated through the cold and impersonal workings of a clue. One of the murder weapons, a knife, has been traced to him. He borrowed it from the decedent's co-worker, who has also disclosed that Yang is the jilted boyfriend of the girl the decedent was about to marry. Yang lost the girl's affection while serving a sentence of reform-through-labor. Is the co-worker telling the truth, though?

Police work now confirms Yang's checkered past. He has threatened his "ex" and even Liu Zhi himself, several times in the past. Yet, background investigation has also created some sympathy for the suspect. His father committed suicide after an unjust Cultural Revolution struggle session. Yang started to go bad only after he was sent down to the countryside following high school graduation, a common but unhappy fate for a promising young man. The wise detective, Gao Si, breaks into the runaway speculation of his young, overeager protégés with dramatic coolness when he observes, with superior objectivity, "Maybe Yang Huting is *one* of the murderers" (*ZT*, p. 7).

Only when this world of many possibilities has been created is Yang Huting introduced in person; the police go to his house for questioning. Even Yang's mother, who by now dreads visits from the police, suspects he may be guilty. A young detective has snooped in Yang's tool bag, too, and found a hammer, possibly the second murder weapon. One cannot help sympathizing with the young man a little; fate itself seems against him.

When Yang finally appears on the scene, he turns out to be 24 or 25, long-haired, and wearing a dirty old army uniform. He makes a bad impression; he smokes during the interview, answers haltingly, and sits glumly, seemingly beaten. He lies that he lost the knife used on Liu Zhi, is exposed, and comes up with the story that he lent it to one Hu Weijun. Junior detective Liu Zhengbin pronounces the young dropout incorrigible. So he seems. Yet the formula reader, on seeing Yang made to look guilty three times over, by his background, his activities the night of the murder, and his bad attitude towards the police, suspends judgment. Yang is just too obvious; the real murderer would have selected him as the perfect fall guy.

In fact, Yang Huting *was* framed; he is more innocent than half the characters in the story. He is not just a middle character; he is a negative character, fully exonerated within the framework of the story. The classical detective story implies nothing about society, and, if this convention is accepted, many socialist clichés may be transcended, even by a formula.[30]

One begins to see the possibility that Yang has been framed long before the murder is solved, as the finger begins to hover over Hu Weijun (*ZT*, pp. 12-13, 16-19). Hu is the classic villain of an exposure piece or rule-of-law story, the son of a deputy commander of the local military sub-region. He too is 25, discharged from the army (which he probably entered through his father's connections), and a Party member, now doing organization work for the municipal Youth League committee. 'His political bearing is good," observes Detective Gao without irony, reminding the reader that this is not a melodramatic world of corruption, but an ordered society whose compact has been disturbed by this one, vicious crime (*ZT*, p. 12). But the fact is, Gao's subordinate says, Hu's mother spoiled him. He arrogantly presumes on his family's power, as when he chased the deceased's pretty fiancée himself, and vowed he would get her in the end, even after she refused his advances. Just when new evidence comes in to refocus investigation on the hoodlum Yang—the hammer in his bag turns out to have been the second murder weapon—Gao, with uncanny insight, proclaims Yang innocent.

Sure enough, Hu Weijun is subsequently incriminated, by a servant's testimony. Hu is detained, and now the reader enjoys his first encounter with this suspect. In jail, wearing a Western-style suit to show off, Hu is scared but displays the arrogance that goes with his position. He questions the authority of the police to detain him, and wants to call the army command. He lies about the knife. Deluded by his own presumptions of special privilege, when cornered he finally admits that he gouged out the eyes of the deceased. To him the crime is not too serious ("I stabbed him a couple of times, because the jerk had it coming to him. Are you going to arrest me for *that*?" *ZT*, p. 18). He still thinks his parents can get him off, until he learns that his victim has died. In a melodrama, one would still want to see whether Hu's confidence that he is beyond the reach of the law is correct or not, but, in this classical whodunit, his admission of guilt gets him locked up, and that is enough. So the author of "Saturday Night" has chosen a classic post-Mao villain for his criminal without making it obvious. And yet Hu Weijun, however evil, did not "do it." Liu Zhi's real murderer acted after Hu committed his foul deed and is quite unguessable, to all but Gao Si; the one sought is a little old lady, Liu Zhi's mother-in-law-to-be. She wanted a better match for her daughter.

In this genre, the criminal is typically just as ordinary as the little old lady in "Saturday Night." Not professionals, juvenile delinquents, traitors, nor in most cases even cadres (in the course of their exercise of power), but unremarkable people commit the crimes. They do so not for political but for personal reasons, such as greed, ambition, or a need to cover up past indiscretions. Lust is evidently still too sensitive to be treated. Young people may commit the crime; a precious antique is stolen with the aid of a young girl in "The Case of the Golden Buddha," but, far from being a street hood, she works behind the counter in an exclusive shop which turns out to have been victimized by an inside job.

Furthermore, the victim typically lacks political significance. The investigation narrated may progress rather far without the victim even being identified, as in "The Case of the Strange Yuan River Corpse" by Yang Rongfang, in which the detectives must account for an anonymous body from up in the national minority territory of West Hunan which has washed up on shore. That victim turns out to be of significance to the characters in the story, but only because of a domestic relationship—as often is the case. The deceased is the long-lost father of one of the detective protagonists, who was raised by foster parents after being left on a doorstep.

In short, the crime in this kind of story is not political; it is even treated with romantic and aesthetic detachment.[31] The theft will have been from an antique shop (catering to whom, foreigners?) or the corpse will have been discovered in a setting whose serenity comes as close to that of the bourgeois vicarage and upholstered railway carriage as socialism will allow. In "The Case of the Three Front Teeth," and in "Saturday Night," the corpse is discovered in a well-manicured park. The body is found submerged in a lovely lotus pond in "The Death of Bai Ying-ying." The fabled headwaters of the Yuan River, which bears a corpse, are up near veteran novelist Shen Congwen's idyllic Frontier City, and the body is clad in minority dress—literary license, since male dress is not ethnic-specific.

There is no taboo on the corpse's being horribly defiled, or on describing a mutilation with detailed, clinical objectivity. We are introduced to Liu Zhi in "Saturday Night" as one whose eyes have been gouged out with a knife, his temple perforated with a hammer. Corpses to be examined are often bloated by water; Bai Yingying's young female body is found naked, with a weight attached. In "The Case of the Three Front Teeth," by Su Yunxiang, an investigating party that has initially come to examine two other bodies discovers a middle-aged cadre's body, hanged from a tree; "It seemed to be smiling at you" (*ZT*, p. 39). In this and other stories, neither moral nor political indignation is extracted from the reader—only curiosity, which is reinforced by the professionalism of subsequent police inquiries. When the hanged cadre, one Long Zhenting, is found to have had three of his front teeth knocked out, there seems to be a bizarre and macabre M. O., perhaps even a Zodiac-murder sort of signature. A hint of Gothic mystery is an established way of focusing reader curiosity on the crime rather than its significance. [32]

"The Three Front Teeth" breaks the formula in some respects, for its victim, Long Zhenting, was a provincial-level cadre. Only at the end does one learn that Long was murdered for revenge, by the son of a man he persecuted in the days of the Gang of Four. At the last moment, the story changes from an apolitical whodunit to a melodrama with a message. More interesting is the spectacle of an aristocratic theater of crime, including Long's luxurious private quarters being expertly penetrated by detectives who socially are a rung below it. The bureaucratic class's manners (not its politics or morality) fascinate senior detective Lao Zhao, and particularly his sidekick, though, as intelligent outsiders, they understand provincial cadres well enough to predict their behavior. They take special interest in Long Zhenting's daughter, whose function in the story is minor, but is one of the "beautiful people," a "proud princess" and "fairy from Heaven," as the sidekick-narrator admits, admiringly. Lao Zhao is by nature impatient with those slower than he, and prone to lecture his subordinate, but even he changes character and becomes a gentleman in her presence (*ZT*, pp. 40–41).

Lao Zhao typifies the Great Detective protagonist of the Chinese formula. He is of the cerebral type; the name of Sherlock Holmes (not Judge Bao) appears in some of these stories, as a comparison, though the Chinese detective is always a Great Investigative Cadre, a public servant. Conventions left over from socialist realism may be responsible for his being less colorful than either Bao or Holmes. Usually the detective is a senior, male policeman or procurator (a few women do play the role), domesticated enough to inform his wife before going out on a mission, and with decidedly uneccentric hobbies, such as reading law books.

With so little scope for individuality—in this sensitive job, which carries with it enormous powers to deprive a person of his civil liberties, as well as simply crack a case—the detective finds his powers of deduction being highlighted as truly the major interest, through exaggeration, and frequent reference to exterior signs of the detective's ratiocination. Such signs are personal quirks indicating withdrawal inward for purposes of seeing the world anew, says Elliot Gilbert, who traces them to Western romanticism.[33] Unfortunately, in China the idiosyncratic indications are so conventional that they function as textual punctuation rather than impart romance. Gao Si of "Saturday Night" rubs the scar on his chin (a reminder of his suffering in the Cultural Revolution, as in so many other stories); "As if it were a sign, Li Zhengbin asked him, 'Lao Gao, what are you thinking?'" (*ZT*, p. 4). Not much of a one for mystery, Li later explains to a colleague, "When [Lao Gao] snuffs out his cigarette, it's a sign that his idea is fully formed" (*ZT*, p. 26).

Exaggeration occurs directly in drawing the character of the detective, and in the reflection of his brilliance through a more commonplace mind, a Watson (like Li Zhengbin), or client, who "tries to assimilate the unusual and fails."[34] "Don't use the word *seem*. We need exactitude," importunes Lao Zhao of "Three Front Teeth," as he gives *his* "Watson" a lesson about the perils of the first impression being the strongest. Zhao ratiocinates in a rapture, with "eyebrows dancing and face radiant" (*ZT*, p. 40), keeps to himself what he calls "some of the magician's tricks of the trade" (*ZT*, p. 40), and likes to greet a person he has never laid eyes on before with an abrupt and authoritative "You're Long Zhenting's daughter" (*ZT*, p. 41). Yet his sidekick, who functions, like the original Watson, as the first-person narrator, describes Lao Zhao's investigative talent as he would a musical gift. He marvels at it, addressing the reader rhetorically. He is happy to be apprentice to a man who, he says, "loves" his work. Lao Zhao, like many a major protagonist, is not the first detective to have been called in on his case, either. He belongs to the same "Scotland Yard," China's one and only, as the fellow who came before him, so he cannot draw any institutional implications, but he can at least call the other fellow a "Dumbbell, idiot, suffering from the aftereffects of a cerebral inflammation" (*ZT*, p. 40).

A conventional way of establishing the detective's intelligence is a "preamble," in which he deduces an obscure and possibly perfectly irrelevant fact from the most ordinary clues, or seemingly no clues at all.[35] "The Case of the Strange Yuan River Corpse" offers an example. The protagonist is Zeng Jinian, former deputy head of the local Public Security Bureau, but now, in 1967, a menial laborer under the supervision of Shen Zhaozhang, a young radical who has "seized power." The story starts with an atypical political dimension as it depicts the relationship between these two protagonists, who will come to cooperate in investigating the murder of a still unidentified person washed up from the river. The murder and murderer have no political importance though, so the Cultural Revolution background functions almost as local color in this otherwise quite standard whodunit. First, Zeng must, with Shen's help, become a fugitive from his de facto custody status if he is to be able to sleuth. Thereafter, politics will be forgotten. It is by a few quick feats which command young Shen's respect that Zeng gets the lad to become his apprentice instead of his taskmaster. After observing the corpse, Zeng calculates in a flash which fork of the river it came down and the distance of its journey. He can deduce this from the color of the sand under the victim's fingernails. He reasons that the deceased was a boatman, not a peasant, since his feet are calloused but not cracked. From the color and condition of the dead man's betrothal pouch, he concludes that he had been in love for twenty years:

"Then is he married?"
"Married, yes."
"Does he have any children?"
"Probably one."
"How—how can you know?"
"Later. Perhaps we'll meet this child." (*ZT,* pp. 163–164; the child is Shen himself, who has never known his father)

Elsewhere, the collectivist ideal limits the contrast between the main protagonist and his subordinates. The Watson is a Great-Detective-to-be; his insight must not be too inferior unless he has a lesson coming to him (like the Yuan River radical, Shen, who straightens out after finding both a father and a mentor).

The Great Detective must act as didact, testily, in the manner of Lao Zhao of "The Three Front Teeth," or more likely constructively, as when the detective arranges evidence so that his subordinates can deduce things for themselves and even teach each other. "What can you learn from this clue?" says Lao Zhao to his aide (*ZT,* p. 38)—and Chief of Detectives Lao Tan to *his* picked subordinate, in "A Gold Buddha" (*ZT,* p. 48).

Other conventions of the formula rivet reader attention on the case at hand. Lao Tan of "The Three Front Teeth" gathers several suspects together in one room for a dramatic revelation— he exculpates all concerned. The hero of "The Strange Case of the Watch that Had No Brand Name" gets out of two classical "locked rooms," a secured train compartment, and a death prison run by Gang-of-Four-type villains.[36] This is a "detective" device employed by what is more nearly a counter-conspiracy, or "spy" story.

Some stories do manage to transcend formula through interesting, if sparing, sorties into comedy of manners. A comparatively serious example is the love between cadre Long Zhenting's "fairy princess" daughter and the boy who will murder Long, a young man condemned to live in the countryside, under "priority surveillance." This recreates a typically nineteenth-century Western theme, of love across a "class" barrier.

More humorous is satire of the police, who are fair game because, in this genre, they are never corrupt. Here we observe one of China's finest, pinning the blame on the wrong people:

> The longer I was there, the more I suspected them, and, the longer I suspected them, the more questions I asked. Finally the woman began to weep. Her grief was my pleasure. We had them where we wanted them. With the help of a little trick, I soon had them in the people's militia headquarters, which gave us the chance to search their house. Heaven smiled on us then! I found clothes inside a closet which contained a calendar watch and a leather wallet with a few bills in it. They were Department Head Long's. With the stolen goods in custody, we had an ironclad case that loomed up before us like a mountain! If we achieved anything whatsoever, it all goes to the help from our leadership and the joint efforts of everybody, with credit due the Party, Chairman Mao, tee hee. (*ZT,* p. 42)

China's Western-style detective stories may not carry many lessons in them, but they do demonstrate the perfect irrelevance of Mao Zedong Thought to solving a murder. This much may now be accommodated in comedy,[37] in post-Mao China.

WHODUNITS, POLICE PROCEDURALS, AND POLICE REPORTS

For all the conventions, post-Mao whodunits strive for "realism" of the sort that might endear them to a curious mass audience and Chinese critics. They are very procedural; "Saturday Night" is told in daily segments, with the date and time recorded, as if taken from a police blotter.[38] Characters who, at the outset, gather around Liu Zhi's corpse are described objectively, not named, until the police go to question them and learn the names for themselves.

The detective stories, like Western ones, try *too* hard to tie up every loose end. The murder, for instance, is likely to have been planned too elaborately. Consider how Liu Zhi's future mother-in-law finished him off in "Saturday Night." She invited the hoodlum Yang Huting into her home for a talk, expressly to fan his angry passion. She had already asked her daughter to buy medicine, so that the daughter would take a certain route home, ensuring that she would see Yang Huting pass by in a huff. Finally, the old lady calculated that she herself would have just enough time to intercept and murder Liu Zhi on his way home from the medicine shop, and return home before his escort, her daughter, entered the door.

The most unusual crime is unraveled through the ability of forensic medicine and the microscope to enlarge the sphere of physical reality itself. Criminological science is exaggerated in the process. Fingerprints are recovered from window sills, boat punting poles, and even pipes (when in real life even a metal gun rarely takes up a good print). Bai Yingying's murder is calculated to within a half hour, from the color of her corpse (*ZT*, p. 58).[39] East and West also share a romantic notion that the dead and unconscious bear an expression indicative of their last conscious emotion. (Much is made, for example, of the facial expressions of a young couple who seem dead but really have only fainted—into each other's arms—on encountering Long Zhenting's hanged body, in "Three Front Teeth.")

Human behavior may be excessively traceable too, as R. Austin Freeman noted of the Western genre, which, he wrote, "tends to be pervaded with logical fallacies, and especially by the fallacy of the undistributed middle term. The conclusion reached by the gifted investigator, and offered by him as inevitable, is seen by the reader to be merely one of a number of possible alternatives."[40] Gao Si of "Saturday Night" again indicates how true this still is of the Chinese versions. When he learns that Liu Zhi's head was attacked with two weapons, only one of which has been found, he brilliantly concludes that Liu was assaulted by two different people (*ZT*, pp. 4–5). Why would a single murderer have disposed of one weapon and not the other? He also deduces that the injuries to Liu Zhi's eyes preceded the blow to his temple. Why would anyone mutilate a dead man's eyes? Yet the reader can imagine how a lunatic might have done this, and how the police might have simply failed to find the second weapon. The world in which the crimes take place is a very finite, "nineteenth-century" one; Gao Si reckons time so precisely that he can be certain of a little old lady's opportunity to commit murder simply by retracing her steps with a stopwatch. "The Case of the Gold Buddha" is actually solved with the help of railroad timetables. On the other hand, readers must become immersed in the story and consult the maps provided if they are to be able to follow the detective's train of thought.

The Chinese whodunits are all police procedurals. What if their exaggeration of the powers of criminology comes from overzealousness rather than ignorance—could their authors have inside knowledge of police work—or be policemen themselves, since police work has long been concealed from most Chinese? The authors are rather obscure. We can only assemble a few clues.

Recently, and even during the Cultural Revolution, say informants, the Ministry of Public Security published anthologies of quite detailed case write-ups. They are classified, unknown to most Chinese intellectuals. Yet, they relate crimes suitable for pulp magazines, and unravel their mysteries only a piece at a time, so as to instruct in proper police procedure. One case began with two bags found abandoned on an express train from

Peking. They contained a human corpse, headless and handless. The extremities were severed from the trunk, and each leg was further chopped up into two pieces (the reader is referred to photographs of the bags and the body parts). Exact measurements are given for each object. Pickpocketing became a major case in another instance, because the victim was a foreigner. He lost RMB (People's Currency) 438 while sightseeing in the middle of Chongqing.[41]

A writer of crime fiction might be interested in the devious paths of human behavior pursued in these reports, as well as their insights into police procedure; an obsessive quest to make material objects give up their secrets does characterize some cases, such as that of the dismembered corpse. Peking police ferreted out every retail outlet selling the particular kind of cotton padding used to wrap the corpse, sent the padding to textile institutes for analysis, roughly determined its age (to within five years), then examined *five years'* worth of receipts at the most likely place of sale. They turned up 483 sales of pads precisely 3.5 by 5 meters and 3.5 kilograms in weight, matching the one used by the murderer. Fortunately for Chinese police, they oversee a socialist society with limited and stereotyped distribution of goods, like military systems they are likely to be up against in the counterespionage field. It really is possible, then, to tell by looking at a plastic bag that it was made in the Zhengzhou No. 3 Plastic Bag Factory. There is much of this kind of detection in the whodunits, notably "The Death of Bai Yingying." Whether or not whodunits ever have a real "police" input is problematic, but some have dual authorship. Perhaps one person furnished the "materials" while the other polished, as seems probable for the Hunanese policemen's stories we shall discuss presently.

In the final analysis, the professional viewpoint from which the crime reports depict police procedure makes their world quite different from that of the whodunits. In China, more even than in most societies, "social control" (procuring witnesses) is the major method of solving crimes. The Chinese euphemism for getting the masses to inform on each other is "mobilizing" them. Who has suddenly come into some money? Who has been hanging around with ne'er-do-wells? The pickpocket case was solved by rounding up the usual suspects, increasing police presence and surveillance, and heightening the vigilance of neighborhood activists so that more pickpockets could be caught in the act. Always there were meetings, for internal liaison and external mobilization. Ultimately the criminal was caught because the auxiliary "eyes and ears" of a suburban police precinct had, on hearing about the high-priority case, noticed a similarity between the M.O. and that of a local hoodlum. "Classical detective stories" are reticent about such procedure, to the point of depicting surveillance only in the course of entrapment; they have a separate tradition, and perhaps a different social sensibility.

In Hunan, policemen anxious to tell about difficult cases they have cracked have favored us with detective documentaries from their own hands, collected in *Uncovering the Mystery of the Missing Person*. Depictions of police procedure are sanitized in this book, which was written for the public, although they are more realistic than in the whodunits: Cases are solved with the help of informants more often than through police science. "Mobilization of the masses" is positively a virtue in this innocent genre, since it indicates "solidarity" with them. Indeed, these true case write-ups stick to the bare facts closely enough that they are apt to bore Chinese readers who have alternative reading matter. Perhaps they need not be called literature; yet it is clear that the authors felt they were writing within a "detective-story" tradition, probably that of the old Maoist "detective" fiction which scouted out spies and KMT diehards. Ordinary "bad people" and Red professionals now replace the counterrevolutionaries and proletarian generalists, respectively. Functionally, the works easily meet the former Gang-of-Four literary standards, being prettified ("artistic") eulogies of the Party and the masses. There is one change. The detective-authors lobby, to use the term from Rudolf Wagner's chapter, not just for the Party, but for themselves. They, the police, serve the people, putting their lives on the line, missing meals and sleep and fearing neither rain nor snow.

The existence of works by a police force with its own literary pretensions might put our whodunits under a cloud, were the two genres not totally incompatible. Far from taking an aesthetic attitude towards crime, the Hunanese stories are accompanied

by moralizing characteristic of pre-nineteenth-century Western
writing about crime. A case from *The Newgate Calendar* (1773)
ends, "The story of this wretched malefactor will effectually
impress upon the reader the truth of the old observation, that
'Honesty is the best policy.'" Our Hunanese police procedurals
(mimicking, perhaps, the chapter-driven traditional Chinese
novel) close similarly: "Thus it's truly a case where the gun thief
fell into a trap he laid for himself!" Or, "It's true; crime does not
pay; the people's dictatorship is omnipotent."[42] The ideology
is not Maoist class struggle, but old-fashioned morality. This is
apparent in the stories' observation that criminals are sexually
loose (taboo in Chinese classical detective stories); their en-
vironmental determinist attribution of crime to hanging out
with "bad people" (idlers and profiteers; gamblers, rather than
Newgate's drunkards); and the importance of "good people"
who come forward to turn in social offenders, leaving sleuthing
simply to sort out the facts (police taking the place of the
English Christian jury). Trials and confessions are not depicted,
but didacticism enters the tales directly, through narrators'
asides that say grace to the Party and the masses.

A finger of suspicion is unlikely to hover over more than one
suspect, since people and certainly guns are seldom left unaccounted for. If there is suspense, it is likely to hang on whether
or not the prime suspect, identified by mid-story, can be located. One piece is so didactically inclined that it refers to a
suspect with a traditional kind of moralistic tag, as "Criminal
Zhang" (p. 12), even before the case is wrapped up.

"Recovering a Gun," for example, tells of an arms depot
that was broken into. A mauser was stolen. Bootprints offer
some clues, but the break comes after a gunshot is heard the
next night. One of the masses steps forward. His dog was shot
by two youths, and the bullet is found. It came from the
mauser; the incidents are linked. Now a vigilant militia head
comes forward. He knows of a young man who has a record of
stealing bullets and borrowing guns. The young man's whereabouts at the time of the theft and the gunshot are unaccounted
for, but he was seen with a high-school student who, paralyzed
by his own guilt and fear, confesses that he was an accessory to
the shooting of the dog. This ends the suspense. From there, it's

just a matter of tracking down the other fellow. The police surmise that he will hide out at his sister's, and there he is found.[43] Usually the police are led on a wild-goose chase, leading to a denouement and a chronological recapitulation of the crime, beginning with how the criminal came to do mischief in the first place.

If these pieces make little pretense at being thrillers, they do engage the reader's curiosity as social documentary. Procedurally more realistic than the whodunits, they depict relationships between senior and junior detectives as being quasi-military rather than collegial (p. 9). There are many meetings, and often many faceless detectives rather than a master sleuth. Insignificant clues are paraded before the reader for no other reason than completeness. And crimes are spoken of in bureaucratese, an element missing from most whodunits. Interestingly, although the Hunanese stories lobby for policemen, showing how brave they are, how they help sick children (p. 112), and so forth, they rarely lobby for legal popularization.

The conventionalization of crime and procedure in the Chinese "classical detective story" becomes apparent when one can find greater realism even in these case write-ups differing so little from Gang-of-Four literature. China basically lacks the "naturalism" of police-procedural writers such as Freeman Wills Croft and Ed McBain. Nor is there the realism of the Western spy novel, in which the best detective is not necessarily the good guy.[44] But this excursion into the fantasies of policemen should have proved that realism isn't everything. Is didacticism, then, necessarily conservative and boring?

RULE OF LAW

Chinese literature has known old-line didacticism much longer than it has Judge Bao, but, since the late Qing, some didacts have used literature to promote modern reform. Is the didacticism of post-Mao "rule of law" stories reformist, or does it support the former Maoist status quo?

"Rule of law" is a slogan now co-opted by the Deng Xiaoping regime to popularize everything it does in the legal sphere, reformist or retrograde. It indicates a commitment to a greater role for legal institutions in running society and is indeed linked to such populist sentiments as "equality before the law." "Rule of law" is also a basic legal spirit opposed to "rule by men." The latter refers to China's traditional Confucian and revolutionary Maoist disdain of governing society by "arbitrary" laws, when the state has available to it the more discriminating judgment of wise "men" (Judge Baos and veteran Communists).[45] It goes without saying that the Gang of Four's paradoxical commitment to philosophical Legalism, as opposed to Confucianism, did not lead them to strengthen "rule of law." The pity is that the Deng regime may call virtually any enactment of "legal system," repressive or progressive, a reform, in view of the previous decade.[46] Yet, our literary Hunanese police were cracking cases before the fall of the Gang, just as after; they were never truly "smashed." Nor is "rule of law" an ideology invented by the post-Mao regime. Red Guards, such as "Li Yizhe," called for "socialist democracy and legal system" and referred to "rule of law" as early as 1973 as a way of dealing with the same mob tyranny the Deng regime has now forsworn.[47] No doubt Deng Xiaoping, and our authors, have got hold of a potentially popular issue. But what does "rule of law" mean, concretely?

One thrust of the slogan is libertarian, or at least progressively reformist, in the spirit of 1979 and Democracy Wall. Yet "rule of law" can also mean law and order, with opposite connotations: more social discipline and more thorough police work.[48] (One post-Mao story blames the Gang of Four for having disrupted the surveillance of people!)[49]

Third, when any behavior is newly put on a legalistic basis, that too is done in the name of "rule of law." In particular, administrative decision-making in China's vast public sector is no longer sanctioned just because it is carried out with authority; it is subject to "internal audit," under new rules differentiating between "legal" and "illegal" practices. Here we are in the realm of "economic crime," a priority of the new regime. Waste of the public's money is now a "crime," when before it was merely wrong. Extension of law into these spheres might eliminate a good deal of obviously antisocial behavior, but the apparatus to enforce it might invade citizen privacy.[50] The state's renewed resolve to apply "rule of law" in the matter of premarital sex, which is illegal, exemplifies how "more law" is not necessarily progressive.

Finally, even public accusations can be "rule of law." Legal action becomes a collective appeal to a higher justice, or morality, functioning as an expression of common pent-up frustration, and mass purgative, rather than as a "system." It is a means of last resort, like suicide, or lawsuit in traditional China, by which one hoped to achieve revenge and clear one's ancestors, at the expense of losing one's social dignity and one's fortune.

Traditionally, the appeal has always been to a judge, not to abstract law. The Chinese term for the accusation, now popularly occurring in short-story titles, is *gaozhuang,* which really has two meanings: to file a lawsuit, or to lodge a complaint against someone with his superior.[51] The new rule-of-law melodramas indeed illustrate the positive workings of new, post-Mao law not through the efficacy of institutions, but good judges—"good men."

At the top of society now is the lawgiving Party, an organization of "good men" and women. In fiction, it has provided the good judges, but, in real life, it has asked the masses everywhere not necessarily to go to court, but to *gaozhuang.* Citizens are actually to file suit against corrupt Party members, if necessary, since they are potentially the system's most powerful renegades; more important, though, is the accusation, which will bring into play the Party's own system of discipline. The masses are also to *gaozhuang* through the press, or in popular magazines, if their grievance is important enough to be instructive. They may put their "case" in a still more idealizing medium if it is of universal interest: literature, which is not so much "legal" as "moral popularization." China is too poor to support litigation as a way of life; morality must be the first line of defense against crime, China's leaders feel. *Gaozhuang* in literature thus invokes the spirit of, while in fact obviating, actual courtroom process under "rule of law."

Like Deng Xiaoping, any author of rule-of-law melodramas is bound to fancy himself a progressive reformer. Crime fiction is a grey area, not for those who want to play it safe. Most authors are obscure (some may have public security connections for all we know), but there is also Wang Yaping, a young, onetime "groundbreaking hero" in post-Mao fiction, and the ex-Rightist Cong Weixi, who drew on his own imprisonment experience when writing "Red Magnolias Beneath the Big House Wall."[52] Simply by choosing to write "serious" stories about society, even melodramatic ones, rule-of-law authors produce what is in China "high" literature, something regarded more highly than "low-level" whodunits just for entertainment.

The progressiveness and originality of any given story will nevertheless depend on the vision of "rule of law" behind it and other intellectual factors by which the story is informed. Surely one influence is still socialist realism, which has long furnished models for the writing of melodrama; it directs the artist to look to the state's noncontroversial vision of the future. Another input is Western ideas of law. An American legal scholar has said of China's new *Legal Dictionary*, "There is nothing to show that it was not written by a committee of Westerners."[53] American lawyers helped China write some of her new tax codes, and, in 1979, one could even publish, as a minority view, a scholarly article on behalf of presumption of innocence, a principle contrary to the very spirit of Chinese jurisprudence, and formerly denounced as bourgeois.[54] (We are not aware of literature having discussed any reform so radical.)

A third factor may have been Western novels and detective stories, which depict a foreign idea of the nature of legal process as being adversarial rather than paternal.[55] In China, the trial is not an instrument of fact-finding, but a ritual. It publicizes the successful termination of a social problem by the state, allows the guilty to show contrition, brings to light factors relevant to sentencing, and "educates" the masses, in theory even allows them to participate in passing judgment. An author trying realistically to dissect society would not be apt to choose a Chinese courtroom as the site to play out his drama. He would have trouble observing a trial, and, if he could, there would assuredly be no shocking revelations or adjournments because of the breakdown of a witness. For that to happen in a real Chinese trial would be an indication of the incompetence or corruption of the state, for only a person whose guilt the state has verified is supposed to go to trial. Therefore a verdict of guilty is rendered an astounding 99.97 percent of the time, China's Procurator General has indicated, without embarrassment.[56] Yet, China's new melodramatists still favor courtroom scenes, and use them to frame dramatic reversals pregnant with legal significance.

A fourth influence is quite evident: Judge Bao and the *gongan* tradition, as well as the ancient interest in verdict-reversal. Sherlock Holmes is not referred to in the rule-of-law melodramas; Judge Bao is, in many of them. Traditional, popular influences have no doubt filtered in from many sources, perhaps even from underground crime and spy stories that circulated during the Cultural Revolution. In the next section, we shall analyze relatively daring "serious detective stories" which combine Judge Bao, Perry Mason, and Western civil liberties. But first, let us examine a pair of rule-of-law melodramas which, however bold, are fascinatingly ambivalent about law as we know it.

Power vs. Law is a play dramatizing *gaozhuang*. The crime is an "economic" one of the sort newspapers feature, to arouse mass indignation against bureaucratic corruption. Here, public funds have been used to provide special privileges for cadres instead of famine relief. The criminal is former Party secretary Cao Da, who had his accountant, Ding Mu, doctor the books after the fact. He was also known for bullying people through his dictatorial control of the police (one-man rule, a cardinal sin in post-Mao China). Previously, his authority to spend money and arrest alleged criminals would have been unquestioned except in specific instances, so here we have "rule of law" reaching into a new sphere.

Cao's accountant now feels guilty. She wants to *gaozhuang* (our word) to the new Party secretary, Luo. Meanwhile, villain Cao's niece, a cub reporter, wants to *gaozhuang* about the same improprieties through the press. She calls her uncle "a bureaucrat on the make," though, in fact, he has been demoted to become Luo's deputy, in a typical post-Fall transition of power. As in more overt anti-crime propaganda, the state's interest in preventing crime because of its ill effects rather than its illegality per se is reflected by a referring of the audience to the enormous impact of the crime. Straining to detail the symmetry of cause and effect, the play turns to the fiancé of Ding Mu's daughter, who was on a famine-relief team. He bears witness to the starvation and freezing that stemmed from Secretary Cao's love of luxury (*ZA*, p. 91).

Cao counters by framing Ding Mu for a murder she did not commit, threatening the press, and using his former relationship with the police to silence his opponents through preemptive arrests. There is suspense and a detective interest in uncovering Cao Da's crimes, past and present, although there is no single detective. In the end, Secretary Luo arrests the Cao gang, after pointedly refusing himself the privilege of signing the warrants on his own authority. He goes by the book, referring the case first to the Party municipal committee.

The play is a courageous hypothetical depiction of corruption within the Communist Party, but its idea of "rule of law" amounts virtually to "correct administrative procedure." Although an important step in fulfilling "equality before the law" in China is, as some works now indicate, insuring that criminal Party members are punished by the state's law, not just Party discipline, *Power vs. Law* fails to distinguish between what it refers to in a single breath as "Party discipline and laws of the state" (*ZA*, p. 90); the former seems, if anything, to have priority. Indeed, "law" in this play seems not to be any code at all, but punishment meted out by a political committee. The evil identified is one-man dictatorship over Party organs, not exclusive Party control over who gets arrested. The role of Secretary Luo, the Party's "good man," is essential if any system at all is to prevail. In sum, the play is exciting as social exposure, but intellectually, and as literature, quite conservative.

"Judgment" is another work whose criminal is a public servant. A legal hair-splitter might well sympathize with the culprit for having been caught in the newly extended scope of law. Liu Lei, former director of a water-conservancy project, built his dam too fast, surveying as he went and taking shortcuts, against the advice of his head engineer. The dam was swept away in a storm, with tragic loss of life and property. Yet, the authors make it clear that Liu Lei is not a bad man. Decades ago, when the Japanese threatened, he saved the man who now has been sent to prosecute him, Chen, instead of his own son. We feel Liu's resentment at being imprisoned in a dingy cell next to murderers, traffickers with the Vietnamese, and pornography merchants. His motive in building the project so fast was praiseworthy, although consonant with Leftist voluntarism.

The didacticism of "Judgment" is partly "legal popularization," the self-conscious portrayal of statutes at work; articles of the Constitution are quoted by number to the defendant in his cell. But a propagandistic declamation by the narrators, supposed to celebrate rule of law, actually sins horribly against it, by implying that law exists to promote economic growth rather than justice for its own sake:

Our Party came by many bitter lessons and paid for them dearly before it arrived at the relatively correct ideological and political line of the present, and realized that the Four Modernizations could be achieved only through small-scale production as well as large-scale socialist production. Then it promulgated civil law and criminal law, and now is trying out economic law. It will establish economic courts, in order to guarantee projects of the Four Modernizations through law. This is an epoch-making turn of events. (*ZA*, p. 13)

Apart from the unsettling legal fervor of such passages, the story explores two interesting social issues. One is the conflict between impartial application of the law, and *qing*, "feelings" of partiality towards an accused person (from gratitude or a past connection). The tension is dramatized in the person of Procurator Chen. Will he go too easy on Liu, because he is in Liu's debt? While local citizens argue *qing*'s pros and cons before the reader, Chen remembers his legal training: *Qing* is a curse from Confucius. Unfortunately, the authors get so carried away with the historical symbolism of law vs. *qing* that law, too, reverts to a "feudal" nature. If Liu Lei as an individual is owed *qing* by a friend, so is he as Party member the beneficiary of *qing* from his flock. The community owes him for many years of good service, or even for being such a good fellow as to have been made a Party member, implies a fellow cadre who would have made a good Calvinist. Are the people not wrong in letting such "*qing*" ameliorate the anger at Liu that law mandates? Yet, by this reasoning, relevant legal factors such as extenuating circumstances, good past behavior, or anything that might lessen the harsh, penal aspect of law is designated as *qing*. Perforce the law is something to be invoked only in an extreme situation, as of old (*ZA*, p. 9).

Less ambiguous in its support of the law is another concept that occurs to the procurator: Law is not a tool of a particular class in relation to another, but a universal relationship among equal people, to be enforced impartially. He arrives at this principle backwards. If law were never for use against the "people," only "enemies of the people," then errant cadres, who are classed as the best among the people, would escape legal scrutiny.

Unfortunately, the authors had to have it both ways regarding *qing*. Liu Lei acknowledges the magnitude of his guilt only after learning that his negligence killed an old friend—to whom he owed *qing*. Thus, a web of *qing* dramatically revealed to Liu at his trial is what reconciles him to impartial judgment of himself. Did he get the point? Moreover, Liu Lei's enlightenment comes through what could be called a show trial. The accused repents and actually revels at being able to star in the state's educational drama, to save others. But the state's extraction of educational value from trials (which leads to heavier sentences when the crime in question is politically important) is a fundamental problem of Chinese "rule of law."[57] And, in this very case, the impact of Liu's crime seems more than any code to determine his sentencing. The story is inconsistent about the purpose of law, reflecting the still ambivalent attitude towards the law of the Chinese state itself.

RULE-OF-LAW DETECTIVE MELODRAMAS

Detective-story conventions have proven irresistible even to Chinese who see themselves as writers with a purpose, too serious to construct criminological puzzles for the reader's amusement. The kind of work we discuss now is not the "detective story" of the classical genre, nor comedy of manners, but deadly serious melodrama, like the Chinese spy thriller. Mystery enlarges its audience and resolves many questions of plotting. But a detection interest also frees the story to expose the state's crime-fighting apparatus as its agents sleuth, while the crime that is pursued, perhaps an ordinary and apolitical evil, masquerades as the focal point of the story. Even if unclear about how law actually ought to rule, the piece crusades for justice; by casting the state in the role of obstructor of justice, it makes the authorities reap the opprobrium due the criminal. A second, even more conspiratorial plot type features criminality and cover-up by the state itself as the concealed evil to be detected.

"After Cracking the Case," by Pang Taixi, is a story of the first type. Its title promises a detective interest, and the reader is not disappointed. Pang narrates a mystery: Who held up the store in a rural production brigade? Stealing from the collective is extremely serious from the state's point of view, but only the state would jump to the conclusion that such a crime must be political; it turns out that the robbery was an inside job, motivated by pure greed. The culprit even has a criminal record (not a political one), in the forgotten past. The detective is local militia head Shi Kanghua, not a professional but an upstanding young Communist, so popular with the masses that they are about to send him to college. He is intelligent, but that is not the point. He saves the situation through his steadfast integrity; he must fend off an evil county-level cadre sent down to investigate the crime, who wants summarily to pin the case on a "capitalist roader and renegade." Anxiety mounts, first because the city cadre's prime suspect is a friend of Shi Kanghua, then because it becomes clear to all but the public security cadre that he has the wrong man. Yet, the city man will not desist; he tortures the "renegade" into making a false confession, and at one point descends on the countryside with armed henchmen. A threat of counter-violence against the brutal outsiders looms when the militia surround them, but, just at that point, Shi Kanghua relieves the tension by revealing the real criminal.

The subject of the story is thus not "the crime" pursued through detection, but a much more serious miscarriage of justice, narrowly averted through moral heroism. At the climax, the "renegade" is interrogated by torture. His ankles are beaten, and he is forced to drink kerosene. Such techniques are exposed as not only inhumane, but in no way conducive to justice. There is also a surprise injustice at the end, which reveals the story to be an ingenious fable discrediting *xuetonglun,* the principle of "like father, like son," which eventuates in people inheriting the stigma of their Rightist relatives, and so forth. The criminal whom Shi Kanghua unmasks, to his own amazement, is his father. That the young man still does his duty indicates his commitment to justice; nor is he anything but filial to the traditional nth degree. He blames himself for not having kept his father out of trouble. Yet, Shi Kanghua has made himself unfit for college—by law. He has unwittingly changed his own status, to "son of a counterrevolutionary." He might as well have committed the crime himself.

These melodramas about injustice take place not in the ordered society of Holmes's or Lao Gao's classical detective story, but the more perilous one of Dou E and Judge Bao—perhaps even the hard-boiled world familiar to Sam Spade and Mike Hammer, an urban wasteland where cops are crooked and violent, and judges have been bought. (Nor is Hammer without a strong ideology: anti-Communism.) There are thefts and rapes, and gangs of hoodlums on the prowl. Shi Kanghua's father's elemental greed thus has a social background of sorts. He explains, "I went wrong only after seeing so many years of open robbery of grain stores, highjackings of railway grain shipments, even casual murders that were never followed up" (ZA, p. 224). Mao would have echoed the East German who thinks hard-boiled fiction "hardly conceivable in a socialist state, above all for the lack of corresponding social phenomena,"[58] but depictions of conspiracy by Lin Biao and the Gang of Four (literary inheritors of the treachery of Soviet spies) have now opened the back door to melodrama of a society that is not only hard-boiled but run by gangsters.

Wang Yaping's "Sacred Duty" (1977) pioneered the literary pursuit of crimes devolving from the top of the power structure. Wang's hero, a policeman himself just back from confinement at a May Seventh Cadre School, devotes himself to helping a man physically broken by police brutality and eight years on a labor farm, following his frame-up by a conspiracy of provincial public security officials and other power-holders of the Cultural Revolution era. The authorities attempt to thwart the good policeman's sleuthing, going so far as to make an attempt on the life of his star witness. The hero prevails in the end only by sacrificing his own life.

The crusade for justice in "Sacred Duty" and its successors is so moving to Chinese readers that such rule-of-law melodramas have become an exciting formula in their own right. State criminality, superficially like the ordinary crime in a whodunit, is stealthy, needing first of all to be exposed. The air is so thick with conspiracy that even the street hoodlums are part of it. They turn out to be children of leading cadres, with protection way upstairs, not the dislocated and under-employed young people one would expect.[59] When there is a murder, the melodrama that might be extracted from its elemental horror is slighted; murder becomes horrible rather for furthering the designs of social tyrants. Hence, the crime to be exposed might well be unjust imprisonment rather than murder.

The "mean," quasi-naturalistic nature of the world depicted may even gratify the reader's taste for "realism."[60] And yet, by tracing all criminality to revisionist Lin Biao types (as to Sicilian Godfathers), the theme of gangster conspiracy tends to exculpate "actual Chinese society" (as it does "real" Americans). Such a formula titillates but does not seriously probe the social origins of crime or the nature of guilt. It even continues the socialist-realist tradition that political malefactors and criminals must be one and the same. Moreover, in post-Mao as in Maoist fiction, human frailty scarcely hinders the victory of abstract good over evil. The new Chinese detective melodramas part company from American hard-boiled detective fiction chiefly in the unflinching morality of their detectives, and the fact that justice prevails not through the individualism of the dick, but through law itself, an abstract social and moral force. Proper legal procedure is the strength behind Shi Kanghua and the good cop of "Sacred Duty." They would never echo Raymond Chandler's cynicism about law: "Lawyers write the laws for other lawyers to dissect in front of other lawyers called judges so that other judges can say the first judges were wrong and the Supreme Court can say the second lot were wrong. Sure there's such a thing as law. We're up to our necks in it. About all it does is make business for lawyers."[61]

They might nonetheless agree with Chandler that justice is achieved by an uncorrupted man of action, never by a lawyer. The good detective has a code of his own, "Serve the people." It is nostalgically chivalrous for the corrupt world he inhabits, as is, indeed, that of the outwardly hard-boiled American dick.[62] Inevitably, the Chinese version is a "wounded" cadre severely tested during the Cultural Revolution, imprisoned, at least.

But the Chinese detective in the rule-of-law melodrama is hard-boiled rather than cerebral in that, like Mike Hammer, he must learn to fight back.[63] He is pursuing people, not physical clues. They will make him their target, so moral distance from the crime in the manner of the classical sleuth is virtually impossible. Because the reader is morally engaged in this melodrama, not just participating in a puzzle, he or she actually wants the detective to pass from the role of investigator to that of judge and executioner[64]—which the Chinese dick, under "rule of law," is not free to do.

Inevitably, the detective is a loner who must keep his own conscience. His erstwhile friends and army buddies may have turned counterrevolutionary during the ten years of the Gang's "feudal fascism." Hence, the typical Chinese detective is a romantic hero, *in* the state's crime-fighting apparatus, but not *of* it; those in power are unlikely to be untainted by the Gang's great inhuman conspiracy. This is increasingly certain as one ascends the power hierarchy. The hero of Shen Zhiwei's "Law Enforcer," deputy chief of public security, has to look no farther than his boss, who is concurrently first secretary of the Party committee. An honest detective's subordinates, even if uncorrupted, are likewise gadflies testing their boss's grit, rather than supportive Watsons waiting to be tested by him.[65]

Being a loner, himself a target, the detective may well have to become a fugitive, like the good cop of "Sacred Duty." He may even be thrust into anti-hero status. While it is evidently taboo for the detective to make deals with criminals, he may make contact with underground elements in society (without reforming them). When a highly professional Chinese counterspy becomes a fugitive in "The Passenger in Handcuffs," and hides above a lavatory in a railway car, he runs into a genial young social dropout. The boy tramp has fun at the expense of the pro, since the older man obviously knows so little about China's pre-existing underground way of life and those who live it. The dropout turns out to be the son of chief of security for a sensitive city in Chinese Turkestan!

The lone-wolf, superficially Western-looking character of sleuthing in these stories is a formulaic departure from social reality, as the police reports remind us. But "Inside the Court and Beyond" is interested in the reality, and its consequences. In heroine judge Shang Qin's world, no crucial decision about investigative procedure is made without a prior judicial committee meeting, which itself follows a judiciary-procuracy liaison meeting. Taking a hint from their superiors, committee members slow investigation of a crime in which officials are implicated; it is easy for them to shirk responsibility when they do so collectively. Undeterred by their cowardice, Judge Shang Qin doggedly pursues truth and justice by herself, morally in conflict with her own bureaucracy.

Realistic or not, the detective hero in this formula is lent integrity by an archetypal Chinese role model—Judge Bao. Cyril Birch has likened heroism in Chinese socialist realism to ancient Chinese conventions for heroism; a similar legacy in the relatively native rule-of-law genre is not surprising.[66] Exemplifying the model Judge Bao or Archibald Cox of post-Mao China is Yang Qingtian, the title hero of "Public Procurator from Beijing." Wise, incorruptible, and pointedly overworked (taking trains when he could fly, the authors tell us), Yang is called by duty to cast a suspicious eye over a municipal Party secretary in the South. The accused is Yang's old war buddy and superior, Du Ping, towards whom he feels partiality (*qing*), as he ought. However, Du Ping's son has killed a young girl with an automobile (a favorite deadly weapon in these stories exposing the high and mighty); his father has managed a cover-up. A person who witnessed the evidently deliberate act has appealed upward for justice—by writing a letter to the Beijing prosecutor.

Yang's given name, Qingtian ("Blue-increase") is homophonous with the nickname "Clear-sky" traditionally used to salute upright judges in old China, notably (Judge) Bao Qingtian. The writer of the letter has the word *just* in his name, too, so the good guys are clearly distinguished by their white hats. Procurator Yang Qingtian must still expose a cover-up. As in traditional stories, suspense hangs on how Yang Qingtian will build his case. He succeeds through his adeptness at cross-examination and assembling witnesses to confront each other's stories. Through clues in the dead girl's diary, and his understanding of human nature, Yang uncovers a prior connection between the killer and his victim, hence a motive for the homocidal driving. Cutting through all obstructions of his investigation, he elicits the confession. A little comedy and realism break the formula at the end. One of Du's henchmen asks a crucial question, now that Du Ping's son is to be reinvestigated: Who will do the reinvestigating? Du Ping? And he asks the modern-day censor: "How long will you be staying here?" (ZA, p. 29).

Plot in the Chinese detective melodrama may have recurrent violent crime, chases, and other aspects of adventure which tempt and test the protagonist. It is chiefly in this formula, not the classical story, that we enter the make-believe Chinese courtroom, wherein trials have unexpected conclusions. The reader also wants to see the criminals actually punished; society as portrayed might let the powerful among them escape. The criminal may even repent, as in socialist realism.

Traditional verdict reversal (pingfan) themes are ubiquitous in these crusades for justice. The plotting of "Sacred Duty" follows a typical pingfan pattern; although a wise policeman is instrumental in reversing the verdict of the story's chief victim, the revised verdict is implemented only with a deus ex machina equivalent to heavenly intervention—the fall of the Gang of Four. In "The Story of the Criminal Li Tongzhong," the posthumous reversal of the subject's verdict acts as a frame for the telling of his "crime" in flashback. And, in "Red Magnolias Beneath the Big House Wall," victims of injustice wail for justice in their own voices, like Dou E. The chief victim is the former director of a reform-through-labor camp who now finds himself thrown in prison and persecuted. He and fellow patriot-victims are severally shot, imprisoned, or put in the camp mental ward during the film scenario's penultimate moments (deleted from the official English translation). Their pingfan, like Dou E's and Li Tongzhong's, will be posthumous: They smuggle out of the camp a full report on how the prison system is being misused by the local authorities.

Social observation in the rule-of-law melodramas is varied, as is the purview of the detective. In *Save Her,* a play about a juvenile delinquent victimized both by society and the power structure, it is a wise teacher who acts as caseworker and also sleuths deep enough to uncover the connections of gang leaders to education-bureau cadres.

Wang Yaping's "Defender" is notable for the legitimacy it tenders adversarial action, through having a lawyer, Lei Meng, act as its positive detective hero. Lawyers are not well thought of in China. As Lei Meng explains, people feel they serve the rich and powerful against the common man.

Lei Meng indeed defends young Tang Xiaobo—son of a prefectural committee secretary—on a murder charge. Lei's credentials are good; he is literally a "wounded cadre," having been left a cripple by the Cultural Revolution. Yet, several devices lead one to worry at first that he may be an F. Lee Bailey, skilled enough at the law to get his client off even if he is guilty. He makes the narrator nervous. Su Ning, aunt of the narrator's wife and procurator, has a convincing case against Tang, while Lei Meng seems to be creating a diversion when he insists on finding out whether or not the deceased, Tang's pregnant young girlfriend, was pregnant even before she met the accused. When Lei Meng comes to interview the narrator, who knew the deceased, the procurator eavesdrops from within a closet (a fanciful arrangement, but inadvertently symbolic of how few rights the accused in China actually has). Finally caught in a lie, the narrator ceases to stonewall and explains what happened.

The deceased was blackmailing Tang Xiaobo, at the narrator's suggestion, although she realized she was pregnant not by Tang, but by his father's henchman, a corrupt food-commissary chief (her boss), who had seduced her. The local food czar had spread false rumors about her, driving her to suicide, except that young Tang had found and saved her, fallen in love, then taken advantage of the helpless girl in his turn. The narrator had discovered the girl as she lay on train tracks, during a second suicide attempt. He suggested that she turn her pregnancy into a weapon suitable for bringing down young Tang and, through him, his father and the food czar. The plan was frustrated by young Tang's willingness to resort to ultimate means.

The lawyer has brought the truth to light; the procurator, won over, emerges from hiding. Lei Meng understands the difference between morality and appropriate use of legal process. He warns the procurator not to launch a lawsuit against the Tangs until she has evidence of their guilt that will stand up in court. This makes good practical sense; the elder Tang is powerful enough to fend off all but the most irrefutable case against him.

Yet this clearheaded use of law is rejected by the procurator, who plans to go ahead and put "socialist law" into action, since it can *educate* the people, even if the case is not proved. This is actually a vote of no confidence in the legal system. The procurator seems to think that the truth will be self-evident when the people hear it, and that court decisions, being often enough influenced by sheer power rather than truth, are not definitive.

Lei Meng, moreover, pleads to serve the now rather compromised narrator as his faithful defense, since the narrator is not really a bad person, and was aiming at a real villain. The lawyer ends up shaking hands with the procurator, agreeing to assist with her new mission of unraveling the Tang conspiracy. What, then, has happened to the sanctity of Lei Meng's defense of the young Tang? The involvement of Tang Xiaobo with his corrupt father should heighten, not blunt, the issue of Tang Xiaobo as a bad man who, even so, has rights. Lei Meng is faithful to the young Tang by Chinese standards, since all lawyers in China are state employees, enjoined to serve the state before serving their clients, but he falls short of furthering "rule of law" as we know it.

The stories in general are strong in arguing against torture and summary justice, and for due process during arrests, searches, and seizures. They ask for authentication of evidence used against the accused and criticize the "Hitler-like raids" of the Gang-of-Four years,[67] without going so far as to say that evidence illegally acquired should not be used. A few pieces also open fire on the indeterminate sentence as in principle inhumane. Particularly remarkable are stories critical of Chinese penology, which acknowledge that prisoners have mental lives of their own, perhaps something of a counterculture, and depict the frighteningly totalitarian surveillance of criminals even after they are safely locked up.[68] There is a rich variety of social exposure in the melodramas, but what interests us in conclusion is what Chinese crime fiction lacks.

CONCLUSION: WHAT IS MISSING?

Chinese crime fiction is partly distinguished by the formulas it omits. There are no completely hard-boiled detective stories; evidently authors are free to probe law's controversial limits, but not any form of justice beyond the law. Nor do full-time detectives star in anything but police procedurals. Perhaps Wang Yaping's "defender" and the teacher of *Save Her* have broken ground for future detectives who will sleuth as an avocation rather than a profession. A Shanghai medical doctor has been featured in the popular nonfiction legal magazine, *Democracy and Legal System,* for having apprehended 1,074 pickpockets in his spare time.[69] Any avocational crime-fighter would, of course, have to be a trusted person in a position of authority—we have just named a doctor, a lawyer, and a teacher.

Also missing from Chinese crime fiction are certain kinds of crimes. Melodramatic though it may be, rule-of-law fiction cannot approach the frankness with which "reportage literature" (journalism presented literarily, as narrative) has exposed hideous crimes of the Party and state, some of them committed after 1976. *Tribulations before the Trial (Shenpan qian de jiaoliang),* a book of reportage about real-life Chinese Watergates, speaks freely of dozens of innocent people killed, maimed, or tortured in a particular county's "people's militia command" and "study classes"—and links the crimes to deliberate policy decisions.[70]

It seems appropriate to compare fiction and nonfiction. Not only is crime reportage of the late 1970s anything but matter-of-fact in tone; some works are structured like detective stories. An example is the title piece, "Tribulations before the Trial," about the notorious Bohai No. 2 oil rig. Its sinking claimed 72 lives and forced the resignation of China's petroleum minister. A fairly low-level cadre begins the episode by sorting out conflicting testimony about the tragedy. Soon he discovers himself in the midst of a high-level cover-up; the Petroleum Ministry has acquired a list of the investigators and begun a coordinated assault of threats, buy-offs of witnesses, and rigged meetings beside which the Watergate cover-up looks timid. The investigator thus changes from sleuth to hard-boiled crusader for justice. A suspenseful courtroom process and punishment of the guilty cap off the piece. Presumably authors may write so forcefully because, when challenged, they can defend their works as factual. As to the book, it must have helped to have had the Ministry of Public Security's outlet as publisher.

Many smaller crimes and civil disputes are missing from China's formula fiction, too, even though the nonfiction press shows great interest in bringing them under "rule of law." We speak of thefts, wife-beatings, abuse of the elderly, and cases of divorce, disputed inheritances, and parental interference in their children's choice of spouse. This time the clue comes from "The Court of Morality," a supposedly instructive human-interest legal column in *Democracy and Legal System* which relates disputes among the masses so sensationally that readers shower it with fan mail, supporting one side in the case or the other. Typically there is a terribly wronged party who has sought in vain to get the courts to take up his or her case, and so cries out to the magazine readers as the "court of last resort." The cases take titles like "Love and Hate," "Men and Wild Beasts," "He's a Love Swindler," "Mama, How Cruel Can You Be?" "Why Is She Driven to Commit Arson?" and "She Died Amid Scorn and Contempt." They disclose such unedifying social behavior as quick divorce and wife-beating by a college student who married only as part of a scheme to get himself transferred to Shanghai, maltreatment and starvation of her helpless old mother by a well-to-do lady, and torture of her daughter (driving her twice to the brink of suicide) by a mother offended by the poverty of her daughter's boyfriend. Yet these little stories, however tawdry, deal with an issue important to the definition of "rule of law": if the courts are to be given a greater role in society, how can they ignore these frightful injustices at the local level? No doubt the masses are interested in at least imagining how "rule of law," something more abstract and solemn than the mediation at the mercy of their neighbors to which they are accustomed, might change their everyday lives.[71] So far, there is no fiction to satisfy them, even at the soap-opera level. These legitimate legal concerns are left to break out, *National Enquirer* style, in the press.

The elements missing from China's new crime fiction indicate some of the paradoxes that result when genuinely popular literary subject matter overlaps an important ideological concern of the state. The whodunit, a form that is "merely" popular, has been free to elaborate most of the conventions found in the West. The "serious" stories, perhaps because of their moral and social pretensions as "high" literature, as well as the extra ideological scrutiny they must bear, seem restricted to suitably "high crimes and misdemeanors." Crime literature in China still has much unexploited potential; no doubt its authors look forward to further relaxations in literary policy.

1984 Postscript: In the cooler climate for Chinese literature these past two years, crime fiction and social exposure have nearly withered away.[72] But genres that survived the Cultural Revolution will surely rise again. Before long, China will have to cope with modernization, improved communications, rising crime, her Cultural Revolution generation, and the absorption of Hong Kong.

PART TWO

Literary Art

CHAPTER FOUR

"Obscure Poetry": A Controversy in Post-Mao China

WILLIAM TAY

Post-Mao Chinese poetry, in particular the works of some of the young poets, has exhibited much innovation. Partly indicative of the new trends, but otherwise rather distracting in its disparagement of the new efforts, has been a controversy surrounding some of the poems that has raged fiercely since 1979. Dubbed by the critics as *menglong shi* or "obscure poetry"— occasionally also labeled as *guguai shi* or "eccentric poetry"— these works have been praised by some as "realization of new aesthetic principles" and deplored by others as "anti-socialist" deviations from the Four Modernizations program.[1]

All the leading poetry journals (*Poetry* [*Shikan*], *Stars* [*Xing xing*], and *Explorations in Poetry* [*Shi tansuo*]), several influential publications (for example, *Wenhui Daily* [*Wenhui bao*] and

Literature and Art Gazette [*Wenyi bao*]), and some reputable local periodicals (for example, *Shanghai Literature* [*Shanghai wenxue*], *Anhui Literature* [*Anhui wenxu*], and *Yalu River* [*Yalu Jiang*]) have been involved in the ongoing debates. Since no manifesto has been proclaimed or poetry society formed, identifying the "obscure" poets is not an easy task, and some confusion has already arisen. The names most often mentioned by critics and editors in connection with "obscurity" are: Gu Cheng, Bei Dao, Xie Yicheng, Ji Xiaowu, Wu Lijun, Li Gang, Gao Falin, Xu Jingya, Wang Xiaoni, Liang Xiaobin, Shu Ting, Jiang He, Chen Suoju, and Yang Lian.[2] The most controversial figure in this group of so-called "obscure" poets appears to be Gu Cheng, a factory worker who is in his mid-twenties and is the son of the old poet Gu Gong. Our discussion of "obscure poetry" will particularly feature this young poet and his works.

To anyone who has read some mainland Chinese poetry, one obvious characteristic is its length. This feature is even more prominent when compared with contemporary Chinese poetry from Taiwan, where the long narrative poem is relatively rare. But we must remember that, when narrative verbosity is intertwined with propaganda and didacticism, the result is not only tedious but also artistically disappointing. In contrast to narrative prolixity, which had become rampant, the poems by several other young mainland poets are definitely some of the shortest ever written since 1949. Take, for example, Gu Cheng's "One Generation" ("Yidai ren"):

> The black night has given me black eyes,
> Yet I use them to search for light.[3]

> 黑夜給了我黑色的眼睛，
> 我却用它寻找光明。

Or Cai Kun's "Wrinkles" ("Zhouwen"):

> Ruts left on my body
> By the reversed wheels of history.[4]

這是歷史倒轉的車輪，
留在我身上的轍印。

The shortest of all is, of course, Bei Dao's "Life" ("Sheng-huo"):

Net.[5]

網

While many longer poems in praise of the "brightness" of socialism are replete with explicit slogans and abstract didacticism, short pieces are, in comparison, more subtle and indirect. But they certainly are not, as some of their critics have charged, "drifting away from reality" or "indulging in purely individualistic expressions." The two main images in Gu Cheng's and Cai Kun's poems—"black night" and "reversed wheels"—can be read as allegorical references to the Cultural Revolution. Such political allegory can also be found in "Photo" ("She"), a slightly longer poem by Gu Cheng:

The sunlight
Flashes once in the sky
And is covered again by black clouds.

The rainstorm is developing
The negative of my soul.[6]

陽光
在天上一閃
又被烏雲埋掩。

暴雨冲洗着
我靈魂的底片。

Different readers may assign different symbolic interpretations to the situation described by the poet, but the politically-minded undoubtedly can view the first stanza as a reference to the brief moment of liberalization in the post-Mao era and the second stanza as a representation of the poet's internal struggle.

The most impressive quality of these poems, however, perhaps is not their symbolic subtlety or absence of didacticism but their occasional emphasis on imagistic perspicuity, which is very prominent in Gu Cheng's "Feeling" ("Ganjue"):

> The sky is grey
> The road is grey
> The building is grey
> The rain is grey
>
> In this blanket dead grey
> Two children walk by
> One bright red
> One pale green [7]

> 天是灰色的
> 路是灰色的
> 楼是灰色的
> 雨是灰色的
>
> 在一片死灰之中
> 走过两个孩子
> 一个鲜红
> 一个淡绿

To those familiar with modern Anglo-American poetry, the interplay of color in this poem will certainly remind them of the Imagist experiments. For example, a similar use of color images which contrast and otherwise interact with each other can be easily found in the poems of the Imagists:

"Green," by D. H. Lawrence

The sky was apple-green,
The sky was green wine held up in the sun,
The moon was a golden petal between.

She opened her eyes, and green
They shone, clear like flowers undone,
For the first time, now for the first time seen.[8]

"In Time of War," by Amy Lowell

Across the newly-plastered wall,
The darting of red dragonflies
Is like the shooting
Of blood-tipped arrows.[9]

Though introductory discussions of Imagism have appeared in China in recent years, the translation of Imagist poems is still very sporadic.[10] It remains unclear whether Gu Cheng has been influenced by these Anglo-American poets who, in the 1910s, were considered avant-garde writers revolting against the Victorian tradition. In his article "Two Generations" ("Liang dairen"), Gu Gong raises this issue—which probably is on many people's minds—of possible Western influence on his son's poetry. According to the father's testimony, Gu Cheng has never encountered either the Crescent School (Xinyuepai) or Western modernism and, like most young people of his generation, has grown up in a cultural desert.[11] Nevertheless, the existence of influence, if it is not outright imitation, can sometimes be a difficult case to argue, even if there can be found actual *"rapports de fait"*; for every work of art, being sui generis, is not explicable solely in extrinsic and positivistic terms.[12] The irony of Gu Cheng's case, however, is that the Imagist experiments, having long been assimilated into the modernist convention, have by now been largely neglected in the West. They can no longer elicit the kind of "defamiliarizing" effect which they once had, such as Gu Cheng's experimentation is arousing in China, and, with it, all kinds of negative criticism. Even in the modernist poetry from Taiwan, which was once heavily indebted to various avant-garde movements of the West, such concentrated color imagery has long been considered passé. For the purpose of comparison, let me quote a passage from Fang Xin, a Taiwan modernist poet of the early 1960s:

Rich beauty of goose yellow
Is laid on the porcelain plate of early autumn whiteness
And pierced with a fork of steel-grey melancholy.[13]

盛鵝黃的豐美
於早秋白色的磁盤
以鋼灰色憂鬱的餐叉刺取

Some of Fang Xin's early poems, as two critics have rightly observed, are very much indebted to Imagism.[14] But in the case of Fang, a scholar of foreign literature who had spent a decade studying in Canada, such indebtedness is more conscious and understandable. The same cannot be said about Gu Cheng. The astounding resemblance between the two poetic experiments seems to indicate that the modernist phase of Taiwan's Chinese literature in the 1960s is only now beginning to take shape on the mainland.

But Gu Cheng's affinity with Imagism seems to go much further. In its use of unconnected, montage-like juxtaposition of images, another poem by Gu entitled "Curve" ("Huxian") actually employs the most fundamental technique of Imagism:

A bird in the gusty wind
Deftly changes direction

A youth tries to pick up
A penny

The grapevine in fantasy
Stretches its tentacle

The wave in retreat
Arches its back[15]

鸟儿在疾风中
迅速转向

少年去捡拾
一枚分币

葡萄藤因幻想
而延伸的触丝

海浪因退缩
而耸起的背脊

This small exercise in imagistic presentation employs four analogous images but refrains from linking them explicitly. Without any linguistic connection, the four images are simply juxtaposed. The basis for the juxtaposition clearly lies in the curve, a shape shared by all the images. Though Gu Cheng's poem may not surprise anyone familiar with Imagism, it has jolted many readers and critics on the mainland, a result not unlike that created by the first appearance of the "Imagistes." Undoubtedly, the technique informing Gu's poem is that of juxtaposition, first demonstrated by Ezra Pound in his poem "In a Station of the Metro":

The apparition   of these faces   in the crowd:
Petals   on a wet, black   bough.[16]

First published in 1913, the poem was analyzed by Pound in his "Vorticism" manifesto as "haiku-like." In the same article, Pound also cites a Japanese haiku by Moritake Arakida as illustration of his argument:

The fallen blossom flies back to its branch:
A butterfly.[17]

Pound goes on to observe that both the haiku and his own poem employ "a form of super-position." What Pound means by "super-position"—a term later replaced by "ideogrammic method"—is the juxtaposition of the two discrete imagistic lines without any explicit linguistic connection. The two lines remain, on the surface, independent entities not conjoined by explicit links. The analogical relationship between the two is implicit and unstated; the imagistic correspondence awaits the active participation of the reader. It is obvious that Gu Cheng's method in "Curve" is basically the same, with the analogy running through all four stanzas.[18]

Juxtaposition, however, does not necessarily appear in every Imagist poem. Very often the poem is characterized only by sharp, perspicuous imagery. "Oread," by H. D. (Hilda Doolittle, 1886–1961), is a quite famous example:

Whirl up, sea—
Whirl your pointed pines,
Splash your great pines
On your rocks,
Hurl your green over us,
Cover us with your pools of fir.[19]

The Oread, a nymph dwelling in the greenness of the hills and mountains, sees a resemblance between the lifted waves and her own environment. On that basis, a metaphoric comparison is made in lines 2, 3, and 6. The effect of lines 2 and 6 following immediately lines 1 and 5 is one of surprise, created by the unexpected metaphoric transference. The literalness of lines 1 and 5 is transformed by the figurativeness of lines 2 and 6, because literal interpretation is frustrated by the poet's violation of selection restriction.

A similiar strategy can also be found in the first stanza of Gu Cheng's "A Walk in the Rain" ("Yu xing"):

Clouds that are grey
Can no longer be washed clean.
We open the umbrella
And simply paint the sky black.[20]

云，灰灰的，
再也洗不干净。
我们打开布伞，
索性涂黑了天空。

Like H. D.'s rather unexpected metaphoric transference, line 2 of this stanza turns the clouds into dirty laundry. Similarly, line 4 transforms the black umbrellas into paint brushes. Lines 1 and 3 (grey clouds and black umbrella), like the first and fifth line of "Oread," are ordinary images which normally evoke no particular response from the reader and are in no way surprising and arresting. But, with the strategy of sudden metaphoric transference, a common situation of walking in the rain under an umbrella is given a concrete and refreshing renewal, an effect not unlike that created by H. D.'s poem.

H. D. and other Imagists, though generally considered to be pioneers in Anglo-American modernist poetry, are, in fact, fairly lucid and intelligible poets. Some Imagists—such as Pound and William Carlos Williams—eventually became "difficult" poets who needed guides and annotations. When the Imagists started as a movement, they clearly did not qualify as "obscure" poets. Neither does Gu Cheng. Moreover, in comparison with modernist poetry produced in Taiwan or the symbolist poems of Li Jinfa, a poet famous for his difficulty in the 1930s, the poems by Gu Cheng are, at least to me, far from "obscure." This is not, however, the view of many old poets. While the criticism leveled by the old poets is superficially against "obscurity," the main concern actually appears to be the content of the so-called "obscure poetry."

Gong Liu, an old poet who had been silenced for twenty years since the Anti-Rightist Movement, first described Gu Cheng as "walking a dangerous path" in an article that ignited the whole debate.[21] In a 1981 interview, several lines by Gu Cheng were attacked by Gong Liu. They are:

The junk in mourning
Slowly passes by
And unrolls the dark-yellow shroud . . .

戴孝的帆船
緩緩走過
展開了暗黃的屍布。。。

The metaphor here compares the Jialing River, which meets the
Yangzi at Chongqing, to a shroud: Gong Liu thinks that this is
"disgraceful" and "denigrating." His reasons are: "The Chinese
people grow from the milk of the Yangzi and the Yellow River.
Who, upon seeing these two rivers, is not proud of the glory of
the motherland's landscape? Who has ever heard of Indians
disparaging the Ganges, or Egyptians the Nile? *Even Americans*
compare the Mississippi to a motherly river."[22] Though Gu
Cheng's lines are gloomy and even "ugly," they can hardly be
seen as "unpatriotic"; instead they can be interpreted as a concerned young man's metaphor for the violent clashes and their
aftermath during the Cultural Revolution.

Gong Liu's accusation against these lines, which obviously
can be interpreted in a totally different way, lends some support to one explanation of the need to be "obscure." Writing to
Poetry, one teacher has pointed out that obscurity is partially
the result of hiding a strong political content behind startling
poetic devices and a special mode of presentation.[23] Indeed, all
the "obscure" poets have written about the Cultural Revolution and its aftermath. Though less explicit than the stories of
"the wounded," these poems are undoubtedly their poetic
counterparts. Take, for example, Mei Shaojing's "Greenness"
("Lü"):

On this poor and barren land,
Like fire lighting up the night,
Greenness also lights up the day.

When will the greenness be able
To cover forever the yellow earth here?
Ah, in those days of yellow ground and yellow sky
I once thought of
A strange, green sun.[24]

在这贫瘠的土地上，
象火照亮了黑夜，
绿色也把白天照亮。

什么时候让绿色
永远盖住这儿的黄土？
啊，在那地黄天也黄的日子里
我曾想：有一个
奇异的绿色的太阳。

What the sixth line refers to is quite obvious. In contrast to yellow, green appears to be a color of life (line 3) and hope (lines 4 and 5). The concluding image of the "green sun," in a surrealistic and concrete way, subtly reveals the desire of the poet.

Equally powerful but linguistically more explicit is Liang Xiaobin's treatment of the Cultural Revolution in "China, My Key is Lost" ("Zhongguo, wo de yaoshi diu le"):

China, my key is lost.

More than a decade ago,
I ran wildly along the red boulevard,
And cheered in the rural wilderness,
Later,
My key was lost.
. . . .
The sky is starting to rain again,
Oh my key,
Where might you be?
Wind and rain must have eroded you, I suppose,
And you are already very rusty;
No, I don't really think so,
I want to search stubbornly,
Hoping that I can recover you.[25]

中国，我的钥匙丢了。

那是十多年前，
我沿着红色大街疯狂地奔跑，
我跑到了郊外的荒野上吹叫，
后来，
我的钥匙丢了。
. . . .

天，又开始下雨，
我的钥匙啊，
你躺在哪里？
我想风雨腐蚀了你，
你已经锈迹斑斑了；
不，我不那样认为，
我要顽强地寻找，
希望能把你重新找到。

Perhaps the best work by Liang Xiaobin, and one of the most memorable pieces by the young poets, this poem is constructed upon a simple metaphor. The simplicity enhances the poem's impact, for it harmoniously matches the strong yet ordinary desire. There is also a delicate balance between the private, lyrical core of emotion and the narrative progression of the poem.

Despite the obvious merits of some of these poems, which probably rank among the best in the hundreds of thousands of "political" poems written since 1949, they have not been warmly received by many critics, when compared with the initial reception of the "fiction of the wounded." This justly provokes Shu Ting, perhaps the most popular woman poet now writing in China, into making this criticism:

I believe that creative writing and literary criticism should be allies; the task force of poetry is now invading forbidden areas and is in need of artillery support. . . . [It is not convincing] that fiction be allowed to write about the "wounds" but poetry forbidden to deal with the sighs; or to stress that everything is fine now and poets need only joyfully sing the praises of spring; or to discuss the problems of youth and condemn the depression, helplessness, and bewilderment of the young people without attacking the social factors that cause this mental state.[26]

Shu Ting's feeling, however, is not shared by the old poets. Tian Jian, the Honorary Chairman of Hebei's Association of Writers, not only thinks the content of poetry must be positive and "uplifting," but also that poetry must serve as the "clarion for the age":

While poetry may be diverse in form, it still must sing for the age. Poets, as revolutionary art workers, must not forget this. Can "obscure poetry" really serve the people? Can it serve socialism? Is it needed by socialism? If poetry is written only for oneself, or for other poets, that is far from enough. Literature and the arts are class-bound.[27]

Tian Jian's statement is just a rehash of the basic tenets of Mao's Yan'an Talks. This orthodox view of the role and function of poetry—and literature in general—in a socialist country still has a strong following among many critics and writers.

Li Ying, a famous soldier-poet in charge of *People's Liberation Army Literature and Art* (*Jiefangjun wenyi*), endorses this view by stating that "the masses" should be the main concern of poetry. Citing an interesting personal example, Li tries to illustrate how the masses can be served by poetry. He reports that, during the recent Sino-Vietnamese war, a poem of his entitled "About Life" ("Guanyu shengming") was copied and memorized by a PLA soldier. The poem not only gave the soldier "a lot of strength and courage," but also solved his questions about "life and death, and honor and disgrace." Subsequently, the soldier "accomplished much and joined the Party."[28] More in tune with the government's current concern, the critic Li Yuanluo, in a short essay, observes that what is needed is poetry that can "promote the great enterprise of the Four Modernizations."[29] Offering a similar view, with a twist, is Ding Li, who correctly points out that obscurity is an artistic style that can be found in all countries at all times. However, Ding believes that, in the last analysis, all the discussion about obscure poetry must be based on one criterion: Can the work serve the masses and socialism? Despite his assessment of the "obscure" style as quite inevitable, Ding's conclusion is negative: "Poetry that cannot be understood, accepted, and appreciated by the masses is either bad or not poetry at all."[30]

Countering Ding is a moderate opinion put forth by Liu Zhanqiu. While arguing that poetry should be "the voice of the people" and should "sing for the age," Liu thinks that "class struggle" and "promotion of productivity" are not inherently the only subject matter for the poetry of a socialist country. Poetry should be able to deal critically and truthfully with social reality. Liu also thinks that "art for art's sake" should be tolerated to a certain degree. He pleads that some of the poets who insist on writing just the more "artistic" poems should be permitted to do so, for the "blooming of a hundred flowers," when translated into individual creativity, may be "the cultivating of one kind of flower by one poet."[31]

The most unorthodox and courageous argument, however, is given by Sun Shaozhen in a symposium organized by the magazine *Poetry* and attended by critics and representatives from *Literature and Art Gazette, Stars, Ocean Rhythms (Haiyun)*, and *Explorations in Poetry.* Arguing that "art has its internal laws of development," Sun points out that literary criticism "cannot focus just on the reflection of life and ignore the art of poetry." More provocative, however, is Sun's "revisionist" evaluation of the poets largely ignored by critics and anthologists since 1949: "In the 1920s and the early 1930s, the poets who made important contributions to the art of modern poetry actually happened to be Dai Wangshu and Xu Zhimo, poets who have been considered as non-revolutionary and cut off from the life of the masses."[32]

With the publication of "New Aesthetic Principles Are Rising" ("Xin de meixue yuange zai jueqi") in March 1981, Sun himself has become as controversial as the young poets that he is defending. In this article, which has created a storm of furor, Sun observes that the emergence of the new poets is not the usual kind of literary succession, but represents the rise of some new aesthetic principles hitherto unheard of in the PRC. These principles are: 1. The new poets are "scornful of being clarions for the age." They "avoid writing about the brave struggles, the work scenes, and the experience of characters whom we are familiar with. . . . Instead of directly glorifying life, they search for the secrets of life already dissolved in the heart and mind." 2. The new poets emphasize expressions of the self. They believe that "the individual should enjoy a higher status in society, since it is man as individual who creates society." Quite boldly Sun goes on to explain that expressions of the self are now surfacing because the state apparatus is no longer as dominant as before. Sun even sees the melancholy in some poets—for example, Shu Ting—as a reflection of the distortion of human relationships, a legacy of the Cultural Revolution. 3. Quoting Gu Cheng's statement that poetry must challenge usual expectations and familiar reading habits, Sun observes that the main task facing the young poets is still the liberation from the "stubborn grip of artistic convention."[33]

Sun's formulation of the second principle apparently has hit a nerve and touched off a separate debate. The critics who challenge Sun's view generally see the "expression of the self" as an idea that contradicts the collective role of literature in a socialist country. Ruan Zhangjing, another old poet known for his simulations of folk songs, openly condemns "works that advocate personal feelings and are not accountable to society, because objectively they create 'spiritual pollution.'"[34] On this issue, however, Sun's opinion is shared by many young poets. In a personal statement, Gu Cheng says:

The old kind of poetry has always propagandized about a "non-individual" "I" or "self," an "I" that is self-denying and self-destructive; an "I" that is constantly reduced to a grain of sand, a road-paving pebble, a cogwheel, a steel screw. In short, never a person, a human being who can think, doubt, and have emotions and desires. . . . In short, a robot, a robot "I." This kind of "I" may have a religious beauty of self-sacrifice, but, as an "I" who has eradicated his most concrete, individual being, he himself finally loses control and is destroyed. The new kind of "self" is born on this heap of ruins.[35]

The young woman poet Wang Xiaoni echoes Gu's view by saying that two kinds of people now exist in the society—a generation of youth who have become aware of the existence of the "self" and are "depressed and bewildered," but are "thinking and groping." Then there are "the many peasants who don't even feel that they are existing in this society as 'human beings' [ren] and are entitled to the rights of human beings." [36]

More specifically, what Gu, Wang, and most young poets plead for is free rein for the imagination and relaxation, allowing writers to treat private desires and feelings. But, even before formal publication of their works was possible, poets had been putting their personal emotions and attachments into words. Some of Shu Ting's love poems, far more personal than the selfless devotion to the motherland and Chairman Mao, were first hand-copied and privately circulated among the young people. One of these poems, "Dedication" ("Zeng"), was written in 1975 and published only in 1980:

> I was very sorry for you
> Beside the gunwales, in the floating moonlight
> on the roads, in the light rain
> you arched your shoulders and hid your hands
> You hid your thoughts deeply
> as if afraid of the cold
> You were not aware of
> my footsteps beside you
> following so slowly
> If you were fire
> I wish I had been coal
> Thus I wanted to comfort you
> Yet I dared not
>
> I was very happy for you
> for the light flickering on your window at midnight
> for your bending posture in front of the bookcase
> When you revealed your awakening to me
> and said that spring torrents had flooded again
> your banks
> you never asked
> how I thought nightly
> when I walked by your window
> If you were a tree

I would be the soil
Thus I wanted to remind you
Yet I dared not[37]

我为你扼腕可惜
在那些月光流荡的舷边
在那些细雨霏霏的路上
你拱着肩,袖着手
怕冷似地
深藏着你的思想
你没有觉察到
我在你身边的步子
放得多么慢
如果你是火
我愿是炭
想这样安慰你
然而我不敢

我为你举手加额
为你窗扉上闪熠的午夜灯光
为你在书柜前弯身的形象
当你向我坦露你的觉醒
说春洪重又漫过了
你的河岸
你没有问问
走过你的窗下时

每夜我怎么想
如果你是树
我就是土壤
想这样提醒你
然而我不敢

Compared with the love lyrics of the 1930s and the 1940s, or
those from Taiwan, this poem is not particularly remarkable in
terms of linguistic skill and poetic devices; but, in its social and
political context, it is quite an unusual and rare piece of work
which has probably evoked for many readers similar murmurs
of the heart.

While some critics and poets are at most unfavorably disposed
towards poets' intimate "expressions of the self," they are
vehemently opposed to what they perceive as Western modernist influence. In a rejoinder to Sun Shaozhen, Cheng Daixi, a
critic who is currently the chief exponent of Georg Lukács in
China, has tried to equate "expressions of the self" with "bourgeois or petit-bourgeois individualism and anti-rational anar-
chism." Cheng thinks that, with the self or the ego preoccupying
the artistic imagination at the expense of the objectivity of the
real world, reality is inevitably replaced by the subjective consciousness of the individual artist. The results are then "obscurity, absurdity, vagueness, and difficulty"—supposedly the
common "sins" of Western modernism. Echoing Lukács, Cheng
views modernism as a reflection of the "hopelessness, emptiness, and desperation" of the Western capitalist system. His
conclusion is that "the aesthetic principles" are "strongly colored
by idealism" and "exuding heavily petit-bourgeois individualism."[38] Cheng's condemnation is very severe and in the old
days would have signaled the beginning of a purge. Equally
scathing is the attack from Zang Kejia. Giving a distorted version of the Chinese poetic tradition, Zang oafishly criticizes

the so-called "obscure poetry" as "a perversion of the centuries-old tradition of realism in Chinese poetry," "a trend that ruins the name of vernacular poetry, poisons some people, and is deeply resented by many readers." Zang goes on to charge the young poets' works with "a betrayal of tradition through imitating foreign 'dregs.' "[39]

Ai Qing, like Zang, is another poet who rose to fame in the pre-1949 days. Approaching the issue from a formalistic perspective, Ai Qing argues that, since modernism in Chinese poetry from Taiwan has already reached a "dead end," and many "intelligent writers" "have begun to return to the path of realism," it does not make sense for poetry on the mainland to try the same experiments. In a rather simplistic fashion, Ai Qing reduces the complexity of modernist Chinese poetry from Taiwan to three features: 1. "Horizontal transplantation" from the West; 2. Intellectualism vs. lyricism; 3. Poetic purity.[40] Echoing Ai Qing's view is Li Yuanluo, who also cites the modernist development in Taiwan to buttress his opposition. Without quoting directly from Wai-lim Yip, Li ascribes the following opinion to him: "Once considered as one of the ten great modernist poets, Wai-lim Yip later believed that classical Chinese poetry was the main stream of world literature, and, because it absorbed the Chinese mode of presentation, Western modernist poetry managed to shatter its own old tradition."[41] This statement is factually wrong, historically ignorant, and conceptually befuddling.[42]

Wai-lim Yip was once included in an anthology entitled *An Anthology of Ten Great Contemporary Chinese Poets (Zhongguo dangdai shi da shiren xuanji)*,[43] but the anthology is not limited exclusively to the modernists. To students of Chinese-Western comparative literature, Yip has been well known for his studies of Ezra Pound, Chinese landscape poetry, and Taoist aesthetics.[44] While Yip's recent works are all concerned with classical Chinese poetry's influence on and affinity with certain aspects of Anglo-American modernist poetry, Yip has by no means made any claim about the dominant role of Chinese poetry in world literature. Neither is it true to credit the Western modernist breakthrough to Chinese poetry, when Pound is the only major figure heavily indebted to the Chinese tradition. In fact, in *The Cantos,* Pound uses the "ideogrammic method" to construct an extremely difficult poetry. But difficulty has always been seen as the hallmark of Western modernist poetry, so it is paradoxical and self-defeating for Li to assign a prominent role to Chinese poetry in the making of modernism.

In the same article, Li also quotes, again without acknowledgment, from an essay by Xiao Qian on Ao Ao (Dominic C. N. Cheung), and presents Cheung as another Taiwan "modernist" now in "repentance": "I am against modernism, for I see the smallness of the self and the greatness of history."[45] Li's failure to understand this statement clearly stems from his lack of historical knowledge. Cheung, a poet who started writing in the 1960s when modernism was dominant and seldom challenged, eventually managed to move beyond it to establish his own voice precisely because of his earlier submersion in the modernist discourse. In other words, Cheung is an insider who breaks away, a case of what Harold Bloom would describe as "the anxiety of influence." Such a case is markedly different from that of the young poets on the mainland, where modernism in any form has long been considered taboo.

Coming to the defense of the young poets is Xie Mian, who compares the new generation to the one that emerged in the first decade of modern Chinese literature. By asserting that the Western poetic forms were models for the May Fourth poets, Xie tactfully defends the Western influence as potentially positive. Xie even argues that, after the productive first decade, the "popularization" (*dazhonghua*) debates in the 1930s, the "native" or "national forms" (*minzu xingshi*) discussions in the 1940s, and the "new folk song" movement in the 1950s have limited the growth of modern Chinese poetry.[46] In an article written roughly at the same time, Xie proclaims that folk songs and classical Chinese poetry do not necessarily constitute the only tradition for the contemporary poets; instead, the quest for form which resulted in all kinds of experimentation from 1919 to 1949 should be seen as the "new tradition," one begun by Hu Shi, Liu Bannong, Liu Dabai, Kang Baiqing, Guo Moruo, and developed by Wen Yiduo, Xu Zhimo, and Dai Wangshu. Citing the indebtedness to Whitman of the early Guo Moruo—still a safe and "venerable" name—Xie reaffirms that foreign poetry can also be a healthy and enriching influence.[47]

A similar view is expressed by the young poet Xu Jingya, who calls for "the translation and study of different trends and schools of foreign poetry—especially the modern and contemporary works." Besides foreign poetry, Xu believes, the young writers can also learn from those Chinese poets of the 1930s and 1940s who have largely been ignored since 1949.[48] Yuan Kejia, a poet who started writing in the 1940s and has spent 1980–1982 teaching and pursuing research in the United States, thinks that the modernist concern with language and poetic devices can be an important phase of training. Guo Moruo, Dai Wangshu, Ai Qing, and He Qifang, Yuan points out, are poets whose early works were inspired by Western models. Without their experimental venture, Yuan argues dialectically, the later works of these poets, generally considered by mainland critics as "realistic," would certainly not have been so interesting and readable.[49]

The opposition since 1949 to experimentation with form—the only exemption being poetry in the mode of Majakovski—has grown into such inveterate aversion that any promotion of or practice in this direction is bound to encounter fierce resistance. As Xie Mian has rightly observed, the theoretical conclusion based on the Yan'an Talks has "obvious limitations." This theory—that "the new poetry must develop on the foundation of folk songs and classical Chinese poetry"[50]—has made the use of rhyme, perhaps the only formal element shared by the two poetic traditions, a predominant feature of contemporary Chinese poetry.

Surely rhyme has always been found in modern poetry of both the East and the West, and no mutual exclusiveness has existed between rhyme and modernism.[51] But, when rhyme is employed to give empty political slogans and didactic statements the semblance of poetry, the result is often what some mainland critics and poets have dubbed "poetic illustrations of politics." Here is one typical product:

Three years are not very long,
The present and the past, what a change.

Truth always lies with the Communists,
I certainly won't drown myself like Qu Yuan!

The roads are long, but I'll keep searching,
My search for truth is for the Party.
Punished and dismissed, I am not daunted,
For the truth will reach the Party Central Committee.[52]

"三年时光不算长,
今非昔比感沧桑。
共产党人真理在,
岂效屈子投大江!

"路漫漫,吾求索,
追求真理为吾党。
获罪免职终不悔,
下情上达党中央。"

Divided into quatrains and using the end rhyme (*abcb*), "Night at the Xiang River" ("Xiang Jiang ye"), from which these two stanzas are quoted, is a narrative poem of 200 lines glorifying Marshal Peng Dehuai, whose name has recently been rehabilitated. Unfortunately, the worthiness of the subject does not automatically translate the poem into successful art; instead, the lifeless traditionalism and the trite didacticism simply fail to provide a moving portrait. The fact that such a poem is one of the 35 award-winning works chosen from hundreds of thousands published in the year 1979–1980 indicates that critical taste has remained very much unchanged, despite the emergence of the young poets.

The critics and poets who are negative about "obscure poetry" are in general supporters of the "native form," with rhyming as its cornerstone. From the perspective of comparative literature, however, though it is the most significant marker distinguishing poetry from prose in traditional Chinese literature, rhyme is by no means confined to the Chinese tradition. And free verse has its defenders. On this issue, Ai Qing parts company with Zang Kejia, the most vocal advocate of "native form." Offering a more sophisticated view, Ai Qing says that free verse, "being less restrained by meter and rhyme, is more flexible in expressing thoughts and feelings. With a larger capacity, it is more appropriate for a rapidly changing age. Form must obey the demands of content. . . . As a product of the new world, free verse is more liberated than meter and rhyme, easier to adopt, and more in tune with revolutionary needs."[53] In an interview, Ai Qing has also stated that the different forms should be allowed to coexist and that no form should be established as the only foundation of development.[54]

Ai Qing's view is indirectly substantiated and the popularity of free verse fully demonstrated by a poll conducted by *Yalu River.* Sending out questionnaires to 300 poets, poetry critics, and poetry editors, the editorial office of this journal asked them to answer six sets of questions—one concerning the future development of poetic form. Of the 199 responses, 129 (64.8 percent) were in favor of "the blooming of a hundred flowers with free verse as the dominant form"; only 12 (6 percent) were for "new meter-and-rhyme forms," and a dismal 1 (0.5 percent) for "folk songs and classical forms."[55] These figures appear to indicate that, even among some of the belligerent critics of "obscure poetry," a majority are for free verse.

Among the various criticisms of "obscure poetry," the most widely raised is its alleged "difficulty." The hostile critics of course claim that the obscurity is simply beyond their comprehension. Even among the sympathizers, however, the same point has been made. For instance, Zhou Liangpei, a critic who is genuinely for the "blooming of a hundred flowers," confesses that he has difficulty understanding the "logic" behind Gu Cheng's "Curve."[56] Commenting on three short poems by Gu Cheng, a columnist of *Ocean Rhythms* states that he is puzzled by at least two of them. They are:

Red Coral

Red coral,
You are loyal love flames,
You want to light up the sea.

Pearl Oyster

You have your own sky,
You embrace the pearl,
Like clouds embracing the sun.[57]

红珊瑚

红珊瑚，
你是赤诚的爱焰，
你要把大海点燃。

珠贝

你有自己的天空，
你拥抱着珍珠，
象云朵拥抱着太阳。

Fairly lucid comparisons, these two poems are concrete, concentrated descriptions embodying no particular message. Perhaps it is this lack of message that has prompted the columnist to say that "the themes are befuddling." He has probably forgotten that *yong wu shi* (thing-describing poems) abound in classical Chinese poetry.

Equally "incomprehensible," according to the critic Zhang Ming, is a line in a poem on autumn by Du Yunxie, a fine poet of the 1940s who has been largely silent since 1949. The line in question is again metaphoric: *Qiu yang zai shangmian saomiao fengshou de xinxi* or "The autumn sun . . . is painting the message of harvest." The query posed by Zhang is this: "Since a message is not a material entity, how can it be painted?"[58] Zhang has apparently forgotten that personification and metaphor do not exist in poetry alone, but also in daily language. Interpreted in his "materialist" and literal fashion, many everyday expressions are probably just as "obscure" and "incomprehensible." Defending this poem by Du, Huang Shang offers an explanation about the appearance of this sort of "materialist" criticism: "People are so used to reading political essays that, when they encounter certain kinds of literary works, the feeling of 'obscurity' inevitably arises."[59] Discussing the same hermeneutical issue of understanding, Yuan Kejia also believes that the key lies in the reader's adjustment to and familiarity with a different kind of discourse.[60]

But, despite the efforts of these well-intentioned critics, the controversy surrounding "obscurity" is far from being resolved. Opposing each other with equal vehemence, the two sides appear to be in a stalemate. The rational course, from an outsider's viewpoint, is clearly that of open-minded tolerance and peaceful coexistence. "Since the founding of the People's Republic," as Xie Mian has aptly observed, "poetry has been interfered with too constantly by politics—to the extent that poetry has been identified with politics. The excessive control of poetry has almost killed poetry by suffocation."[61]

The current blooming of the young poets has undoubtedly given contemporary Chinese poetry another fresh and promising start. Some of the works, needless to say, are crude and uneven, but, among the "hundred flowers," this sprout of a new species perhaps deserves more cultivation.

The Politics of Technique: Perspectives of Literary Dissidence in Contemporary Chinese Fiction

LEO OU-FAN LEE

In a pioneering essay published some years ago, Mark Schorer spoke of the importance of the technique of fiction in the following memorable words:

Modern criticism has shown us that to speak of content as such is not to speak of art at all, but of experience; and that it is only when we speak of the *achieved* content, the form, the work of art as a work of art, that we speak as critics. The difference between content, or experience, and the achieved content, or art, is technique.

In this sense, technique "is not the secondary thing . . . some external machination, a mechanical affair, but a deep and primary operation"; it not only *"contains* intellectual and moral implications . . . it *discovers* them."[1]

Schorer's remarks, now taken almost as basic premise in Western literary criticism, still prove refreshingly relevant to Chinese literature in the People's Republic of China since 1976. For the tradition of the past three decades in imaginative writing in China was precisely one that emphasized content—or prescribed content—to the utter neglect of technique. Insofar as technique was acknowledged at all, it meant only "some external machination, a mechanical affair." A close look at Mao Zedong's Talks at the Yan'an Forum on Art and Literature—the basic canon for all creative literature and literary criticism until 1976—reveals, remarkably, that Mao as a literary critic gave only lip service to literary technique. While he mentioned the "contradiction between political content and artistic form" (chiefly in reference to reactionary literature), he clearly considered the former "primary" and the latter "secondary"; and technique, which is presumably what separates art from propaganda, meant in Mao's view merely some decorative "touching up" by writers, who were thereby transformed into "literary workers."[2] In Jiang Qing's radical application of the Maoist canon, the writer became in fact a mechanical "reproducer" who with his "technique" brought the general guidelines provided by the Party cadre to bear upon the material of life provided by the people. Most of these injunctions were, of course, extrinsic to literary technique—to the art of literature itself as Schorer defines it.

Even before Mao's politicization of literature, the May Fourth tradition of imaginative writing had given prominence to content, particularly as personal experience and social history. With few exceptions (primarily in poetry), ideologically self-righteous critics discouraged conscious experiments in technique or even attacked them outright as empty formalism. What C. T. Hsia has so aptly called "obsession with China" —or preoccupation with China's contemporary social conditions, scarcely leavened by a clinging hope for the nation's future—led to a consensus that "realism," however vaguely defined, ought to prevail as *the* correct approach to literature. Even before the more prescriptive socialist realism was introduced from Russia, the concept of "realism" had already taken on an ethical weight, a kind of patriotic pan-moralism which tended to govern creative writing, especially in the 1930s. This is not to suggest that all realistic writing in modern Chinese literature is technically deficient; rather, the obsession with social reality served to perpetuate a new didacticism which encouraged message-giving and literature's "social effect" at the expense of the "achieved content" of the literary text. Especially in fiction, the distance between experience and technique was all but nonexistent.

Given this general legacy of modern Chinese literature—its moral weight, ideological thrust, and its later appropriation by politics—it is most significant that, after the downfall of the Gang of Four, a number of writers—both the middle-aged generation of newly rehabilitated "Rightists" and a younger generation of "non-official" writers in their twenties and thirties—are beginning to pay renewed attention to technique as a subtle (or not so subtle) antidote to political ideology. They demand of literature and imaginative writing a degree of independence unprecedented in the history of the People's Republic. And they labor conscientiously with technical innovations, despite the limitations of their own craftsmanship and the much less obtrusive pressures from the new Party leadership. In a sense, this new phenomenon can be viewed as a literary form of dissidence, of departing from and thereby challenging the long-established theory and practice of imaginative writing.[3] To some extent, it also poses a potential threat to the Maoist orthodoxy of revolutionary literature. In a society in which politics has permeated every sphere of life, this "artistic" stance inevitably has its political connotations, and the "social effects" of this new challenge are only beginning to be felt.

The word *technique,* of course, means different things to different people. Mark Schorer, following T. S. Eliot, gives the broadest possible definition of fictional technique, as

any selection, structure, or distortion, any form or rhythm imposed upon the world of action, by means of which, it should be added, our apprehension of the world of action is enriched or renewed. In this sense, everything is technique which is not the lump of experience itself.

However, Schorer reduces the amorphousness of this broad definition to refer specifically to two aspects:

the uses to which language, as language, is put to express the quality of the experience in question; and the uses of point of view not only as a mode of dramatic delimitation, but more particularly, of thematic definition.[4]

Insofar as the selection or distortion of reality has largely been prescribed or conditioned by extra-literary factors, technique in contemporary Chinese literature is itself intruded upon by political considerations. In Mao's Yan'an Talks, the injunctions are concerned more with the *what* and *why* than the *how* of literary writing: the correct attitude of the writer, the need for a popular language comprehensible to the masses, the prerequisite of "extolling" and not "exposing" revolutionary reality, and so forth. These extrinsic, yet confining, criteria leave little room for the writer to manipulate his material. In general, precedents of past practice bequeath two possible areas of concentration—language and characterization. More politically defined, language denotes the uses of popular phrases and dialects in line with the demand for "popularization," and characterization is expected to observe the rules of typicality and black-and-white contrast, with prominence given, of course, to the positive traits of the heroic characters. As a result, individuality in both language and characterization tends to be deemphasized. During the past three decades, literary policies and debates have often revolved around the issue of characterization (the "middle characters," "three prominences," and so on), but seldom, if ever, around the uses of language as expression of the quality of the experience depicted in a literary work. In other words, the use of language as style—the particular manner of linguistic expression evolved by the writer—did not enter into general discussion until after 1976. It is for this reason that I should like to single out the fiction of Wang Meng and Gao Xiaosheng for discussion, for each has attempted, with varying degrees of success, to evolve a language of his own in order to realize an individual fictional vision of contemporary Chinese reality.

WANG MENG

Of all the established writers who have emerged or re-emerged since 1976, Wang Meng was the first to distinguish himself not solely through creating an ethos of exposure, which characterized the so-called "literature of the wounded" of 1977–1978, but by the radical experimentalism of his fictional language. In fact, his linguistic adventures have gone so far as to elicit criticism from other writers and critics, who fault Wang's recent fiction for being too abstruse, ambiguous, foreign-sounding, and difficult to understand. For his experiments with depicting the protagonists' inner feelings and thoughts he has been branded, sometimes with gentle malice, as an imitator of the Western "stream-of-consciousness" fiction. In his several public speeches and published essays, Wang Meng has defended his artistic stance, which is derived from two bold premises: that the social and political function of literature has been over-emphasized in China; and that the reality of life—the basic material of literature—is so complex, changeable, and multifarious that it cannot be fitted into the simplistic, bifurcated categories of exposure and glorification.[5] Both these premises, familiar to a Western reader, nonetheless represent a revision of, if not a direct challenge to, the Maoist canon of imaginative writing.

The way to recapture life's complexities, in Wang Meng's view, lies in the use of language. He is convinced that the Chinese language is sufficiently rich for such purposes. But the writer nevertheless must first of all be "relaxed" (*fangsong*): In imaginative writing, as in "labor, athletics, or dancing, only by being relaxed can one do well. Tightening of fists and staring with wide open eyes are but expressions of strained force."[6] (Though Wang does not explain, he may have been referring to the familiar dramatic gestures in the revolutionary operas.) In his own fiction published since 1978, Wang Meng has certainly let himself loose with a variety of experiments in language.

Wang Meng's early works are fairly conventional in technique: his novel, *Long Live Youth* (*Qingchun wansui*, written in 1953 but not published until 1978), gives a generally straightforward narrative of student life in its naive idealism.[7] His first short story, "Little Bean" ("Xiao-douer") published in *People's*

Literature in 1955), has a simplicity of language as befits a young girl, from whose point of view the story unfolds. (This is probably the story's only technical novelty.) The protagonist, together with her brother and mother, uncovers two KMT spies in the persons of her father and "uncle" (the father's close friend). The most controversial of all Wang Meng's early works, the story "Young Newcomer in the Organization Department" ("Zuzhibu laile ge nianqingren," written in 1956), is not distinguished by its technique.[8] However, the sincerity with which the author depicts the relationship between the newcomer, Lin Zhen, and the married woman, Zhao Huiwen, who works in the same department, imbues the narrative with a certain intensity of feeling. Contrary to Wang's own intentions, the story's gentle criticism of the work-style of Party cadres (which is not central to the emotional matrix of the story) brought the author political disaster: Wang Meng was silenced for twenty years. Except for a short story published in 1957 and two other stories in 1962, he published nothing.

Reading these early works against what I have known of Wang's recent accomplishments, I must admit to a sense of disappointment. These stories are crudely crafted and (save for the "Newcomer" story) almost totally lacking in subtlety of both language and characterization. The only spots where Wang Meng's prose seems to shine through his rather formulaic ideological content are those dealing with nature—both its sights and sounds. The story, "Night Rain" ("Yeyu") is mildly interesting because of its depiction of rain and the transformative power that this aspect of nature exerts on the protagonist, an 18-year-old peasant girl who decides against marrying a worker in the city in order to stay in her village and work in the commune.[9] Wang Meng's artistic agility—an early manifestation of a "relaxed" style—is evidenced by the use of onomatopoeia: for example, *xixi suosuo, dididada,* and *bataer* to describe the sound of rain, and *zhisha* and *buteng* for the sound of the movement of birds. These words are not easy to write, and some may have been the author's own inventions, but they serve to give a colloquial ring, a sense of intimacy and familiarity, to the "reality" of the story. From these colorful—and sometimes tuneful—words are formed clusters of words and phrases which weave a pastoral tapestry. In the opening part of his more recent story, "God of Song" ("Ge shen," 1979), for instance, this pastoral idyll fits nicely into the author's paeans to an exotic landscape, the Uighur-speaking region of Keshiger in Xinjiang (Sinkiang).[10]

One of Wang Meng's consistent hallmarks, visible even in the early works, is his gift for words; his descriptive language is, above all, a profusion of words and word compounds fraught with audio-visual effect. He freely employs, aside from onomatopoeia, repetitions, alliterations, long series of adjectives and adverbs, and strings of Chinese characters containing the same radicals which convey a striking visual splendor. At its best, this florid yet fluid style is enlivening and even spellbinding. It gives his text rhythm and color; it imparts an aura of pastoral beauty to his landscape portraits; it invests his characters with individuality and humanity. All these features present a refreshing contrast to the stereotypical ideological fiction of the recent past. One distinguishing difference between Wang Meng's early and later works lies in his increasing attention to the multi-hued texture in which he attempts to delineate the thoughts and feelings of his individualized characters. He does so with an intense subjectivity that borders on the "stream-of-consciousness." One of the best illustrations of this refined technique is the story 'The Eye of the Night" ("Ye de yan"), published in 1979. In this work, Wang Meng applies a heightened visual sensitivity to the depiction of the modern city at night with all its hubbub and excitement. Especially in the beginning paragraphs, his prose approximates the roving eye of a movie camera which seems to be positioned right at the eye level of the protagonist, thus unfolding a nocturnal kaleidoscope infused with a kind of kinetic rhythm:

Naturally, the streetlamps were all lit in an instant. But Chen Gao felt as if two streams of light were being cast out from the crown of his head. The light flowed down the street in both directions, no end in sight. Locust trees cast an abundance of simple shadows, and the people waiting for the bus laid their own dense or meagre shadows onto the sidewalk as well.

Large cars and small ones. Trolleys and bicycles. Sounds of bells, conversation, and laughter. Nights in the big city still epitomized its vitality and uniqueness. Scattered but eye-catching neon lights and the revolving swirls of color in front of beauty parlors were beginning to appear. There were permanent waves and long hair, high heels, semi-high heels, sleeve-less dresses, the scents of perfume and facial cream. The city and its women were just beginning to dress up a bit, and already some people couldn't sit still.[11]

As the story develops, the reader gradually realizes that the protagonist has become unused to the city landscape after twenty years spent in the countryside. Dazzled by the glitter of the night, he feels lost, both psychologically and spatially, as he stumbles into a newly constructed compound of houses in order to deliver a message from the leader of his work unit in a distant region, who wants to acquire certain automobile parts. And he walks right into the new lifestyle of decadence and corruption in the person of the son of a high-ranking cadre. While the story is, strictly speaking, not told entirely from the protagonist's point of view, the total impression achieved by Wang Meng's prose is nevertheless highly subjective: By the sheer force of imagery, the author makes us join the protagonist in a laby-rinthine journey into the heart of city life. Typically, Wang Meng juxtaposes sight and sound effects: the noises from a foot-ball game on television mixed with those of the watchers; foot-steps in the dark corridors; waltz music by Franz Lehar from a tape recorder, and so on. At the end of the story, as the pro-tagonist stumbles out of the building, it seems as if both he and the reader have been led through a nightmare. Due to the author's subtle distortion of perception (hence, perhaps, the artistic implication of "eyes"), and his manipulation of atmo-sphere, this basically realistic work is tinted with touches of surrealism.

"The Eye of the Night" is a groundbreaking work in the sense that, through fictional technique, Wang Meng has transformed an ordinary real experience into a nightmarish vision. Despite several contrived details, including the overworked symbolism of a streetlamp, the story encapsulates this highly subjective vision in a few pages—a brevity of form that matches the temporal brevity of the described experience itself (a few hours in one night).

In another story, "Kites" ("Fengzheng piaodai"),[12] he tries to achieve a similar effect of impressionistic realism by using a more complex method. The setting is again the big city, in which a pair of young lovers are lost; they have nowhere to go for their rendezvous until they stumble into a newly constructed empty high-rise building. The story begins with the young girl waiting for her boyfriend; her reveries lead into flashbacks of their first and subsequent meetings. Halfway through the narrative, he finally shows up, and the two embark upon an almost futile search for shelter—to find a temporary haven for their love. Wang Meng himself once explained that in this story he uses the "multi-linear, cross-jumping" technique of organization in order to capture the "rapidly changing colors of life."[13] But the work is not so complicated, at least to this reader. The temporal scheme is only slightly more "multi-linear" than that of "The Eye of the Night," and the jerky rhythm does not really bring out a youthful cadence as the author intended. What is more remarkable about the story seems to be its intimate and emotional tone. While the story unfolds primarily from the young girl's point of view, it is narrated by an outside voice that is close to the mental processes of the young lovers; the narrative voice is so empathetically situated vis-à-vis the lovers that it occasionally whispers comments like this:

Look, look, and a whole night is used up. Our vast and boundless sky and land, our magnificent three-dimensional space—is there any corner for the young people to talk, embrace and kiss? We only need a very small place. And you—you have room for towering heroes and earth-shaking rebels, for vermin and villains that besmear heaven and earth, for so many battlefields, detonation fields, broad squares, meeting grounds, execution grounds . . . but you have no room for the passionate love between Susu and Jiayuan: one 160 centimeters tall and weighing 48 kilograms; the other barely 170 centimeters in height and weighing 54 kilograms.[14]

This invocatory passage is obviously overdone. It reveals an overeagerness on the part of the author to command our sympathy towards the young lovers. It is an extreme example of Wang Meng's penchant for emotionalism. Both the power and weakness of his style seem to rely on the reader's emotional response and even identification with the fictional characters and situation. This is, of course, nothing new in modern Chinese literature. What is more unique to Wang Meng's style is that it does not impose or exhort (as in the typical fare of

Chinese Communist fiction) or confess to the authenticity of the author's own experience (as in most May Fourth fiction); rather it seeks to lure us with its intense subjectivism. We are gently asked to enter the hearts of these protagonists, most of whom are neither heroes nor villains, and empathize with them. The emotional appeal of a story like "Kites" depends very much on the predisposition of the reader, which in turn is conditioned by the degree of experience shared with the author and the text. In short, Wang Meng's fiction does not spring from a sense of detachment; his is a style of sincerity and florid emotionalism.

Much of this discussion of Wang Meng's emotional style has bearing on his experiments with stream-of-consciousness. Strictly speaking, none of the examples cited above can be analyzed in the same vein as, say, Virginia Woolf's stories and novels. While Wang Meng does attempt to capture "the full spectrum and flow of a character's mental process, in which sense perceptions mingle with conscious and half conscious thoughts, memories, feelings and random associations,"[15] his own emotional personality nevertheless intrudes upon his fictional universe. It is difficult for him to be totally "relaxed," to let go of his characters so that, as in Joyce and Faulkner, they can move in seemingly disconnected directions and enter into a full spectrum of conscious and half-conscious thoughts. It seems that Wang Meng feels compelled to "interfere" with the mental processes of his fictional characters from the standpoint of his own humanistic proclivities, to affirm their stature as Chinese people despite their foibles and weaknesses. Thus, from a Western modernist point of view, Wang Meng's "stream-of-conscious" fiction does not break down the conventional narrative structure; his characterization is not "dehumanized" by intense, sometimes sickly, psychology (as in Faulkner's *The Sound and the Fury*). For all his technical experimentation, Wang Meng's recent fiction has not relinquished its grip on Chinese reality; rather, it serves to liberate that reality from the grip of political ideology. To this extent, he can still be regarded as something of an artistic dissident.

The issue becomes more ambiguous, however, when we attempt to assess Wang Meng's technique as art in terms of the relationship between his fictional form and his humanistic-realistic content. One of the intriguing side effects of Wang Meng's prose style is that, owing to the ornateness of his typical sentences, which are not so much broken up as lengthened into a seemingly endless flow of imagistic adjectives, it does not contribute to economy and restraint. In my view, Wang Meng's longer works—the novelettes *Butterfly* (*Hudie*) and *Bolshevik Salute* (*Buli*)[16]—are less effective than his best short stories because, being longer, they provide more room for his linguistic self-indulgence. When comparing the two novelettes, we discover that in theme they are quite similar: Both narrate the life and tribulations of a loyal Party member across a long time span. But in structure Wang Meng obviously experiments with two different approaches to storytelling. *Butterfly* is more involved with the mental processes of the hero, whereas *Bolshevik Salute* is cast in a more complex temporal structure which tends to constrain somewhat his display of purple prose. The latter work is composed of seven sections which do not form a linear time sequence; rather, each is subdivided into different non-sequential time periods marked by year, month, and date, so as to effect a "jumping rhythm" through flashbacks and flashforwards. The device is very similar to that of Ru Zhijuan's "Mis-edited Story" ("Jianjie cuole de gushi"), and the inspiration from film editing is manifest in both works. With more emphasis on temporal structure than on language, *Bolshevik Salute* reads more smoothly because Wang Meng is nevertheless narrating a story. (It is reported that Wang Meng, in his initial conception of the novelette, wanted to use a straightforward narrative but discarded this conventional technique because the story read like an "account book.")[17] And like "Mis-edited Story," this new temporal device betrays a measure of contrivance. A conventional reader may still secretly wish that the story were told from beginning to end without artificial editing, or he may "re-edit" the various fragments back into sequence in his own mind. In rearranging the time sequences, Wang Meng of course wants to bring out comparisons between past and present in the protagonist's experience: The juxtaposition of his activities as a revolutionary and underground Party worker shortly before Liberation, with his persecution in 1958, 1966, and

1970, reveals the utter absurdity of the charges against him. The out-of-sequence structure thus brings more heightened drama to his testimony of loyalty. However, with its happy ending—the protagonist's rehabilitation in January 1979 and his final "Bolshevik Salute" to Hua Guofeng, Ye Jianying, and Deng Xiaoping—one begins to wonder whether the story may not also be the author's roundabout way of "tendering his heart" (*jiaoxin*) to the Party.

Still, in spite of its predictable content, *Bolshevik Salute* is preferable to *Butterfly* because it contains a lesser dose of extravagant language. The monologues and impressionistic portraits (examples of the "stream-of-consciousness" technique, according to Chinese critics) are relatively less frequent. Interestingly, the one concentrated piece of imagistic writing (in section 6), which seems unconnected with the plot, bears the caption "Year unclear," which some readers in China consider incomprehensible.[18] The strength of the work, despite its unconventional temporal structure, rests on its conventional plot. *Butterfly,* on the other hand, is less concerned with telling a story than showing the subjective feelings of the protagonist: It plays on memories he gathered during his seemingly interminable journey to assume a new office after being rehabilitated. The details of his past rush back at every convenient moment, as in his bus and train rides, which are depicted with an abundance of decorative words and phrases laden with metaphors, some of them clichés. The total effect becomes, for this reader at least, not so overwhelming as overloaded. The duality of the past and present roles of the protagonist—old-man Zhang and Vice-Minister Zhang, peasant and cadre—is overdrawn, while the pun in the title, derived from the familiar legend of Zhuang Zi and the butterfly, to refer to the mutual transformation of the two roles, is tendentious. Again, the reader is expected to ride with the protagonist and share his joys and sorrows. His emotional response is presumably engineered by waves of lyricism such as this:

Ah, ah, ah? Haiyun's [literally, "sea-cloud"] tears, raindrops on lotus leaves, eaves with melting snow, for the first time, the spring rain that is no longer sufficient to nourish the dry and thirsty earth! Spring 1945, across the rain drizzle he saw Dongdong's [literally "winter-winter"] face squeezed against the windowpane—flat nose, blue, white, clownish, lovable. Everywhere there was fresh coolness, moistening wetness, comfort to the dry and thirsty heart. Immortal spring, eternally fresh green leaves, the rain drizzle that never congeals, consolidates, freezes![19]

This lavish description of spring and rain, which by now has become a cliché even in Wang Meng's own work, is supposed to trigger "surging waves" in the protagonist's heart. But this reader remains unstirred. We are faced with the familiar problem of rhetorical overkill, a display of language drawn from an effusive imagination which, alas, is no longer fresh. Similarly, we find a tendency towards verbal excess in two recent stories—"Voice of Spring" ("Chun zhi sheng") and "Dreams of the Sea" ("Hai de meng"). In a paragraph in the latter story, there are eight verbs depicting the impact of the sea: "She has never changed her heart, she has never tired, she has never gone away. She always *welcomes* him, *embraces* him, *kisses* him, *carresses* him, *pounds* on him, *storms* into him, *cleanses* him, *crushes* him."[20] (emphasis added) Whatever residual eroticism is left in this sentence is "washed out" by those worn-out metaphors, which serve also to make an unintentionally corny mockery of the hero's heaving thought: "Oh, sea—I—love—you." And the reader is battered by the familiar devices of temporal framing of a train ride, the juxtaposition of audio and visual effects, even by references to foreign sights (Stuttgart factories, the Munich Opera House, the autobahn along the Rhine, children in Frankfurt) and sounds (Strauss's waltz "Voice of Spring," Rimsky-Korsakov's "Scheherazade")[21] and literature (the sea as described by Gorki, Hans Christian Andersen, Jack London, and Hemingway).

If we attempt to relate Wang Meng's language to the overall quality of human experience depicted in his fiction, we are likely to conclude that his florid prose, while imparting an emotional tinge to his characterization and blurred beauty to his narrative in the manner of an impressionistic painting, also tends to soften the blow of the harshness of reality. In other words, the socio-political subject-matter treated in his stories tend to lose their sharp edges. Evil and villainy are "toned down" into many shades of gray; and pain and suffering become engulfed in a welter of adjectives. The net result is a certain lack of depth of thought and feeling. The dimensions of darkness in the Cultural

Revolution—surely a fitting subject for a Dostoevski or even a Conrad—are not conveyed in Wang Meng's fiction with the same degree of shattering impact as can be found in the reportage of Wang's colleague, Liu Binyan. Liu is a far less artistically conscious writer, but his long documentary piece, "Between Men and Monsters" ("Ren yao zhi jian"), is exceptionally powerful in its accumulated details of human corruption and corruptibility.[22]

Perhaps unlike the more ruthlessly honest Liu Binyan, Wang Meng still wishes to retain or recapture some youthful idealism, just as his "newcomer," Lin Zhen, strove to do, despite his bitterness and frustration. After twenty years of literary exile, Wang Meng returns as a man with a renewed faith in his Party and his people. He is too eager to forgive, if not to forget, past errors committed by his compatriots. When he remembers, as the intellectual protagonist does in so many of his stories, it is a remembrance of youth, love, devotion, and trust—in short, the very best of human qualities. When he attempts, on the other hand, to expose the negative sides of that experience, his prose becomes curiously inadequate, in spite of its stylistic flourishes.[23] In one of his recent pieces, a story composed of three separate anecdotes, one of the narrators is a linguist by profession and tries to make an ironic comment on the rich terminology of ugly vituperation in the language of the Cultural Revolution: ox demons and serpent ghosts, foreign slaves, evil dregs, parasites, shattered dogs' heads, reactionaries to the core, and on, and on. But it remains a terminological catalogue of evil. Neither the narrator nor, it seems, the author is intent on pursuing it further by seeking the deeper and surely more ironic nexus between language and reality during the Cultural Revolution. Instead, Wang Meng resorts to his typical metaphors: These ugly terms are like "raindrops pouring down" and "scores of sharp daggers, each capable of piercing my heart."[24] One wonders whether, as the dagger hits the heart, the Chinese reader reading this passage feels really hurt! Thus, Wang Meng's very flowery language—a hallmark of his technique—becomes an ironic comment on his very inability to confront the darker side of genuine reality and to probe the inner sources of this "heart of darkness" in the Chinese national character.

Leaving aside the issue of whether or not a conscientious Chinese writer, having survived the Cultural Revolution, should distinguish good from evil more sharply and profoundly, my reading, based entirely on his texts, has led me to believe that Wang Meng's style has made the experience he describes somewhat superficial, even glamorous; and that, somewhere along the way, amidst the display of his linguistic fireworks, a part of Chinese life is somehow compromised in the very process of transforming experience into achieved content. The radicality of form is, in Wang Meng's case, ultimately in the service of a humanistic vision which affirms the innate decency of the Chinese people, in spite of all the catastrophes inflicted upon their bodies and souls. Such an optimistic vision is at odds with the potentially more pessimistic kind in Liu Binyan's reportage and in some of the pieces of "literature of the wounded."[25] On the other hand, Wang Meng's demonstrative endorsement of the importance of literature is closer to the position held by some younger dissidents, such as the group associated with the magazine *Today* (*Jintian*). The crucial matter for both then becomes: Is this assertion of art and artistic independence made to protest the intrusion of all forms of politics, including the political thrust of the underground exposés? Or is it made to conform to a larger political objective of the present Party leadership—"Let the Hundred Flowers Bloom," so long as they are flowers of art and style that do not contain any "poisonous weeds" of dark and vicious content?

GAO XIAOSHENG

The "political" past of Gao Xiaosheng is similar to Wang Meng's. Because of a "manifesto" he wrote with a group of friends associated with a new literary journal, he was branded a "Rightist" in 1958 and sent down to the countryside in Jiangsu province for more than twenty years. He did not resume writing until 1979. As most critics have pointed out, this prolonged experience living with the peasants has forged a characteristically "peasant style" in his fiction which, in its vivid rusticity, is comparable to that of Hao Ran, the reigning novelist during the Cultural Revolution, although the ideological orientations of the

two writers are markedly different. Gao's style is also qualita-
tively different from Wang Meng's. On the superficial level,
Gao is a very traditional realistic writer. His prose has little of
Wang Meng's fancy imagism and undulating lyricism. Nor does
he even pretend to write in the manner of "stream-of-consciousness." Compared with Wang's "foreign-flavored" syntax, Gao's
language is exclusively rooted in native soil: Its vividness is inseparable from the earthiness of the peasant milieu he describes
in almost all of his stories. Yet, for me, Gao is a more accomplished stylist; his seemingly simple and transparent language
has the oral cadence of a Chinese folk epic. Consequently, I find
his prose not only eminently readable but almost "hearable."
His stories can be "told" to a live audience, in the centuries-old
tradition of oral storytellers.

The best illustration of Gao Xiaosheng's style is provided by
his best work to date, "Li Shunda Builds a House" ("Li Shunda
zaowu"), published in 1979. The story is told in a traditional
manner by an implied oral storyteller. Its folksy tone is set from
the beginning by a peasant proverb followed by a seemingly
effortless flow of simple sentences:

> Old-generation folks who tilled the land used to say, "Three years of
> eating light gruel is enough to buy an ox." It's easier said than done.
> Imagine, for three years you can't bear to eat any rice. Don't you want to
> save on the other expenses wherever you can? Besides, this is mostly
> empty talk! If you can't afford to eat, what's there left to save?
> Li Shunda's family was like this before. So, before Liberation, he never
> dreamed of buying an ox. But after Land Reform he vowed to apply the
> spirit of "three years of eating gruel is enough to buy an ox" to build a
> three-room house. [26]

As the reader reads on, or rather listens to, the narration, the
story becomes a saga of one peasant's efforts to fulfill his humble
dream in the three decades since Liberation. Gao Xiaosheng's
remarkable feat is derived from his ability to tell a vivid, detailed
story and keep within the length of a short story. In about 20
pages he gives us an account of the impact of successive political
campaigns on Li Shunda's life. Every time Li has enough resources to build his dream house, his effort is frustrated by a
new campaign, until, at the story's end in 1977, he is finally

within reach of his goal, after having illegally acquired the building materials through the "back door."

The interesting point about this simple story is that within its realistic frame are contained other layers of meaning. Li Shunda's thwarted attempts at building his house may be seen as an embryonic myth of Sisyphus, Chinese style—of forever striving and failing in a seemingly unending process. While Sisyphus's fate is cosmically determined, Li Shunda's is the consequence of constantly changing Party policies. The characterization of Li Shunda has not only the rustic humanity of an individual peasant but also the political mentality of a "true follower." As Gao himself explains, for thousands of years Chinese peasants have been true followers. They have been searching for an object of faith, first in divinities and emperor; then they found it in the Chinese Communist Party, which they worshiped like an idol. "It is not easy to find an object of worship," Gao adds: "once it is established it is hard to shake it. Accordingly, even when the Party practiced wrong lines of policy, [the peasants] likewise worshiped them."[27] From Li Shunda's very blind persistence in following the Party's policies we also derive the lesson that honesty does not pay, that he is finally able to succeed only by an act of dishonesty.

As I have argued elsewhere, this mythic characterization of the protagonist also brings to mind Mao Zedong's revolutionary reinterpretation of the figure of the "Foolish Old Man" ("Yugong") in traditional Chinese mythology.[28] As is well known, Mao gave a positive twist to Yugong's effort to remove the mountains (imperialism and feudalism). In Mao's version, the Chinese Communist Party is so persistent in the ceaseless task of removing the two mountains that the effort finally moves God, who is no other than the Chinese people. Gao Xiaosheng in his story not only trivializes such ideological grandeur by reducing it to the labor of an ordinary peasant building a house ("God" arrives in the person of a new daughter-in-law). He also juxtaposes Li Shunda's experience against Mao's Yugong to reveal the utter discrepancy between ideological fantasy and the raw reality of peasant life. Mao's peasants are moved to fight against imperialism and feudalism; Gao's peasant wants only to build a three-room house for his family and himself. Thus, as a concrete symbol of peasant idealism, Li Shunda's "house" also takes on a larger significance. Evidently the selfish need for comfort and shelter takes priority over the collective claims of populist ideology. If building socialism is like building a house (as is implied in the story's metaphorical meaning), the objective has not been realized because of the erroneous policies of the Party, which the docile peasants have blindly followed. The story's achieved vision, based on "true reality," therefore becomes an ironic comment on the Party's ideological vision.

We can, of course, go on in this vein to explore additional ironies of content directed against the Maoist orthodoxy. But the important point I would like to argue is that these ironic readings of the text, whether or not intended by the author, are made possible by the author's consummate technique, which intricately combines two modes of representation, the mimetic and the allegorical. This is, in turn, achieved by a supple language composed of many elements: popular idioms and aphorisms, colloquial *baihua* prose, folk lyrics, and slightly formulaic classical (*wenyan*) expressions of a kind found in traditional Chinese fiction. In fact, as Gao Xiaosheng himself admits, his language is enriched by both contemporary and traditional Chinese syntax.[29] Here are a few choice samples of Gao's aphoristic style:[30]

In his eyes, doing socialism is nothing but "both upstairs and downstairs, both electric lights and telephones." It is basically a matter of building houses. But, he thinks that a two-storied house is not as convenient as a one-story bungalow. He would rather prefer downstairs to upstairs, so he wants only to build a bungalow. But then he isn't sure whether building a bungalow can be considered socialism. Electric lights he is in favor of having, but telephones are not necessary. He doesn't have that many relatives or friends, so what's the use of a telephone? When the children break it, it costs money to repair. Isn't it an unlucky thing for the household?

Since he once said that a two-storied house is not as convenient as a bungalow and it costs too much to repair a damaged telephone, this is proof that he viciously attacked socialism.

In these years the revolution was so earth-shaking that it pretty much scorched the earth.

Nowadays, "rounded heads" [official seals] are not as good as "nodded heads" [personal connections].

Big officials have it delivered to their doors, small officials must open back doors; and the common people can only implore other people.

Labor—it's still laboring, but reform—it's not reformed.

It is clear that the above aphorisms, maxims, and puns are not used solely to enhance the mimetic qualities of the story; they also contain gentle mockery and satire. However, when these folk idioms are concretely visualized, the ironic impact becomes devastating. The description of Li Shunda's nightmare of the "black pan"—a visual image stemming from the political metaphor of "shouldering a black pan" (*bei heiguo*, i.e. "black-listed")—is a *tour de force* demonstration of Gao Xiaosheng's technique:

He is a little shocked, thinking it's all right for him to be turned into an ox or a horse, but not a "revisionist." What sort of thing is a "revisionist"? It is a "black pan" that cannot be used for cooking but can only be carried as a decoration. It is a "household treasure" which can be passed on from generation to generation because it is not alive and therefore will not die. ... As Li Shunda thinks of this he feels both alarmed and superstitious. From childhood he heard many stories; among them were stories about people turning into different things. The storyteller always put it this way: "After the night was over, he turned into a _____." Also, before the transformation there was always a bizarre sensation, such as his bones would ache all over, or his skin would become burning hot and so on. So, whenever Li Shunda feels uncomfortable in his body, he dreads the dark night, afraid that he will fall asleep. He always opens his eyes wide to prevent himself from turning into a black pan in his slumber. His capacity for alertness is good, and consequently until now he has not been transformed.[31]

This vivid passage is both realistic and surrealistic. In it, the author turns the psychological fear of his protagonist into a fitting metaphor. It has none of the "stream-of-consciousness," but its dimension of absurdity easily brings to mind Kafka's famous story "Metamorphosis." But Gao Xiaosheng definitely has no knowledge of Kafka; rather, his frightening metaphor is the result of an effortless reworking of contemporary and traditional Chinese motifs by giving the political term *black pan* its literal image, as seen from the peasant's point of view. The ironic import of the metaphor is even more hard-hitting when we recall that some of the Cultural Revolution terminology is, in fact, taken from traditional Chinese folklore and fiction (for example, "ox demons and serpent ghosts"). By placing this new political term "naively" in a traditional frame of reference, Gao Xiaosheng cleverly performs the same trick from a counter-perspective. It is, in my view, an example of technique as dissidence at its ironic height.

As aphorisms and metaphors such as those cited above are interposed into the story's narrative prose, they serve the purposes of both description and verbal irony. Moreover, the story does not merely consist of a series of folk wisdoms; it is further reinforced by the heroic cadence of classical phrases, which seem to elevate the story's "low mimetic" level to a higher plane of the epic or the romance, thereby impregnating its surface realism with other layers of meaning. The following passage, strung together by a succession of four-character classical phrases, is most illustrative of what I mean: [32]

And so it came to pass that Li Shunda's mastery of architecture reached the very summit of excellence, and was requited with the acclaim it deserved. But lo, is the world vast and the ingenuity of the Creator boundless. Events worthy of special transcription for posterity flowed on and on, like the waters of the turbid Yangzi. One could not bear to avert one's gaze. Forgive us if we spare our readers the trifling and inconsequential details.

到此為止，李順大对於建築学的知识，本来已经登峰造极，叹為观止了。想不到天地渊博，造化無窮，值得大書特書的事情，如長江濁流，滾滾而来。竟无法忍心不看。那雞零狗碎的事，想不細说。

Yet, this heroic-sounding language is not adapted to heroic characters (as in traditional knight-errant novels or historical novels like *Romance of the Three Kingdoms*). On the contrary, it is used to describe the experience of Li Shunda, a common peasant. The effect of this interplay of language and characterization is to place the entire story in an anti-heroic light. Because of the heroic prose, Li Shunda's experience is elevated to an allegorical level: as noted earlier, he is the counter-example of Mao's "Yugong"—he does not wish to move any ideological mountains but merely seeks security and well-being by constructing a house of shelter. His task assumes Sisyphean proportions because it is made insurmountable by the political milieu. This allegorical level of meaning, which springs from the realistic plane, thus informs the entire story with a persistent ironic force. It seems to fit into what M. H. Abrams defines as "structural irony" in that "the author, instead of using an occasional verbal irony, introduces a structural feature which serves to sustain the duplicity of meaning. One common device of this sort is the invention of a naive hero, or else a naive narrator or spokesman, whose invincible simplicity leads him to persist in putting an interpretation on affairs which the knowing reader—who penetrates to, and shares, the implicit point of view of the authorial presence behind the naive persona—just as persistently is able to alter and correct."[33]

Gao Xiaosheng himself, of course, would not have agreed entirely with this ironic reading of the story, perhaps for reasons not directly connected with literary technique. "Li Shunda Builds a House" is also unique among Gao's stories. His other works published in 1979 and 1980 are not so consistently ironic. Most of them are less ambitious character sketches. The most successful of these are the stories revolving around the same protagonist, Chen Huansheng: "The Head of the 'Leaking Household'" ("Loudou hu zhu"), "Chen Huansheng Goes to Town" ("Chen Huansheng shang cheng"), and "Chen Changes Jobs" ("Chen Huansheng zhuanye").[34] Like Li Shunda, Chen Huansheng is an ordinary peasant, very down-to-earth, yet something of a "misfit." His characterization in the first story has more of an ironic edge because of the discrepancy between his action and official policy. Perhaps due to its more concentrated focus (the story takes place in 1971), it does not have the epic quality and allegorical depth of "Li Shunda," although its language is still characteristic of Gao Xiaosheng at his best. The prize-winning story "Chen Huansheng Goes to Town" has been well received by Chinese readers and critics. But the story's appeal lies more in characterization and situation than in irony.

It is an example of what Gao himself calls "putting a character in a special environment," thereby rendering him in sharper relief.[35] In this case, the "special environment" is the expensive room in a hostel for cadres in town, where the protagonist by chance finds himself spending the night. It is not a terribly original device, for Chen Huansheng's misadventure is but another variation of the "country-bumpkin-in-town" formula. While his folk wisdom endears him to the readers, Chen Huansheng as a fictional characterization suffers from a humanistic "toning-down" process similar to what we have found in Wang Meng's stories. It seems that the author no longer maintains the necessary detachment vis-à-vis his protagonist: Chen Huansheng cuts a sympathetic rather than an ironic figure because he does not possess the naiveté and passivity of Li Shunda. Instead of the "dumb follower," he becomes somewhat self-righteous about the correctness of his own vision of reality (which, of course, is shared by the author and reader). In one episode in the story "The Head of the 'Leaking Household'," Chen Huansheng is so motivated by his self-respect that he goes to ask the country schoolteacher to write a letter to the newspaper on his behalf. The following dialogue takes place:[36]

> Teacher: I cannot write this.
> Chen: Why?
> Teacher: In socialist society the fact you have just described does not exist.
> Chen: This is something that happened to me, can I fool you?
> Teacher: I know you are not lying to me, but you don't understand. Facts are in the service of necessity, and all the facts must prove that socialism is paradise. Therefore what you have just told me is not fact.

This exchange is meant to be satirical, but the point is too explicit to have its critical impact. In fact, Chen Huansheng's action, in its persistence of right over wrong, is reminiscent of Hao Ran's hero, Gao Daquan, in the novel *The Golden Way* (*Jinguang dadao*), who some years ago also embarked upon what he considered to be the right course of action. The two writers in the short story genre make a fascinating comparison, but here I would point out that, whatever similarities may be established in the rustic tone, epic proportion, and rich cadence of the language of both writers, Hao Ran's fictional world is envisioned primarily from an ideological perspective, whereas Gao Xiaosheng's fiction, as he himself has said several times, is solidly grounded in the fabric of reality. The "fictional" dimension in Gao's work is largely a product of artistic restructuring. Insofar as both form and content are united in an ironic vision, I have found the Li Shunda story a prime example of implied dissidence. Perhaps the "achieved content" of this particular story has gone beyond the author's original intentions.[37] If this is, in fact, the case, then "Li Shunda Builds a House" may well serve as a unique testimony that Gao Xiaosheng's fictional technique not only "contains" intellectual and moral implications of a dissident nature, it also "discovers" them.

TECHNIQUE AS DISSIDENCE

I have discussed the works of Wang Meng and Gao Xiaosheng in some detail because they were among the first writers to pay utmost attention to literary technique as a way to break away from the orthodoxy of politicized and formulaic writing. Their consciousness of technique itself represented, it seems to me, an initial challenge to the Maoist canon in literature. However, in the rapidly changing socio-political milieu of post-Mao China, a process of de-Maoification has already been underway, and the novelty of this challenge now no longer looks so daring. This is partly because the literary scene since 1977 did witness an unprecedented "thaw," which reached a height in 1979, with the convening of the Fourth Congress of Writers and Artists. In this more relaxed climate, imaginative writing took a new turn by breaking into many hitherto "forbidden areas." The result was not only a spate of social exposés but an increasing attention on the part of some writers to more personal, non-political subjects, such as love, friendship, and the comforts or conflicts of ordinary life. Thus, the regime's subtle application of the "Two Hundreds" policy ("Let a Hundred Flowers Bloom, Let a Hundred Schools Contend") has catapulted writers like Wang Meng, who are technically inventive but politically "tame," to official fame; they have become the newly established "models" for public adoration. Gao Xiaosheng attained a comparable fame, but his "Li Shunda Builds a House" did meet considerable criticism. Interestingly, as the liberalization trend waned after 1980, neither Gao Xiaosheng nor Wang Meng has written anything as politically explosive as "Li Shunda Builds a House" or Wang Meng's "The Barber's Tale," both published in 1979.

In this changed atmosphere, literary experimentation alone no longer constitutes a dissident posture. The contrasting examples of Wang Meng and Gao Xiaosheng have shown that a new, Western-oriented technique can still be used to serve a rather conformist outlook, whereas an unassuming story in the native, peasant mold can be transformed into a highly dissenting vision. Moreover, the establishmentarianism of the middle-aged and older writers has become a subject of considerable dissatisfaction among younger, anti-establishment writers—former Red Guards, workers, and intellectual youths in their late twenties and early thirties—who have taken up imaginative writing in the so-called "unofficial journals" (*minjian kanwu*). In their counterperspective, the older generations have once again submitted to political power, thus confirming "the historical weakness of the Chinese intelligentsia" as a whole.[38] They also suspect that, once established or re-established, the older writers are co-opted by the new political leadership with the security of money and prestige and, consequently, are losing their critical intelligence.

The challenge from the younger generation is expressed in two different, though interrelated, positions, which give a new dimension to the meaning of literary dissidence. The more politically oriented position argues that literature's function of social criticism must be upheld to the point of "interfering" with the existing social structure. The notion of an active "delving into life," which literally has the force of "interference with life" (*ganyu shenghuo*), was first raised by Liu Binyan, who is still a widely respected writer among the young for his moral integrity and his bold journalistic investigations. But the younger writers of such unofficial works as "Feitian" and *In the Annals of Society* (*Zai shehui de dang'an li*) wanted to go farther than Liu Binyan in their scathing and sometimes sensational critique of the darker aspects of society: not only corruption, special privileges, backdoorism, and vicitimization of veteran cadres but also rape, murder, and juvenile delinquency caused by dislocation and disillusionment. It was towards the repercussions from this kind of exposé literature that Hu Yaobang was compelled to give the first of his talks at a "playwrights' forum" in February 1980. With the criticism of Bai Hua and the crackdown on the democracy movement and the arrest of its leaders shortly afterwards, the new leadership has also put an end to this underground exposé movement in literature.[39]

The second position, echoing Wang Meng's but more outspoken, was put forth by the members of the underground journal *Today*. As Pan Yuan and Pan Jie eloquently state in their chapter, the *Today* writers argue that the demand of politics on literature in the past half-century "constitutes a stranglehold on literature." Accordingly, literature, in their opinion, must be totally separated from politics. Out of this utter disgust with political ideology they have come to the position that literature should, above all, depict the "uniqueness of the human individual."[40] In an interesting twist of the meaning of *alienation*, they argue that the political campaigns in the last three decades have forced them to emulate so many "revolutionary models" of exemplary behavior that they have been gradually "alienated" by the collectivist ideology from their essence as human individuals. Thus, they wish to go more deeply into the inner self in order to rediscover a more authentic humanity of which they have been deprived. An eloquent statement of this sentiment can be found in the afterword of a controversial novel, *Man, Ah Man* (*Ren a ren*), written by a young literature instructor in Shanghai by the name of Dai Houying. The novel was rejected by several publishers before it was published in Canton in late 1980 and immediately generated sharp controversy over the author's thesis that "Marxism and humanism are compatible." (That this notion, long accepted by European Marxists, is still "sensitive" enough to create a controversy says something about the rigidity of ideological orthodoxy in China.) But Dai's fundamental claim in matters concerning literature itself is that realism is not the only method to arrive at artistic truth. In her view, "artistic truth is not the same as imitation of life's facts" and, "strictly speaking, the highest function of artistic creation does not lie in representing reality, but in truthfully and imagistically expressing the perception, attitude, and feeling towards reality on the part of the artist-writer." Thus, she wishes to lay special emphasis on the "important meaning of the writer's subjective world" and welcomes the trends of Western modernism because she thinks that "the serious modernist artists are also seeking an artistic truth; they sense that the realistic method has constrained their search for truth, and therefore they embark upon a reform in art." Her own novel is, consequently, an experiment in human subjectivity and inter-subjectivity, as it is written from a number of points of view, and her "stream-of-consciousness" technique combines "the characters' feelings, fantasies, associations, and dreams" because "in this way it is closer to the reality of their psychological states."[41]

Dai's intellectual intentions deserve our attention, for she has argued boldly against the omnipotence of realism as *the* creative method. The term itself has had a checkered history: As noted earlier, it was firmly established in China in the 1930s and, after a period of relative eclipse in which the more ideological varieties of socialist realism and revolutionary romanticism held sway, it has been reasserted since 1976 by formerly victimized writers and critics in reaction against the radical excesses.[42] Thus, having served as a potential heterodoxy, realism is now so widely trumpeted that it seems to become a new orthodoxy. Against this historical background, Dai Houying's position, which reflects those of a sizable number of young poets, novelists, and painters, may be seen as a newly emerged stance of dissidence more "radical" (in the non-ideological, nonconformist sense) than what has been said of Wang Meng and Gao Xiaosheng.

Unfortunately, Dai Houying's lofty ambitions are not realized in her novel, due largely to the inadequacy of her fictional technique. Compared to Wang Meng, she is a novice writer. Her experiment in inter-subjectivity consists in having the story (the individual experiences of a group of young students after they graduate) told respectively and sequentially by each of the main characters. And her dream sequences, which she claims contain "symbolic meaning," are very derivative. The center-piece of the novel is a "dream" written up by the heroine, in which a special disease suddenly takes hold of the city popula-tion (traces of Camus's *Plague*?) and causes everyone to take out his or her heart. She is apparently living with her husband who has somehow lost his heart. The man whom she secretly loves and from whom she maintains a platonic distance in real life, left his heart in a pocket of his leather jacket, which she picks up on the street amidst the coats, shoes, "colored glasses," "hats of all sizes which one can wear or put on other people's heads," and "sticks with which to climb up or to beat people." She nurses the dead heart to health and swallows it, thus becoming insane in the eyes of her neighbors (traces of Lu Xun's "Diary of a Madman")—she has contracted a different disease, the source of which is his heart.[43] The "symbolic meaning" of the dream is too obvious to need any explication: We can easily find references to the Cultural Revolution campaigns (including of course the movement of *"jiaoxin"*—to hand out one's heart to Chairman Mao) and, counter to the ideological madness, the significance of the human heart as a symbol of love and humanity. The only novelty of the episode is the visual and surrealistic pun on the heart, which, upon further recollection, is not so novel after all. The blueprint lies, of course, in Chapter 82 of *The Dream of the Red Chamber.* The same device as Gao Xiaosheng's "black pan," this dream sequence is in my judgment a miserable failure due to the overeagerness of the author to get her hidden messages across to the reader. The intrusiveness of her humanistic didacticism has all but ruined the effectiveness of the novel as art. Despite her claim that she has "put in considerable literary effort in adopting a different way of expressing these contents,"[44] *Man, Ah Man* remains, alas, a crude and rather conventional realistic novel.

   This phenomenon of discrepancy between technique and intention—of form failing to measure up to the intellectual unconventionality of content—bears further analysis, especially when compared with a reverse sort of discrepancy in Wang Meng's work, in which we have found a more unconventional, though excessive, technique serving an increasingly conformist outlook. This is one of the "contradictions" mentioned in Mao's Yan'an Talks (although Mao had in mind the case of technically good art which is ideologically reactionary) and, in fact, one of the thorny issues in Marxist aesthetic criticism. Neither Mao nor his ideological followers have solved this contradiction, since they have basically de-emphasized literary technique in favor of "politics in command." But the more conscientious writers in China are becoming aware of the problem and the possible choices allowed them. There are those who, like Liu Xinwu, the renowned writer of "literature of the wounded," are trying to improve upon their rather crude technique (as exemplified in most specimens of "literature of the wounded") in order to substantiate the weight of their content. Liu's recent work, a novelette with a fancy title, *Elevated Highway Bridge* (*Liti jiaocha qiao*), is an elaborate examination of the lack of physical and psychological space of Peking residents.[45] While still uninventive in language, it is a far more solid work than his earlier cause célèbre, "The Homeroom Teacher" ("Banzhuren"). On the other hand, the woman writer Zhang Jie, renowned for her depiction of the intricacies of feeling, has in her recent work, "Heavy Wings" ("Chenzhong de chibang"), produced a blunt, problem-oriented study of the young workers of a car factory and their generational conflict with elder cadres—an explosive documentary purposely shorn of fictional technique.[46] As expected, the novelette has already elicited a barrage of political criticism. The underlying issue for the more conscientious of established writers still has to do with the functions of "realism": Should literature directly reflect reality as part of the writer's social responsibility or should literature reflect a more artistically conceived reality without the burden of social responsibility? Technique naturally occupies a higher place in the scale of priorities of the latter orientation. Only rarely, however, do we find works that are dissident in both content and form—a daring critique of present and past realities coupled with a mature but inventive technique. In my judgment, "Li Shunda Builds a House" comes close to such an "ideal," although formalistically it is not so daring.

While, for all their differences in priorities, the established writers are united by their advocacy of realism, the new dissidence of the younger, less well established writers lies in their position that, in both content and form, creative literature must go beyond the political and artistic strictures that realism in the Chinese context inevitably entails. So far, their efforts in this direction have not succeeded. Dai Houying, as mentioned earlier, suffers from a case of "thesis comes first" (*zhuti xian xing*), a remnant of her erstwhile Cultural Revolution mentality. Nor can we regard *Today* writers as accomplished novelists, despite occasionally interesting pieces by Zhao Zhenkai and Chen Maiping.[47] Their achievements in writing "obscure poetry" are comparatively more advanced, as the "obscurity," which proves incomprehensible to some older poets, consists precisely of surrealism and symbolism.[48]

For the young writers who rebel against Chinese traditions, the preferred avenue lies in Western modernism. As Dai Houying's manifesto indicates, she welcomes Western modernism because the realistic method constrains her search for truth. Zhao Zhenkai has moved from Soviet to contemporary European and American literary works for guidance, because in them "there existed a more profound exploration of the problems confronting the whole human race and transcending the problem of different political systems."[49] With the gradual introduction through translation of more Western literature, these younger writers are stimulated to attempt another "breakthrough" into the long-established "forbidden zones" of the present and the past. Two short stories by the writer Zong Pu are worth noting. Though technically still deficient, they are both determinedly Western. One story, entitled "Who Am I?" ("Wo shi shei"), is directly influenced by Kafka's "Metamorphosis"; the characters are all turned into worms.[50] In another, "Snails' Abode" ("Wo zhu"), the inspiration from Kafka and Ionesco can be noted in the story's absurd setting.[51] The narrator enters a nightmarish landscape in which people become snails and hide in their shells. They are chased and attacked, their shells crushed, by nameless authoritarian figures. The rebel leader is a young man who becomes headless as he descends into hell. Yet, he nevertheless leads a group of headless rebels in a march towards the far horizon. The background source for both works is, of course, the Cultural Revolution, and, like Dai Houying, Zong Pu cannot resist adding a touch of hope: The headless rebel leader proclaims at the story's end that, "someday, truth will be acquired without the exchange of heads."

Despite its humanistic tinge, these two stories perhaps come closest to the spirit of Existentialism and the tenets of the

European avant-garde. Zong Pu's ferocious parody of the Cultural Revolution has turned itself into a portrait of alienation and loss of identity. Social order and political authority are shown to be monstrous shams which keep human beings walled off from what is most distinctly human in themselves. Unlike Ionesco, however, Zong Pu does not envisage a breakdown of language (a potential channel for a more inventive style, expressable by breaking down typical sentence patterns, for example) as a sign of the fundamental failure of human communication; if she had, the two stories would have constituted genuine breakthroughs, at least in the Chinese literary context. The failure lies again in technique, but Zong Pu has failed more "successfully" than Dai Houying.

In sum, we are confronted with an ironic fact: Most younger writers simply do not write as well as the older, more experienced writers; at the same time, the works of the younger writers, though artistically flawed, are more daring in intention and content. The more established writers have become basically conformist, despite their relative maturity in literary technique. This intriguing phenomenon may be explained "historically": Most of the established writers born before Liberation share the same "revolutionary background" with the political cadres despite their past differences in literary matters. In order to rally the intellectuals behind it, the Deng-Hu leadership has incorporated some of their dissenting views raised in the past into the new policy, which does allow for a degree of freedom for writers to experiment with new techniques and to evolve more subjective forms of expression. Consequently, the middle-aged and older-generation intellectuals and writers, now enjoying unprecedented prestige, no longer feel any need for dissidence. On the other hand, the younger writers, more politically vocal and discontent, are receiving harsher treatment from the Party leadership. The gradual tightening of control since 1981 has sufficiently curbed the trend of excessively negative exposure and crushed the semi-underground democracy movement. There is, therefore, currently no political dissidence in China comparable to the Soviet situation: no intellectual figures of major stature who speak out against the new regime, no *samizdat* literature (after all the wall posters and unofficial journals, including the unpolitical *Today,* have been banned). The Chinese translation of the term *dissident* is strictly political: *chi butong zhengjian zhe*—one who holds a different political opinion. And "political opinions" in China continue to be shaped and carefully controlled by the Party. Since political dissidence is not allowed to exist, the literary varieties of dissidence I have described become the only alternative for individual expression.

Is artistic dissidence separable from political dissidence? In view of the May Fourth tradition of modern Chinese literature— in which a writer considers himself a spokesman of critical conscience vis-à-vis the political establishment—it can be said that all modern Chinese writers are ipso facto dissenters in a broad sense. As Lu Xun once said in a memorable speech, literature invariably takes a divergent path from politics because it always expresses discontent with society, whereas the politicians wish to maintain the status quo.[52] It is, therefore, to be expected that writers and artists in modern China would have invariably been viewed as troublemakers by leaders of successive governments, and they suffered most during the Cultural Revolution. In the changed atmosphere of the early 1980s, can a writer be content merely with stylistic experimentation while remaining ideologically "safe"? Here the generational gap becomes, in my view, a crucial factor. The underlying political impulse of the younger generation, whether they argue for more social exposure or for artistic independence, is much more unrestrained. It definitely disagrees with the official position of blooming within the bounds of the Four Principles. Thus, whatever the deficiencies in their literary technique, one finds a true spirit of dissidence in their works. This does not mean that their preferred route of Western modernism necessarily provides the answer to their quandaries. The point, however, is that this pro-Western orientation constitutes a rebellious stance which, when combined with an outlook less burdened with the weight of social or socialist realism, may provide the ground for new visions which depart radically from the hagiographical or realistic tradition.

What will happen to the young writers as they grow older? Will their modernism generate a nativist reaction as the precedent of Taiwan *xiangtu* ("native-soil") literature has indicated?[53] Is such a reaction, occurring on the mainland, likely to be intertwined with a political backlash from "conservative" radicals against "bourgeois liberalization"? Or does it prove again the everlasting grip of realism on the Chinese imagination? Whatever the outcome—and no one can be certain of any outcome—the present varieties of artistic dissidence deserve our close attention. In view of the long history of orthodoxy and conformity in Chinese literature, even a limited form of literary dissidence should be encouraged. For I believe that only through this nonconformist mode of writing, critical in spirit and unconventional or experimental in form, can there be the possibility of originality and, consequent to it, the genuine flowering of great literature.

PART THREE

The Sociology of
Publishing and Reading

The Non-Official Magazine Today and the Younger
Generation's Ideals for a New Literature

PAN YUAN and PAN JIE

In the late 1970s, literature in the People's Republic of China
entered a new era. For the first time since the founding of New
China, there emerged a literature of social criticism that was not
initiated by the political authorities. This literary movement began after the fall of the Gang of Four in 1976, following the
death of Mao, and dwindled and disappeared after the country's
political situation was completely controlled again by the Deng
Xiaoping leadership.

The critical thrust of this literary movement was basically
aimed at two things. One was the political tyranny and ideology
of the past decade, when political pressure had been extremely
strong. In a sense, the criticism of this aspect was similar to the
"thaw" period in Russian literature in the late 1950s. The other

target of this movement was the negative side of the nation's morality, culture, and mentality. After the nightmare of a nationwide catastrophe called the Cultural Revolution, the writers of this new critical literature attempted to point out the connection between this catastrophe and the Chinese national character. In this sense, the solemnity of self-criticism could be likened to the so-called literature of "Ruins" in Germany after World War II.

These two major features of the new critical literature were based on different perspectives and not necessarily embodied in a single work or author. Literature of the first type emphasized the response of people to a particular political environment, while the second type focused on scrutinizing people's nature as it was derived from their culture and history. If it can be said that the "literature of the wounded" (a label after the title of the first published short story of its kind, "The Wound") by and large was at the level of politics, describing the "wounds" of a normal person that resulted from physical and mental suffering incurred during political turmoil, then the second type of critical literature, which was at the level of history and culture, argued that such a person might not be sound, that his suffering was the inevitable result of something deeper in him, a congenital deficiency or malfunction.

After "The Wound" was published in October 1978, the first type of critical literature rapidly became dominant in the literary scene. Works of this sort were published in all kinds of official newspapers and magazines.

The critical literature at the level of history and culture first appeared in the unofficial publications of that time. A leading representative of these unofficial journals was Today (Jintian), which advocated the independence of literature from any political forces.

THE ARTISTIC VIEWPOINTS OF TODAY

What made the literary work of Today distinctive from most works of the "literature of the wounded" was its strong awareness of the potential independence of literature from politics. Writers of Today insisted that literature should not be a mere political statement or let itself be used as a tool for political struggle, as had often been the case in the past. Literature should serve as a vehicle to express people's feelings, as a bridge between souls, and as a means of purifying people's natures. The *Today* writers were rather critical about the nature and mentality of the Chinese nation as a whole. They argued that traditional Chinese culture, from which the distinctive Chinese character and mentality had derived, was, to be sure, old enough to be proud of, but at the same time too old to be vital. As a part of this culture, Chinese literature could not be expected to flourish unless it underwent a change—one of assimilating foreign cultures. The tradition of Chinese literature could no longer suffice for depicting people's feelings or for probing human nature in modern Chinese society. It was time, *Today*'s writers believed, to re-evaluate the old tradition of Chinese literature and infuse new blood into it by learning from foreign literatures. This pursuit of depoliticization and nontraditionalism can be found throughout the writings, as well as in the other activities, of the *Today* writers.

The Relationship between Literature and Politics

The *Today* writers held that, since the 1920s, Chinese literature had not enjoyed the freedom to develop that it deserved; it had been basically fettered by politics. The New Chinese Literature of the 1920s dawned in a period of the country's transition from feudalism to bourgeois democratism. The New Literature bore first and foremost its political importance and, only secondarily, a literary importance. After the 1920s, the struggles among feudal, capitalist, and Communist forces formed a vortex into which all people were drawn. Under such social conditions, literature lost its independence, for the Chinese writer at that time could not escape the urgent and pressing need to subordinate himself or herself to certain political objectives. The pressure to dedicate oneself to political struggles in other roles besides that of writer of literature was well nigh inescapable.

Thus, after the 1920s, most writers began to take social responsibility as the first priority. Literature became merely a means of expressing particular political and social claims. The political messages contained in a literary work became an important criterion of literary criticism. For example, the distinction between "progressive" and "reactionary" literature was often made by leftists as the number one criterion in judging those literary works. This was obviously solely a political distinction. Works considered successful at that time were, in fact, based on the strength of their ideology on behalf of political or social change.

Some writers were aware that, under such historical conditions, the political function of literature was contradictory to its independence. But they voluntarily gave up claims that were purely artistic. Lu Xun, for instance, in his later years, gave up his pursuit of achievement in literary technique, adopting almost exclusively the form of *zawen* (essay) to serve his social and political purposes. There were other people who, insisting on the apolitical character of literature, attempted to employ literature to express their personal emotions. However, their emotional whispers were drowned out by the battle cries of the soul-stirring contemporary class struggle.

Since the founding of New China in 1949, the subordination of literature to politics has been further confirmed in the new state ideology. Based on the Marxist premise of the class nature of literature and art, it has been taken for granted that literature is but a tool for class struggle—writers must write for the progressive class and their work must be a "clarion call for the new era." The *Today* writers held that such a demand constituted a strangle hold on literature. They argued that, just as the same cloud would evoke different responses in the minds of a meteorologist and a poet, images of society should be different in the eyes of a writer and a politician. There was always a contradiction between the pragmatic virtues of politics and the non-pragmatic function of literature as an expression of the emotions and feelings of an individual. Politics in an authoritarian system is centralized, while the emotions of people that are sought out and portrayed in literature are myriad. Writers should be entitled to express their own feelings and thoughts in their own ways.

This was the basis of *Today*'s literary principles. It reflected an understanding of the value of the individual different from what had been taught in China. The *Today* writers also held that, in literature, the uniqueness of the human individual had long been supplanted by his social character and class character —an official conceptual system that overrode the real lives of the people. In their discussions of poetry-writing, which were published in *Today* and other magazines, the young poets remarked:

Having poetry serve as political propaganda is a misfortune that should have been stopped long ago! Too long has poetry remained enslaved, subject to the juggling acts of political careerists furthering their own ambitions. If some today still require that poetry bear a "political label," they are either muddleheaded or malicious![1]
I'm opposed to "tradition," and I'm opposed to stereotyped style and its strangle hold on people's souls.[2]
Poetry has no boundaries, not those of time, space, or the self. But the starting point of poetry should be the poet's self.[3]

To portray people's true feelings and to pursue communication between kindred souls were the goals of the *Today* writers. Shu Ting, a female writer renowned for the delicacy of feelings found in her writings, once said:

Through my own experience, I've fully realized that people today are in sore need of mutual respect, belief, and warmth. I'm ready to use poetry to express my concern for the human race to the fullest. Obstacles must be removed, masks should be torn off. I'm convinced of the possibility of mutual understanding between human beings, for it is after all possible to find others' souls.[4]

When such a principle, of art based on humanitarianism, emerged in a country where the doctrine of class struggle prevailed, it met with resistance and criticism. Adhering to such a principle, the *Today* writers were not without contempt in their views of the older generation of writers. In their youthful minds, the older generation's submission and self-subordination to political forces reflected the historical weakness of the Chinese intelligentsia. Therefore, in its announcement "To Our Readers" in its first issue, *Today* boldly declared that "they, the older generation as a whole, have fallen behind the times."

The *Today* writers also objected to the excessive employment of literature as a tool of political expression by some of their contemporaries. In 1979, a liberal poet in the army, Ye Wenfu, wrote a poem to expose and attack the privileged stratum in the army.[5] This poem triggered enormous repercussions throughout the country. It was regarded as a successful literary work, although it had little literary merit. Yet Zhao Zhenkai, chief editor of *Today,* commented:

His poem does not represent the goal of our pursuit. In a sense, he is a fighter, too, but only a fighter for politics, not for art. A fighter for art should fight for the truthfulness of art.[6]

The Re-Evaluation of the Chinese Cultural Tradition

In the Preface to *Today*'s first issue, the editors wrote:

Today, as we open our eyes anew, we would not just look vertically at our cultural legacy from millennia past, but begin to cast our gaze horizontally, at the other intellectual horizons all around us. Only by so doing can we truly understand our own values.[7]

One of the most significant points of divergence between the older and younger generations in China lay in their attitudes towards their cultural tradition. The younger people of *Today* held that the ancient Chinese civilization, while rich, revealed certain aspects of rottenness. The easy acceptance of totalitarianism in China, for instance, was inseparable from ideas derived from the traditional culture. New ideas and new thinking, which could lead China to a thorough transformation, could not be conceived within the old civilization itself. Aware of all this, *Today*'s writers were seeking appropriate means of self-expression. Humanitarianism, the basis of their literary creation, was the result of such a pursuit. In regard to the future development of Chinese literature they, not unlike their predecessors in the May Fourth era, had a theory opposing such "inbreeding"; they believed that, if the new Chinese literature of the future were to remain a mere repetition of the old, then its artistic offspring would be increasingly feeble. Only by getting fresh blood from other nations could Chinese literature possibly flourish. *Today* writers had their own understanding of the "literature that is national in form"; Zhao Zhenkai once said:

Our poems must absorb the techniques of Western poems, while the mood and emotion must be national. In this case, "national" should not be mechanically understood as referring to traditional Chinese literary forms, such as Chinese folk songs, but as trials and tribulations uniquely experienced by the Chinese nation.[8]

The application of this theory can be found in the poems in *Today*. The feelings that had long existed in people's hearts but never theretofore been given literary expression appeared in unexpected yet effective forms. These new poems caused immediate and widespread interest and controversy, which testified to their very success, for people were for the first time since the founding of the People's Republic involved in a debate about the forms of literature per se, not the social or political merits of the literary works.

This emphasis on technique and on the influences of foreign literature turned out to be the start of the experiments with what some later called "obscure poetry"; the controversy it generated has continued until today.

Just like the debate on the relationship between politics and literature, the problem of new literary forms became the center of a confrontation between the two generations of writers. Ai Qing, one of the renowned poets of the older generation, unambiguously expressed his aversion to this kind of "bizarre" poetry. He said, "Poems cannot be evaluated as good or bad unless they are understandable in the first place. . . . The incomprehensibility of some poems results from their mechanical imitation of Western poetry."[9] He once mocked a poem in *Today* in the following way: "The writings by young people nowadays are quite strange. Take one poem for example. It is only half as long as its title; the title contains two characters meaning 'life,' while its content consists of only one word, with one character—'net.'"[10]

Today was prepared for such reproaches. The editors and authors considered the risk of being incomprehensible to some people as a price necessarily paid by any literary pioneers. Mang Ke, one of *Today*'s main poets, once said: "Poems, after all, are not popular cookbooks."[11] Another *Today* woman poet said, not without pride, "If you cannot understand, your son or grandson will understand some day."[12]

TODAY'S FOUNDING AND ACTIVITIES

Today was based on an informal organization in Beijing of young people who were devoted to literature. The group, mostly male, had gradually come into being since 1969. It came to be considered by the authorities as an "underground literary circle."

In the late 1960s, those who would become the core of the "Today" group were students at several different Beijing middle schools. Their parents were mostly intellectuals—professors, writers, poets, and so forth, although some were ordinary working people. What the young people shared was being sent together, in 1969, to Baiyangdian Lake, a rural area in Hebei province. There they were to "settle down and join the production brigade."[13]

The young middle-school graduates felt negative about farming, and had little basis for communication with the peasants. For the first time in their lives, they saw how backward the countryside was, and how numb and ignorant the peasants seemed to have remained, despite thirty years of socialism. The peasants, under "the dictatorship of the proletariat," were deprived of basic rights that the young city folk had not thought much about previously—not only the right to voice their opinions on policies and government leaders, but the right to choose the very crops they would plant. The "Baiyangdian Lake group," like educated youths in similar straits all across China, were assigned to live by themselves, in a special corner of the brigade. They could, however, continue with their literary creations in their spare time, after the day's farm work. Most of their writings were poems. Since there was no opportunity to publish them, these poems were circulated among young people in the form of handwritten copies. They enjoyed a certain following. These poets were called the "Baiyangdian Lake School."

The "Baiyangdian Lake School" of poetry, like the "Today" group which succeeded it, consisted of several major writers, and their permanent readers, a "periphery" (waiwei) who were also close friends and "sympathizers." Later, the poets returned to Beijing to work in the factories; they did not stop writing.

After the downfall of the Gang of Four in 1976, the Third

Plenary Session of the Tenth Central Committee of the Chinese Communist Party allowed a temporary "liberalization." The Democratic Movement developed rapidly. Democracy Wall in Xidan, Beijing, which became a symbol of this movement, served as the forum for all kinds of reformers. Around October 1978, Zhao Zhenkai, Mang Ke, and some others met in the home of Huang Rui, who later became the art editor of *Today*. They decided to set up a non-official magazine by the name of *Jintian*, meaning "Today."[14] (The English translation of the name that appeared on the first issue of the magazine was "The Moment," but it was changed to "Today" after the second issue.) On 23 December 1978, *Today*, as one of the first non-official magazines during the Democratic Movement, appeared in the form of big-character posters on the walls of the Ministry of Culture in Beijing, on the gate of the institute publishing *Poetry* (*Shikan*), an official magazine, and on Democracy Wall. It aroused a great sensation.

Today absorbed some of the poets of the "Baiyangdian Lake School," such as Zhao Zhenkai and Mang Ke, but not all of them, for the original comrades had split up, due to differing opinions on the proper relationship (or non-relationship) between politics and literature. Outsiders also joined, such as Chen Maiping. Later, about 30 people were involved in the daily activities of *Today*. The new magazine's "periphery" again consisted of young people, mostly college students who were interested in *Today*'s literature and art. Sometimes they would take part in the magazine's activities.

The editorial board worked regularly in the home of a young worker in Beijing, holding discussion meetings once a week. The literary contributions were read aloud and chosen through discussion. When the author was present, he or she would do the reading, and solicit comments from the group. When opinions differed about a work's publishing potential, a vote was taken. In accepting or rejecting a piece, the members tended to act so as to reaffirm their literary ideals, giving preference to works notable for their aesthetic qualities and absorption of Western literary techniques, rather than for their politics. At least one article rejected by *Today* was later printed by the major official literary magazine *October; Today*'s editor-in-chief, Chen

Maiping, nevertheless felt "no regrets." That he and others carried on literary activities unofficially did not mean that they never published in the official magazines. Chen's own "In Snow Mingled with Rain," for instance, was printed in an official publication subsequent to its appearance in *Today*.

After the writings that would be printed were selected, the editors managed to do the plates, using stencils and a Chinese typewriter owned by a certain state-run unit. Unofficial use of loosely supervised state property was not only necessary to unofficial publishing; it was a common practice, an open secret.[15] After cutting the stencils, members of the editorial board would, with the help of some supporters around them, do the printing and binding themselves. Then they would go into the streets to sell them. The cost of the magazine was comparatively high, because of the large amount of time and labor required to print it. The price of a single copy varied from 50 to 80 *fen* (cents), higher than that of an official magazine by nearly 50 percent. This hindered the greater circulation of the non-official magazines in general.

From December 1978 to September 1980, 9 issues of *Today* were published. More than 1,000 copies were printed of each issue. The *Today* editors also published some collections of poems and short stories, such as *The Unfamiliar Beach* by Bei Dao (Zhao Zhenkai), *The Secrets of the Heart* by Mang Ke, and the novelette *Undulation*, also by Zhao Zhenkai (pseud. Ai Shan). And the editors twice held mass poetry readings in Beijing parks, events unprecedented since the Revolution thirty years before.

Although *Today* declared itself an organization in pursuit of pure art, it nevertheless risked political persecution because of being in a country where politics takes command in every field. Under these political pressures, *Today* and other non-official publications shared a common fate. *Today*'s quest for mere survival inevitably became a political act. The editorial board of *Today* took part in the 1 October 1979 demonstration on the occasion of the thirtieth anniversary of the founding of the People's Republic, which was started by some non-official publications in Beijing (including *Exploration*, which had Wei

Jingsheng as its chief editor). *Today*'s participation came about as follows.

On 27 September 1979, a group of young painters, headed by Huang Rui, the art editor of *Today*, had set up a non-official painting exhibition in front of the Chinese Art Gallery, located in the center of Beijing. Western painting techniques quite different from the styles of the Russian oil paintings that had shaped contemporary Chinese oil painting styles were liberally adopted. The exhibition took the name of "Star." Most of its motifs had never been on display before, in an official exhibition. Offering a striking contrast to the official exhibition on display within the gallery at that very time, "Star" attracted much attention.

On the morning of 29 September, the Public Security Bureau sent about 100 policemen to close the "Star" painting exhibition. Its organizers raised a protest, but received no reply at all from the authorities. On 1 October 1979, the National Day (considered to be one of the most important political occasions in China), several non-official magazines held a joint assembly, followed by a demonstration march. This march was the only one in all the National Day celebrations since Liberation that ran counter to the official parades. At this counter-procession, slogans appeared such as "We Want Political Democracy and Freedom for Art!" Although this demonstration was never approved by the authorities, the "Star" painting exhibition was later allowed to continue in an officially designated place.

In the spring of 1980, on the pretext of "removing the obstacles to achieving national stability and unity," the authorities banned some political organizations like the editorial boards of *Beijing Spring* and *The April Fifth Forum*. The "Today" group did not feel any need to take precautions against official threats, for they would have considered it strange for the government to bother with such a small, informal organization of young people. But there were, indeed, subtle sanctions against some members. Officials also denounced, in speeches and in print, the poetry *Today* published, as being "obscure"; the magazine's short stories escaped such criticism.

Ultimately, in August 1980, the Public Security Bureau

ordered *Today* to stop publication, under the pretext that *Today* "had not registered before." As a matter of fact, there had never been an official ministry where non-official publications could be registered. Any non-official magazine could by definition be declared illegal. In order to help *Today* survive, the editorial board began to go around campaigning for it. In "An Open Letter to the People of Beijing in All Walks of Life," distributed in the form of leaflets, they rejected the charge of "not having registered," arguing that "it is not that we have deliberately opposed the law, rather there is no appropriate law for the registration of non-official publications for us to abide by." However, due to the political pressure and general atmosphere at that time, they did not get much response or support from the populace. The editorial board decided to resume its activities by setting up another organization by the name of the Research Association for Literature of Today (Jintian Wenxue Yanjiuhui). The Association was founded on 2 November 1980, with Chen Maiping, then a student at the Beijing Teachers College, as its head. Altogether this association had 33 members. *Today*'s publications continued to be circulated in the form of loose-leaf selections of "Reference Materials for Internal Distribution."[16] After the third issue in its loose-leaf format, *Today* faced greater political pressures. Problems of funding and dissension among some of the members added to the problems; the Association's activities came to an end.

BRIEF ANALYSIS OF WORKS PUBLISHED IN *TODAY*

Today published mostly poetry and short stories, with occasional literary criticism, essays, and introductions to foreign literature. In its 9 issues, the magazine offered to its readers 87 poems, 28 short stories, and 1 novelette, as well as lesser numbers of works in the other forms.

Generally speaking, these works were based on the personal experiences of the writers, especially their life during the Cultural Revolution (1966–1976). In the main, these young people had had a comparatively peaceful childhood and had received a politically orthodox education. However, in their adolescent years, they had become disillusioned, as a result of trials and

and tribulations in their own lives, and their exposure to selfishness, cruelty, and ruthless struggle. All this imbued their writings with skepticism and encouraged their use of literature for pondering major questions of life. The authors meditated on problems of history and culture rather than politics. That is to say, they did not think that the Cultural Revolution—the recent tragedy of the Chinese nation—was merely a circumstantial political phenomenon resulting from some individuals' actions. What they were seeking to establish in their writings was the connection between this disaster and the nation's traditional culture and mentality. In their works, some untraditional ways of expression fittingly served as a better form in which to express their untraditional ideas. We shall examine the works, focusing on *Today*'s poems and short stories.

Poetry

The influence of the poetry, in terms of the extent to which it aroused controversy, stands out much more than that of the stories. To most Chinese readers, who were used to the tributes paid to the leaders of the country and to the upholding of a certain policy of the Party, such as had appeared frequently in the poetry of the thirty previous years, *Today*'s poems seemed very unusual. The feelings buried in people's hearts were displayed in a novel, most unexpected way. The readers were stunned by the poems and by the images of themselves they found in the poems.

The general atmosphere in China's poetry circles had become increasingly oppressive since Liberation. Apart from the direct influence of the belief that "literature is a tool of political struggle," new poetry also had had some problems within itself. Since Liberation, poetry writing had been bound by the slogan of "nationalization" (*minzuhua*). In fact, even earlier, since the birth of New Literature in the May Fourth period, poetry had constantly been faced with two divergent futures: a popular poetry, closer to folk songs and more easily understood by the masses, or a new poetry, which would absorb foreign literary influence to find new methods for individual expression. The most attention-getting characteristic of *Today*'s poetry was the representation of painful reflections. The upheavals of the time and the vicissitudes in their personal lives made the younger generation question the world around them:

> A starless night, town and village have tightly shut their windows.
> The soundless plains are deserted,
> As desolate as the people's wisdom and feelings;
> Frigid air engulfs me.
> Deep in my head,
> Pitch-black coal forms slowly, layer by layer.[17]

This poem reflects a kind of historical and political meditation on the Chinese nation. The poet implies that the political atmosphere, combined with the longstanding Chinese traditional frame of mind, has become a burden to the Chinese people. The two have stifled thinking and rendered the people's minds inert and in a way morbid.

The Great Wall, as depicted by Chinese poets in the past, was always a symbol of the nation's culture, of which they were proud. Yet, for the poets of *Today*, the Great Wall engendered a sense of oppression:

> Solemnly I place the Great Wall on the northern peaks,
> Like a shuddering chain of several thousand years.

About the long heritage of China's history, they wrote:

> Well why should we have
> Let the emperors' chariots lay down their ruts in history,
> Let the people grow as lean and thin as ciphers;
> To go on showing off our past, I can't,
> I can only give a wide-eyed stare,
> Watching our bronze civilization slough off layer by layer,
> Like arid land, callouses on my hand,
> Or honest wind-whipped lips.[18]

The fact that the people had grown "as lean and thin as ciphers" was what prompted the *Today* poets to challenge the tradition of several thousand years. They had a deep love for those "honest, wind-whipped lips," but they could not bear to remain silent about the grievances of the Chinese people—one of which was to have their arduous struggle and suffering regarded as a virtue, that of "diligence." This kind of virtue was a passive characteristic, imposed by the backward and primitive living conditions of China. It was something to be changed instead of regarded with pride. One poet wrote:

> I curse sweat, wood, and callouses,
> May the sound of metal
> Riffle the fields and mountains like the wind.[19]

They were expecting a sonorous sound of a new life that would break the stagnancy of China, a society based on an agricultural economy.

This questioning of tradition and authority was a result of these young people's thoughtful meditations. It was manifested in many of their poems, as in the following:

> To the heavens rich as satin I proclaim:
> This isn't morning, your blood has already congealed.[20]

> Surely, even if you donned the heavens' raiments,
> I'd still undo the starry clasps.[21]

On the other hand, the young poets always cherished hope for the earth on which they lived and worked. Though they sometimes felt disappointed, they never despaired:

> If every corner of the earth were sun-drenched,
> Who would be in need of stars?
> Who would stand alone and burn up in the coldness,
> Searching for a twinkle of hope?
> Who would, year in and year out,
> Write stanzas of bitterness and miseries?[22]

The unyielding struggle in the darkness was represented thus:

> Your eyes are veiled,
> Your gutteral, angry voice
> Bursts out in clammy darkness:
> Release me![23]

And by deep sighs in darkness:

> If everywhere were rubble and ruins,
> How could I say that the way out lay at our feet?[24]

> Maybe we can have no friends who can read our minds.
> Maybe the way we took was wrong from the beginning, and can only lead
> us further astray.
> Maybe we lit lanterns one after another, only to have them blown out, one
> after another, by gale-force winds.
> Even though we burn out our lives to light up the dark,
> We haven't any fire to warm ourselves.[25]

In solitude, they yearned for warmth, love, and communication between souls:

> On the unending road of life,
> We've suffered too many astringent rains;
> Lean your head on my chest, dear,
> I want to hold with both hands, your hair, like a bonfire.[26]

> A solid shoulder is wanted
> By the fatigued head seeking a place on which to lean;
> A pair of hands is needed
> To hold up under the most oppressive moment.[27]

Poems portraying the true feelings among people could scarcely be found in the official poetry circles. Poems under the title of "Mother," for instance, were often tributes to the Party. Among the *Today* poems, we find a real poem for Mother, in which the special love of a Chinese girl for her mother is revealed:

> Your pale fingertips smoothed the hair on my temples,
> I could not help, as I did in childhood,
> Hanging on tightly to your dress,
> Ah, Mom,
> To hold on to your receding figure,
> Though dawn light has cut my dream into vanishing pieces,
> I dare not open my eyes even now.
> . . .
> Once I cried and screamed at you because of a little thorn in my hand,
> But now, though I wear a crown of thorns,
> I dare not, dare not utter a single groan.

Ah, Mom. . . .
My deep and tender memory of you
Is not a cascade, not a torrent,
But an ancient well that cannot sing from beneath the overgrowth.[28]

These excerpts represent a part of the *Today* poets' impressions of and contemplations of their lives in the past. The mood that characterizes their poems is unprecedented in Chinese history since Liberation. And the way this mood is expressed is also unique. Political ideology, which suffused the poetry of the recent past, all but disappears in *Today* poems. Naive optimism is discarded. The elaborately regular, yet overcautious, rhymes and meters found in classical Chinese poetry are also replaced by a kind of natural and elastic rhythm. Objective descriptions give way to subjective imagination. Stereotyped expressions are replaced by bold and fresh ones; ordinary concepts of spatial and temporal relationships, by intertwined sense perceptions; and the real world, by a new one filled with symbolic and suggestive implications. In short, by getting rid of the dominance of politics and receiving fresh blood from foreign literature, the young poets of *Today* rejuvenated the ossified organism of contemporary Chinese poetry. Their works led to aversion among those who would have kept literature a slave of politics forever. These critics accused *Today*'s poems of being "low in spirits"—in China, this meant politically unhealthy—and of being "nebulous." However, they could not but admit that *Today*'s poems were truthful and unique. In view of these two characteristics, the poetry of *Today* is entitled to its own existence and development.

Short Stories

The short stories in *Today* often aimed at exploring the truth of human life and condemning the evil behavior that had twisted people's souls. In many stories, the period depicted was not exactly specified. In writing technique, efforts were made to reveal the protagonist's inner world, thus offering a great contrast with the traditional narrative method of storytelling.

The stories of *Today* mainly portray people's miseries in harsh environments. The heroes and heroines are mostly young people. Many stories show traces of autobiography. Due to the varied personal experiences of the authors, their writings also offered different themes and styles.

THE PORTRAYAL OF MUTUAL TRUST BETWEEN PEOPLE IN HARDSHIP. The younger generation in present-day China is portrayed as a disillusioned generation. They are disillusioned with their previous political ideals and also with some of the people around them. During the cruel political struggles, people deceived and told on each other; sincerity was utilized by politicians for their mean purposes; kind and upright people were regarded as foolish, while villains easily succeeded. With such disappointments, the *Today* writers turned to a new pursuit of sincerity and nobility in true human sentiments.

The story "In Snow Mingled with Rain," by Chen Maiping, describes a young man who happens to meet a girl at a bus stop on the night of a storm. Both await the last bus. "She stood far away from me [the young man], with the street lamp in between; our shadows were cast apart." The bus fails to show up, and the young man offers the shelter of his umbrella to the girl. After a terse refusal, she finally agrees to share the umbrella with him. In the darkness, they remain silent. And in their silence they are sure that a mutual trust is emerging. The author writes:

Darkness of the night sometimes would make people on guard against each other, with their bolts and locks, with tightly shut windows and widely opened eyes. But it sometimes could make people trust each other, with their hearts, their breath, their shining eyes . . . No other language was needed, we said nothing more. I was aware that, after parting, we would be no more than passers-by to each other. So what would be the point of more conversation? The intersection on which the two lives had met was a mere bus stop, on a night when the snow was mingled with rain. I did not know who she was, or where she might go. Yet she began to trust me. Trust—it made me light-hearted. It was something unachievable during daytime. I wished I could live always in just such a night of mingled snow and rain.[29]

Another short story depicts the lives of some educated young people during the Cultural Revolution. These urban youths were deprived of a chance for education and self-development.

They were told that they were to spend the rest of their lives in the remote countryside. They lived in the abyss of despair, feeling like social outcasts; and yet they felt they could do nothing about it. Qiu Xia, a girl from one of the youth groups, cannot bear such a life, but she tries every way possible to cheer up her friends. She holds a party for them. She wears bright clothes, talking and laughing, in the hope that others might feel better. She does not allow her companions to say anything depressing. At dinner time, she suggests that each one of them tell about the happiest event in his or her life. When it comes her turn, she says:

As you know, I love to read on top of the dam. Several days ago, when I was there reading alone, I saw what looked like a little squirrel running back and forth along the side of the dam, as nimbly as one of those motorcycle acrobats. I stood there frozen, staring at it, for what I saw reminded me of human life—a single slip and you are drowned, or broken into pieces. . . . Suddenly I heard someone calling, "Young lady, young lady!" I raised my eyes and saw an old shepherd with his sheep on the hillside. He cried and ran to me desperately, "Young lady, young lady . . ." "What has happened?" I asked. "People told me that a girl student settling down in another village threw herself into a well," he wheezed. "Silly girl, why abandon life? How nice it is to live. . . ." I suddenly understood: he was afraid that I was about to jump into the reservoir! Waves of gratitude swelled up from the bottom of my heart. On this desolate autumn day, I had run into a total stranger who was concerned about me.

A year later, Qiu Xia died—"She was alone, reading on the dam when, no one knew why, she fell into the water and drowned."[30]

The despair felt by Qiu Xia was not unrepresentative of the predicament that had once confronted the "Baiyangdian writers" themselves. They saw some of their friends degenerate under such conditions, even commit petty crimes (as in *Undulation*). One of the few positive points of contact with the peasants was indeed the latter's occasional kindness and concern for the "new settlers."

SEARCH FOR THE TRUTH OF LIFE. What is the true value and significance of the individual? This question is extremely hard to answer in a society that advocates collectivism. What is the relation between an individual and the society to which he belongs? What are his obligations and rights? How are national activities (such as war) linked up with an individual's real life? These are some of the questions the *Today* writers have raised and tried to answer.

In the short story "The Open Terrain," the protagonist is a man who used to be a KMT soldier and once fought against the Communist army. He stands in front of the open terrain, years after the war is over. The land before him is the battlefield on which he and his fellow men were trained and armed by U. S. military advisers before fighting the Communist army. His fellow soldiers were all killed in the battle, while he was captured. Now, all that has passed. Construction is going on here. A new project with U. S. aid is to start. Beside the old fortress, where grass now grows, he digs out the bones of his fellow soldiers. He can tell to whom each piece of bone belongs:

Attached to this skull were two big front teeth; it belonged to the heavy machine gunner. With the two front teeth, he had gnawed other bones. . . . This thigh bone was a sot's, familiar by its length. This man had wept in the middle of the night, out of loneliness for his wife. . . .

Now he piled up these bones anew. Unquestionably these were bones of those who had been in the pillbox with him, stubbornly holding out. When the shots had died down, corpses on the victorious side were carried away and buried over there, under a monument. Glory was with them. They guarded peace, tranquility, and happiness! The corpses of the defeated were buried here, beside the fortification, sins along with them. They embodied death, shame, and disaster![31]

What is the reason for these kinds of conflicts among human beings? What is the true meaning of glory and shame that have been passed on to posterity, and what is the true meaning of the individuals' lives? Are people entitled and able to understand the real meaning of their actions? The official literature contains no work that discusses such questions about war.

EXPLORATION OF THE NATION'S MENTALITY. Like its poetry, the short stories of *Today* also explored the relationship between the people's mentality and the nation's history. The historical legacy was seen to be declining, yet it still lingered on. In the eyes of *Today*'s youth, complacency and forbearance were the factors that had made society relatively stable; these were the main objects of their criticism and self-criticism.

The short story "Under the Striking Clock" is a piece of symbolic writing. It depicts an old couple who sit under an age-old clock in the center of the city and listen to it at a fixed time every day. "They always looked solemn and serene. Whenever the clock struck, they would close their eyes as if they were enjoying fascinating music." Every time the narrator drives past this couple, he envies their leisure, thinking that "their figures indicated to people the concrete existence of the universe." As the years go by, the clock becomes worn out. The trees alongside the clock die. Yet the old couple always sit there as before, "peaceful and satisfied," listening to the striking of the clock without fear. One day, the narrator finally feels that he is "not so comfortable seeing the couple sitting there. They could not satisfy a certain feeling in my heart." Later the old man dies, and the old woman looks even more senile. Her body is shrinking, stiff. Still, she sits peacefully under the striking clock. The narrator begins to feel sad. "From then on I began to resent this old woman who clung to the past. . . . I even hoped that the turret would collapse one day, with the striking of the clock."[32]

Contentment with the status quo and forbearance towards misery have always been regarded as virtues of the Chinese people, yet it was these virtues that became the basis for the miseries, as in the case of the Cultural Revolution. The future renaissance of the Chinese nation must be based on the nation's serious and thorough self-criticism, thought the *Today* group.

The techniques of representation in the *Today* short stories did not cause as great a sensation as the *Today* poems. Most *Today* stories did not go beyond realism. However, in some stories, obviously non-traditional techniques are adopted, and the effects were fairly successful.

For instance, in the novelette *Undulation*,[33] by Zhao Zhenkai, different narrators appear by turns, and the points of view from which the story is told are similar to those in some films in which people with different identities and experiences express their different impressions of the same event. In Yi Shu's *Hatred*,[34] the style is almost dream-like, and, by cross-cutting in space and time and by mixing the subjective and objective worlds, the unusual relationship between a brother and sister is represented. Although few in number, these works using non-traditional techniques did represent the beginnings of a certain new literary trend.

Works in Other Genres

The fables published in *Today*'s first issue were quite exceptional. In general, Chinese fables have been mildly didactic, but the fables in *Today* are full of pungent sarcasm, assailing morbid social phenomena. The following are some examples:[35]

> A Moth:
>
> Hey man! Just listen—
> Take heed of what I've done.
> Don't go mistaking every candle for the sun.

> A Spider:
>
> I've built a superstructure,
> Nothing does it bear
> But the bodies of the careless
> Who've wandered into there.

> A Scorpion:
>
> When your eyes are on me
> I'm a dependable friend and true.
> But turn your back an instant
> And I'm the first who's after you.

> A Cat:
>
> My tongue's so clever
> So adaptable you see
> That there's no way
> To dish the dirt on me.

> A Cuckoo:
>
> When I call you in the morning,
> I'll wake you early on.
> Then while I lie in the cool shade,
> You can labor in the sun.

The illustrations in *Today* were also quite exceptional. Constrained by the magazine's printing facilities, they were mostly ink drawings with simple lines. Corresponding to the style of the poems, these illustrations were of ample imagination and symbolism. For instance, a drawing entitled "Pondering" depicts the head of a woman pensively looking up at the starry firmament. Yet her eyesight is blocked by her hands, which represent all kinds of thoughts; the light of stars, a symbol of freedom and wisdom, is hidden by these hands. The picture's mood is oppressive; it symbolizes the arduous experience of those young people who constantly seek truth. Another drawing, entitled "Youthfulness," portrays a girl stark naked. The nude is a symbol of youthfulness; she also signifies what the *Today* writers were pursuing—the natural, unconcealed beauty of human beings.

FUTURE PROSPECTS

The literary activities of *Today* are now past history. In spite of the authorities' reluctance to recognize it, *Today* evidently has secured its own place in contemporary Chinese literature.[36] However, it may be too early to give a definite appraisal of *Today*'s significance and influence, for it was naturally impossible for a small magazine like *Today* to bring about essential changes in Chinese literature during its two-year existence. The most meaningful thing about *Today* is that it represented a latent trend of literary development. The prospect of this trend and the realization of this possibility will depend on many factors, among the most important of them, politics.

Today's pursuit of the independence of literature from politics undoubtedly represents the ultimate direction of the development of Chinese literature. Yet this pursuit is obviously tinted with idealistic colors which contrast with the real conditions of China. The wishes of the *Today* youth to change the inert components in the Chinese national character has also placed excessive stress on the role of literature. Without a change in the material conditions of Chinese society, it is hard to imagine fundamental changes occurring in the mental outlook and moral concepts of the Chinese people. The very prerequisites for such change are in the first place politically controversial in a country like China.

Today's pursuit of new literary technique is limited by other social conditions as well. Without the raising of the whole nation's level of culture and education, *Today*'s poetry will remain in the "ivory tower" and may lose its vitality.

Limited by social conditions, the new type of literature advocated by *Today* cannot become dominant in the Chinese literary scene; however, it does suggest a possibility for the co-existence of more than one type of literature—both politically oriented literature and literature independent from politics; both literature stressing the Chinese cultural tradition and literature stressing the assimilation of foreign cultural traditions. These diverse facets should all become part of Chinese literature. For the first time since 1949, the Chinese people are promised by the government that "no large-scale political struggle will occur in the future" and that "the raising of the Chinese people's level of living and culture will be given the top priority." Perhaps we can cherish some hope that the kind of literature advocated by *Today*'s writers may enjoy the unrestricted development it deserves.

APPENDIX
BACKGROUND ON SOME MAJOR MEMBERS OF *TODAY*

Zhao Zhenkai

Zhao was the chief editor of the *Today* magazine. His pseudonyms are Bei Dao, Ai Shan, and Shi Mo. His main works include the novelette *Undulation,* the short stories "Return of a Stranger" and "Melody," and a poetry collection, *The Unfamiliar Beach.* He is now working as an editor for the official magazine *The New Observer* (before that, he was a worker in the Sixth Construction Corporation of Beijing).

He was born in 1949 into a family of intellectuals, and received his secondary education at one of the best middle schools in Beijing. At the beginning of the Cultural Revolution, he actively participated in the Red Guard movement. After he was assigned to work in the construction corporation in 1969, he had second thoughts about the Cultural Revolution. He divorced himself from political activities and buried himself in reading during his spare time. He regarded young writers in Russia in the 1960s as his model for modern literature, saying that works by young Russian writers were more attractive to him than some American novels like *The Catcher in the Rye* (by J. D. Salinger), because the ideology and social structures of Russia and China were similar.[37] Later, Zhao gained more access to contemporary European and American literary works, and he found that in these works there existed a more profound exploration of the problems confronting the whole human race and transcending the problem of different political systems. Hence, they became increasingly appealing to him. Zhao began to compose poetry in 1970 in order to vent his discontent with the hostility that existed among the people at that time. He commenced short-story writing in 1972, experimenting with various non-traditional techniques. Some of his writings in this period were quite remarkable. His poems offer highly condensed images of life. Zhao's accomplishments in literature made him representative of the younger generation of writers writing in the new style in present-day China.

Chen Maiping

Chen was the acting chief editor during the later period of *Today*. His pseudonym was Wan Zhi. *Today* published his short stories "The Statue," "In Snow Mingled with Rain," and "The Open Terrain." Now he is a graduate student in the Department of Drama and Literature at the National Drama Academy. Chen was born into a professor's family in 1952. His stories emphasize the sensations and feelings of people caught up in their concrete situations and their destinies. Most of his stories use the night, storms, or unbearable heat as natural settings. In these situations, people are confronted with unusual pressures and have to make unusual choices. Thus they reflect the pressures of environment and the realities facing human beings. His writings also evince a deep sympathy for mankind, mixed with a certain disappointment. Chen is obviously critical of some aspects of the Chinese national character.

Chen believes that literature and art should be subordinate not to politics, but to the sensations and feelings of human beings themselves; they should express what human souls are eager to express. He thinks that the main task of literature and art is to depict the true feelings of people in real situations. Chen quite agrees with the Japanese "New Sensational School," and he esteems the "psychological-realistic" methods of the American woman writer Joyce Carol Oates, who stresses the inner world of people and reflects reality largely by probing into people's psyches.

Chen spent his early years in a rich area in South China, where the tranquil and idyllic life made a deep impression on him. When the Cultural Revolution began, he, like many other young people, showed fanaticism and rebelled against his family. In 1970, he was sent to a remote area in Inner Mongolia, where he was in touch with people of the lowest social strata. He began to feel the bitterness of their lives and the uncertainty of their destinies. His thoughts turned increasingly dark. The work he did as laborer, teacher, and barefoot doctor all left an imprint on his writings. Around 1975, while he was working in Inner Mongolia, Chen began to write short stories. He joined the *Today* group in 1979, and gradually became one of the main contributors to the magazine.

Mang Ke

Mang Ke was the deputy chief editor of *Today*. He was born in 1951 and is now a worker in Beijing's Yanjing Paper Mill. He was a member of the "Baiyangdian Poetry School" during the Cultural Revolution. He took part in the preparations for *Today*'s founding. His writings are mostly poems, which were published in the collection *Secrets of the Heart*. It is generally held that, among all the *Today* poets, Mang Ke is the most Westernized and the most impressionistic in technique. Generally speaking, his poems are short; many consist of only two lines, and are characterized by striking images and jarring rhythms. The mood of Mang Ke's poetry vividly evokes that of the wandering and depressed youth of the mid-1970s. Because of his obvious divergence from the traditional method of poetry-writing, the authorities never approved of him, nor did they allow his writings to be published in official magazines.

CHAPTER SEVEN

Fiction and the Reading Public in Guangzhou and Other Chinese Cities, 1979-1980

PERRY LINK

The grey tones of a city like Guangzhou may not suggest an active cultural life or much of a reading public. Bookstores are often less crowded than the sidewalks; people seldom read on buses or in a park; everyone seems preoccupied with daily life. Beneath these appearances, though, there is an active market for fiction and a complex pattern of readership. Perhaps for residents of a dull-looking city, fictional escape is even more important than it otherwise might be. Perhaps the very impossibility of reading on a bus increases one's desire to read at home, where one's elbowroom, both physical and political, is greater. Perhaps an empty bookstore is the most dramatic of evidence that all the attractive books have long since been sold out. In any case, fiction has an important place in the life of the city.

The reading of fiction is, of course, only one of many spare-time cultural and entertainment activities in any society. Various groups—analyzed by age, sex, education, occupation, and so forth—show differing tendencies in the amounts and uses of their spare time, and we shall consider below certain of these questions as they relate to the fiction readership. But here, because of the element of arbitrariness in selecting fiction as a topic, we might best begin, albeit briefly, by placing fiction in the more general context of alternative forms of diversion.

THE PLACE OF FICTION IN THE
ENTERTAINMENT AND CULTURAL SCENE

The thirst for amusement that supports fiction-reading also supports a wide range of other activities, and it would be fascinating to compare these systematically. Here we shall review only "fiction-related" items, such as films, stage performances, television, and the reading of other literary genres, while passing over "non-fiction-related" activities like sports and games, visiting parks, exhibitions, museums, and restaurants, window-shopping, drinking, sex, and—by no means least, since it is so common—simply strolling the streets looking for something unusual.

Gossiping, or "chatting" (*liao tian* in Mandarin, *king gai* in Cantonese), broadly understood as it is in China, is only partly related to fiction, but is such a basic institution in popular culture that we must not overlook it. In addition to the workaday gossip that is normal in any society, in China friends drop in on one another (*chuan men*)—unannounced but not entirely unexpected—for the sole purpose of "chatting," a mode of entertainment that has remained extremely common in a society where easy access to television, films, or books is still unusual. Chatting focuses not only on neighbors and workmates but, at least in the cities, very often on national leaders and the affairs of state as well. Discussion about famous people, which of necessity is oral in China, resembles in certain of its functions the gossip press in the West. For example, when the rumor mill reported in autumn 1979 that Marshal Ye Jianying had enjoyed an extravagant 80th birthday party, the details of the story may have been as questionable as if published in the *National Enquirer;* but the breadth of the rumor's circulation was also comparable to that of a major tabloid in the West. Other items on the national grapevine in 1979–1980 included serious and often accurate pieces of news that could not be printed in the controlled press: that Wang Dongxing and others were about to be demoted; that soon Kang Sheng would be identified by name as an associate of the Gang of Four; and so on. But, regardless of whether the items for gossip are big or small, people who are good at telling stories—embroidering and dramatizing them—become known as skilled chatters and even a bit honored as such. In sum, the institution of chatting is partly recreation, partly a social grace, and partly a supplement to the press.

Its connections with fiction are basically two. First, it is closely parallel to fiction in some of its psychological functions: It allows readers to escape the boredom of normal daily life, or, if they choose to face daily life, allows them to vent their irritations and frustrations. (The fiction of 1979–1980 was particularly well suited to both these functions.) Second, the grapevine itself carries fiction. This is sometimes called *koutou wenxue* or "word-of-mouth" literature. Chen Guokai's tremendously popular story called "What Should I Do?!"[1] had actually been circulating in various forms across China for several months prior to its publication in February 1979. *What If I Really Were?*[2] written in the summer of 1979, was never published in China in media available to the general public, but the whole story, in many versions—some reputedly true and others unabashedly fictive—was known by millions and hotly debated throughout the autumn of 1979. The distinctions among fiction, news, and gossip are blurred on China's grapevine. Each feeds off the other two inside the one great cornucopia of "stuff to talk about."

The autumn of 1979 was one of the freest times for expression in China since 1949. People could relax somewhat (but never entirely) about who might be overhearing their chatting and gossiping. In the stricter times before and after, more care had to be taken to ensure confidence among one's listeners, and under these stricter conditions the written word was in certain ways superior to gossip as an outlet. When one communes with a book, one can think any thought one wishes in the privacy of one's own mind. Besides, gossip among a close circle of trusted friends can grow stale; to increase one's supply of stimuli, a new book is not only more trustworthy than a new acquaintance but, in a sense, more flexible as well: One can use it as much or as little as one wishes, with no worries about what its reaction will be. The oft-remarked lack of privacy in China has not prevented people from cherishing their own, if they can get it.

The more formal fiction-related media of film, television, the stage, and so on should also be briefly compared here with fiction in terms of their advantages and disadvantages from the audience's point of view. These advantages and disadvantages may be analyzed as the absence or presence of impediments to communication such as illiteracy, cost, and political controls. No good statistics on illiteracy in China are available,[3] but, clearly, for the great majority of people in the cities as well as the less literate countryside, watching a film is much easier and more fun than reading a book. It is normally cheaper as well. A novel might cost 2 or 3 yuan and a literary magazine 0.30–1.00 yuan, but admission to a film, 0.30 yuan at most. When films are shown in one's own work unit (or school), they cost as little as 0.05 yuan and are often free. In Guangzhou in 1979–1980, the attractions of film gave rise to a serious problem of roving bands of youth "crashing" film shows at Zhongshan University and other units. Officials in charge of the political control of cultural media are aware, of course, of the popularity of film, of the directness of its impact, and of the potentially incendiary fact that large crowds watch films together. Political controls are, accordingly, tighter on films than on fiction, and in 1979–1980 films did not match fiction in outspokenness. An interesting exception to the tighter control on films is the special category of "internal-reference-only" showings of many kinds of foreign films. These showings are open only to high officials, or persons in film-related units, and their families. The intense excitement that attaches to the very phrase "internal film tickets" is indirect testimony to audience resentment of controls on the publicly available films.

In recent years, television has come to rival films in audience size. Officials at the Central Radio and Television Stations in Beijing stated in October 1979 that there were 2.5 to 3 million television sets in China.[4] Though they had no breakdown of this estimate, it is obvious that television sets are concentrated in the major cities. Guangzhou, in particular, may have the highest concentration of sets because such a large portion of its populace has connections in Hong Kong. Once the cost of obtaining a television set has been met, it then becomes the least expensive of the entertainment media. Those who do not have their own sets (still the great majority, of course) can often watch for free with neighbors or in such places as the labor-union offices in their work units. The public library in the city of Jiangmen in Guangdong charges 0.04 yuan per evening to watch color television. The brigade auditorium in the village of Xian'gang in Kaiping county charges 0.02 yuan to watch two black-and-white sets placed side by side. But a disadvantage of television, compared with films, is that one often cannot hear well, or at all. In the village of Xian'gang, for example, perhaps 200 people came each night to watch those two television sets. Besides watching, they chewed sugar cane, spat melon seeds, spanked screaming children, and commented loudly and independently on what they saw on the magical flickering screen. Yet this was, even without audio, obviously superior to staring at the wall at home, and not unlike the traditional social experience of watching village opera. In private homes and in smaller crowds, it was more possible, in varying degrees, to link sound with image, but nothing assured this quite as well as the booming dominance of a film's sound track in a public theater. Another disadvantage of television was that, beginning in early 1980, new films were not shown on television because of the outcry from theater managers who, under the new rules of Deng Xiaoping's economic regime, were now required to answer for their own debts. Owners of television sets protested that, having invested all their savings in buying a set, they could not well afford to go out to theaters. But officials decided in favor of the theaters, requiring that first runs (of 50 to 60 showings) be protected from television.

Stage performances of both modern drama and Cantonese opera were very well received in Guangzhou in 1979–1980. The popularity of the local opera needs no explanation, especially after ten years of nearly total repression. The popularity of modern drama was partly the result of a series of unusually lively and bold "problem" plays about juvenile delinquency, corruption, official hypocrisy, the Gang of Four, and so on, which came to the Guangzhou stage during 1979-1980.[5] Perhaps because of the limited audience size for modern drama, political controls on it were looser than on films or television, making it in this respect more comparable to fiction. But the reasons for looser controls were apparently somewhat different for fiction and drama: While fiction has a larger audience, and therefore a larger political impact, that danger was balanced by the fact that the fiction audience is dispersed, not concentrated like the stage audience in theaters.

The stage audience was relatively small not only because of the intrinsic physical limitations of the stage, but because ticket prices were high. A ticket to a stage performance in Guangzhou in 1979-1980 cost from 0.30 to 0.80 yuan, and free viewings arranged by one's unit were much less common than for films or television. A cost of this magnitude was a bigger barrier between art and audience even than illiteracy. A survey of 74 literature students at Zhongshan University, who were certainly better off than average economically, shows that a student went to a play, on the average, about 3.2 times per year (see Appendix 2). This compares with seeing a film about once a *week* (4.2 times per month), and an estimated 12.8 hours per week reading literature.

Reading, for the broader public of Guangzhou city and elsewhere, involves only the minority who have the time, inclination, and ability to read anything beyond the occasional sign or poster. But the reading material available to the urban populace is much more varied than in any of the other media discussed above (excepting gossip). There are newspapers, magazines, pamphlets, and books which are official, unofficial, or underground, and modern, ancient, or foreign. The major newspapers are without doubt most widely read. The Guangzhou evening newspaper *Yangcheng wanbao,* which had been very popular before the Cultural Revolution, was revived in early 1980 and grew in circulation from 200,000 to 510,000 in less than three months.[6] Circulation was frozen at that level by the State Publication Administration, not only because of a paper shortage but because the Post Office complained that postal workers' delivery bags were getting unmanageably heavy. Under these conditions, feisty crowds gathered at local post offices to compete for the copies of *Yangcheng wanbao* sold at retail. Crowds also gathered at post offices every month on the day that the immensely popular *Masses Cinema (Dazhong dianying)*, with its color photos of movie stars, arrived at local post offices. Certain popular science magazines, like *Radio (Wuxiandian)*, were also in great demand.

But, in general, except for daily news, fiction was the most sought-after reading material in China in 1979–1980. It overshadowed even the news when the news was dull. (The popularity of newspapers like *Yangcheng wanbao* cannot be taken as indicating a preference for news as opposed to fiction, because one of the paper's most attractive features was its fiction column.) I base my estimate of fiction's popularity on statistics on borrowing from public libraries and libraries in work units, as well as on the estimates of editors, publishers, and personnel of the monopoly New China Bookstore. Editors and publishers learn of reader preferences from (1) letters to the editor; (2) surveys that some magazines conduct by putting questionnaires in the backs of their November and December issues; and (3) a system of "reviewing stations" *(pingshu dian)* that some magazines use, by which certain people are given free subscriptions to the magazine in return for periodic reports on reader response in their local areas.

My most complete statistics are from the public library of a county seat not far from Guangzhou (see Appendix 1). The library includes 130,000 volumes and serves a small city of about 80,000 people as well as a county of perhaps ten times that number. For the three months of January through March 1980, an average of 5,313 books were borrowed per month, of which 74.95 percent were literature books. Other humanities comprised 6.68 percent of the borrowings; natural sciences and technology, 16.09 percent; social sciences, 2.18 percent. Among the 18 specific categories the library recognized, the lowest borrowing rate was for "Marxism-Leninism-Mao Zedong Thought," with .013

percent or 2 books in the three months. The library kept no records on the breakdown of borrowing within the large category called "literature," but the librarians were emphatic that fiction predominated. This point was unanimous among librarians that I interviewed at several other places and levels; at the huge Shanghai Municipal Library, for example, 74.82 percent of the books borrowed in May 1980 were literature, and the librarians again were confident that most of these borrowings were of fiction, especially full-length foreign novels. [7] But contemporary Chinese fiction was also popular, especially periodicals such as, in the Guangzhou area, *Literary Works* (*Zuopin*, Guangzhou), *City of Flowers* (*Huacheng*, Guangzhou), *Harvest* (*Shouhuo*, Shanghai), and *People's Literature* (*Renmin wenxue*, Beijing). Poetry seems to have been the least borrowed genre, especially foreign and modern poetry. Tang and Song poetry still drew a faithful few. From an examination of library shelves and card catalogues, it was obvious that the high rate of borrowing fiction did not reflect a proportionate imbalance in library collections. There were plenty of books to borrow in other fields, but readers preferred fiction. The only kinds of fiction they did not borrow from libraries were the two kinds that all libraries in the People's Republic on principle do not lend out, except to carefully appointed "researchers," that is, pornographic fiction and "reactionary" fiction. To judge from the fiction market in society as a whole, readers would no doubt have borrowed fiction in these two categories, too, if they could have. But let us now look at the wider market more systematically.

THE SOURCES OF FICTION IN SOCIETY

Bookstores

The national network of New China Bookstores (Xinhua Shudian) handles the sales of all new books—through its own retail stores in most cases, but also by contract with other shops in rural areas or with street vendors in certain cities. Theoretically, there are two other bookstore systems parallel to the New China system, namely the China Bookstores (Zhongguo Shudian) that sell used books published before 1949, and the Foreign

Languages Bookstores (Waiwen Shudian); but in many places this tripartite division has not actually been made. As of May 1980, there were about 5,000 retail bookstores in all China, or about one per 190,000 residents. In the large cities, the ratio of bookstores to population was two to three times higher than this average. [8]

It is somewhat difficult to characterize what was in these bookstores, except to note that the Marxist-Leninist-Maoist classics were usually available. This unpredictability may seem strange, since the bookstores drew from a single supply network, and the network drew on a fixed group of publishers governed by a carefully modulated system of quotas designed to bring a balanced supply of books to most places. [9] A major problem was that desirable books sold out so quickly that the shelves normally contained only various sorts of leftovers. Ironically, one sometimes could find in a relatively remote bookstore a highly sought book of fiction that would last only minutes or hours on the shelf of a downtown or university bookstore. Much sought-after books often sold out, through orders to work units or through "backdoor" sales, even before they reached bookstore shelves.

It is more interesting, therefore, to enquire what was supplied to bookstores than what was present in them. (Neither question is equivalent to that of what readers preferred, of course.) From January 1977 through June 1980, at least 629 novels were published in China, of which 259 were newly written Chinese works, 126 were republications of earlier Chinese works, and 244 were foreign works in translation, mostly republications. [10] These figures are based on all publishers in China, but the titles with the largest printing runs are nearly all from two publishers: the People's Literature Publishing House and the China Youth Publishing House, both in Beijing. A basic indication of the large volume of output of these two presses is that, for the three years 1977–1979, they together used 33.7 percent of all the paper officially allocated for literature in China. [11] Data from these two publishers make it possible to compile a list of the 20 most circulated novels and plays for the period January 1977 through June 1980. (Publications from the other major literary publishers—Wenyi Publishing House in Shanghai and Baihua

Publishing House in Tianjin—normally ranged up to 200,000 at most, and hence would not make this list.) [12] To make the list more amusing I am listing ancient, modern, and foreign works together, based solely on their printing runs. The printers' "top 20" were: [13]

Author and Title	Copies printed
1. Zhang Yang, *The Second Handshake*	3,300,000
2. Luo Guangbin and Yang Yiyan, *Red Crag*	2,000,000
3. Yao Xueyin, *Li Zicheng*	1,820,000
4. Feng Menglong, *States of the Eastern Zhou*	900,000
5. Luo Guanzhong, *Romance of the Three Kingdoms*	900,000
6. Wu Jingzi, *The Scholars*	870,000
7. Ethel Voynich, *The Gadfly*	800,000
8. Zhou Libo, *The Hurricane*	800,000
9. Alexandre Dumas (père), *The Count of Monte Cristo*	780,000
10. William Shakespeare, *Plays*	720,000
11. Wu Cheng'en, *Journey to the West*	700,000
12. Honoré de Balzac, *Eugénie Grandet* and *Father Goriot* (in one volume)	700,000
13. Li Boyuan, *Panorama of Officialdom*	700,000
14. Yang Mo, *The Song of Youth*	680,000
15. Ba Jin, *Spring*	650,000
16. Ba Jin, *Autumn*	630,000
17. Daniel Defoe, *Robinson Crusoe*	600,000
18. Yuan Jing et al., *New Tales of Young Heroes* (*Xin ernü yingxiong zhuan*)	600,000
19. Li Ruqing, *Redness Throughout the Land* (*Wanshan hongbian*)	600,000
20. *One Thousand and One Nights*	600,000

Zhang Yang's *The Second Handshake,* first on the list, is a popular-style novel that combines the well-established appeals of a triangular love story, a martial-arts tale, a detective story, and exploration of the West; it also incorporates the theme of China's contemporary policy of national strength through modernization through science. Having originated as a hand-copied underground text during the Cultural Revolution, it was reprinted in vast quantities in 1979–1980—partly, it seems, to cement popular support for the new regime and opposition to the old.[14] Number 7 on the list, Ethel Voynich's *The Gadfly,* is well known in the Soviet Union and Eastern Europe. According to editors at the China Youth Publishing House, who published it in China, it became widely known to Chinese readers through its mention in the Soviet novels *How Steel is Tempered* by Nicholas Ostrovskii and *The Story of Zoya and Shura* by Lyubov Timoteyevna Kosmodemyanskaya, which were published in runs of 1.4 and 1.6 million copies respectively in the 1950s.[15] That Ethel Voynich was an early supporter of the Chinese Communists certainly also helps to explain why her novel was introduced in the 1950s. *The Count of Monte Cristo,* a somewhat different case, was popular before Liberation and was given an extra boost during the Cultural Revolution by Jiang Qing, who listed it with about 7 other foreign works as highly recommended reading.[16] We might also note some strange absences from the above list. Why are Ba Jin's *Spring* and *Autumn* represented, but not the famous *Family,* the first part of the *Torrent* trilogy? *Family* was, in fact, printed in 580,000 copies, slightly fewer than its two sister volumes, apparently because it was already much more widely available than they. The absences of *Dream of the Red Chamber* and *Water Margin* are different cases, both interesting. *Dream* has never been published in the People's Republic in numbers that reflect its stature or popularity. During 1949–1966, it was published in 660,000 copies, only 23rd among all novels for those years. During 1977–1980, the number added was 400,000, a figure that tied *Dream* with *Tom Sawyer* and Du Pengcheng's *Defending Yan'an* at 31st for those years. *Dream* has likely been penalized for its supposedly unrevolutionary effects on youth. But *Water Margin* is clearly a different story. During 1949–1966, it was published in 1,580,000 copies—tops among pre-modern works. This presumably was because Mao Zedong liked it. Its neglect during 1977–1980, in turn, is almost certainly related to the general neglect of Mao.

Officials of the People's Republic often made the point in 1979–1980 that there has been a "socialist renaissance" in literature since 1977, and that this has been reflected in "mushrooming" literary publication. If we set aside for a moment the questions of content and literary quality, and ask only what the increase in volume was, the most fundamental measure we have is the amount of paper used on literary publication. In 1977, the figure was 596,000 reams for all of China. In 1979 this figure had risen to 1,476,000 reams, an increase of 148 percent in two years.[17] But a fact that was seldom pointed out is that, in 1976, the last year the Gang of Four's publishing policies were in effect, 36 percent more paper was used for literature than in 1977. (Publishers apparently had not known quite which way to proceed during the transitional year of 1977, and had published conservatively.) When the dip in 1977 is accounted for, the actual three-year increase from 1976 to 1979 is only 59 percent. This increase is noteworthy, to be sure, but by comparison the change in the *content* of published literature was much more dramatic. Measured in terms of the numbers of titles on bookstore shelves, the "renaissance" has also, in comparison with pre-Cultural Revolution years, been more qualitative than quantitative. In 1978, the largest bookstore in Shanghai had only 4,000 titles on its shelves (including everything, not just fiction); by April 1980, this had risen to 6,800, but was still considerably short of the highpoint of 12,000 reached before the Cultural Revolution.[18]

Whatever the quantities, the distribution of book supplies was very complex. In the quasi-capitalist economic regime of 1979–1980, bookstores were encouraged to advertise their holdings, and in Guangzhou they did, both in newspapers and on blackboards outside storefronts. For the most part, this was an entirely formalistic exercise, however, because there was no elasticity in the market; books that were in demand sold with lightning speed anyway, and books that were not in demand would not sell—anyway. As parts of the New China Bookstore's (or other) large national system, individual bookstores had no flexibility in pricing. Retail stores earned 22 percent of the price of every book sold, while another 8 percent went to the wholesale level. The retail prices of all new books were also "fixed prices"—determined by complex formulas that, although changeable from province to province, were basically the same everywhere.[19] Every publisher had to employ the formulas, which determined a book's price according to its number of pages, quality of paper, size of characters, number of illustrations, number of colors used in illustrations or on the cover, quality of binding, and—most interestingly—nature of content. (For the Guangdong formula, see Appendix 3.) Materials were ranked in 6 categories according to content; and the price per page was fixed in increasing steps between 0.055 yuan and 0.080 yuan. To a certain extent, the ranking reflected the regime's interests and priorities, and, to a certain extent, the cost of production. The lowest price, for example, was allowed to primary-school textbooks and mass political propaganda. Most expensive were technical and specialized works (because of low circulations and the difficulty of typesetting) and the "internal-circulation" books that were so sought after that hardly any price would have been too high. Modern and contemporary Chinese literature cost 0.065 yuan per page. "Traditional literature worth recommending" was set at 0.070 per page, and other traditional literature (not worth recommending?) at 0.075 per page.

With price out of the question as a mechanism for regulating distribution, competition for limited supplies naturally shifts to the sphere of privileged access. The system of "internal" publications we have just referred to is one major way in which privileged access is secured. Several levels of "internality" correspond to the stations of those who are allowed access. Originally, the rationale for this system was to prevent the masses from reading materials the leadership felt they might misinterpret politically. And this rationale, to be sure, is still important in the control of books like Richard Nixon, *Six Crises,* Winston Churchill, *The Second World War,* and so forth. But the system has also been used to assure privileged access to highly sought books: Michener's *Centennial,* Haley's *Roots,* Margaret Mitchell's *Gone with the Wind.* (It is amusing that nearly all fiction stamped "internal" [*nei*] is in fact foreign [*wai*].) Edgar Snow's *Red Star Over China* should hardly be considered poison for the masses by the Communist leadership, yet it too was "internal" until 1979.[20] If there was any doubt about whether something should be classified "internal," a publisher was well-advised to so stamp it, in order to avoid possible future criticism. At some publishing houses, more than 50 percent of all titles were "internal."[21]

The larger branches of the New China Bookstore, such as the ones on Beijing Road in Guangzhou or Wangfujing in Beijing, have two or even three "counters," that is, special rooms where successively higher ranks are necessary for entry. There are also separate stores limited to officials of certain ranks.[22] For the majority of the books that are not "internal," the Bookstore has other mechanisms to assure various kinds of privileged access. In general, a work unit has priority over an individual if it wants to order a book for its reading room or library. If a book is related to a unit's work, as a foreign novel might be to a university's foreign languages department, the priority is higher. Certain officials are also given priority. In addition, people who have received remittances of foreign currency, which is so important to China, are given priority in buying many hard-to-buy things, not just books, through a system of "purchasing coupons." In 1979, 21 of these coupons were issued for every foreign remittance equivalent to 100 yuan. To buy a copy of *The Count of Monte Cristo* in Shanghai, one needed to use 20 of these coupons in addition to the purchase price in yuan. Four years earlier, in 1975, one needed 60 coupons plus the purchase price. In addition to these various formal regulations of access, there have been many varieties of "backdoor" arrangement by which powerful people, people who work in the bookstore, or people with friends or relatives who work in the bookstore, and so on, can put in "orders" for a book before it arrives at a store. When the appearance of a desirable book was rumored in advance during 1979–1980, it could happen that none ever appeared on a bookstore shelf.

When hard-to-get books did appear, bookstores would be temporarily packed with people scrambling to buy them. I occasionally saw lines in Beijing bookstores during 1979–1980, but only hands and elbows in Guangzhou. When the first issue of the magazine *City of Flowers* appeared in bookstores in April 1979, it was sold out in one morning. (Ironically, in nearby Hong Kong, *City of Flowers* and other hard-to-get books and magazines rested in great piles in the left-wing bookstores.) The whole system of book sales plainly puts at a severe disadvantage anyone who lacks special status and lives beyond running distance from a bookstore. Recognizing this fact, the New China

Bookstore system has established "postal purchasing sections" at its major branches. These allow readers in remote areas to order by mail, with the bookstore paying the postage. But to get one of the more sought-after books this method was almost impossible during 1979–1980.

Borrowing from Libraries, Reading Rooms, and Friends

The works of fiction most consistently in demand at libraries in 1979–1980 were those by contemporary Chinese writers who were seeking to expose and examine China's social problems. Some libraries simply decided not to cater to demands for these materials, because much trouble was involved in acquiring sufficient quantities and in handling the heavy demand for their use. Libraries that did try to meet the demand had to find ways to get multiple copies of the most popular magazines. The Jiangmen Library in Jiangmen, Guangdong, which managed to get a few dozen copies of each issue of the magazines *City of Flowers* and *October* to serve its city of 130,000, still found the pressure to borrow these magazines extremely heavy. Second most borrowed among fiction materials were generally the full-length novels of socialist realism published between 1949 and 1966. These were not as infectiously popular as the contemporary magazines, but, because of their political acceptability and large library holdings, were widely available and relatively easy to borrow. Libraries did not offer pre-1949 publications to the general public; the availability of pre-revolutionary works was limited to a few traditional novels that had been reprinted after 1949. The various provincial and municipal literary magazines from 1949–1966 were also seldom available to the public in libraries, although, when they were, those from the liberal Hundred Flowers period in 1956 were invariably the most worn, indicating heaviest use. Materials from the Cultural Revolution years of 1966–1976 were offered only selectively, and were quite unpopular in any case, although Hao Ran's novels were still read.[23] In sum, it is possible to get a first approximation of what novels were most available to the public in Chinese libraries in 1979–1980 by drawing up another list of most published works—this one of the novels published

during 1949–1966 (including reprintings done during 1977–
1980):[24]

Author and Title	Copies printed
1. Luo Guangbin and Yang Yiyan, *Red Crag*	6,850,000
2. Jin Jingmai, *The Song of Ouyang Hai*	3,800,000
3. Luo Guangbin, Liu Debin, and Yang Yiyan, *Immortality in the Raging Flames*	3,280,000
4. Qu Bo, *Tracks in the Snowy Forest*	3,040,000
5. Yang Mo, *The Song of Youth*	2,930,000
6. Luo Guanzhong, *Romance of the Three Kingdoms*	2,380,000
7. Li Yingru, *In an Old City Ablaze*	2,220,000
8. Wu Cheng'en, *Journey to the West*	1,760,000
9. Liu Liu, *Intrepid in the Flames*	1,740,000
10. Lyubov T. Kosmodemyanskaya, *The Story of Zoya and Shura*	1,600,000
11. Shi Naian, *Water Margin*	1,580,000
12. Liang Bin, *Keep the Red Flag Flying*	1,490,000
13. Wu Qiang, *Red Sun*	1,450,000
14. Nicolas Ostrovskii, *How Steel is Tempered*	1,410,000
15. Du Pengcheng, *Defending Yan'an*	1,360,000
16. Zhou Libo, *The Hurricane*	1,280,000

Eleven of these 16 mainstays of the contemporary Chinese
library shelf are works of Chinese socialist realism written during
the first fifteen years of the People's Republic. They are sum-
marized and interestingly analyzed in Joe C. Huang, *Heroes and
Villains in Communist China* (London, 1973). The dominance
of *Red Crag* is especially noteworthy. *Immortality in the Raging
Flames*, number 3 on the list, is but another version of the *Red
Crag* story in earlier and less fictionalized form. A total of the
printings of these two books containing the same story exceeds
10 million, not counting at least a million of a comic-book version. In the 1950s, Sister Jiang, the martyred heroine of *Red
Crag* who withstood torture in a Nationalist prison, was so well
known as to become a standard term in ordinary speech.
Ostrovskii's *How Steel is Tempered* (number 14) is the outstanding example of Chinese circulation of Soviet socialist realism, or indeed of foreign fiction generally.[25] The three famous

traditional novels on the list (numbers 6, 8, 11) demonstrate the political acceptability of these books as much as popular demand for them. If reader demand had been a dominant criterion in printing decisions, *Dream of the Red Chamber* would certainly be on the list, as would Chinese novels from the 1920s and 1930s. Although a book's availability and reader preferences for it are both important factors in how often it is borrowed from libraries, the two questions in themselves are importantly different. An indication of which of the above works were preferred in 1979–1980 among one group—university students in Guangzhou—can be gleaned from Appendix 2.

Public libraries in China differ in function, depending on their size. The major municipal libraries in cities like Beijing, Shanghai, and Guangzhou concentrate on expanding their collections and serving specialized researchers. In 1979–1980, Beijing Library did not lend fiction to the general public at all. Zhongshan Library in Guangzhou (not to be confused with Zhongshan University and its several libraries) theoretically did lend fiction to the public, yet, according to one staff member, commonly saved itself much trouble by telling would-be borrowers that it did not have certain highly sought works of fiction even if it did have them. The Zhejiang Provincial Library in Hangzhou did not allow a person even to read inside the library unless he could show that he was a university student or a university graduate, that is, part of a very small portion of the reading public.[26] The Shanghai Library did lend fiction to the public in 1979–1980, and did have reasonable stocks on hand; but it issued only about 11,500 borrowing cards for a city of over 10 million people,[27] or about one card for each 9,500 citizens. It was not always true that people in the biggest cities were best served by libraries. At the county library in Xinhi, Guangdong, there was one borrowing card for every 13.5 people in that small city.

University libraries were surprisingly hard to use, even for university students. One copy of *Gone with the Wind* in translation was locked inside the Beijing University Library, like a caged worm inside a pool of trout, limited to borrowing by faculty only. At the Foreign Languages Department library at Zhongshan University in Guangzhou, students were barred not only from borrowing but even from using the library's seven

English dictionaries and other books in English. Students could borrow from the Chinese Department library, but there were many restrictions.

The difficulty of securing borrowing privileges at major municipal and university libraries was both the cause and the effect of efforts to gain such privileges through the back door. Of the Shanghai Library's approximately 11,500 borrowing cards in June 1980, about 10,000 were for individuals and the rest were for work units.[28] There was a rule that no new cards for individuals could be issued unless someone turned in an old card. But, since there was no charge for holding a card, nor even fines for overdue books (only the threat of revoking one's privileges), cards were seldom, of course, relinquished. The back door thus became one's only practical hope for getting a card, even though few had the clout necessary to open such a door. Hence, the majority of would-be fiction borrowers were referred to smaller libraries at the district and street-committee levels.

In Guangzhou, as of late 1979, slightly over 50 street committee "culture stations" (*wenhuazhan*) had been partly or fully reactivated, having been closed during the Cultural Revolution. Before the Cultural Revolution there had been about 90.[29] The purpose of libraries at this level, in sharp contrast to the research libraries, was precisely to supply fiction and other popular materials to the reading public. Still, the would-be borrower was often frustrated, and for several reasons. First, there were no effective incentives for the people in charge of district and street libraries to acquire books that readers really wanted. Why fight to acquire copies of *The Count of Monte Cristo* when it was so much easier to pick up a song book of national-minority tea-pickers praising Chairman Hua? One got the same pay whether there were many borrowers or few, and more leisure time if there were few. Second, even if some good books came in, they did not stay in. The two-to-three-week borrowing periods, which frequently lacked fines to enforce them,[30] were commonly ignored as readers hungrily shared their goodies through private arrangements with friends and acquaintances. Third, since libraries did not have open stacks, it was often difficult to determine what was available for borrowing. It was frustrating to ask a library attendant time and again to go in search of books that were not on the shelves. This circumstance put an obvious premium on cultivation of personal relationships with library staff, who could be very helpful in reporting what "hot" books were available, as well as in discreetly setting them aside. Some libraries sought to prevent these practices by using so-called "half-open stacks," where books were placed behind sheets of glass with only an inch-wide crack left open, to allow one to push a desired book inward far enough to indicate it to an attendant on the other side. But most libraries could not afford to construct half-open stacks, and to open the stacks entirely would have been folly. For several reasons, then, district and street-committee libraries were often far from ideal.

But, when a library was well stocked and well run, it was heavily used. At the small library referred to on p. 227 and in Appendix 1, the maximum number of books that could possibly be borrowed at one time, to calculate from the number of borrowing cards and the number of books allowed per card, was about 12,600 per month. The actual number borrowed per month averaged 5,313 for January-March 1980, indicating a very intense use of borrowing cards.

Besides public libraries, various work units and branches of the Communist Youth League had reading rooms from which members could check out books. At one Youth League reading room near Guangzhou, the borrowing period was one month with a 0.50-yuan fine for late return of books. All workers at the local unit could borrow, but formal priority went to League members. A much larger factory, the No. 27 Locomotive Plant in Beijing, had in 1979 a library of 90,000 volumes housed in 35 separate reading rooms for use by 10,300 workers. Two-thirds of the books were literature, primarily fiction.[31] The best work-unit libraries were in units concerned with education or entertainment, where sometimes good collections of even "internal-circulation" fiction were on the shelves. Yet many work-unit libraries, though easier to use than the public libraries, experienced the normal problems of procuring popular items and distributing them fairly.

It is almost certainly true that many more books were borrowed from friends in the late 1970s than from libraries. It is even likely that more *library* books were borrowed from friends than from libraries. Library books so popular as to be passed around without revisiting the library were called "flying books" (*feishu*), and there was little that libraries could do to stop them from flying. To levy fines was to tilt against windmills, because "sub-borrower's fees," which the library borrower could charge to his friends, could easily cover the fines. Even at the prestigious Academy of Social Sciences, someone checked out the only copy of *The Count of Monte Cristo* from the Academy library and set up his own system of waiting lists. The four-volume edition was lent out sparingly, one volume per person per day, lest the precious book "fly" elsewhere. To be sure, *Monte Cristo* is not a typical case. It is very difficult to estimate an average number of readers per instance of borrowing from libraries, but I asked this of librarians in China wherever I could and got estimates that averaged between two and three. For flying books the figure could be in the hundreds.

Subscriptions to Literary Periodicals

Except for a handful of unofficial publications, which eventually disappeared, all newspapers and magazines in China that came out with reliable periodicity in 1979–1980 were distributed through the Post Office. As of April 1980, there were about 1,500 such periodicals, of which 110 were literary. Each periodical was assigned a maximum circulation figure by the State Publication Administration, which also readjusted these ceilings from time to time and helped enforce them through allocations of paper. *Literary Works,* Guangdong's provincial literary magazine, began with a ceiling of 50,000 when it was revived in 1972.[32] The ceiling rose quickly, partly because paper is plentiful in Guangdong and partly because the comparatively daring editorial policy at *Literary Works* created a large nationwide demand for it. The ceiling was 70,000 by mid-1978, 210,000 in early 1979, and 500,000 in early 1980.[33] The actual circulation of *Literary Works* was 460,000 in early 1980, and at no point was far below the permissible ceiling figure. It was true of most literary magazines that their actual circulations hovered near the permissible limits, but *Literary Works* was very unusual in the height of its limits. At 500,000 it was the largest in China for a provincial-level literary publication, above the norm by a factor of about 10. *Guangzhou Literature and Art,* the city-level literary magazine in Guangzhou, also had, at 300,000, the biggest circulation in China for a literary magazine of its kind.[34] Every time the ceilings were raised for these two Guangzhou magazines, they would place newspaper advertisements aimed at raising their actual circulations. When the actual circulations neared the limits, the Post Office would instruct the magazines to cease advertising.

But, regardless of how high or low the ceilings were, how were magazines actually distributed? The Post Office coordinated an elaborate system of quotas that specified how many copies of every publication should go to each province and city. For *Harvest,* published in Shanghai, for example, 60,000 copies were kept in Shanghai as of June 1980, and 68,000 copies were allocated to nearby Jiangsu province, but only 4,000 to Sichuan province; 9,000 copies were given to Beijing, where many "leading comrades" resided, while only 1,000 went to Guangzhou. The quotas were not necessarily the last word, however. Cities and provinces could trade for higher allotments, either by relinquishing their rights to certain other publications or by trading other material goods. In 1979, Hunan province traded 15 tons of its paper allotment in exchange for 12,500 extra copies of *Literary Works.*[35] Besides this kind of flexibility, there was an unwritten understanding in most provincial capitals that local favoritism would be winked at. For example, *Literary Works* and *Guangzhou Literature and Art* could be supplied to Guangzhou residents well in excess of Guangzhou's quotas. Thus, in April 1980, Guangzhou was getting more than its quota of 60,000 copies of *Literary Works,* more than its quota of 30,000 copies of *Guangzhou Literature and Art,* but exactly its quota of only 1,000 copies of *Harvest* from Shanghai.[36] With similar imbalances in other cities, a kind of "grass is greener on the other side" mentality could develop among readers from the mere fact of relative scarcity. For example, in January 1980, *Literary Works* carried a story by Liu Binyan called "Warning,"[37] in which the ghosts of four deceased followers of the Gang of Four grumble to one another from inside the still-faintly-warm ashes in their cinerary caskets, thereby delivering the author's allegorical warning that political extremism is not dead. The story raised considerable furor in Shanghai and Beijing, but not in Guangzhou. Around the same time, Guangzhou readers were running to one another with word of Wang Ruowang's "Hunger Trilogy," published in Shanghai in *Harvest*,[38] a work that compares the author's experiences in a Kuomintang prison in the 1930s and in a People's prison in the 1960s.

Distribution within cities was governed by Post Office policies that allocated separate portions of each supply to subscriptions and to retail sales.[39] Periodicals with technical, scholarly, or politically sensitive uses went exclusively to approved subscribers. Such periodicals were a numerical majority of the total of 1,500 handled by the Post Office in 1979–1980, but few literary magazines were in this group. Subscriptions to literary magazines were dispensed in basically a two-tiered system of priorities. Certain officials and work units had first claim, especially if their work was in any way related to literature. In Guangzhou, for all literary magazines except local ones, *City of Flowers, Literary Works* and *Guangzhou Literature and Art,* demand from work units and other priority subscribers used up the entire supply of subscriptions and left few copies, if any, for retail. Ordinary citizens could get subscriptions to the local literary magazines, but there were waiting lists for that privilege, and many would-be subscribers complained that connections were a more reliable means of access than waiting lists. Even those who managed to get individual subscriptions were limited (unless they were special people) to three months. The reason for the three-month rule was to try to maintain reader morale by sharing the privilege of a subscription and avoiding the impression that access was a closed system.

For basically the same reason, the Post Office made a special point of ensuring that a good portion of local literary magazines, usually approaching 50 percent, was reserved for retail sales. This way even non-subscribers could aspire to personal ownership of a copy or two. Retail sales in Guangzhou were made at the local post offices on Beijing Road, on People's Road, and at Dongshan, where many well-placed families resided. In 1979–1980, news of the impending arrival of an issue of *Literary Works* or *Guangzhou Literature and Art* would spread quickly, and the retail supply of these magazines sold out in a matter of hours. When retail sales were indeed maintained near 50 percent, the result was to put even more pressure on the non-priority individual three-month subscriptions. For a person without pull, it was, ironically, far easier to subscribe to *Literary Works* in California than in Guangzhou.

Renting

Just as it was before 1949, the renting of fiction in books, magazines, and comic books has clearly been important in the People's Republic. But, compared to sales, it is very difficult to get a systematic picture of renting. The New China Bookstore system regulated much of the book renting by providing books to street-side stalls which, though not formally part of the New China system, worked on a commission basis and under guidelines set by the system. But an otherwise fruitful interview at the headquarters of the New China Bookstore in Beijing turned up no statistical information on renting, and I believe none exists. The renting situation was too ad hoc to be easily measured. To hazard a rule, the larger bookstores in the cities did not rent books, but the smaller the bookstore and the remoter the location, the more likely it was that renting was an important activity. In the village of Xian'gang in Kaiping county in Guangdong, there was no New China Bookstore in 1980, but there was a "Rising Sun Book and Cultural Supply Store" that, in addition to selling pencil sharpeners, thermos bottles, and many such items, sold and rented many books of fiction, mostly contemporary Chinese fiction. A book could be rented for a week or so for only 0.02 yuan, and was secured by a deposit of roughly the price of the book. At certain "Youth Culture Palaces" in towns and cities, books were also rented by the week for about 0.02 yuan and required a deposit of 2 yuan or, if a book was priced above 2 yuan, then slightly more than the fixed price. Some towns and cities had sidewalk bookstalls entirely devoted to the renting of comic-book fiction. Many of these comics were adaptations of the major Communist novels of the 1950s, like *Red Crag* and *Tracks in the Snowy Forest,* and some were based on post-1977 short stories by writers like

Liu Xinwu and Jiang Zilong. It is clear from the back covers that these comics were printed in hundreds of thousands of copies, and therefore were an important source of fiction for the marginally literate portions of the reading public. On the streets of Huhehot in summer 1980, it cost only 0.01 or 0.02 yuan to rent a comic book, and sidewalk stalls provided little benches where one could sit and read on the spot, thus avoiding a security deposit.

But, in general, books that were rented at stores, Youth Palaces, and bookstalls were not the most intensely sought-after books. And, if they had been, the normal deposit of roughly the purchase price would not have been sufficient to hold them. When the Beijing Post Office experimented in 1979 with renting popular items like *Masses Cinema* and *Harvest*, deposits in excess of the purchase prices proved to be insufficient.[40] It was partly because of the security problem that the Guangzhou Post Office, as of April 1980, had not tried to rent periodicals. *Harvest*, after all, could sell on the black market above its fixed price, and begin to circulate in any number of ways outside the official state-approved distribution system.

Unofficial and Underground Sales, Rental, and Exchange

We must begin this topic with a modest "rectification of names," because there has developed in Taiwan, Hong Kong, and other Chinese communities outside the PRC a misleading use of the term *underground*. The unofficial publications that appeared during 1978–1980 in China, such as *Today (Jintian)* in Beijing and *The Future (Weilai)* in Guangzhou, were a far cry from the "underground" or "dissident" literature of the Soviet Union and other Communist countries. In China, these publications were not, during the years they appeared, illegal; they could be exchanged openly, and the risk of "illegality" was only that the permissive policy towards them might change in the future. To call such publications "underground" not only misdescribes their status but obscures an important distinction between them and another kind of publication that truly *was* underground. But let us consider the whole picture systematically.

In 1979–1980, there were four basic kinds of reading materials corresponding to four different modes of distribution. We might call these (1) official restricted, (2) official unrestricted, (3) unofficial aboveground, and (4) unofficial underground. The two official categories represented the overwhelming majority of materials, and the distinction between them was whether they were "internal-circulation" materials or not. Of course, there are many gradations of "internality"; even materials that are unrestricted inside China admit a distinction between those that can be exported and those that cannot. For the intellectually curious reader in China, at least in 1979–1980, the forbidden reaches of "internal-circulation" literature (which might be called "overhead" if not "underground") were the most mysterious and alluring sources of fiction in society. These reaches, accessible only to winged cadres, contained highly coveted contemporary foreign literature, which was very scarce either on the ground or under.

The category of "unofficial aboveground," including journals like *Today* and *The Future,* can be defined in terms (to take a cue from Chinese mnemonics) of three lacks: lack of official support, lack of official control, and lack, at least in 1978–1980, of official proscription. For student literary magazines, such as *The Red Bean (Hongdou)* at Zhongshan University in Guangzhou or *Unnamed Lake (Weiminghu)* at Beijing University, it is useful to speak of "semi-official" status. *The Red Bean,* for example, began with a 1,000-yuan subsidy from Zhongshan University, and did "consult" with professors in the Chinese Department on its choice of manuscripts. Yet, it and other student magazines were close to the purely unofficial magazines in their relatively bold content as well as in their very low circulations. The government limited the circulation of unofficial publications by denying them permission to use the Post Office to reach subscribers, thus effectively limiting them to sale on the streets. (*The Red Bean* reached 10,000 per issue and *Unnamed Lake* 20,000.) In 1980, when all unofficial and semi-official publications were extinguished, it was not their publication per se that was banned but their last small market: Street sales were declared illegal.

The "underground" category consists of materials from basically three sources. Secretly written materials circulated in hand-copied (or mimeographed) form. Although very occasionally something handwritten turns up that had a serious political or artistic aim, the bulk of handwritten fiction was entertainment literature and of very poor quality. There were detective stories, horror stories, spy stories, love stories, and pornography. The manuscripts usually had been copied in several different people's handwritings, a few pages per person, and were bound together with string. The obvious clues to origins are that official stationery was sometimes used, reading "Zhanjiang District Revolutionary Committee," or "Revolutionary Committee of the Second People's Hospital of Kaifeng City," and so forth. But such clues are almost useless in tracing an author, because hand-copied stories were copied and recopied many times and at different places, all secretly. All hand-copied fiction has been technically illegal in the People's Republic. During the Cultural Revolution, when there was so little else to read, hand-copied fiction seems to have circulated much more than either before or after. In Guangzhou, many hand-copied volumes were turned in during 1978 when a call was issued, under a promise of amnesty, to hand them over to authorities.

The second kind of material that circulated underground was material from outside China brought in secretly. Guangzhou had more of such material than other cities because of its proximity to Hong Kong, from where it was possible, although not entirely simple, to carry books past customs inspectors. There is no way to estimate the size of this influx. The third source of underground material was, ironically, the officially restricted "overhead" material. When a high-ranking cadre could get *The Rise and Fall of the Third Reich,* so could his family members; and if they could, so could their friends, and so on, until Shirer's massive work became an underground commodity. Interestingly, both restricted materials and materials brought in from outside sometimes spread underground in hand-copied form.[41] Restricted materials sometimes came to circulate underground when workers at printing presses would compile extra copies surreptitiously. This required cooperation, since a given worker was normally assigned to print, say, only pages 1–10 of a book; but, if other workers were doing pages 11–20, and 21–30, and so on, copies could be assembled and strung between card-board covers.

There are no rules that limit literary works to a certain one of the four categories of materials I have outlined above. Not only could the "official restricted" category become "underground," as we have just seen; it could also be declassified to become "official unrestricted," something that happened to a great extent in the late 1970s with books ranging from Alex Haley's *Roots* to Edgar Snow's *Red Star Over China.* In addition, stories from "unofficial aboveground" publications like *Today* and *The Red Bean* were occasionally selected by progressive-minded editors for publication in official journals of both the "restricted" and "unrestricted" types.[42]

Clearly, the most important means of dissemination of fiction in 1979-1980 was borrowing. If a piece was popular, it mattered little whether it was official or unofficial, bought, rented, or purloined; it was passed around. No popular piece was ever available in nearly enough copies so that everyone could have his or her own. I asked editors of literary magazines in several cities to estimate the number of readers per issue of their magazines, and, while some were wise enough to point out that the question was so difficult as to be unfair, most estimated about 10; some said as high as 30. For library books, librarians estimated about 2 or 3 readers per borrowing. The proportions of the black market are equally difficult to estimate, though it is clear that the more popular literary magazines in 1979-1980 could sell at double or more their "fixed price." Prior to the dramatic increase in the late 1970s in the supply of relatively interesting reading material, items such as *The Count of Monte Cristo* commanded a rent on the black market in Beijing of as much as 8 yuan for 24 hours. In Guangzhou in the mid-1970s, *Monte Cristo* could be exchanged for a Fenghuang Brand bicycle from Shanghai.

Oral Fiction

Most oral storytelling, like other kinds of popular performing arts (*quyi*), has been "organized" in the People's Republic.

Instead of gathering a crowd at a marketplace or in a teashop, the storyteller often stands on stage, before a microphone, and the audience sits in rows, sometimes even in numbered seats. These changes in the situation of *quyi* performance have affected tone and content as well as more external matters. Other *quyi* forms, such as comedians' dialogues (*xiangsheng*) and fast tales (*kuaiban shu* and *Shandong kuaishu*) have changed to suit modern political and technological demands. But traditional-style storytelling has adapted less well: Its main audience (excepting an occasional radio audience) are older people who listen nostalgically. Scholars are concerned to "preserve" storytelling.[43]

The younger generation, meanwhile, has become quite attached to what might be viewed as the storytellers' functional replacement—modern-style storytelling on the radio. The Central People's Broadcasting Station, which broadcasts throughout the country, used 9–10 percent of its air time in 1979 on fiction. It broadcast primarily modern-style narrations, frequently with violins or other Western music in the background. (Occasionally, when a story involved much description and little dialogue, old-style storytellers were used to make the narrative livelier than a "straight" modern narrator could.)[44] Well-known short stories like Liu Xinwu's "The Homeroom Teacher," Zhang Jie's "A Youth Like This," and Lu Xinhua's "The Wound" were presented in slightly saccharine narrations of 20 to 30 minutes each. Yao Xueyin's voluminous novel *Li Zicheng* was done in 30-minute installments reliably at 12:30 p.m. every day, so that listeners could count on picking up the continuation of the story during their lunch and siesta breaks. Officials at the Central People's Broadcasting Station in Beijing reported receiving a great number of letters about the timing of these broadcasts. Youth, in general, insisted that the noon hour was best, while older people complained that noontime naps had become impossible because of blaring radios.[45] Being entirely oral-aural, radio fiction was closely related to "word-of-mouth" literature (*koutou wenxue*), which we have mentioned above in connection with gossip. Popular stories heard on the radio spread quickly by word of mouth. In fact, the radio audience in China in 1979–1980 was very likely the biggest fiction audience of all, given the relative pervasiveness of radio (broadcast over loudspeakers even in small villages, at least in Guangdong) and its circumvention of the barriers of literacy and cost.

TYPES OF READERS AND THEIR PREFERENCES

It is not easy to define a fiction readership, and even less easy to measure one after it is defined. Yet, in contemporary China, as in other places and times, the place of fiction in society cannot be understood without at least some reference to levels and types of readership. Impressions of readership groups are easy to come by in China, because readers themselves often claim rather formulaically that "educated youth" read the fiction magazines, workers prefer detective stories, young women prefer love stories, and so on. But, while these commonly accepted formulas may hold at a high level of generality, there is certainly no purity in the correspondence between readership groups and certain kinds of fiction. University students, for example, who in 1979–1980 eagerly read all the contemporary Chinese literature they could find, also visited the library for Soviet detective stories from the 1950s, borrowed any foreign fiction they could, and saved their hand-copied love stories from the Cultural Revolution just for good measure. The difficulty of procuring reading materials prevented the development of highly specialized interests among all but the most privileged readers. Most were limited to whatever they could lay hands on. But, despite overlapping interests among readers, and many ad hoc reasons for their reading choices, it is still important to analyze levels of readership. Four basic categories are useful.

The Masses

The peasant masses do not read. This is not to denigrate them, obviously, or to say they do not occasionally read signs, posters, parallel couplets at doorways, family genealogies, debit notices, and other things that require various kinds of "functional" literacy. It is simply to say they seldom if ever read fiction or other kinds of literature. (I am not counting urban youth who have been relocated in the countryside as peasants. They will be included in other categories below.) Even within cities, including cities like Guangzhou with comparatively good school systems, we still cannot say that the masses read fiction, if *masses* is taken to mean the majority of the population. In Guangzhou in 1979–1980, radio fiction came closer to having a truly mass audience, and films and television were quickly approaching the same audience breadth.

One way to conceive the non-reading portion of the populace is to view them as those who are prevented or deterred from reading by various impediments. The most important of such impediments appear to be (1) illiteracy, (2) cost of reading materials, (3) difficulty of access to materials, and (4) availability of alternative amusements.

Measuring literacy is notoriously difficult, and part of the difficulty comes from the problem of definition. Estimates of adult literacy in China in the early 1980s as high as 76.5 percent and even 95 percent[46] only beg the question of what kind of literacy is being measured. If we assume that education at least through six years of primary school is normally necessary to produce a fiction reader, it would appear that about 30 percent or 50 percent of China's population as a whole had this level of education in 1979–1980.[47] Exceptional cases of self-taught literacy do exist, but are far outnumbered by cases of what one researcher has called "recurrent illiteracy,"[48] meaning the loss later in life of reading skills acquired in schools. Lower rates of primary education and atrophy of reading skills have both been more severe in the countryside than the cities. In major cities such as Guangzhou, in fact, literacy was good enough that it clearly was not the most important barrier to the reading of fiction.

Among the more important problems was the cost of fiction. A young worker in Guangzhou in 1979–1980 was typically paid about 40 yuan per month, about half of which was necessary to cover one person's food. After clothing, rent, and utilities were paid for,[49] many young families could not consider buying fiction; even a single worker or a working couple without children had to make hard choices before doing so. Editors at the jumbo-sized literary periodical *City of Flowers* were rightly proud in 1979–1980 to point out how many young workers sought to buy their journal in spite of the considerable asking price of 1 yuan per copy.

But, in spite of the price problem, would-be buyers of popular books and magazines, at least in 1979–1980, usually far exceeded the supply for sale, leading to the fast sell-outs we have noted previously.[50] Thus, if cost was a greater barrier than illiteracy in the cities, the problem of access was often more important than cost. The access problem was especially crucial for the many who could not afford to buy at all and had to rely upon borrowing, thereby encountering the several problems of borrowing we have already discussed.

The comparatively easy availability of alternative amusements in major cities, such as Guangzhou, Beijing, and Shanghai, inevitably reduced fiction reading in 1979–1980 from what it otherwise would have been in these comparatively literate communities. In cities such as these, whether in China or in the modern West, a lower-than-possible rate of fiction readership does not suggest illiteracy so much as the fact that many people who could be reading a book if that were their choice are watching television, film, or something else instead. In 1979, 95 percent of the 2,000 workers at the No. 3 Universal Machine Works in Beijing preferred films to fiction, according to an officially approved estimate.[51] The preference for films was probably even stronger among Guangzhou workers, who had more access to television, and in particular to television from Hong Kong, than workers in other cities.

While non-readers of fiction appear to have been a majority in the cities, although not a very large one, we leave as the estimate of their numbers the remainder after the following groups have been accounted for.

The Popular Readership

This group can be defined as those who had sufficient literacy to read fiction, who could afford it and get access to it, and who chose to read it instead of (or more commonly in addition to) various alternative amusements, but who did not qualify for the more elite readership groups we shall discuss below. The popular readership in the cities were mostly young people (under

35) who were workers, either industrial or clerical. According to statistics at the Shanghai Library, in May 1980 "workers" or their units were responsible for 62 percent of all book-borrowing, most of which was borrowing of fiction.[52] Statistics on borrowing by sex are not available, but librarians at Shanghai and elsewhere estimated a rough parity between the sexes,[53] at least up until normal marriage ages in the mid-twenties are reached. (After marriage, according to librarians at the Jiangmen Library in Guangdong, men use the library more than women because the women become "busier.")

The size of the popular readership can be estimated only roughly. For a city like Guangzhou, one way to construct an estimate is from circulation figures for the local literary magazines. In 1980, *Literary Works* was easily the most circulated literary magazine in Guangzhou at 60,000 copies per issue, including both subscriptions and post office sales. Assuming an average of about 10 readers per copy (the estimate of the magazine's editors) the readership of *Literary Works* in Guangzhou may have been about 600,000 or about 12 percent of the city's population. Beyond this number one must account for perhaps an equal number of readers of popular detective, adventure, or love stories, who would find *Literary Works* too difficult, or too political, for their tastes. Correspondingly, 100,000 or 200,000 would have to be subtracted from the total figure to count among the more elite readers we shall discuss below. In sum, the popular readership in Guangzhou would seem to be about a million readers or slightly more—around 20 percent of the population. Other ways of estimating the size of the popular readership point towards approximately the same result.[54]

The tastes of the popular readership in 1979–1980 (as, no doubt, in many years before and after) were for detective and anti-spy (*fante*) stories, tales of daring adventure, and tearful love stories. With the lone exception of Zhang Yang's *The Second Handshake* (see pp. 230–231), the official Chinese press was not publishing works of this kind by Chinese authors.[55] Readers had to look to foreign fiction in translation, which the Chinese press did publish in considerable amounts, or to the hand-copied fiction that had circulated widely during the Cultural Revolution.

The Count of Monte Cristo and *The Adventures of Sherlock Holmes* were clearly among the most popular works in many of China's major cities. The evidence for this is impressively widespread.[56] Ellery Queen was also "hot" during 1979–1980, as was Agatha Christie, partly because a film of her *Death on the Nile* was being shown so successfully. The Jiangsu People's Publishing House published *Murder on the Orient Express* in 1980, while Shanghai municipal officials were complaining that "some publishers pay no attention to quality" as they print detective stories in batches of "hundreds of thousands at a time."[57] Although translations of Soviet anti-spy stories, which were widely available in the 1950s, were not being reprinted in 1979–1980, they were still circulated by libraries and informally among friends, and were quite popular. Readers in Guangzhou unabashedly expressed fondness for "KGB novels," despite the anti-Soviet policies of the Chinese government in 1979–1980. In the 1950s, many Chinese anti-spy stories had been written in imitation of the KGB novels (except that the KMT joined the CIA as villains), and these, too, were still very popular in 1979–1980. But, on the whole, the political messages in these stories, both Soviet and Chinese, were unimportant. Other than labeling clearly the "good" and "bad" people, a structural requirement of the genre, the political labels were quite aside from the interest of the storytelling.

The nature of popular tastes suggested by the foreign and foreign-influenced entertainment fiction published in the People's Republic is confirmed by underground hand-copied volumes. All but one of the nine hand-copied stories I have been able to find betrays strong influences from Western popular fiction. Four are actually set in foreign countries, and the others in Westernized Chinese cities like Hong Kong, Shanghai, or wartime Chongqing (Chungking), where foreigners and foreign things are naturally part of the scene. For example, in "An Embroidered Shoe" ("Yizhi xiuhua xie," author unknown), the young hero uncovers a KMT plot to blow up Chongqing by using his romantic liaison with the daughter of a KMT official. In "The Annihilation of the Underground Stronghold" ("Dixia baolei de fumie"), stalwarts from public security, also in Chongqing, untangle a fantastically complex web of intrigue and finally locate, beneath a graveyard, an underground American chemical research laboratory whose mission is to develop poisons for use in the Korean War.[58] The stories also reflect strong interest in technological gadgets (such as Rolex watches that double as secret radio transmitters); in clever deception (a tough detective's disguise as a foppish Overseas Chinese); and in the macabre (a dingy house where blood oozes under doors at midnight, a corpse leaps to its feet, and rows of coffins are prelabeled for the living).

But, for all the obvious debts the stories owe to Western entertainment fiction, they also employ, not surprisingly, certain established Chinese values and ideas. Assistant detectives always defer to their chief, even to the extent of abandoning a chase in order to report to headquarters for authoritative instructions. Dance halls are considered slightly barbarian, and the women one finds in them suggest the fox-fairy temptresses of traditional stories and, sometimes, the aggressive, overly Westernized women in much modern Chinese popular fiction. Occasionally, some explicit tenets of the Communist Revolution are observed, for example, that a "worker" is bound to be an honest person, or that counterrevolutionaries, "as Chairman Mao has taught us,"[59] must be entirely annihilated; yet politics, as noted above, is not vital to the storytelling. The two love stories I have seen among hand-copied volumes are tearful triangular affairs, some of whose cultural roots are easily located in Chinese tradition.[60] Although I have seen no example, pornographic fiction clearly also circulated in hand-copied form in 1979–1980.[61]

Nearly everything that hand-copied stories have to offer is in their plots, which are complicated, very fast-moving, and full of crucial coincidences. Episodes are loosely linked in the manner of traditional Chinese vernacular novels, although shifts of direction can be truly startling. There is no warning when the character one presumes to be the main protagonist (for example, because of his long and splendid record of catching spies) is suddenly shot dead and the story line moves to someone else.[62] These unceremonious jolts, along with numerous contradictions, omissions, mistaken characters, and so on, are all signs of the hasty and casual creation (or re-creation, since they were recopied many times) of hand-copied volumes.

Concerned Educated Youth

The term *educated youth* (*zhishi qingnian*) is used in China to mean secondary-school graduates who are working, or going to college, or waiting for either work or college.[63] Many of them in 1979-1980 were part of the popular readership just described. But some—whom we might call "concerned educated youth" and who were a large portion of educated youth in Guangzhou and other major cities—read fiction for more than entertainment. They enjoyed, sometimes passionately, reading political and social criticism in fiction, and were the core readership of the contemporary Chinese stories that "revealed the dark side" of society and "spoke for the people." They also enjoyed foreign fiction, including popular works, but were much more interested than the popular readership in seriously learning about Western life and literature. They frequently saw the West as offering attractive alternatives to Chinese ways of doing things. Many in this group had grown up as Red Guards in the Cultural Revolution and later came to feel deeply resentful that they had been deceived and ten years of their lives wasted. They were articulate and highly conscious of themselves as a distinct generation, comparatively free from what they perceived, in various degrees, as the hypocrisy of the older generation. They talked to one another about literature more than the other readership groups. Word of an exciting new story often spread among them well in advance of actual access to the book or magazine in which it appeared. When they believed that a certain story spoke for "us," they consciously championed it.

A more detailed sense of their reading habits and specific preferences can be gained from the results of surveys among 74 literature students at Zhongshan University in spring 1980 (Appendix 2), although the circumstances of the surveys' administration probably introduced a certain bias towards giving the "right" answer—what one ought to prefer rather than what one does prefer. The answers to questions 4 and 5, which asked what the students had been reading in the two weeks previous to the survey, are tabulated as numbers of titles in three categories rather than as lists of all titles cited by the respondents, because the latter listing would have been too cumbersome. In general, the lists reveal that Zhongshan students had been reading a wide range of materials whose idiosyncrasies probably reflect the chance of what was available more than any finely honed preferences. But it is certainly significant that most items were either (1) contemporary Chinese stories and plays, especially ones containing sharp social criticism, or (2) foreign works in translation, including classics (*Wuthering Heights, Anna Karenina*), more popular works (*Gone with the Wind*), and contemporary entertainment (*From Russia with Love, Star Wars*). Some had been reading the Taiwan writer Bai Xianyong, whose works were newly available in the People's Republic. In response to question 9, about their favorite works of all time, 61 percent listed *Dream of the Red Chamber*, yet one must wonder how much this represents merely the bestowal of accolades upon the definitive Chinese novel. In their answers to question 4 about what they actually had been reading recently, no student mentioned *Dream*—or even, with the exception of one mention of *The Golden Lotus*, any traditional Chinese fiction of any kind. Equally surprising, no modern Chinese works from before 1976 were mentioned.

Educated youth at Zhongshan University, and in Guangzhou generally, were probably not completely representative of their cohort elsewhere in their interest in Western fiction and traditional Chinese fiction. More and easier access to foreign works and to Hong Kong culture gave Guangzhou youth a better informed and more diversified interest in life and literature outside China. To be sure, fads in Western things (rock 'n' roll, sunglasses) swept Chinese cities everywhere in 1979–1980, but in Guangzhou youth were more accustomed to foreign culture and consequently more relaxed about it. They too observed fads, but against a background of broader interests.[64]

A first approximation of the numbers of "concerned educated youth" in a city like Guangzhou is possible by estimating the number of college students (about 40,000–45,000 in 1979–1980)[65] and multiplying by 3 to 5 to account for would-be college students. (based on application-to-acceptance ratios)[66] who were basically similar to college students in their reading habits. For Guangzhou this yields an estimate of about 120,000 to 225,000. To be sure, there were some college students and would-be students, especially in the sciences, who did not read much fiction; but there were also some fiction-readers among educated youth who did not apply to college. Hence the estimate is still probably serviceable.

It is perhaps an indication of the relish with which the university students in the surveys pored over their fiction that, in fact, they seem to have read very slowly. They estimate themselves to have read an average of 12.8 hours a week (question 5), and the equivalent of about 5 short stories per week,[67] or about 2.5 hours per short story. Short stories in contemporary journals were usually about 10-20 printed pages.

Elite Readers

This group of high-level intellectuals is even harder to estimate in numbers than other groups, although it is certainly small—at least an order of magnitude smaller than the preceding group of "young intellectuals." If, as a broad generalization, we say that the popular readership read fiction mostly for entertainment, and that intellectual youth frequently read it for socio-political involvement, then the elite readers, in general, read it as art. These people, usually well placed in society (at least after the Cultural Revolution), could often participate in privileged access to "internal circulation" materials and therefore read widely in Western as well as Chinese literature. They cannot be characterized by generation, as the other groups can, but were often part of a *family* culture that spanned generations. Many children of high-level intellectuals did manage to get through the Cultural Revolution without denouncing their parents as "stinking" bourgeois authorities, and continued to learn from their parents things they never could have learned elsewhere.

The three categories of readership distinguished above are not entirely comprehensive, of course. The first two both basically consist of young people, and the third group is very small. Does this mean there were hardly any middle-aged or elderly readers? While there is no doubt that youth predominated in fiction-reading, older generation non-elite readers certainly did exist. The oft-heard claim that "old workers" like to read things like *Romance of the Three Kingdoms* and *Dream of the Red*

Chamber doubtlessly had some living examples, although I
never found one. Certainly the readers of detective and adventure entertainment fiction included some old and middle-aged
people, as did the group that reads fiction for contemporary
socio-political commentary.

FURTHER RESEARCH

In broad terms, the picture of reader preferences that tentatively
emerges suggests strong continuities with pre-revolutionary
times. The excitement of twisting plots, coincidence, surprise,
and intrigue in "hand-copied volumes" is similar to that of popular stories from the late Ming era and earlier. At a slightly
higher readership level, the delight in exposing corrupt officials,
which was magnified in 1979–1980 by complaints about the
Cultural Revolution, is also continuous with the tradition of Wu
Jingzi's *The Scholars* and late-Qing "castigatory fiction," as well
as with an important strain in May Fourth fiction. The interest
in exploring Western fiction likewise has clear precedents in the
late Qing and May Fourth periods. These basic components in
the popular appeal of fiction—exciting storytelling, exposure
of wrongdoing, and exploration of the West—emerge as constants
through much modern social turmoil and political change, even
including putative "revolutions" in literature or culture.

By 1979–1980, very heavily politicized literature, especially
that from the Cultural Revolution, was thoroughly unpopular.
Yet the "classics" of socialist realism from the 1950s and early
1960s still did command some respect, and there can be little
doubt that they enjoyed a genuine popularity in their time. To
be sure, official sponsorship contributed to this "popularity";
but, measured by the basic wellsprings of popular appeal that
we find re-emerging in 1979–1980, the socialist realism of the
1950s and early 1960s may not have been too exceptional after
all. These works included exciting storytelling and intrigue
(*Tracks in the Snowy Forest* was certainly in part this); exposure
of corruption (*Morning in Shanghai* did this, as did most other
novels in portraying their villains); and even exploration of the
West (after all, for the popular-level Chinese reader, Russian
socialist realism like *How Steel is Tempered,* or Chinese works

written in this tradition, were as "new" or "Western" as anything they had ever found appealing before.)

The difficulty of doing field work in China will probably prevent us, for the foreseeable future, from completely understanding questions of popular preferences in fiction. Studies based on circulation figures alone, rather than data on actual preferences, will always be hostage to the objection that what readers buy depends primarily upon what is available to them; in 1979–1980, the problem of short supply was the major fact of the fiction market. The reading-preference surveys presented here are limited to university students in the humanities, and as such give us much less than the range and detail we need for understanding the readership as a whole. Many of our impressions of popular preferences must be gathered through less direct means, for example by assuming, as I have here, that hand-copied volumes must have been appealing in order to have been so widely and laboriously produced; or that *Sherlock Holmes* must hold obvious attraction for masses of readers if publishers are able to rely on it to fill their coffers quickly. But a great distance remains between such inferences and a detailed grasp of popular tastes in fiction. Even something as basic as literacy rates remains unclear; existing estimates not only vary widely but beg the question of what kind of literacy is at issue.

Clearly, another worthwhile approach to this field, as the chapter by Rudolph Wagner in the present volume shows, is comparison of contemporary Chinese popular fiction with that of the USSR and Eastern Europe. Some of the conventions of socialist fiction are basically the same everywhere; in China there was, moreover, direct borrowing of Soviet traditions in the 1950s. Yet, for both the Soviet and the native strains in contemporary Chinese fiction, we need to pay more attention to the question of how readers read: What, to paraphrase Jonathan Culler,[68] are the working assumptions the reader consciously or unconsciously brings to a text in interpreting it? The implicit codes shared by writers and readers need not be the same among cultures, and could reward comparative study. When a Chinese reader watches Liu Binyan expose social problems, he or she expects him to "speak for the people" in a sense that by no means duplicates the expectations of an American who reads the "muckraking" of Upton Sinclair or Woodward and Bernstein. Assumptions about the writer's role and moral duty are different in China, and, since they are revealed in textual signs, they can be studied. But, if the study of the reading process of Western fiction is still in its infancy, it is not yet *in foetus* for the China field, where some of the basic facts of who reads what still remain largely to be discovered.

APPENDIX 1

Borrowings per month from a *xian* library in Guangdong

Field	January 1980	February 1980	March 1980*	Total
Marxism-Leninism-Mao Zedong-Thought	2	0	0	2
Philosophy (including political)	5	5	4	14
Government	12	6	17	35
Military Affairs	5	11	8	24
Economics	7	9	10	26
Culture and Education	89	59	77	225
Language	153	102	168	423
Literature	3,874	3,621	4,141	11,636
Art	115	145	129	389
History and Geography	92	77	84	253
Natural Science (general)	50	48	11	109
Mathematical Sciences and Chemistry	412	246	316	974
Astronomy and Earth Science	10	13	6	29
Biology	9	3	7	19
Medicine and Hygiene	87	62	84	233
Agriculture and Forestry	14	22	25	61
Industrial Technology	347	320	360	1,027
Communications, Transport, and Space Travel	17	14	15	46
Totals:	5,300	4,763	5,462	15,525

*Figures for March include only borrowings through March 28; the library was also open on March 29 and 30.

APPENDIX 2

Results of a survey at Zhongshan University, Guangzhou, among Chinese Department class of 1981 (59 respondents) and Foreign Languages Department class of 1980 (15 respondents), April 1980.

Question	Chinese Dept. (59)	Foreign Languages Dept. (15)	Total (74)
1. How many novels have you read in the past three months?	(avg.) 3.5	(avg.) 5.2	(avg.) 3.8
2. How many short stories have you read in the past three months?	43.5	22	39
3. How many plays have you read in the past three months?	2.7	2.8	2.7
4. What works have you read in the past two weeks?			
Number of contemporary (post-1976) Chinese titles listed*	108+	10+	118+
Number of earlier Chinese titles listed	1	0	1
Number of foreign titles listed*	31+	34+	65+
5. How many hours per week do you spend reading literature?	12.3	15	12.8
6. How many movies do you see per month?	4.3	3.7	4.2
7. How many modern-style plays do you see per year?	3.4	2.3	3.2

* The "+" sign indicates that these figures are minimums; they are based on lists of titles, some of which I have not been able to identify.

Question	Chinese Dept.	Foreign Languages Dept.	Total
8. How many hours per week do you spend watching television based on literary works?	1.8	1.9	1.8
9. What are your favorite literary works of all time, Chinese or foreign?			
Work			
Cao Xueqin, *Dream of the Red Chamber*	37	8	45
Luo Guanzhong, *Romance of the Three Kingdoms*	12	6	18
Stendhal, *The Red and the Black*	9	8	17
Shi Naian, *Water Margin (All Men Are Brothers)*	7	7	14
Yang Mo, *The Song of Youth*	8	3	11
Tolstoi, *Anna Karenina*	7	2	9
Nicholas Ostrovskii, *How Steel Is Tempered*	7	2	9
Qu Bo, *Tracks in the Snowy Forest*	7	1	8
Ethel Voynich, *The Gadfly*	6	2	8
Ba Jin, *Family*	6	1	7
Balzac, *Father Goriot*	6	1	7
Mao Dun, *Midnight*	6	0	6
Lu Xun, "The True Story of Ah Q"	6	0	6
Liu Qing, *The Builders*	6	0	6
Dumas (fils), *La dame aux camélias*	5	1	6
Balzac, *Eugénie Grandet*	5	0	5
Tolstoi, *Resurrection*	4	1	5

APPENDIX 2 *(Continued)*

Question	Chinese Dept.	Foreign Languages Dept.	Total
Work			
Dumas (père), *The Count of Monte Cristo*	1	4	5
Luo Guangbin and Yang Yiyan, *Red Crag*	4	0	4
Pu Songling, *Strange Stories from a Chinese Studio*	3	1	4
Some respondents preferred to mention an author or a kind of work, rather than a specific title, in response to the foregoing question. Most frequently mentioned were:			
The stories of Lu Xun	13	1	14
The stories of Chekhov	13	0	13
The works of Tolstoi	9	0	9
The plays of Shakespeare	7	1	8
Tang and Song dynasty poetry	6	1	7
The plays of Cao Yu	6	0	6
The works of Maupassant	6	0	6
The works of Balzac	5	0	5
10. What are your favorite pre-modern (pre-1919) literary works?			
Cao Xueqin, *Dream of the Red Chamber*	42	10	52
Luo Guanzhong, *Romance of the Three Kingdoms*	34	7	41

Question	Chinese Dept.	Foreign Languages Dept.	Total
Work			
Shi Naian, *Water Margin*	33	7	40
Wu Cheng'en, *Journey to the West (Monkey)*	16	4	20
Sima Qian, *Historical Record*	13	0	13
Poems of Li Bo	10	1	11
Wang Shifu, *Romance of the Western Chamber*	7	1	8
Works of Su Shi	7	0	7
Pu Songling, *Strange Stories from a Chinese Studio*	6	1	7
Poems of Du Fu	6	1	7
Poems of Li Qingzhao	5	0	5
Qu Yuan, *On Encountering Sorrow (Li sao)*	4	1	5
Anon., *Wonders New and Old (Jingu qiguan)*	4	1	5
Classic of Poetry (Book of Odes)	4	0	4
Some respondents chose to answer in more general terms, as follows:			
Tang dynasty poetry	24	0	24
Song dynasty poetry	21	0	21
Tang-Song essays	6	0	6
Ming-Qing fiction	4	0	4

APPENDIX 2 *(Continued)*

Question	Chinese Dept.	Foreign Languages Dept.	Total
11. What are your favorite works from the period 1919–1949?			
Work			
Ba Jin, *Family*	16	8	24
Cao Yu, *Thunderstorm*	20	2	22
Mao Dun, *Midnight*	20	0	20
Lu Xun, "The True Story of Ah Q"	12	0	12
Lao She, *Camel Xiangzi*	9	1	10
Cao Yu, *Sunrise*	5	1	6
Mao Dun, "Spring Silkworms"	5	0	5
Cao Yu, *Peking Man*	4	0	4
Mao Dun, *Eclipse*	3	0	3
Lu Xun, "Remorse"	3	0	3
Some respondents answered with reference to a particular writer, as follows:			
Lu Xun's works	36	5	41
Cao Yu's plays	17	0	17
Mao Dun's fiction	12	4	16
Ba Jin's fiction	13	1	14
Guo Moruo's plays	7	0	7

Question	Chinese Dept.	Foreign Languages Dept.	Total
Work			
Lao She's works	4	1	5
Zhu Ziqing's essays	4	0	4
Zhao Shuli's works	3	0	3
Wen Yiduo's poetry	3	0	3
Ai Qing's poetry	3	0	3
Yu Dafu's fiction	3	0	3
12. What are your favorite works from the period 1949–1966?			
Yang Mo, *The Song of Youth*	31	6	37
Qu Bo, *Tracks in the Snowy Forest*	30	5	35
Liu Qing, *The Builders*	30	0	30
Luo Guangbin and Yang Yiyan, *Red Crag*	20	3	23
Wu Qiang, *Red Sun*	18	1	19
Zhou Libo, *Great Changes in a Mountain Village*	9	1	10
Hao Ran, *Bright Sunny Days*	5	5	10
Liang Bin, *Keep the Red Flag Flying*	8	1	9
Li Yingru, *In an Old City Ablaze*	7	2	9
Essays of Yang Shuo	9	0	9
Feng Deying, *Bitter Roots*	3	4	7
Zhou Erfu, *Morning in Shanghai*	5	1	6
Fragrant Flowers Reblooming (1979, a collection of 1956–1957 stories)	6	0	6

APPENDIX 2 (Continued)

Question	Chinese Dept.	Foreign Languages Dept.	Total
Work			
Zhi Xia, *Railroad Guerrillas*	3	3	6
Chen Canyun, *Fragrance Pervading Every Season*	1	4	5
Poems of He Jingzhi	5	0	5
Poems of Guo Xiaochuan	5	0	5
13. What are your favorite works from the period following the Gang of Four (after 1976)? (Titles below, which lack generally accepted English equivalents, refer to short stories unless otherwise indicated.)			
Jiang Zilong, "Qiao changzhang shangrenji" (Manager Qiao takes his post)	19	0	19
Chen Rong, "Ren dao zhongnian" (long story) (When you get to middle age)	12	0	12
Wang Jing (pseud.), *Zai shehui de dang'an li* (film scenario) (In the annals of society)	11	0	11
Liu Binyan, "Ren yao zhi jian" (reportage) (Between men and monsters)	10	0	10
Chen Shixu, "Xiaozhenshang de jiangjun" (The small town and the general)	8	0	8

Question / Work	Chinese Dept.	Foreign Languages Dept.	Total
Zhang Jie, "Ai shi buneng wangji de" (Love cannot be neglected)	7	0	7
Zhang Yang, *Di'erci woshou* (novel) (The second handshake)	3	3	6
Wang Yaping, "Shensheng de shiming" (Sacred duty)	5	0	5
Ru Zhijuan, "Caoshang de xiaolu" (Path through the grasslands)	5	0	5
Lu Xinhua, "Shanghen" (The wound)	4	0	4
Gao Xiaosheng, "Li Shunda zaowu" (Li Shunda builds a house)	4	0	4
Li Kewei, *Nüzei* (film scenario) (The girl thief)	4	0	4
Ye Wenfu, "Jiangjun, buneng zheyang zuo" (poem) (General, you just can't do such things)	4	0	4
Xu Huaizhong, "Xi xian yishi" (A story from the western lines)	4	0	4
Cui Dezhi et al., *Bao chun hua* (play) (Harbinger of spring)	4	0	4
Kong Jiesheng, "Zai xiaohe nabian" (Across the river)	3	0	3
Zong Fuxian, *Yu wusheng chu* (play) (In a land of silence)	3	0	3
Chen Guokai, "Daijia" (long story) (The cost of it all)	3	0	3
Liu Xinwu, "Banzhuren" (The homeroom teacher)	0	3	3

APPENDIX 2 *(Continued)*

Question	Chinese Dept.	Foreign Languages Dept.	Total

Many other works were mentioned once or twice. Many residents volunteered that they preferred works "that expose the dark side," or "that make you think hard," or "that press you to action," etc.

14. What kind of foreign literature do you like?

Work			
Stendhal, *The Red and the Black*	8	3	11
Balzac, *Father Goriot*	8	0	8
Dumas (fils), *La dame aux camélias*	6	1	7
Ostrovskii, *How Steel is Tempered*	5	2	7
Dumas (père), *The Count of Monte Cristo*	4	2	6
Tolstoi, *Anna Karenina*	4	2	6
Voynich, *The Gadfly*	4	2	6
Tolstoi, *Resurrection*	3	3	6
Balzac, *Eugénie Grandet*	4	0	4
Rolland, *Jean Christophe*	4	0	4
Mitchell, *Gone with the Wind*	3	0	3

Many respondents answered with reference to writers, as follows:

Question Work	Chinese Dept.	Foreign Languages Dept.	Total
Shakespeare	22	4	26
Balzac	21	1	22
Tolstoi	17	1	18
Chekhov	14	0	14
Maupassant	8	1	9
Mark Twain	7	2	9
Hugo	7	1	8
Gorki	5	0	5
Dickens	3	1	4
Dumas (fils)	3	1	4
O. Henry	3	0	3
Shelley	3	0	3
Pushkin	3	0	3
Jack London	3	0	3

APPENDIX 3

Standards for the Fixing of Prices for New Books in Guangdong, May 1979

A. Charges for Texts

Category	Nature of material	Price per Printing Sheet[1] (in yuan)
1	Elementary and secondary school textbooks High-circulation[2] political propaganda or study materials	0.055
2	Popular reading materials Children's reading materials High-circulation[2] modern literary works Books on the social or natural sciences for educating general audiences High-circulation[2] scientific or technical books for educating general audiences	0.060
3	Reference books for elementary and secondary school teachers Ordinary books on the social or natural sciences Modern literary works Musical scores (numerical) of songs for the masses Books on science or technology for educating general audiences (including books on policy and regulations)	0.065
4	Secondary specialized teaching materials Relatively specialized books on the social or natural sciences Modern poetry, folk songs, and literary theory Musical scores (numerical) and ordinary books on music Ordinary books on science or technology Reference books on Chinese Traditional literature worth recommending Cartoon strips on modern topics	0.070
5	Secondary specialized teaching reference materials Specialized teaching materials for higher education Specialized scholarly works Traditional literature Cartoon strips on traditional topics Specialized regulations, standards, and handbooks	0.075

A. Charges for Texts

Category	Nature of material	Price per Printing Sheet[1] (in yuan)
6	Specialized teaching reference materials for higher education Internal circulation works on Chinese or foreign topics Special-use dictionaries	0.080
7	Children's reading materials in color:	
	from regular press	0.160
	from offset	0.200

1. A "printing sheet" (yinzhang) refers to a sheet of 0.86 square meters, from which 16 pages of a standard-sized literary periodical or 32 pages of a standard-sized book can be printed. When printing sheets of different sizes are occasionally used, the prices listed here vary proportionately. In all categories, prices can be higher for books with special bindings or designs, for specialized books with unusually small print runs, or for books more than 30% of whose lines are in a foreign language. Prices can also vary with quality of paper.

2. "High" circulation means print runs of 100,000 or more.

B. Charges for Paper-Bound Covers (per cover)[3]

Size of Cover (sq. cm.)	Length of Accompanying Texts	One to Three Colors (yuan)	Four Colors or More (yuan)
155	320 pp. or less	0.020	0.025
	321 " " more	0.025	0.030
269	160 " " less	0.030	0.040
	161 " " more	0.035	0.045
310	160 " " less	0.040	0.050
	161 " " more	0.045	0.055
537	80 " " less	0.050	0.070
	81 " " more	0.070	0.090

3. Hard covers are priced according to the materials used and standards set by the national-level presses. There are additional charges for sculptured or glossy surfaces and other special features.

APPENDIX 3 (Continued)

C. Charges for Illustrations and Lining Pages (per page)

Size of Page (sq. cm.)	Number of Colors	By Regular Press (yuan)	By Offset (yuan)	By Copperplate (yuan)
155	blank sheet	0.003	0.005	—
	one color	0.005	0.009	—
	multi-color	—	0.013	0.015
269	blank sheet	0.005	0.008	—
	one color	0.008	0.015	—
	multi-color	—	0.020	0.025
310	blank sheet	0.006	0.010	—
	one color	0.010	0.018	—
	multi-color	—	0.025	0.030
537	blank sheet	0.008	0.015	—
	one color	0.015	0.030	—
	multi-color	—	0.040	0.050

Notes
Glossary
Index

Introduction, by Jeffrey C. Kinkley

1. Huang Yongyu is the artist who got into trouble for his painting of an owl. Lao She's widow, Hu Xieqing, student of Qi Baishi, painted only in reds, greens, and yellows, for the reason cited; Geremie Barmé, "Flowers or More Weeds? Culture in China Since the Fall of the Gang of Four," *The Australian Journal of Chinese Affairs* (*AJCA*) 1:128, 132n10 (January 1979).

2. On China's imports of foreign culture, see Leo Ou-fan Lee, "Recent Chinese Literature: A Second Hundred Flowers," in Robert B. Oxnam, ed., *China Briefing, 1980* (Boulder, Westview Press, 1980), p. 66; and Marián Gálik, "Foreign Literature in the People's Republic of China between 1970–1979," *Asian and African Studies* 19:55–95 (1983). On underground and other non-official literature, see articles written by Bonnie S. McDougall and others in an issue McDougall co-edited of *Contemporary China* 3.4 (Winter 1979); Leo Ou-fan Lee, "Dissent Literature from the Cultural Revolution," *C.L.E.A.R.* 1.1:59–79 (January 1979); Chen Ruoxi, *Democracy Wall and the Unofficial Journals* (Berkeley, Center for Chinese Studies, University of California, 1982); and David S.G. Goodman, *Beijing Street Voices* (Boston, Marion Boyars, 1981).

3. Standard references, all distributed by the Harvard University Press, are Chow Tse-tsung, *The May Fourth Movement* (1960); Merle Goldman, ed., *Modern Chinese Literature in the May Fourth Era* (1977); Leo Ou-fan Lee, *The Romantic Generation of Modern Chinese Writers* (1973); and Benjamin I. Schwartz, ed., *Reflections on the May Fourth Movement* (Harvard University, East Asian Research Center, 1972). The standard history and criticism of the period's fiction is C. T. Hsia, *A History of Modern Chinese Fiction, 1917-1957*, 2nd ed. (New Haven, Yale University Press, 1971).

4. Hu Yaobang's maiden speech quashed optimism that Chinese literary policy, in its recurrent oscillations, might ever re-approximate the freedom of 1979-1980; Hu Yaobang, "Zai Lu Xun dansheng yibai zhounian dahui shang de jianghua" (Speech at the centenary celebration of the birth of Lu Xun), *Guangming ribao,* 26 September 1981. More moderate was Hu Qiaomu's 8 August 1981 speech to the Party Central Committee Propaganda Department; Hu Qiaomu, "Questions on the Ideological Front," *Beijing Review* 1982.4:15-18 (25 January 1982). Leo Ou-fan Lee thinks the current leaders intend a "middle course" in regard to literary freedom. See his "Chinese Literature for the 1980s: Prospects and Problems," in Norton Ginsburg and Bernard A. Lalor, eds., *China: The '80s Era* (Boulder, Westview Press, forthcoming in 1984). For updates on Chinese literary policy, by Winston L. Y. Yang and Nathan Mao, see the *Encyclopaedia Britannica Yearbooks,* "Literature: Chinese."

5. Rudolf G. Wagner, "The Cog and the Scout," in Wolfgang Kubin and Rudolf G. Wagner, eds., *Essays in Modern Chinese Literature and Literary Criticism* (Bochum, Brockmeyer, 1982), pp. 334-400. References on the Hundred Flowers are Merle Goldman, *Literary Dissent in Communist China* (Cambridge, Harvard University Press, 1967); D. W. Fokkema, *Literary Doctrine in China and Soviet Influence: 1956-1960* (The Hague, Mouton, 1965); and Hualing Nieh, ed., *Literature of the Hundred Flowers* (New York, Columbia University Press, 1981).

6. Quoted in Kam Louie, "Between Paradise and Hell: Literary Double-Think in Post-Mao China," *AJCA* 10:2 (July 1983).

7. Bai Hua (1980), cited in Michael S. Duke, "The Second Blooming of the Hundred Flowers: Chinese Literature in the Post-Mao Era," in Mason Y. H. Wang, ed., *Perspectives in Contemporary Chinese Literature* (University Center, Michigan, Green River Press, 1983). Also revealing is Sylvia Chan's interview with writers Chen Dengke and Cong Weixi; Sylvia Chan, "'Blooming and Contending': Chinese Writers' Responses on Chinese Literature," *AJCA* 8:127-136 (January 1983). For systemic constraints, see Perry Link, "On the Mechanics of the Control of Literature in China," in his *Stubborn Weeds: Popular and Controversial Chinese Literature after the Cultural Revolution* (Bloomington, Indiana University Press, 1983), pp. 1-28, and Bonnie S. McDougall, *Mao Zedong's "Talks at the Yan'an Conference on Literature and Art"* (Ann Arbor, Center for Chinese Studies, 1980).

8. Perry Link, ed., *Stubborn Weeds;* Link, ed., *Roses and Thorns: The Second Blooming of the Hundred Flowers in Chinese Fiction, 1979-80* (Berkeley, University of California Press, 1984); Liu Binyan, *People or Monsters? And Other Stories and Reportage from China after Mao,* ed. Perry Link (Bloomington, Indiana University Press, 1983); Helen F. Siu and Zelda Stern, eds., *Mao's Harvest* (New York, Oxford University Press, 1983); Lee Yee, ed., *The New Realism: Writings from China after the Cultural Revolution* (New York, Hippocrene Books, 1983); Mason Y. H. Wang, ed., *Perspectives in Contemporary Chinese Literature;* Edward M. Gunn, ed., *Twentieth-Century Chinese Drama: An Anthology* (Bloomington, Indiana University Press, 1983); Bonnie S. McDougall, ed. and tr., *Notes from the City of the Sun: Poems by Bei Dao* (Ithaca, Cornell University China-Japan Program, 1983). Special issues of *Renditions* (Hong Kong) and the *Bulletin of Concerned Asian Scholars* will focus on post-Mao literature, as will a book by Michael Duke. Official translations of new literature appear in *Chinese Literature* (Beijing) and under the imprint of Panda Books (Beijing), e.g., Gladys Yang, ed., *Seven Contemporary Chinese Women Writers* (1982), which translates stories by Zhang Jie and Chen Rong mentioned in this book. See also Liu Xinwu, Wang Meng and others, *Prize-Winning Stories from China, 1978-1979* (Beijing, Foreign Languages Press, 1982). German translations of controversial recent writings appear in Rudolf Wagner, ed., *Literatur und Politik in der Volksrepublik China* (Frankfurt, Suhrkamp, 1983). Many 1942-1977 works are available in Kai-yu Hsu, ed., *Literature of the People's Republic of China* (Bloomington, Indiana University Press, 1980). For analysis of Mao-era works, see Bonnie S. McDougall, ed., *Popular Chinese Literature and Performing Arts in the People's Republic of China, 1949-1979* (Berkeley, University of California Press, 1984).
9. Colin Mackerras, "The Taming of the Shrew: Chinese Theatre and Social Change Since Mao," *AJCA* 1:1-18 (January 1979). On the ideological skirmishes, see Irene Eber, "Old Issues and New Directions in Cultural Activities Since 1976," in Jürgen Domes, ed., *Chinese Politics After Mao* (Cardiff, University College Cardiff Press, 1979), pp. 203-227; Sylvia Chan, "The Blooming of a 'Hundred Flowers' and the Literature of the 'Wounded Generation,'" in Bill Brugger, ed., *China since the "Gang of Four"* (New York, St. Martin's Press, 1980), pp. 174-201.
10. Barmé, p. 131. For stories in translation, see Geremie Barmé and Bennett Lee, trs., *The Wounded: New Stories of the Cultural Revolution, 77-78* (Hong Kong, Joint Publishing Co., 1979). For background: Joseph S. M. Lau, "Literature that Hurts: The World of *Shang-hen* Fiction," *Journal of Oriental Studies* 20 (1983), forthcoming; Marián Gálik, "Some Remarks on 'Literature of the Scars' in the People's Republic of China (1977-1979)," *Asian and African Studies* 18:53-76 (1982); Richard King, "'Wounds' and 'Exposure': Chinese Literature after the Gang of Four," *Pacific Affairs* 54.1:82-99 (Spring 1981); and

Geremie Barmé, *"Chaotou wenxue*—China's New Literature," *AJCA* 2:137-148 (July 1979).

11. Kam Louie, "Youth and Education in the Short Stories of Liu Xinwu," *Westerly* 3:115-119 (September 1981). A more remarkable, in China, infamous case of a young person who switched from an extreme Maoist "my-Party-right-or-wrong" position to an extreme skeptical stance is Li Jian. See Kam Louie, "Between Paradise and Hell." To conservatives, Li was a traitor; to libertarians, an opportunist seeking to become a cause célèbre, so instead he became an "anti-cause célèbre."

12. Leo Ou-fan Lee discusses this story at greater length in his chapter in this volume and in "Gao Xiaosheng de 'Li Shunda zaowu' yu fanfeng yiyi," *Dangdai* (Hong Kong) 4:4-8 (15 December 1980). The most exciting literature of 1979 is surveyed in W.J.F. Jenner, "1979: A New Start for Literature in China?" *China Quarterly* 86:274-303 (1981).

13. Liang has published his autobiography; Liang Heng and Judith Shapiro, *Son of the Revolution* (New York, Knopf, 1983).

14. Howard Goldblatt, ed., *Chinese Literature for the 1980s: The Fourth Congress of Writers and Artists* (Armonk, M. E. Sharpe, 1982).

15. Leo Ou-fan Lee, "Chinese Literature for the 1980s."

16. We are blessed with a translation of a one-minute story (that's how long it takes to read it) which won a prize: "A Spring Night," *Beijing Review* 26.2:28-29 (10 January 1983). Summary: A kind stranger fixes a girl's broken bicycle. Lee, "Chinese Literature for the 1980s," points out another carrot dangled before writers: They are handsomely remunerated, both for their works and for membership in the Chinese Writers' Association.

17. Li Yi (editor prefers Lee Yee), ed., *Zhongguo xin xieshizhuyi wenyi zuopin xuan* (Selections from China's new realistic literature; Hong Kong, The Seventies, June 1980). This book is now but the first volume in a series. See also vol. 2, ed. Lee Yee and Bi Hua (Kee Fuk Wah; September 1980); vol. 3, ed. Bi Hua and Yang Ling (Hong Kong, Tiandi tushu youxian gongsi, May 1982); and vol. 4, ed. Bi Hua and Yang Ling (Hong Kong, Dangdai wenxue yanjiushe, December 1983). (Readers of Lee Yee's and Bi Hua's essays will note that these two pioneers in the study of post-Mao literature differ in their interpretations of what they both continue to call "new realism.") Also optimistic about continuing production of work of distinction, outside the exposure tradition, is W.J.F. Jenner, "Letter from Peking," paper from the St. John's conference, publication forthcoming. For an in-depth view of the achievement of one writer, see another essay from the St. John's conference, by Philip Williams, "Stylistic Variety in a PRC Writer: Wang Meng's Fiction of the 1979-1980 Cultural Thaw," *AJCA* 11:59-80 (January 1984).

1. Science Fiction, by Rudolph G. Wagner

I am indebted to the Cornell University Society for the Humanities and my 1981-1982 co-fellows there. Criticism and encouragement from St. John's conferees and Cornell colleagues, especially Mei Tsu-lin, Edward Gunn, Alex Zholkovski, and Ted Morris, were likewise of great benefit.

1. Rao Zhonghua, "Yongjiu de meili" (Eternal fascination), in *Zhongguo kehuan xiaoshuo daquan* (Compendium of Chinese science-fantasy fiction; Beijin, Haiyang chubanshe, 1982), I, 1. Rao Zhonghua and Lin Yaochen, *Kexue shenhua, 1976-1979 kexue huanxiang zuopin ji* (Science myths, a collection of 1976-1979 works of science phantasy; Beijing, Haiyang chubanshe, 1979), Introduction, p. 4.
2. Tong Enzheng and Shen Ji, "Shanhudao shang de siguang" (Death rays from Coral Island) received the 25th of 25 awards for 1978. It was published as *kexue huanxiang xiaoshuo* in *Renmin wenxue* 1978.8 (August 1978). On the provincial level, Wang Xiaoda, "Bo" (Waves) received a prize in Sichuan for children's literature for 1979-1980. See *Sichuan wenxue* (Sichuan literature) 1981.10:9 (October 1981). The piece was published in *Sichuan wenxue* 1979.4 (April 1979). Both stories figure also in Rao and Lin, ibid.
3. Rao/Lin; Zhongguo Qingnian Chubanshe (China Youth Publishing House), ed., *Kexue huanxiang xiaoshuo xuan* (Selected science-phantasy fiction; Beijing, Zhongguo qingnian chubanshe, 1980); a variety of science-phantasy fiction also appears in Gao Shiqi and Zheng Wenguang, eds., *(Ertong wenxue) Kexue wenyi zuopin xuan* ([Children's literature]: Selected works of science belles-lettres), 2 vols. (Beijing, Renmin wenxue chubanshe, 1980). Ye Yonglie, *Diule bizi yihou* (After the loss of the nose; Shanghai, Shaonian ertong chubanshe, 1979). Tong Enzheng, *Xueshan modi* (The magic flute from the Snowy Mountains; Beijing, Renmin wenxue chubanshe, 1979).
4. *Kexue wenyi*, ed. Sichuansheng Kepu Chuangzuo Xie'hui (Sichuan Association for Creative Works Popularizing Science), first issue May 1979, appears quarterly. *Beijing zhi chun*, May 1979.
5. Tong Enzheng's "Shanhudao shang de siguang" was made into a filmscript; *Kexue wenyi* 1 (January 1979), Rao/Lin. The film was shown in 1980. Ye Yonglie (and Wen Bianjing), "Fei xiang Mingwangxing de ren" (The man who flies to Pluto) in Rao/Lin is also a filmscript.
6. *Dianying chuangzuo* (Cinematic creations) 1979.3 (May-June 1979).
7. *China News Analysis*, no. 1140 (November 1978). *Asahi shimbun*, 16 September 1979. Meanwhile, a first study of Chinese science fiction has come out; Bruce Doar, "Speculation in a Distorting Mirror: Scientific and Political Phantasy in Contemporary Chinese Writing," *The Australian Journal of Chinese Affairs* 8:51-64 (July 1982).
8. The story by Yan Jiaqi, "Zongjiao, lixing, shijian" (Religion, reason, practice) appeared in the Japanese *SF zasshi* 1979.11 (November 1979). Tong Enzheng's "Death Rays . . ." has been translated into

Japanese in *SF hoseki* 1980.2 (February 1980). The social-science fiction by Su Ming, "Zai 2000 nian keneng fasheng de beiju" (A tragedy that may yet happen in the year 2000), *Beijing zhi chun* (May 1979), is translated in *Paris-Pekin* 1 (1980). I have presented lengthy excerpts from PRC science fiction stories in various radio features in German, in the Federal Republic of Germany.

9. E. Zamyatin, *My* (New York, Mezhdunaodnoe literaturnoe sodvuzhestvo, 1967). This is E. Zamiatin, *We,* tr. G. Zilboorg (New York, E. P. Dutton, 1924). I. Efremov, *Tumannost' Andromedy* (Moscow, Molodaia gvardia, 1958). This is I. Yefremov, *Andromeda,* tr. G. Hanna (Moscow, Foreign Languages Publishing House, no date, 1959?). G. and J. Braun, *Der Irrtum des Grossen Zauberers* ([East] Berlin, Verlag Neues Leben, 1972).

10. Lü Chen, "Fangwen Zhongguo SF zuojia Zheng Wenguang" (Interviewing the Chinese science fiction author Zheng Wenguang), *Kaijuan* (Hong Kong) 2.10:2 (May 1980).

11. The following science-phantasy writers were members in 1980: Gao Shiqi, Zheng Wenguang, Tong Enzheng, Ye Yonglie, You Yi. See Du Jian, "Tantan Zhongguo kexue xiaoshuo chuangzuo de yixie wenti" (Some questions concerning Chinese science fiction), *Kaijuan* 2.10 (May 1980).

12. Cf. Ye Yonglie, *Lun kexue wenyi* (Treatise on science belles-lettres; Beijing, Kexue puji chubanshe, 1980), pp. 95, 101.

13. Tong Enzheng et al., *Wuwannian yiqian de keren* (The visitor from fifty thousand years ago; Beijing, Shaonian ertong chubanshe, 1962).

14. Zheng Wenguang, *Fei xiang Renmazuo* (Flying toward Sagittarius; Beijing, Renmin wenxue chubanshe, 1979). Du Jian says it sold 300,000 copies in a few days; the edition I have consulted is the second, published in April 1980. It went from 50,000 (the first ed.) to 180,000. There might be regional reprints.

15. Ye Yonglie, "Kexue huanxiang xiaoshuo de chuangzuo" (Creation of science-phantasy fiction), *Kexue wenyi* 1980. 4:66 (April 1980). See his *Lun kexue wenyi,* p. 93.

16. Ye Yonglie, *Lun kexue wenyi,* pp. 95 ff.

17. Zheng Wenguang, "Chi You dong" (Chi You's cave), *Beijing wenyi* (Beijing literature and art) 1980.5 (May 1980). Tong Enzheng, *Xueshan modi;* Zheng Wenguang, "Taipingyang ren" (The human from the Pacific), in Rao/Lin.

18. Ye Yonglie, "Fei xiang Mingwangxing de ren."

19. Ye Yonglie, "Kexue huanxiang . . .." Cf. *Lun kexue wenyi,* p. 98.

20. Zheng Wenguang, *Fei xiang Renmazuo,* p. 282.

21. Tong Enzheng, "Shanhudao shang de siguang."

22. Zheng Wenguang, "Shayu zhenchabing" (The shark patrol fish), *Shaonian kexue* (Science for young people) 1979.5-6 (May-June 1979), summary in Rao/Lin, pp. 504 ff. Sima Chunqiu, "Juting chenmo" (The sinking of the giant ship), *Yalu Jiang* (Yalu River) 1979.9 (September 1979). Wang Xiaoda, "Bo."

23. Tong Enzheng, *Guxia miwu* (The puzzle of the old gorge; Shanghai, Shaonian ertong chubanshe, 1960; rev. ed. Shanghai 1978).
24. Liu Zhaogui, "B zhege mi" (The beta secret), in Rao/Lin.
25. Tong Enzheng, "Shanhudao shang de siguang," pp. 109, 131 ff. It should be mentioned that Soviet science-phantasy authors have not been remiss in countering these charges in the same vein. Efremov describes the world as happily Communist in his *Cas byka* (Moscow, 1970); only one group of humans has retired to a planet and established there a pseudo-socialist "ant-hill type" society, a clear reference to the Chinese. Cf. G. V. Grebens, *Ivan Efremov's Theory of Soviet Science Fiction* (New York, Vantage Press, 1978), p. 82.
26. See Zheng Wenguang, *Fei xiang Renmazuo*, p. 9; note the title of Wang Chuan's "Zhenjing shijie de Ximalaya-hengduanlong" (The Himalayan dinosaur that amazed the world), in Rao/Lin, pp. 202 ff.
27. Zhou Yang, "Xin minge kaituole shige de xindaolu" (New folk songs have opened a new road for poetry), *Hongqi* (Red flag) 1958.1 (January 1958); Guo Moruo, "Langmanzhuyi yu xianshizhuyi" (Romanticism and realism), *Hongqi* 1958.3 (March 1958). Zheng Wenguang says science phantasy uses "the method of romanticism" in his interview with Lü Chen, pp. 4, 5. Lou Qi, "Yinggai huanxiang" (Phantasy is needed), *Renmin wenxue* 1979.6:112 (June 1979), declares fable and "phantasy fiction" (*huanxiang xiaoshuo*) to be "romantic" works. Zheng Wenguang, "Kexue he minzhu de zange" (Paean to science and democracy), *Dushu* 1979.1 (January 1979) also says that Jules Verne already "used the method of romanticism," p. 69. In Tong Enzheng and Xiao Jianheng, remarks of this kind are conspicuously absent; cf. Xiao Jianheng, "Shilun woguo kexue huanxiang xiaoshuo de fazhan" (A tentative review of the development of Chinese science-phantasy fiction), *Kexue wenyi* 1980.4:61 ff. (April 1980); Tong Enzheng, "Tan-tan wo dui kexue wenyi de renshi" (Some words on my opinion about science belles-lettres), *Renmin wenxue* 1979.6 (June 1979).
28. *Kratkaia literaturnaia enciklopedia* (Sovietskaia Enciklopedia, 1968), *sub nauchno-khudozhestvennaya literatura*, V, 143. I have studied the "Soviet connection" of modern Chinese literature in other contexts, as in my "The Cog and the Scout: Functional Concepts of Literature in Socialist Political Culture: The Chinese Debate in the Mid-Fifties," in Wolfgang Kubin, Rudolf Wagner, eds., *Essays in Modern Chinese Literature and Literary Criticism* (Bochum, Brockmeyer, 1982); "Xiao Jun's Novel *Countryside in August* and the Tradition of 'Proletarian Literature'," in Fondation Singer-Polignac, ed., *La littérature chinoise au temps de la Guerre de Résistance contre le Japon* (Paris, Fondation Singer-Polignac, 1982); and "Der Moderne Chinesische Untersuchungsroman," in J. Hermand, ed., *Neues Handbuch der Literaturwissenschaft*, vol. 21 (Wiesbaden, Athenäum, 1979).
29. M. Gorki, "O Temakh," *Sovr* (Moscow, Gosudarstvennoe izdalst'vo chudozestvannoy literatury, 1953), XXVII, 97 ff. Il'in (pseud.) (1895–1953) was a Soviet writer of science popularization. In the 1930s,

Dong Chuncai translated his *Story of the Five-Year Plan* as *Wunian ji-hua;* cf. Xiao Jianheng, p. 65b.

30. On the Chinese translation, see Ye Yonglie, *Lun kexue wenyi,* p. 41. On Il'in, see Zheng Wenguang in Lü Chen, p. 5; Du Jian, p. 9; Ye Yonglie, ibid., pp. 37 ff.

31. K. E. Tsiolkovski (1857–1935) is mentioned as a classic by Zheng Wenguang, *Fei xiang Renmazuo,* Postface, p. 280.

32. Zheng Wenguang explicitly states in his interview with Lü Chen, p. 7, that most of the science-phantasy writers in China today are scientists. This is true for him, an assistant researcher at the Beijing Astronomical Station (p. 2), and for Tong Enzheng, an archeologist; see Tong Enzheng, "Wode shenghuo he chuangzuo jingli" (My experiences in life and creative writing), orig. in *Yuwen jiaoxue tongxun* (Language teaching bulletin) 1980.1 (January 1980), reprint in *Kaijuan* 2.10:14 (1980). For Ye Yonglie this is stated in Ni Ping, "Zhishi de bozhongzhe, ji xianjin kepuji gongzuozhe Ye Yonglie" (Of wide learning: Remembering the advanced science pop writer Ye Yonglie), *Dushu* 1979.3:124 (March 1979); no proof is necessary for such a well-known scientist as the dean of *Kexue wenyi,* Gao Shiqi.

33. *Lu Xun quanji* (Complete works of Lu Xun; Beijing, Renmin chubanshe, 1973), XI, 9. Sydney Finkelstein, "Kexue xiaoshuo de shijie" (The world of science fiction), *Yiwen* 1957.5 (May 1957). Ye Yonglie, *Lun kexue wenyi,* p. 89, complains that the only science phantasy of his that was published during the Cultural Revolution (in 1976) came out without the word *phantasy* (*huanxiang*). Lu Xun's old term was used again.

34. See Grebens, p. xviii, who based himself on *Enciklopediceskii slovar* (Moscow, Sov. Enciklopedia, 1960), III, 789.

35. E. Parnov, *Sovremennaia nauchnaia fantastika* (Moscow, Znamie, 1968), p. 4, quoted by J. Glad, *Extrapolations from Dystopia, a Critical Study of Soviet Science Fiction* (Princeton, Kingston Press, 1982), p. 137. See also p. 135 for statistics on readers of Soviet science fiction, and Darko Suvin, "Ein Abriss der Sowjetischen Science Fiction," in E. Barmeier, ed., *Science Fiction* (Munich, W. Fink, 1972), p. 318; H. Heidtmann, "A Survey of Science Fiction in the German Democratic Republic," in *Science Fiction Studies* 6.1:92 (1979).

36. A. Tolstoi, *Giperboloid inzenera Garina,* in *Moscow Sovietskaia literatura* (Moscow, 1933). In Chinese, A. Tuoersitai, *Jialin gongchengshi de shuangquxian.* Tolstoi's *Aelita* also appeared in Chinese.

37. S. Ivanov, "Fantastika i dejstvitel'nost," *Oktjabr* 1959.1:159, 155 (January 1979), quoted from J. Glad, p. 24. On Verne, cf. L. Heller, *De la science fiction soviétique, par delà le dogme, un univers,* tr. A. Coldefy (Lausanne, L'Age de l'homme, 1979), p. 52.

38. Heller, p. 46.

39. V. V. Maiakovskii, *The Bedbug,* tr. M. Hayward (New York, Meridian

Books, 1960). M. Bulgakov, D'javoliada-rokovye jajca (Moscow, Nedra, 1925). This is M. Boulgakov, Diablerie—les oeufs fatidiques, tr. Y. Hamant (Lausanne, L'Age de l'homme, 1971). See Heller, p. 43. M. Slonimski, "Masina Emeri," in Rasskazy (Leningrad, Gosudarstvennoe izadelst'vo, 1924), p. 71, quoted after Heller, p. 42.

40. Heller, pp. 131 ff.
41. Cf. Soiuz pisateli'SSSR, Proizvedeniia Sovetskikh pisatelei v perevo-dakh na inostrannje iazyki, 1945-1953 (Moscow, Vsesoiuznaia gosu-darstvennaia biblioteka inostrannoi literatury, 1924), p. 226.
42. Heller, p. 52.
43. Xiao Jianheng, "Bu shuijiao de nüxu" (The son-in-law who didn't sleep), in Rao/Lin. Cf. also Tong Enzheng's Xueshan modi, wherein the reliability of old travelogues is affirmed; and his pre-Cultural Revolu-tion Wuwannian yiqian de keren, which asserts the same for old Chinese astronomical records.
44. A. Britikov, Russkij sovetskij nauchno fantasticeskii roman (Russian Soviet science phantasy fiction; Leningrad, Izd. Nauka, 1970), p. 361. Heller, p. 251.
45. Yu Zhi, "Gediao bizi de daxiang" (Elephants sans proboscis), in Gao/ Zheng, I, 1 ff.
46. Zheng Wenguang, "Taipingyang ren," in Rao/Lin, pp. 48 ff.
47. Jean Chesneaux, The Political and Social Ideas of Jules Verne, tr. Th. Wikeley (London, Thames and Hudson, 1972), p. 43.
48. Chesneaux, pp. 168-174. In Tong Enzheng's Xueshan modi, reprinted in Rao/Lin, p. 356, the leadership of the "higher Party levels" is men-tioned.
49. Chesneaux, pp. 70 ff. The quotation is from p. 88.
50. Franceville is described in The Begum's Fortune. See Chesneaux, p. 72. Wang Xiaoda, "Bo," in Rao/Lin, p. 16. Liu Zhaogui, "B zhege mi," in Kexue huanxiang xiaoshuo xuan, pp. 283 ff.
51. Cf. R. Mathewson, The Positive Hero in Russian Literature, 2nd ed. (Stanford, Stanford University Press, 1975), ch. 3. The original illustra-tions supervised by Verne frequently contained pictures of these defi-ant heroes standing, arms folded, alone on a rock and gazing into the distance. See Chesneaux, pp. 79, 99.
52. This is explicitly referred to by Ye Yonglie in his "Kexue huanxiang xiaoshuo de chuangzuo," p. 67b.
53. Xiao Jianheng, "Shilun woguo kexue huanxiang xiaoshuo de fazhan," Kexue wenyi 1980.4 (April 1980). Ye Yonglie, Lun kexue wenyi.
54. "Bat": Ye Yonglie, ibid., p. 4; Zheng Wenguang, "Yinggai jingxin peiyu kexue wenyi zhege zhuhua" (We ought carefully to cultivate the flower of science belles-lettres), Guangming ribao, 20 May 1978. Gong Zhi, "Tichang kexue wenyi" (For science belles-lettres), Guangming ribao, 23 February 1979. "Pills": Ye, ibid., p. 6; Gao Shan, Jin Hai, "Shitan kexue wenyi de chuangzuo" (A tentative discussion of the creation of

science belles-lettres), *Guangming ribao,* 20 May 1978. The last created the happy formula that belles-lettres should be as closely bound in with science as "sugar which dissolves in water."

55. *Lu Xun quanji* (Beijing, 1973) XI, 10 ff. Lu Xun translated, or rather rewrote, Verne's *De la terre à la lune,* from a Japanese translation. He also translated *Voyage au centre de la terre.* Incidentally, he took the author of the first book for an American called Peilun, and the author of the second for an Englishman transcribed as Weinan. Much later, he planned to translate Fabre's magisterial work on the insects, but he died too early. For Lu Xun's later attitude toward science, see Leo Lee, "Genesis of a Writer: Notes on Lu Xun's Educational Experience, 1881–1909," in Merle Goldman, ed., *Modern Chinese Literature in the May Fourth Era* (Cambridge, Harvard University Press, 1977), pp. 172 ff.

56. The history of the *kexue xiaopin* is told in great detail by Ye Yonglie in *Lun kexue wenyi,* pp. 51 ff. The same book reprints Gu Junzheng, "Heping de meng" (Dream of peace), pp. 193 ff. For the others, see pp. 58 ff, 67.

57. Ye Yonglie, *Lun kexue wenyi,* pp. 86 ff. *Gediao bizi de daxiang* (Shanghai, Shaonian ertong chubanshe, 1956) is a tale of the time. The American article is the one by Finkelstein.

58. Zheng Wenguang, "Yinggai jingxin."

59. Ye Yonglie, *Lun kexue wenyi,* p. 86.

60. See *Xiaoshuo congbao* (Thicket of fiction) 1915.11 and 1915.12; *Xiaoshuo daguan* (The grand magazine) 1915.1; *Xiaoshuo yuebao* (The short story monthly) 1912.2 and 1912.4.

61. Liang Qichao, "Xin Zhongguo weilai ji" (The future of the new China), in his *Xiaoshuo zhuanji wuzhong* (Five pieces of fiction and biography; Shanghai, 1936); also in A Ying, ed., *Wan Qing wenxue congchao* (Anthology of late Qing literature) I, 1 (Beijing, Zhonghua shuju, 1960). Liang's translation, *Huanyou yueqiu,* is referred to by Xiao Jianheng, p. 62. The "utopian fiction" category appears in *Xiaoshuo shibao* (The fiction times) 1909.1; *Xiaoshuo congbao* 1915.7–13, 1916.21. Edward Bellamy, *Looking Backward 2000–1887* (Boston, Houghton Mifflin, 1888); Chinese under the title *Huitou kan* in *Wanguo gongbao* (Review of the times) XXV–XLIX, December 1891 to April 1892. Cf. Martin Bernal, *Chinese Socialism to 1907* (Ithaca, Cornell University Press, 1976), pp. 25 ff.

62. Gaoyangshi bucaizi, "Dian shijie" (Electric world), *Xiaoshuo shibao* 1909.1. Lao She, *Maocheng ji* (Cat country; Shanghai, Fuxing shuju, 1936). This is Lao She, *Cat Country,* tr. William Lyell, Jr. (Columbus, Ohio State University Press, 1970).

63. Yan Jiaqi, "Zongjiao, lixing, shijian," *Guangming ribao,* 14 September 1978. Zheng Wenguang, "'Bai mayi' he yongdongji" (The "white ant" and the perpetuum mobile), *Kexue wenyi* 1:19 ff (January–February 1979). Wei Yahua, "Wenrou zhi xiang de meng" (Dream of the cosy

home), *Beijing wenxue* 1981.1 (January 1981), also in *Xiaoshuo xuankan* 1981.3 (March 1981), with "Editor's Words," p. 59.

64. Zhao Shuli, *Sanliwan* (Beijing, 1955), ch. 25. In the 1973 edition of the *Lu Xun quanji*, Lu Xun's 1932 criticism about the flood of science fiction and Sherlock Holmes stories is also omitted. Cf. Lu Xun, "The Ties between Chinese and Russian Literature," in Lu Xun, *Selected Works*, ed. Yang Xianyi and Gladys Yang (Beijing, Foreign Languages Press, 1980), III, 209. Ye Yonglie published a collection of science tales (*kexue tonghua*) in Shanghai under the title *Yancong jian bianzi* (The chimney cuts off the braids) and a science-fiction story in 1976. Ye Yonglie, *Lun kexue wenyi*, pp. 89, 112.

65. Zheng Wenguang states so in his interview with Lü Chen, p. 4.

66. Ye Yonglie, *Lun kexue wenyi*, pp. 85 ff.

67. Ibid., p. 106.

68. Objections quoted by Xiao Jianheng in his "Shitan woguo," pp. 61 ff; Lu Bing, "Linghun chuqiao de wenxue" (Literature about ghosts darting from the cave), published in *Zhongguo qingnianbao* (China youth gazette), 14 August 1979; Dong Dingshan, "Kaerweinuo de huanxiang xiaoshuo" (The phantasy fiction of Italo Calvino), *Dushu* 1981.2:102 (February 1981). Dong refers to an article he had written "some months before" in the Hong Kong *Dagong bao,* in which he had been "criticizing the excessive attention given to detective stories and science fiction" (in China). Dong is a Chinese correspondent residing in New York.

69. Quoted by Ye Yonglie, *Lun kexue wenyi,* p. 5. Gao Shan, Jin Hai, "Shitan."

70. They are Ma Shitu, the first secretary of the Sichuan branch of the Chinese Writers Association; Ai Wu, the well-known author of the *Nanxing ji* (Southern journeys; Shanghai, Wenxue congkan, 1946) and of *Bailian chenggang* (Steeled and tempered; Beijing, Renmin wenxue, 1959); and E Hua, who wrote a middle-length science phantasy I have not seen (see Lü Chen, p. 4). See also Gao/Zheng, I, 378 ff. and II, 788 ff.

71. Xiao Jianheng, "Shitan," explicitly demands that the "family name" be changed. Ye Yonglie in his "Kexue huanxiang," pp. 66 ff., treats science-phantasy stories mainly as literature. Zheng Wenguang asks for recognition of science phantasy as literature in his interviews with Lü Chen. Tong Enzheng, "Shitan wo dui kexue," p. 110, pleads for science phantasy as a literature furthering a "scientific world view," but maintains that its basis is "thinking in images" as literature. Cited in Ma Shitu, "Zhu kexue yu wenyi de jiehe" (Congratulations to the marriage of science and literature), *Kexue wenyi* 1:2 (January 1979). Science-phantasy writers are conscious of the fact that "mainstream writers" do not write science phantasy. Meng Weizai, who does not seem to come from the science community, may be an exception. I have not seen his science phantasy published in *Beifang wenyi* (Northern literature and art).

72. Darko Suvin, *Metamorphoses of Science Fiction: On the Poetics and History of a Literary Genre* (New Haven, Yale University Press, 1979), Chapter 1, "Estrangement and Cognition." Heller, pp. 61ff.
73. Although the theory is not widely repeated, I think it reflects the attitude of science-phantasy writers quite well. It is explicitly developed in Zheng Wenguang's postface to his *Fei xiang Renmazuo*, p. 280.
74. Examples, respectively, from Ye Yonglie, "Fei xiang Mingwangxing de ren," in Rao/Lin, pp. 90ff; Tong Enzheng, "Xueshan modi," in Rao/ Lin, pp. 342ff. Tong Enzheng, *Wuwannian yiqian de keren* (Shanghai, Shaonian ertong chubanshe, 1962). Zheng Wenguang, "Shayu zhenchabing," *Shaonian kexue* 1979.5-6 (May-June 1979). Wang Xiaoda, "Bo," in Rao/Lin, pp. 16ff. *Kexue huanxiang xiaoshuo xuan*, pp. 283ff.
75. Ye Yonglie, *Fei xiang*, p. 168; Tong Enzheng, "Xueshan modi," p. 345; Tong Enzheng, *Wuwannian yiqian de keren*, p. 12; Xiao Jianheng, "Bu shuijiao de nüxu," in Rao/Lin, p. 303.
76. See Wei Yahua, p. 52, and Liu Zhaogui, p. 298.
77. See Wang Xiaoda.
78. Zheng Wenguang, "Kexue he minzhu de zange," *Dushu* 1979.1:72 (January 1979).
79. For analysis of these texts, see my *Literatur und Politik in der Volksrepublik China* (Frankfurt, Edition Suhrkamp, Band 1151, 1983).
80. Ye Yonglie, "Fushi" (Corrosion), *Renmin wenxue* 1981.11 (November 1981).
81. Mo Lilin, "Qiyi di licheng" (Strange course), *Guangxi wenyi* 1979.12: 17 (December 1979).
82. Sima Chunqiu, p. 39.
83. Zheng Wenguang, *Fei xiang Renmazuo*, pp. 24, 74.
84. Zheng Wenguang, "Taipingyang ren," in Rao/Lin, pp. 49ff.
85. Cf. Zheng Wenguang, *Fei xiang Renmazuo*, p. 68; Liu Zhaogui shows rich historical knowledge when he writes his "B zhege mi" in order to refute Samuel Butler's *Erewhon* and *Erewhon Revisited;* see p. 295. A similar cross-reference to a Western science theory is in Xiao Jianheng, "Shaluomu jiaoshou de miwu" (Professor Solomon's delusion), *Renmin wenxue* 1980.12 (December 1980).
86. "It is the main function of science-phantasy fiction to inspire (*qifa*)," says Ye Yonglie, *Lun kexue wenyi*, p. 95.
87. Su Ming, "Zai 2000 nian keneng fasheng de beiju."
88. Ai Wu, "Mantan kexue yu wenxue" (A leisurely chat about science and literature), *Kexue wenyi* 1980.4:4 (April 1980).
89. Rao/Lin, p. 15.

2. Love Stories, by Kam Louie

1. This chapter is concerned only with literature published officially. There have, of course, been many underground stories on love and other topics written during the Cultural Revolution period. The best-

known example is Zhang Yang's *The Second Handshake* (*Di'erci wo-shou*), mainly because it was later officially published and promoted.

2. Qian Hai and Li Yan, "Wenxue de fanrong he zuojia de zeren: dui sinian lai wenxue chuangzuo fazhan qingkuang de huigu yu tantao" (A flourishing literature and the responsibility of writers: a retrospective look and investigation of the literary works and developments of the last four years), *Renmin ribao* (People's daily), 25 May 1981.

3. Su Liwen, "'Aiqing re' manbu Zhongguo wentan" (A 'love craze' floods the Chinese literary scene), *Qishi niandai* (The seventies) 2:76-79 (1982).

4. "Tigao shehui zeren, zhengque miaoxie aiqing" (Raise our sense of social responsibility, write about love accurately), *Renmin ribao*, 11 November 1981.

5. The Cantonese magazine *Zuopin* (Literary works), for example, seems to feature more stories about Hainan Island and Overseas Chinese than the other magazines.

6. In a sense, writers must act as spokespersons for Party policies, as their works must be officially approved for publication. They have also often pledged to "contribute to the construction of the socialist spirit" and other official ideals. See, for example, "Wenyi gongzuozhe gongyue" (The literary and artistic workers' convention), *Renmin ribao*, 26 June 1982.

7. Zhang Jie, "Ai shi buneng wangji de" (Love cannot be neglected), *Beijing wenyi* (Beijing literature and arts) 11:19-27 (1979).

8. Quoted in He Zi, "Aiqing, hunyin ji qita" (Love, marriage and other things), *Dushu* (Reading) 8:54 (1980).

9. By "accuracy," I do not imply that the stories necessarily correspond to reality, but that they focus on the thinking of "concerned people" of a particular period. My own perceptions in 1978-1981, when I was teaching and studying at Nanjing and Beijing Universities, certainly very closely paralleled those expressed in the stories.

10. Li Weishi, "Sikao, dan biewangle wenxue . . ." (Think, but don't forget literature . . .), *Guangming ribao* (Guangming daily), 6 March 1979.

11. Some of these letters were later collected into a book—Liu Xinwu, *Rang women lai taolun aiqing* (Let us talk about love; Shanghai, Shanghai renmin chubanshe, 1979).

12. Liu Xinwu, "Aiqing de weizhi" (The place of love), *Shiyue* (October) 1:129 (1978).

13. This is also true of his early stories about other aspects of life. See my article "Youth and Education in the Short Stories of Liu Xinwu," *Westerly* 3:115-120 (1981).

14. The novel, *The Song of Youth*, for example, discusses this question in some detail. See Yang Mo, *Qingchun zhi ge* (The song of youth; Beijing, Zuojia chubanshe, 1958).

15. Guan Gengyin, "Bu chenxin de jiefu" (The unsatisfactory brother-in-law), *Yalu Jiang* (Yalu River) 7:10 (1978).

16. The expression "Gang of Four" is used here for the sake of brevity. It refers more to a political line than to Jiang Qing, Zhang Chunqiao, Yao Wenyuan, and Wang Hongwen.

17. The stories "Mingyun" (Fate) and "Baoyu yan" (Baoyu Cliff) have been reprinted in the book *The Wounded* (Hong Kong, Sanlian shudian, 1978).

18. Da Li, "Shiqu le de aiqing" (Lost love), *Yalu Jiang* 12:48-62 (1978).

19. This is a very popular theme, as seen in Lu Yanzhou "Tianyun Shan chuanqi" (A legend of the Tianyun Mountains), reprinted in *Zhongpian xiaoshuo xuan* (Selected long stories; Kunming, Yunnan renmin chubanshe, 1980), pp. 1-96. This novelette was made into a popular movie.

20. Zhu Shucheng, "Wo ai zhe yi hang" (I love this kind of work), reprinted in *Aiqing xiaoshuo ji* (Collected love stories [*AX*]; Shanghai, Shanghai wenyi chubanshe, 1979), pp. 177-196.

21. Li Tuo, "Xiangshui yuegui" (Chinese roses), *AX*, p. 249.

22. Liu Fudao, "Yanjing" (Glasses), *AX*, p. 5.

23. See W.J.F. Jenner, "1979: A New Start for Literature in China?" *China Quarterly* 86:274-303 (1981).

24. In 1978, Kong Jiesheng had already written about romance between a factory worker and a returned Overseas Chinese, a theme which, for that time, was new. See Kong Jiesheng, "Yinyuan" (A destined marriage), *AX*, pp. 197-217.

25. Kong Jiesheng, "Yinwei youle ta" (Because of her), *Renmin wenxue* (People's literature) 10:52 (1979).

26. Kong Jiesheng, "Zai xiaohe nabian" (Across the river), *Zuopin* 3:31-42 (1979).

27. Chen Guokai, "Wo yinggai zenme ban?" (What should I do?), *Zuopin* 2:37-50 (1979).

28. Zhang Kangkang, "Aiqing de quanli" (The right to love), *Shouhuo* (Harvest) 2:103 (1979).

29. Ibid., p. 111.

30. Zhang Jie, "Love Cannot Be Neglected," p. 27.

31. See, for example, Li Huixin, "Lao chunü (Old spinster), *Beijing wenyi* 3:10-21 (1980).

32. "Du 2,354 feng guniang yingzheng xin" (On reading 2,354 letters from girls who responded), *Qingnian yidai* (The young generation) 2:22 (1981).

33. Qian Yan, "Buyao gei daguniang yi yali" (Don't put pressure on old maids), *Qingnian yidai* 2:24 (1981).

34. See, for example, Wang Wei, "Jianshe shehuizhuyi hunyin daode" (Build socialist morality in marriage), *Guangming ribao*, 22 November 1981.

35. "Love Cannot Be Neglected," pp. 26-27.

36. Luo Xin, "Aiqing miaoxie zhong de yige wenti" (A problem in the writing of love), *Wenhui bao* (Wenhui daily), 18 August 1981.

37. Tony Walker, "China Feels for Liu's Lonely Heart," *Sydney Morning Herald*, 20 March 1982.

38. Jin Fan, "Gongkai de qingshu (Open love letters), *Shiyue* 1 (1980).

39. Wang Ye, "Ke bu keyi zheyang zhuiqiu aiqing?" (Can love be sought this way), *Qingnian yidai* 4:30-31 (1981). Letters in response to this and the editor's comment are found in nos. 5 and 6 of this magazine.

40. See, for example, Jing Fengliang, "Wo dui buqi ta" (I have wronged her), *Zhongguo funü* (Chinese women) 1:6-7 (1982).

41. Liu Xinwu, "Xie zai buxie de huaban shang" (Written on a petal that does not wither), *Xin gang* (New harbor) 9:4-13, 64 (1980).

42. Chen Kexiong and Ma Ming, "Dujuan tigui" (The cuckoo calls homewards), *Qingchun* (Youth) 6:6-14 (1980). A critique of it and "Love Cannot Be Neglected" is found in Zhong Chengxiang, "Shenghuo aiqing daode" (Life, love, and morality), *Hong yan* (Red cliff) 2:160-165 (1981).

43. Yu Yimu, "Chulian de huisheng" (Echo of the first love), *Shiyue* 2:138 (1981).

44. Yang Ximin, "Zhezhong 'chulian' bixu fouding" (This kind of "first love" must be negated), *Beijing ribao* (Beijing daily), 22 December 1981.

45. This question has already been raised by Lu Xun, "Nuola zouhou zenyang" (What happens after Nora leaves home?), *Lu Xun quanji* (Complete works of Lu Xun; Beijing, Renmin wenxue chubanshe, 1973), I, 143-151.

46. Sha Yexin et al., *Jiaru wo shi zhende* (What if I really were?), *Qishi niandai* 1:76-96 (1980).

47. The incident was reported in Zhang Xutang and Wang Fuchu, "Pianzi xingpian luowang ji" (Account of the swindler's activities and arrest), *Wenhui bao*, 11 September 1979.

48. Ru Zhijuan, "Ernü qing" (The love of sons and daughters), *Shanghai wenxue* (Shanghai literature) 1:21 (1980).

49. Ji Si, "Bu yukuai de hunli" (An unhappy wedding), *Yalu Jiang* 9:60 (1979).

50. See, for example, the cartoon reproduced in Cen Ying, ed., *Zhongguo dalu aiqing xiaoshuo xuan* (Selection of mainland Chinese love stories; Hong Kong, Tongjin chubanshe, n.d.), p. 190.

51. Wang Meng, "Fengzheng piaodai" (Kites), in *Wang Meng xiaoshuo baogao wenxue xuan* (Selected fiction and reportage literature by Wang Meng; Beijing, Beijing chubanshe, 1981), pp. 154-176.

52. Liu Xinwu, "Liti jiaochaqiao" (Elevated highway bridge), reprinted in Bi Hua and Yang Ling, eds., *Zhongguo xin xieshizhuyi wenyi zuopin xuan* (Selections from China's new realistic literature; Hong Kong, Tiandi tushu youxian gongsi, 1982), III, 224-275.

53. Chen Guokai, " 'Chechuang huanghou' " (The "lathe queen"), reprinted in Cen Ying, p. 77.

54. Jiao Qun, "Qidai–Shuqing de shouji" (Waiting–Shuqing's manuscripts), *Anhui wenxue* (Anhui literature) 2:40 (1980).
55. Ru Zhijuan, p. 21.
56. This problem is also discussed in other popular magazines, such as *Chinese Women.* See for example, Wang Zangge, "Shuoshuo zenyang duidai popo" (Let's talk about how we should treat our mothers-in-law), *Zhongguo funü* 5:38 (1980).
57. "Zhe zhuang hunshi fumu gai bu gai guan?" (Should parents interfere with this marriage?), *Zhongguo qingnian* (China youth) 2:19 (1982).
58. Bai Hua, "Yi shu xinzha" (A packet of letters), *Renmin wenxue* 1 (1980).
59. Zhang Kangkang, "Beiji guang" (Northern Lights), *Shouhuo* 3:4–61 (1980).
60. Zeng Zhennan, "Ai de zhuiqiu wei shenme xupiao" (Why is the pursuit of love illusory?), *Guangming ribao,* 24 December 1981.
61. Chen Kexiong and Ma Ming, p. 13.
62. Li Binkui, "Tianshan shenchu de 'da bing'" (The "great soldier" of the Tianshan Mountains), reprinted in *1980 nian duanpian xiaoshuo xuan* (Selection of short stories of 1980; Beijing, Renmin wenxue chubanshe, 1981), pp. 560–583.
63. Zhang Xian, "Weiwang ren" (The one who survived), reprinted in Bi Hua and Yang Ling, p. 98.
64. Wang Meng, "Hudie" (Butterfly), reprinted in *Wang Meng xiaoshuo baogao wenxue xuan,* pp. 309–390.
65. Li Jian, "Gu bao nüshen" (The goddess in an ancient castle), *Lu ming* (Deer's cry) 5:6–15 (1980).
66. Zhang Xian, "Bei aiqing yiwang de jiaoluo" (A corner forgotten by love), *Shanghai wenxue* 1:6 (1980).
67. Ibid., p. 13.
68. Ibid., p. 14.
69. Ma Feng, "Jiehun xianchanghui" (The marriage meeting), reprinted in *1980 nian duanpian xiaoshuo xuan,* pp. 80–93.
70. Yu Mei, "A, ren . . ." ("Oh, man . . .), *Huaqi* (Flower creek) 10:13–24 (1980).
71. Li Jian, "Nüer qiao" (Woman bridge), *Fang cao* (Fragrant flowers) 2:10–15 (1980).
72. Zhu Lin, "Wang" (Net), reprinted in Bi Hua and Yang Ling, pp. 23–31.
73. Zhao Yulan, "Changxiang saozi" (Sister Changxiang), *Shanghai wenxue* 8:70–77 (1980).
74. Zhu Lin, p. 23.
75. Li Jian, "Zui ru huacong" (Drunken among flowers), *Zhanjiang wenyi* (Zhanjiang literature) 6:35 (1980).
76. The term *shanghen wenxue* (literature of the wounded) has been used to describe literature that talks about the tragedies caused by the Cultural Revolution. It became a popular term after Lu Xinhua's "Shanghen" (The wound), *Wenhui bao,* 11 August 1978.

77. For a pre-Cultural Revolution example, see Zong Pu, "Hongdou" (Love berries), *Renmin wenxue* 7:14-25 (1957).
78. See, for example, Lu Wenfu, "Xiaoxiang shenchu" (In the recesses of a small lane), first published in *Xin wenyi* (New literature and arts) in 1955. Reprinted in *Chong fang de xian hua* (Fragrant flowers re-blooming; Shanghai, Shanghai wenyi chubanshe, 1979), pp. 201-216.
79. Li Yingru, "Miao Qing," reprinted in Bi Hua and Yang Ling, pp. 104-126.

3. Crime Fiction, by Jeffrey C. Kinkley

I wish to thank colleagues from the St. John's Conference and Harriet Mills. All materials for this chapter were collected at research centers in America.

1. Entry for *zhentan xiaoshuo* (detective story) in *Cihai, shixingben* (Dictionary, draft), *Wenxue, yuyanxue* (Literature, linguistics; Beijing, 1961), X, 11a. I am indebted to Rudolf Wagner for this reference.
2. See the chapter by Rudolf Wagner in this volume.
3. Examples are "Feitian" (Feitian) by Liu Ke, *Zai shehui de dang'an li* (In the annals of society) by Wang Jing, "Jiangjun, bu neng zhe yang zuo" (General, you just can't do such things) by Ye Wenfu, and "Qingshui yamen" (Clear-water yamen) by You Fengwei. These are anthologized in Li Yi (author prefers Lee Yee), ed., *Zhongguo xin xieshizhuyi wenyi zuopin xuan* (Selections from China's new realistic literature; Hong Kong, The Seventies, 1980). See also vol. 2, ed. Li Yi and Bi Hua (1980) and vol. 3, ed. Bi Hua and Yang Ling (Tiandi tushu youxian gongsi, 1982).
4. Examples are *Nü zei* (The girl thief) by Li Kewei, reprinted in ibid., vol. 2 and *Jiujiu ta* (Save her) by Zhao Guoqing, discussed in this chapter.
5. E.g., Jin He, "Chongfeng" (Re-encounter), *Shanghai wenxue* 4:14-25 (April 1979), discussed in William J. F. Jenner, "1979: A New Start for Literature in China?" *China Quarterly* 86:274-303 (June 1981).
6. See Shao-chuan Leng, "Criminal Justice in Post-Mao China," *China Quarterly* 87:452-453 (September 1981). A more pessimistic account of Chinese law is Hungdah Chiu, "China's New Legal System," *Current History* 79.458:29-32, 44-45 (September 1980).
7. The historical derivation of China's Western-style whodunits is beyond the scope of this chapter. All the "late Qing" detective novels Lu Xun speaks of are indebted to the *gongan* and knight-errantry traditions. In 1906, Wu Woyao published a rather unconventional detective tale of Sino-Western inspiration, *Jiuming qiyuan.* See Gilbert Chee Fun Fong, "Time in *Nine Murders:* Western Influence and Domestic Tradition," in Milena Doleželová-Velingerová, ed., *The Chinese Novel at the Turn of the Century* (Toronto, University of Toronto Press, 1980), pp. 116-128. But the detective story was about to become synonymous with

Sherlock Holmes, thanks to Lin Shu's translations from Conan Doyle. As early as the 1910s, there were native Chinese detective stories for the mass urban market. Among the most popular were those featuring "the Chinese Sherlock Holmes," as his creator called him (Perry Link, *Mandarin Ducks and Butterflies: Popular Fiction in Early Twentieth-Century Chinese Cities*, Berkeley, University of California Press, 1981, pp. 22, 140, 147, 158–159, and 260). From then until 1950, a profusion of Western mystery fiction was always available in translation. Detective/spy stories from the Soviet Union, representing another kind of Western influence, were available until the 1960s, and from them came other Chinese imitations. Detective and spy stories circulated underground in China may also have had an impact on recent crime fiction (see Perry Link's chapter in this volume). But, in post-Mao times, one again cannot overlook the reprinting, in great numbers, of the Western classics in translation. Whodunit writing has flourished in Canton, close to Hong Kong, a source of Western and native crime fiction.

8. This view is common among the authorities cited in this chapter, despite its having been best articulated by one, Erik Routley, who has prepared "The Case Against the Detective Story," in Robin W. Winks, ed., *Detective Fiction: A Collection of Critical Essays* (Englewood Cliffs, Prentice-Hall, 1980), p. 166: "the detective story [must take care not to get sidetracked from its main object] or it will collapse. . . . It will gather to itself a seriousness, a message, a mission, and in the end a conscience; and the result of all that will be that no problem [of detection] is solved at all." There are now, of course, all sorts of detective stories, even metaphysical ones by Borges and Eco, but a whole modernist movement came first.

9. Talk with Wang Yaping, New York, 30 May 1982.

10. Chung-wen Shih, *The Golden Age of Chinese Drama: Yüan Tsa-chü* (Princeton, Princeton University Press, 1976). Robert van Gulik, tr., *Celebrated Cases of Judge Dee (Dee Gong An): An Authentic Eighteenth-Century Chinese Dectective Novel* (New York, Dover, 1976), translator's preface. George A. Hayden, *Crime and Punishment in Medieval Chinese Drama: Three Judge Pao Plays* (Cambridge, Harvard University Council on East Asian Studies, 1978). Yau-woon Ma, "The Pao-kung Tradition in Chinese Popular Literature," PhD dissertation, Yale University, 1971; his "Themes and Characterization in the *Lung-t'u kung-an*," *T'oung Pao* 59:179–202 (1973); and his "The Textual Tradition of Ming *Kung-an* Fiction: A Study of the *Lung-t'u kung-an*," *Harvard Journal of Asiatic Studies* 35:190–220 (1975). Ching-hsi Perng, *Double Jeopardy: A Critique of Seven Yuan Courtroom Dramas* (Ann Arbor, Center for Chinese Studies, University of Michigan, 1979).

11. Peter Li, "In Search of Justice: Law and Morality in Three Chinese Dramas," in Richard Wilson et al., eds., *Moral Behavior in Chinese Society* (New York, Praeger, 1981), pp. 104–125. Chung-wen Shih,

Injustice to Tou O (Tou O Yuan): *A Study and Translation* (Cambridge, Cambridge University Press, 1972). On concepts of justice, see also Wolfram Eberhard, *Guilt and Sin in Traditional China* (Berkeley, University of California Press, 1967).

12. Robert van Gulik's Judge Dee novels (inspired by the historical Di Renjie) have been reprinted by the University of Chicago Press and take such titles as *The Chinese Bell Murders, The Chinese Nail Murders, The Chinese Gold Murders*, etc.

Our comparison of the *gongan* with the Western classical detective tradition is intended to be only suggestive; *gongan* are not even a consistent genre (argues Y. W. Ma, "The Pao-kung Tradition," pp. 12-13). Moreover, the characteristics of Judge Bao himself change, over the centuries. In this chapter we mean by *gongan* the well-known and highly popular portion of that tradition, centering on the *Longtu gongan*, the better-known plays such as *The Chalk Circle* and *The Butterfly Dream*, etc. A full study of the meaning of Judge Bao to the folk today would require field research, or at least a survey of Judge Bao in nineteenth century spin-offs from the *Longtu gongan* and *Sanxia wuyi* (Three heroes and five gallants).

13. The bell figures in "Guanyin Pusa tuo meng" of the *Longtu gongan* retold as "The Dream of the Goddess of Mercy," in Leon Comber, tr. *The Strange Cases of Magistrate Pao* (Hong Kong, Heinemann, 1972), pp. 71-81.

14. The caution introduced in note 12 is of relevance here. In some plays, Judge Bao is simply a *deus ex machina* who comes in during the last act, to solve the impossible crime. One of the works that must have done most to popularize Judge Bao in modern times is *Sanxia wuyi;* in this work, Judge Bao solves a number of crimes in the first 27 chapters, but then becomes a minor figure in what is essentially a knight-errantry novel. Ma, "The Pao-kung Tradition," pp. 10, 250-257.

15. Norman Donaldson, "R. Austin Freeman: The Invention of Inversion," in Francis M. Nevins, Jr., ed., *The Mystery Writer's Art* (Bowling Green, Bowling Green University Popular Press, 1970), pp. 79-87.

16. Hanna Charney, *The Detective Novel of Manners* (London, Associated University Presses, 1981), p. 93. John G. Cawelti, *Adventure, Mystery, and Romance: Formula Stories as Art and Popular Culture* (Chicago, University of Chicago Press, 1976), p. 120.

17. Cawelti, pp. 1-7.

18. Ibid., pp. 44-45.

19. Cited by Jacques Barzun, "Detection and the Literary Art," in Nevins, p. 250.

20. Ibid., p. 251.

21. Yau-woon Ma, "The Pao-kung Tradition," pp. 205, 207.

22. Zhao Jingshen regards the tale as having originated in India. Cited by Ma, "The Pao-kung Tradition," pp. 84, 112-113.

23. In the West, prior to professional crime-fighting, criminals were appre-

hended by self-appointed "thief-takers," who assumed disguises and "became a thief to catch a thief." The association in the public mind of the newly formed nineteenth-century professional police detectives with such "spies" was attractive neither to the police nor to those who romanticized them in fiction. See Ian Ousby, *Bloodhounds of Heaven: The Detective in English Fiction from Godwin to Doyle* (Cambridge, Harvard University Press, 1976). On the lack of torture in the Western classical detective story, see Aaron Marc Stein, "The Mystery Story in Cultural Perspective," in John Ball, ed., *The Mystery Story* (New York, Penguin Books, 1976, 1978), pp. 36 ff. For Judge Bao, see Ma, ibid., pp. 86, 223, on disguises; 84–85, 225, on torture.

24. Ma, "The Pao-kung Tradition," pp. 87, 213, 288.

25. Cawelti, pp. 55, 96.

26. Dennis Porter, *The Pursuit of Crime: Art and Ideology in Detective Fiction* (New Haven, Yale University Press, 1981), p. 125.

27. Ellen R. Eliasoph and Susan Grueneberg, "Law on Display in China," *China Quarterly* 88:669–685 (December 1981).

28. Northrop Frye, *Anatomy of Criticism: Four Essays* (Princeton, Princeton University Press, 1957), p. 46.

29. I am indebted to Cen Ying for his anthologies, *Zhongguo dalu zhentan xiaoshuo xuan* (A selection of mainland Chinese detective stories; Hong Kong, Tongjin, n.d. [1981?]), hereafter referred to as *ZT*, and *Zhongguo dalu zuian xiaoshuo xuan* (A selection of mainland Chinese crime stories; Hong Kong, Tongjin, n.d. [1981?]), hereafter *ZA*. The former anthology contains most of our classical detective stories, as follows: Wang Hejun, "Mousha fasheng zai Xingqiliu yewan" (The murder happened late on a Saturday night); Su Yunxiang, "'San ke menya' anjian" (The case of the three front teeth); Cen Zhijing and Wang Wenjin, "Yi zun jin foxiang" (The case of the gold Buddha); Lin Xiao, "Bai Yingying zhi si" (The death of Bai Yingying); and Yang Rongfang, "Yuan Shui qi shi an" (The case of the strange Yuan River corpse). It also has Shi Tongxue, "Wuming biao qi an" (The strange case of the watch that had no brand name), a SF/detective story which turns into a James-Bond-style adventure melodrama; "Zhifazhe" (Law enforcer) by Luo Huajun and Li Zaizhong, a rule-of-law melodrama; and various pieces not referred to in this chapter, including a nonfiction forensic-medicine mystery narrative and several SF/detective stories, some by Ye Yonglie (see Wagner's chapter in this volume). *ZA* contains most of our melodramas, as follows: Li Dong and Wang Yungao, "Shenpan" (Judgment); Su Dezhen, Li Yangui, and Lan Yangchun, "Beijing lai de jianchaguan" (Public procurator from Beijing); Song Yuexun and Chen Dunde, "Fating neiwai" (Inside the court and beyond); Xu Shaowu, "Jianchazhang renxuan" (Candidates for chief procurator); Xing Yixun, *Quan yu fa* (drama; Power vs. law); Wang Yaping, "Bianhuren" (Defender); Wang Yaping "Shensheng de shiming" (Sacred duty); Li Zhaochun, "Shui zhi zui" (Whose crime?); Zhao Guoqing,

Jiujiu ta (Save her); Xu Xiao, "Yi ge nü yushenyuan de zishu" (Statement from a woman preliminary hearing interrogator); Pang Taixi, "Poan zhi hou" (After cracking the case); Zhang Yigong, "Fanren Li Tongzhong de gushi" (The story of the criminal Li Tongzhong); Shao Hua, "Shetou" (The tongue); and Cong Weixi and Liang Jianhua, "Daqiang xia de hong yulan" (Red magnolias beneath the Big House wall). *ZA* also has a spy story by Ji Ming, "Dai shoukao de 'lüke'" (The "passenger" in handcuffs). Other melodramas cited in this chapter were scouted out at random in 1980–1982 literary journals, e.g., Cao Yumo, "Nü tingzhang" (Woman judge), *Zuopin* 1982.2:10–16 (February 1982).

30. By the 1960s, writers in China were permitted to depict only good Red heroes and bad, white class enemies, not people in the middle ("middle characters") whose stance was subject to misinterpretation. See Donald A. Gibbs on "Shao Ch'üan-lin (1905?–   ) and the 'Middle Character' Controversy," in Kai-yu Hsu, ed., *Literature of the People's Republic of China* (Bloomington, Indiana University Press, 1980), pp. 642–652.

31. Students of the Western detective story attribute its appearance to the rise of aesthetic-scientific detachment towards crime, both as a deed and as a social problem; Cawelti, pp. 56–57. Barzun speaks of interest in detection resulting from an age of rationalism *and* romanticism; p. 250. To see how close pre-nineteenth-century Western accounts of crime (e.g., *The Newgate Calendar*, 1773) are to the moralizing of Judge Bao, refer to Stephen Knight, *Form and Ideology in Crime Fiction* (Bloomington, Indiana University Press, 1980), pp. 9–13.

32. Elliot L. Gilbert, *The World of Mystery Fiction: A Guide* (San Diego, Regents of the University of California, 1978), pp. 56–71.

33. Ibid., p. 61.

34. Barzun, p. 253.

35. Cawelti, p. 82.

36. Donald R. Yates, "An Essay on Locked Rooms," in Nevins, pp. 272–284.

37. Although two famous writers have called detective fiction an imitation of the tragic experience, a convincing case has been made for it as comedy, and comedy of manners (cf. Charney). An excellent statement of the case for comedy is George Grella, "The Formal Detective Novel," in Winks, pp. 84–102. Frye seems to have gone before him in this line of thinking. Arguing for tragedy is W. H. Auden, "The Guilty Vicarage," in Winks, pp. 15–24. Dorothy Sayers goes even farther, in her "Aristotle on Detective Fiction," in Winks, pp. 25–34. Those arguing the tragic analogy focus on the catharsis inherent in discovering "whodunit" (relief that one has no part in the guilt oneself), while those who see comedy describe what goes on during the pursuit.

38. Barzun characterizes Western police procedurals as often naturalistic, sometimes self-consciously instructive and sociological; pp. 258–259.

See also Hillary Waugh, "The Police Procedural," in Ball, pp. 163–187.

39. Waugh, pp. 168–170, cites Western exaggerations.

40. Gilbert, pp. 126–127.

41. Peking Public Security Bureau, "27 ci tebie kuaiche shang de wutou suishi an" (The case of the headless and dismembered corpse on Express Train No. 27), pp. 1–23; Chongqing Public Security Bureau, "Aodaliya waibin bei paqie an" (The case of the foreign guest from Australia whose pocket was picked), pp. 261–266, examples from the Public Security Ministry, Third Bureau, ed., *Xingshi zhencha anli xuanbian* (Selected cases exemplifying criminal investigation; Beijing, Qunzhong chubanshe, 1980).

42. Edwin V. Mitchell, ed., *The Newgate Calendar* (Garden City, Garden City Publishing Co., 1926), p. 24. "Hunan Gongan" Bianweihui (The editorial board of "Hunan Public Security"), ed., *Jiekai shizong de mimi* (Uncovering the mystery of the missing person; Changsha, Hunan renmin, November 1980), pp. 59, 155. Knight, pp. 10–12, analyzes the moralism of *The Newgate Calendar*.

43. *Jiekai shizong de mimi*, pp. 147–155.

44. Gilbert, p. 116.

45. Many who in 1979 debated "rule by men" identified it as a basic weakness of Chinese culture. To sample the tenor of the debate, refer to *Fazhi yu renzhi wenti taolun ji* (Discussions of the question of rule of law vs. rule by men; Beijing, Qunzhong chubanshe, 1981).

46. This is not to deny that great progress has been made, including enactment of the PRC's first criminal code and code of criminal procedure ever (summer 1979), training of new lawyers, disavowal of the legality of "disguised torture" such as continuous interrogation, prosecution of corrupt officials, etc.; see Leng. China under Deng Xiaoping still has to preserve social order from youth gangs; smuggling on a scale that could indeed threaten state power, particularly when cadres engage in it; and an occasional mob attack on a police station; Fox Butterfield, "Peking Is Troubled About Youth Crimes," *New York Times*, 11 March 1979; James P. Sterba, "Peking Gang Warfare Is Disclosed by China: 1 Killed as 140 Clash," *New York Times*, 13 December 1979. For the mob attack, on a Hangzhou police station, see BBC *Summary of World Broadcasts* FE/6519/BII/8, 27 August 1980.

47. Li I-Che [sic], "Concerning Socialist Democracy and Legal System" (September 1973–November 1974), in The 70s, ed., *China: The Revolution Is Dead, Long Live the Revolution* (Montreal, Black Rose Books, 1977), pp. 213–241.

48. Ironically, in China, "human rights" rarely refers to civil liberties, a sensitive topic, since the state is not ready to confer some rights; the term more often refers to one's right to be handled by the government according to standard procedure, e.g., to have a preliminary interrogation within 24 hours of arrest, etc. A post-Mao story, like Shen Zhiwei's

"Zhifazhe" (Law enforcer), *Zuopin* 1981.3:7-12 (March 1981)— not to be confused with a story in *ZT* by the same title—can get strangely worked up over this procedural regulation. Xu Shaowu's "Jianchazhang renxuan," *ZA*, p. 71, refers to a "human right" which amounts to freedom from anarchy: One may not be arrested except on the authority of the people's courts and the people's procuracy. This right, essential to liberty, is no less important to the authoritarian bureaucracy, which is concerned that a sense of hierarchy be maintained.

49. Ji Ming, "Dai shoukao de 'lüke,'" *ZA*, p. 142.
50. For the campaign against economic crimes, see *Beijing Review* 1982.8: 3-4 (22 February 1982); Christopher S. Wren, "Peking Executes an Official for Economic Crimes," *New York Times*, 19 January 1983. The problems with such vigilance have unfortunately been manifested precisely in the economic sphere, where there is controversy about what is right and wrong. Some consider bonuses to factory innovators "bribes," and so have been moved to prosecute awardees as "economic criminals." Peking has of course criticized this as a perversion of its intent; Phil Brown (AP), "China Tries to Change Idea that Money Is Evil," *Champaign-Urbana News-Gazette*, 6 January 1983. Again, when factories exchange money informally in return for goods and services, is that a bribe? Chalmers Johnson wonders if the Chinese leaders are not failing "to distinguish between genuine graft, which is a felony and properly dealt with through the criminal justice system, and the bureaucratic self-interest that is an integral and inevitable outgrowth of their particular institutional structure"; Chalmers Johnson, "What's Wrong with Chinese Political Studies?" *Asian Survey* 22.10:925 (October 1982).
51. The two emphases of *gaozhuang* are found respectively in Wu Xuehe, "Liu Jiangyanzi gaozhuang" (One-track-mind Liu files suit), *Beifang wenxue* (Harbin) 1981.6:12-16 (June 1981); and Wang Wenjin, "Jin yisheng gaozhuang" (Dr. Jin files a complaint), *Zuopin* 1981.3:27-30 (March 1981).
52. Sylvia Chan, "'Blooming and Contending': Chinese Writers' Responses on Chinese Literature," *The Australian Journal of Chinese Affairs* 8:132-133 (1982).
53. William C. Jones, review of *Faxue Cidian* (Legal dictionary) in *Journal of Asian Studies* 41.2:323-325 (February 1982).
54. Leng, pp. 456-457.
55. The parental/adversarial distinction is developed in a discussion between Jerome Cohen and Soia Mentschikoff, "The Chinese Legal System," *Chicago Today* 3.2:10-11 (Spring 1966).
56. Procurator General Huang Huoqing told the National People's Congress in December 1981 that 99.97% of all those prosecuted during the first nine months of 1981 were found guilty; reported by Christopher Wren, "China Moves to Resurrect a Credible Legal System," *New York Times*, 5 December 1982, p. 22.
57. In Maoist times, the PRC regarded the administration of the law as

primarily preventive (warning other criminals) rather than curative (achieving justice for individuals already harmed); see Ezra F. Vogel, "Preserving Order in the Cities," in John Wilson Lewis, ed., *The City in Communist China* (Stanford, Stanford University Press, 1971), p. 77. A 1957 Chinese textbook divided the punishment and rehabilitation of criminals into two categories: "special prevention" and "general prevention"; Jerome Alan Cohen, *The Criminal Process in the People's Republic of China: 1949-1963* (Cambridge, Harvard University Press, 1968), pp. 80-81.

58. Ernst Kaemmel, "Literature under the Table," in Glenn W. Most and William W. Stowe, eds., *The Poetics of Murder* (New York, Harcourt Brace Jovanovich, 1983), p. 61.

59. Liang Heng and Judith Shapiro, *Son of the Revolution* (New York, Knopf, 1983), p. 153, shows cadre sons forming gangs of their own and even allying with gangs of street "misfits," but the latter are a motley under-class, sometimes semi-professional.

60. Cawelti, pp. 164, 262.

61. Raymond Chandler, *The Long Goodbye* (New York, Pocket Books, 1955), p. 227. Quoted in Cawelti, p. 143.

62. Cawelti, pp. 152, 157.

63. Ibid., p. 142.

64. Ibid., pp. 142-143.

65. Shang Qin, heroine of "Fating neiwai," has such a gadfly.

66. Cyril Birch, "Change and Continuity in Chinese Fiction," in Merle Goldman, ed., *Modern Chinese Literature in the May Fourth Era* (Cambridge, Harvard University Press, 1977), pp. 385-404.

67. Cong Weixi and Liang Jianhua, "Daqiang xia de hong yulan," *ZA*, p. 263.

68. Notable is Su Ce, "Tongfan" (Cellmate), *Xiaoshuo yuebao* 14:2-12 (1 February 1981) as well as ibid.

69. Gao Shenying, "Yi ge yisheng he 1074 ge pashou" (A physician and 1,074 pickpockets), *Minzhu yu fazhi* ("Democracy and Legal System," Shanghai) 1982.1:26-27 (25 January 1982).

70. Zu Wei, "A, fulao xiongdi!" (Oh, elders and brothers!), in *Shenpan qian de jiaoliang* (Tribulations before the trial; Beijing, Qunzhong chubanshe [The Masses' Publishing House], 1981), pp. 1-19.

71. Zhou Zheng, "China's System of Community Mediation," *Beijing Review* 1981.24.47:23-28 (23 November 1981) glosses over the fact that people must settle their disputes through mediation, since access to the courts is so difficult. Perhaps the greatest infringement of "rule of law" is that the police may send a person to years of rehabilitation through labor without a trial, since the confinement is technically only an administrative punishment; it does not leave the punished person with a criminal record.

72. On 6 June 1984, Radio Hong Kong broadcast New China News Agency

statistics indicating that sales of detective fiction had dropped from 1,170,000 copies in the previous year to a recent low of 25,000. This apparently was induced by the campaign against "spiritual pollution." I thank William Tay for this reference.

4. "Obscure Poetry," by William Tay

1. During the debates, *menglong* is used most often to refer to "obscurity" and "incomprehensibility," but occasionally other meanings such as "nebulosity" and "ambiguity" are also ascribed by a few critics to this term. Since obscurity is the focus of the debates, this paper has used "obscurity" to translate *menglong*. Some of the "obscure poets"—notably Bei Dao, Yang Lian, and Jiang He—had been involved in the "unofficial" journal *Jintian* (Today), which ceased publication after the ninth issue (September 1980). Both Gu Cheng and Shu Ting saw their works in print for the first time in that journal. For a detailed discussion of the journal, see the chapter by Pan Yuan and Pan Jie in this volume. The works of some of the young poets can be found in two anthologies: Perry Link's *Stubborn Weeds* (Bloomington, Indiana University Press, 1983) and Helen Siu's and Zelda Stern's *Mao's Harvest* (New York, Oxford University Press, 1983). *The Bell on the Frozen Lake,* a cycle of poems by Yang Lian, has been translated into English by John Minford and will be published by the Chinese University Press of Hong Kong. *Notes from the City of the Sun,* a selection of poems by Bei Dao, has been translated into English by Bonnie S. McDougall (Ithaca, Cornell University China-Japan Program, 1983). Göran Malmqvist has rendered into Swedish poems by Gu Cheng and Bei Dao and will publish a volume of their poems in Stockholm.

2. My list is derived mainly from the following sources: *Zuopin yu zhengming* (Writings and discussions) 3 (1981), special section on *menglong shi;* "Qing tingting women de shengyin" (Please listen to us), *Shi tansuo* 1 (1980); Xie Mian, "Shique pingjing yihou" (Since the loss of peace and quiet), *Shikan* 12:8-11 (1980). Of the three lists, only that of *Zuopin yu zhengming* is plainly entitled *menglong shi;* Xie Mian identifies the issue he is addressing at the beginning of his essay. The editors of *Shi tansuo,* however, choose to open the personal statements by the young poets with that of Zhang Xuemeng, a not-so-"obscure" poet. This is perhaps done to show some "balance."

3. Quoted in *Shi tansuo* 3:49 (1981).

4. No mainland Chinese editor or critic has named Cai Kun as an "obscure" poet, but, in reprinting this poem, the editors of *Qishi niandai* (The seventies) have chosen to do so. See *Qishi niandai* 11:40 (1981); the poem first appeared in *Shikan* 12:42 (1979).

5. Quoted in *Shi tansuo* 3:71 (1981).

6. *Xing xing* 3:5 (1980).

7. *Shikan* 10:28 (1980).
8. *Some Imagist Poets: An Anthology* (Boston, Houghton Mifflin, 1915), p. 78.
9. *Pictures of the Floating World* (New York, Macmillan, 1919), p. 17.
10. Several early poems by Pound have been translated by Du Yunxie in *Waiguo xiandaipai zuopin xuan* (An anthology of foreign modernist writings), ed. Yuan Kejia et al. (Shanghai, Shanghai wenyi, 1980), I. Five poems by H. D., including "Oread" and "Heat," have appeared in Chinese in *Shijie wenxue* (World literature) 5 (1981). Introductory essays on Imagism have appeared in *Waiguo wenxue yanjiu* (Foreign literature studies) 1 (1980); *Wenyi yanjiu* (Literature and art studies) 6 (1980); and *Shijie wenxue* 1 (1981).
11. *Shikan* 10:49–51 (1980).
12. Cf. Claudio Guillén, "The Aesthetics of Influence," in *Literature as System: Essays Toward the Theory of Literary History* (Princeton, Princeton University Press, 1971), pp. 37–39.
13. *Mobai* (To kneel and worship; Taibei, Xiandai wenxue, 1963), p. 32.
14. Yu Guangzhong's analysis of Fang Xin's *Mobai* can be found in Yu's *Wangxiang de mushen* (Look homeward, satyr; Taibei, Chun wenxue, 1968). Li Yinghao's review of the same volume is in his *Piping de shijue* (Critical vision; Taibei, Wenxing, 1966).
15. *Shikan* 10:29 (1980).
16. *Poetry* 2:12 (April 1913).
17. "Vorticism," in *Ezra Pound*, ed. J. P. Sullivan (Harmondsworth, Penguin, 1970), p. 53. First published in 1914.
18. Pound's method of juxtaposition is actually indebted to, besides haiku, the Chinese ideogram. The method can also be found in classical Chinese poetry. For further discussion, see my articles: "*Ukiyo-e*: Waka, Haiku, and Amy Lowell," *American Studies* 5.3 and 4 (1975); "Fragmentary Negation: A Reappraisal of Ezra Pound's Ideogrammic Method," in *Chinese-Western Comparative Literature: Theory and Strategy*, ed. John Deeney (Hong Kong, Chinese University Press, 1980), pp. 129–153.
19. *Some Imagist Poets: An Anthology*, p. 28.
20. *Shikan* 10:28 (1980).
21. *Wenyi bao* 1:38 (January 1980). First published in *Xing xing* 1 (1979).
22. *Wenyi bao* 16:19–20 (August 1981). Italics mine.
23. *Shikan* 11 (1980); reprinted in *Zuopin yu zhengming* 3:71 (1981).
24. *Shikan* 11:21 (1980).
25. *Shikan* 10:4 (1980).
26. *Shi tansuo* 1:56 (1981).
27. *Wenyi bao* 16:21–22 (August 1981).
28. Ibid., p. 23.
29. *Shikan* 9:48 (1980).
30. *Shikan* 12:6 (1980).

31. *Shi tansuo* 1:29–30 (1981).
32. *Shikan* 12:4 (1980).
33. *Shikan* 3:55–58 (1981).
34. *Wenyi bao* 16:21–22 (August 1980). For summaries of the pros and cons, see *Shikan* 12:4 (1980); *Zuopin yu zhengming* 1:60–61 (1981); *Shi tansuo* 1:43–44 (1981); and *Zuopin yu zhengming* 3:71 (1981).
35. *Shi tansuo* 1:52 (1981).
36. Ibid., p. 53.
37. *Zuopin yu zhengming* 1:56 (1980). First published in *Fujian wenyi* (Fujian literature and art) 1 (1980).
38. *Shikan* 4:3–8, 17 (1981).
39. *Wenxue bao* (Literature gazette) 2:1 (April 1981).
40. *Wenyi bao* 16:19 (August 1981). In his criticism of Chow Tse-tsung, who visited the PRC in 1981 and made some remarks sympathetic to "obscure poetry," Ai Qing reveals that his limited understanding of the poetry from Taiwan actually derives from a speech delivered by Gao Zhun during the 1979 "Chinese Weekend" at the University of Iowa; see *Zhongguo zhoumo* (Chinese weekend; Hong Kong, Cosmos, 1980), p. 63. Entitled "Mihuan yao" (Hallucinatory drugs), Ai Qing's article can be found in *Guangming ribao* (Guangming daily), 20 December 1981, p. 4. Chow's opinions are in *Beifang wenxue* (Northern literature) 11:61–62 (1981). Ai Qing's criticisms of "obscure poetry" are collected in *Ai Qing tan shi* (Ai Qing on poetry; Guangzhou, Huacheng, 1982).
41. *Shi tansuo* 3:38 (1981).
42. Li's confusing and very limited understanding of Yip appears to have come from Xiao Qian's introductory essay on Yip, published in *Wenhui zengkan* (Wenhui supplement) 6:17–21 (1980). Xiao's article, basically a brief survey of Yip's poetry and criticism, is quite accurate, except for the following sentence which has been seized upon by Li Yuanluo: "He [Yip] believes that classical Chinese poetry is the main stream of world literature" (p. 21).
43. Ed. Zhang Hanliang et al. (Taibei, Yuancheng, 1977).
44. Wai-lim Yip, *Ezra Pound's Cathay* (Princeton, Princeton University Press, 1969); *Chinese Poetry: Major Modes and Genres* (Berkeley, University of California Press, 1976), especially the introduction on "The Convergence of Languages and Poetics"; *Hiding the Universe: Poems by Wang Wei* (New York, Grossman, 1972); "Aesthetic Consciousness of Landscape in Chinese and Anglo-American Poetry," *Comparative Literature Studies* 15:211–241 (1978); and "The Taoist Aesthetic: Wu-yen tu-hua, the Unspeaking, Self-generating, Self-conditioning, Self-transforming, Self-complete Nature," in *China and the West: Comparative Literature Studies*, ed. William Tay et al. (Hong Kong, Chinese University Press, 1980; distributed by University of Washington Press), pp. 17–32.
45. *Shi tansuo* 3:38 (1981). This sentence is quoted by Xiao from Cheung's

letter on Taiwan poetry and his own writing career. Li's quotation is a verbatim reproduction from Xiao's essay, which can be found in *Wenxue bao* 3:4 (April 1981).
46. *Shi tansuo* 1:11-14 (1981).
47. *Chang Jiang* (Yangzi River) 2:163-168 (1980).
48. *Shi tansuo* 1:50 (1981).
49. *Shikan* 3:52 (1981).
50. *Chang Jiang* 2:165 (1980).
51. See Donald Wesling, "Modernity and Literary Convention," in *The Chances of Rhyme: Device and Modernity* (Berkeley, University of California Press, 1980), pp. 99-132.
52. Quoted by Bai Hang in *Shikan* 7:16 (1981).
53. *Renmin wenxue* (People's literature) 5:4-5 (1980).
54. *Shi tansuo* 1:8-9 (1981).
55. *Yalu Jiang* 1:72 (1981).
56. *Wenyi bao* 2:9 (January 1981). A similar opinion is also expressed by Qiao Shi in *Shikan* 3:54 (1981).
57. *Haiyun* 3:22 (1981).
58. *Shikan* 8:53-54 (1980). For Du's own explanation, see *Shikan* 9:55-56 (1980).
59. *Dagong bao* (Dagong daily), overseas edition, 9 February 1982, p. 4. For Bian Zhilin's view on this poem and his criticism of Zhang Ming, see *Shi tansuo* 3:10-11 (1981).
60. *Shikan* 3:52 (1981).
61. *Chang Jiang* 2:165 (1980).

5. The Politics of Technique, by Leo Ou-fan Lee

1. Mark Schorer, "Technique as Discovery," in *The World We Imagine: Selected Essays by Mark Schorer* (New York, Farrar, Strauss & Giroux, 1968), pp. 3, 10.
2. Mao Zedong, *Zai Yan'an wenyi zuotanhui shang de jianghua* (Peking, Renmin wenxue chubanshe, 1967), p. 85. For an English translation and analysis, see Bonnie S. McDougall, *Mao Zedong's "Talks at the Yan'an Conference on Literature and Art": A Translation of the 1943 Text with Commentary* (Ann Arbor, Michgan Papers in Chinese Studies, 1980).
3. The word *dissidence* or *dissent* is, of course, loaded with meaning. As will be made clear, my use of the term is different from the official Chinese version and from that treated in a previous article, "Dissent Literature from the Cultural Revolution," *Chinese Literature: Essays, Articles, Reviews* 1:59-80 (January 1979). In that article, I used the term *dissent* to refer to works that "challenged, directly and unequivocally, the authority and infallibility of Chairman Mao," written during the Cultural Revolution. By now, of course, that dissident ethos has become part of an official posture. As in the case of the

previous article, I alone bear responsibility for the present analysis. The Chinese writers discussed are thereby exempted from any possible responsibility on their part, political or otherwise.

4. Schorer, p. 5.
5. See, for instance, his articles: "Weile gengjia chengshou de wenxue" (For a more mature literature), *Wenyi bao* 6:12–15 (1981); "Shenghuo, qingxiang, bianzhengfa he wenxue" (Life, inclination, dialectics, and literature), in Wang Meng, *Dang ni naqi bi* (When you pick up the pen; Peking, Beijing chubanshe, 1981), pp. 47–62.
6. Wang Meng, "Gei Yan Wenjing tongzhi de huixin" (A letter of reply to comrade Yan Wenjing), *Beijing wanbao*, 5 July 1980. I am indebted to Pan Yuan for this reference and other forms of research assistance.
7. Wang Meng, *Qingchun wansui* (Long live youth; Peking, Renmin wenxue chubanshe, 1979).
8. These two stories are included in Wang Meng's story collection, *Dongyu* (Winter rain; Peking, Renmin wenxue chubanshe, 1980), pp. 1–13, 23–64. The original title of the first story is "Zuzhi bu xinlai de nianqing ren."
9. Ibid., pp. 81–93.
10. Ibid., p. 166.
11. Ibid., p. 230. English translation by Helena Kolenda, with my minor corrections.
12. *Wang Meng xiaoshuo baogao wenxue xuan* (Selected fiction and reportage literature by Wang Meng; Peking, Beijing chubanshe, 1981), pp. 154–176.
13. "Buduan tansuo xindi biaoxian shoufa" (Constantly searching for new methods of expression), *Beijing wanbao*, 2 July 1980.
14. *Wang Meng xiaoshuo baogao wenxue xuan*, p. 167. My translation.
15. M. H. Abrams, *A Glossary of Literary Terms*, 3rd ed. (New York, Holt, Rinehart and Winston, 1971), pp. 164–165.
16. Included in *Wang Meng xiaoshuo baogao wenxue xuan*, pp. 222–308.
17. He Xilai, "Xinling de bodong yu qingtu—lun Wang Meng de chuangzuo" (Trembling and confession of the heart—on Wang Meng's creative work), in *Wenxue pinglun congkan* (Peking, Zhongguo shehui kexue chubanshe, 1981), X, 32.
18. Ibid., p. 33.
19. *Wang Meng xiaoshuo baogao wenxue xuan*, p. 335.
20. Ibid., p. 211.
21. Most likely, this is inspired by the author's visit to Germany in 1979. Wang Meng's vocabulary of Western music seems limited to waltzes and the standard nineteenth-century Russian repertoire. In comparison, Wang Wen-hsing, a modernistic writer in Taiwan, uses Mahler's "Das Lied von der Erde" as a thematic motif for one of his early stories, "Dadi zhi ge" (The song of the earth).
22. For a discussion of this piece, see my article in Chinese, "Liu Binyan he 'Renyao zhijian'" (Lin Binyan and "Between Men and Monsters"), *Qishi niandai* (The seventies, Hong Kong) 129:79–82 (October 1980).

23. The notion of "neutralizing" villainous characters and "simplifying" good characters in Wang Meng's fiction is discussed extensively by Chen Youshi in *Qishi niandai* 131:87–89 (December 1981).

24. Wang Meng, "Kuaile de gushi" (Happy story), in *Dongyu*, p. 154.

25. The term is based on a story titled "Scar," also translated as "The Wounded." For a discussion of this literature and related issues, see Joseph Lau, "Literature that Hurts: The World of *Shang-hen* Fiction," *Journal of Oriental Studies* 20 (Hong Kong, 1983).

26. The story, a national prize-winner of 1979, is included in Gao Xiaosheng, *Qijiu xiaoshuo ji* (Stories of 1979; Nanjing, Jiangsu renmin chubanshe, 1980), pp. 12–36. English translation my own. Gao's style also offers an interesting comparison with Zhao Shuli's in such stories as "Li Youcai banhua" (The rhymes of Li Yucai) and "Xiao Erhei jiehun" (The marriage of Xiao Erhei). But I think Gao's technique is more inventive, his story more powerful than Li's folksy works of political conformism.

27. Gao Xiaosheng, " 'Li Shunda zaowu' shimo" (The background of "Li Shunda Builds a House"), in *Gao Xiaosheng yanjiu ziliao* (Research materials on Gao Xiaosheng), ed. Lianyungang shi jiaoshi jinxiu xueyuan (July 1981), p. 40.

28. See my article in Chinese, "Gao Xiaosheng de 'Li Shunda zaowu' yu fanfeng yiyi" (Gao Xiaosheng's "Li Shunda Builds a House" and its ironic meaning), *Dangdai* (Contemporary monthly, Hong Kong) 4:4–8 (15 December 1980).

29. Gao's own discussion of his language can be found in *Gao Xiaosheng yanjiu ziliao*, pp. 70–74. This is part of a talk he gave to the amateur writers of the city of Lianyungang.

30. The Chinese originals of these excerpts are cited in my article in *Dangdai*, p. 6.

31. Gao Xiaosheng, *Qijiu xiaoshuo ji*, p. 25. All translations are my own.

32. Ibid., p. 32.

33. Abrams, *A Glossary of Literary Terms*, p. 81.

34. The first two stories are included in *Gao Xiaosheng yijiubaling nian xiaoshuo ji* (Gao Xiaosheng's 1980 stories; Peking, Renmin wenxue chubanshe, 1981), pp. 17–44. The last story can be found in *Xiaoshuo yuebao* 1981.5:46–56 (1981).

35. *Gao xiaosheng yanjiu ziliao*, p. 65.

36. *Gao Xiaosheng yijiubaling nian xiaoshuo ji*, pp. 37–38.

37. Gao Xiaosheng once said the following: "Sometimes there is something of which you are only 70% in support and 30% opposed, but, once rendered on paper, the result is no longer 70% and 30% but total support or total opposition." (*Gao Xiaosheng yanjiu ziliao*, p. 72).

38. See the chapter by Pan Yuan and Pan Jie below, p. 197.

39. The Bai Hua incident is different from the case of underground journals and was also treated differently by the regime. For an analysis of the Bai Hua case, see Michael S. Duke, "A Drop of Spring Rain Fallen on

the Hard Cold Ice: Humanistic Expression in Pai Hua's Film-Poem *Bitter Love* (*K'u-lien*)," publication forthcoming in *C.L.E.A.R.* I have also discussed the implications of the Party's new literary policy in a paper, "Chinese Literature for the 1980's: Prospects and Problems," submitted to the Conference on China: The 1980s Era, University of Chicago (13-15 November 1981). It will be published in Norton Ginsburg and Bernard A. Lalor, eds., *China: The '80s Era* (Boulder, Westview Press, 1984).

40. Pan Yuan and Pan Jie, p. 197.
41. Dai Houying, *Ren a ren* (Man, ah man; Canton, Guangzhou renmin chubanshe, 1980), pp. 356-358.
42. The *locus classicus* for this reassertion is Qin Zhaoyang's essay "Xianshizhuyi—Guangkuo de daolu" (Realism—the broad way), first published some 20 years ago.
43. *Ren a ren*, pp. 175-183.
44. Ibid., p. 358.
45. Published in *Shiyue* 1981.2:4-55 (1981). It is worth noting that Liu Xinwu and many other writers are experimenting with longer story forms. The novelette or long story (*zhongpian*) presumably offers more scope for developing plot and reflecting a broader reality.
46. Published in *Shiyue* 1981.4 and 5 (1981).
47. Both have "surfaced" and now write for the official journals, since *Today* was banned.
48. See the chapter by William Tay in this volume.
49. Pan Yuan and Pan Jie, p. 217.
50. Published in *Xiaoshuo yuebao* 1980.3:49-53 (1980).
51. *Zhongshan* 1981.1:185-190 (1981).
52. Lu Xun, "Wenyi yu zhengzhi de qitu" (The divergence between literature and politics) in *Jiwai ji* (Addenda collection), *Lu Xun quanji* (Complete works of Lu Xun; Beijing, Renmin wenxue chubanshe, 1973), VII, 470-481.
53. For discussions of Taiwan fiction, particularly *xiangtu* (native-soil) literature, see Jeannette Faurot, ed., *Chinese Fiction from Taiwan: Critical Perspectives* (Bloomington, Indiana University Press, 1980).

6. The Magazine Today, by Pan Yuan and Pan Jie

We wish to acknowledge the guidance and assistance of Professor Leo Ou-fan Lee, who is himself a friend of the "Today" group. Thanks are due also to Professors Philip West and Jeffrey Kinkley, and to Mr. John Coleman, for their assistance with editing and translation. We hope that this chapter may offer consolation to our friends of the "Today" group, who fought for the rejuvenation of Chinese literature.

Note: Issues of *Today* did not always bear a date of publication. No. 1 was published in December 1978. Nos. 2 and 3 followed in 1979. No. 4 was dated June 1979, No. 5 August 1979, and No. 6, November 1979. No. 7

was published in January 1980. Nos. 8 and 9 followed, prior to the October 1980 publication of No. 1 of the *Reference Materials for Internal Distribution of the Research Association for Literature of Today*. No. 2 of the *Reference Materials* was published in 1980 and No. 3, in 1981.

1. Yang Lian, "Wode xuanyan" (My manifesto), *Fujian wenxue* (Fujian literature) 1981.1:64 (January 1981).
2. Ling Bing, "Dafu" (Replies), *Jintian* (Today) 9:61 (1980).
3. Zhao Zhenkai, pseud. Bei Dao, "Dafu" (Replies), *Jintian* 9:61 (1980).
4. See Sun Shaozhen, "Xinde meixue yuanze zhengzai jueqi" (New aesthestic principles are rising), *Shikan* (Poetry) 1981.3:56 (March 1981).
5. Ye Wenfu, "Jiangjun, buneng zheyang zuo!" (General, you just can't do such things!), *Shikan* 1979.8:32 (August 1979).
6. A talk with a friend on 15 June 1980.
7. Jintian Bianjibu (Editorial staff of *Today*), "Zhi duzhe" (To our readers), *Jintian* 1:2 (December 1978).
8. A talk with a friend on 15 June 1980.
9. See Yuan Kejia, "Fangmei shujian" (Letters from the States), *Shikan* 1981.3:51 (March 1981).
10. The author of the poem is Zhao Zhenkai, who later told this to his friends.
11. Mang Ke, "Dafu" (Replies), *Jintian* 9:61 (1980).
12. From Zhao Zhenkai's talk in the summer of 1980.
13. Beginning at the end of 1968, the government sent most students in the cities to the countryside for political purposes, as well as to relieve increasing population pressure in urban areas.
14. Chen Ruoxi, *Democracy Wall and the Unofficial Journals* (Berkeley, Center for Chinese Stuides, University of California, 1982), pp. 52, 107, correctly indicates that Liu Nianchun, a brother of Liu Qing of the *April Fifth Forum*, offered sympathy and much assistance to *Today*. We are not aware of Liu Nianchun's having participated in *Today*'s editorial activities, however, as some might infer from the Chen monograph.
15. In China today, there are basically no privately owned Chinese typewriters; individuals have no need and no access to purchase them. This was one of the reasons why the non-official magazines faced difficulty in continuing publication once the government showed its unfavorable attitude towards them.
16. Cadres and other privileged persons in China may read materials not openly published for the information of the public; these are usually printed under the classification of materials for "internal distribution," and it is understood that the views expressed do not necessarily represent an official consensus. By adopting such a title, *Today* intimated that its publication activities were not necessarily to be judged according to the strict, watered-down standards appropriate to publication for mass circulation.
17. Jiang He, "Cong zheli kaishi" (Start from here), *Jintian* 8:44 (1980).
18. Jiang He, "Zuguo" (Motherland), *Jintian* 4:3 (June 1979).

19. Fei Sha, "Weile" (For the sake of), *Jintian* 8:1 (1980).

20. Jiang He, "Zuguo."

21. Mang Ke, "Xinshi" (The secret of the heart), *Xinshi*, p. 51.

22. Jiang He, "Xingxing bianzouqu" (Musical variations on the stars), *Jintian* 8:43-44 (1980).

23. Mang Ke, "Taiyang luole" (The sun has set), *Jintian* 3:27 (1979).

24. Zhao Zhenkai, pseud. Bei Dao, "Hongfanchuan" (Sailing boat), *Jintian* 8:22 (1980).

25. Shu Ting, "Yexu" (Maybe), *Jintian* 8:11 (1980).

26. Jiang He, "Dong" (Winter), *Jintian Wenxue Yanjiuhui neibu cankao ziliao* (Reference materials for internal distribution of the Research Association for Literature of Today) 3:7 (1981).

27. Shu Ting, "Zhongqiuye" (Night of mid-autumn), *Jintian* 3:36 (1979).

28. Shu Ting, "A Muqin" (Ah, Mom), *Jintian* 1:23-24 (December 1978).

29. Chen Maiping, pseud. Wan Zhi, "Xueyu jiaojia zhijian" (In snow mingled with rain), *Jintian* 4:76 (June 1979).

30. Gan Tiesheng, pseud. Tian Ran, "Juhui" (The get-together), *Jintian* 6:63 (November 1979).

31. Chen Maiping, pseud. Wan Zhi, "Kaikuodi" (The open terrain), *Jintian* 5:55 (August 1979).

32. Chen Maiping, pseud. Wan Zhi, "Zimingzhong xia" (Under the striking clock), *Jintian Wenxue Yanjiuhui neibu cankao ziliao* 2:8 (1980).

33. Zhao Zhenkai, pseud. Ai Shan, *Bodong* (Undulation), *Jintian* 4:31 (June 1979).

34. Yi Shu, *Chouhen* (Hatred), *Jintian* 7:16 (January 1980).

35. Yongyu, "Dongwu yuyan" (Animal fables), *Jintian* 1:33-34 (December 1978). The author of these fables does not belong to the "Today" group. He is the eminent Chinese painter Huang Yongyu, who visited America in 1980. These translations are from David Goodman, *Beijing Street Voices* (Boston, Marion Boyars, 1981), pp. 21-25, published with his permission.

36. When a delegation of the Chinese official literary critics, visiting Indiana University in March 1982, were asked about their evaluation of works published in *Today,* they avoided making a reply and offered no information about it.

37. In the 1960s, some literary works by contemporary Russian and American writers were translated into Chinese by the official publishing houses, but only in restricted publications that circulated among a small group.

7. Fiction and the Reading Public, by Perry Link

1. "Wo yinggai zenmo ban?" *Zuopin* (Guangzhou) 1979.2:37-50 (February 1979).

2. Sha Yexin, Li Shoucheng, and Yao Mingde, *Jiaru wo shi zhende, Qishi niandai* (Hong Kong) 1980.1:76-96 (January 1980).

3. See p. 250 and notes 46-48 for a brief discussion of the literacy question.

4. Interview at the Central People's Broadcasting Station, Beijing, 11 October 1979.

5. These included *Jiujiu ta* (Save her!), *Jiaru wo shi zhende* (What If I Really Were?), *Liaokai nide miansha* (Lift your veil), and *Shenzhou fenglei* (Storms over China).

6. Interview at Guangzhou Municipal Post Office, 30 April 1980.

7. Interview at Shanghai Municipal Library, 13 June 1980.

8. "Publishing in China Past and Present" (Beijing, National Publishing Administration, May 1980), pp. 8-9.

9. But not to all places. When the "35 world literary classics" were republished in the late 1970s, 25% of the whole supply went to Beijing city, because of its "concentration of leading comrades." (Interview at New China Bookstore, Beijing, 30 October 1979.)

10. Interview at the State Publication Administration, 4 August 1980.

11. Ibid.

12. Interview at Wenyi Publishing House, 16 June 1980; and at Baihua Publishing House, 29 June 1980.

13. The figures were provided to me by the State Publication Administration (interview, 4 August 1980). To account for the holdings of Guangzhou bookstores in particular we should supplement the above list with fiction published by the Guangdong People's Publishing House, whose print runs have been generally much higher than average for provincial presses because of the comparatively abundant supply of paper in Guangdong. For example, Guangzhou's literary quarterly *City of Flowers* (which was distributed through the bookstore in the late 1970s because it was too bulky for the Post Office) was printed in 405,000 copies by early 1980. In 1981, the Guangdong People's Publishing House began republication of *The Adventures of Sherlock Holmes* in several hundreds of thousands of copies, partly in order to ensure itself of profits for the subsidy of other books. But I do not have systematic data on fiction runs in Guangdong.

14. I have discussed this novel at somewhat greater length in an "Afterword" to *Mandarin Ducks and Butterflies* (Berkeley, University of California Press, 1981), pp. 236-239.

15. Interview at China Youth Publishing House, 8 October 1979.

16. Other works on Jiang Qing's list included Charlotte Brontë, *Jane Eyre;* Charles Dickens, *A Tale of Two Cities;* Margaret Mitchell, *Gone with the Wind;* Nathaniel Hawthorne, *The Scarlet Letter;* Stendhal, *The Red and the Black.*

17. Interview at the State Publication Administration, 4 August 1980.

18. *Wenhui bao* (Shanghai), 22 April 1980.

19. Interview at New China Bookstore, Beijing, 30 October 1979.

20. Yu Chen, "Jiefang 'neibu shu,'" *Dushu* (Beijing) 1979.1:9 (April 1979).

21. Ibid., p. 8.
22. I had entirely underestimated the sensitivity of such stores until one day a Chinese friend played a practical joke on me. Knowing my interest in bookstores, he told me of an unusually good one at a certain address. I arrived there one noon at, apparently, a moment when the guard who normally sits at the door was taking a break. There was no sign to indicate a bookstore—only a very prettily painted open doorway. When I walked in, a middle-aged woman jumped out of her chair and literally about two feet into the air. She came running towards me waving her arms and shouting "We're closed!" I asked her if this was indeed a bookstore and she shouted back "No! It's an empty room!" Actually, books were piled everywhere, but I was of course in no position to examine them. I left feeling guilty that I had inadvertently caused big trouble for the unoffending storekeeper.
23. Hao Ran, the only novelist published to a significant extent during 1966–1976, still attracted readers in 1979–1980 with his *Bright Sunny Days (Yanyangtian,* which actually was first published in 1964, before the Cultural Revolution). His second long novel, *The Golden Way (Jinguang dadao,* 1972), was less popular, both for its association with Cultural Revolution policies and because reader demand for it had been well saturated before 1977.
24. Interview at the State Publication Administration, Beijing, 4 August 1980. I end this list at 16 instead of going on to 20 because of questions about the data on numbers 16 to 20.
25. Lyubov T. Kosmodemyanskaya's *The Story of Zoya and Shura* was published in 1,600,000 copies, even more than *How Steel Is Tempered,* but this true story of a heroic revolutionary mother counts as nonfiction.
26. Interview at the Zhejiang Provincial Library, Hangzhou, 12 June 1980.
27. Interview at Shanghai Municipal Library, 13 June 1980.
28. Ibid.
29. *Guangzhou ribao,* 26 December 1979.
30. The Zhejiang Provincial Library, like most big libraries, levied no fines but fashioned another interesting disincentive for late returns; a person who returned a book n days late was "fined" n days on his next borrowing.
31. Interview with Beijing readers, arranged by the Academy of Social Sciences, 18 October 1979.
32. From 1972 until June 1978, the same publication was called *Guangdong wenyi.*
33. Interview at *Zuopin* editorial offices, 4 March 1980.
34. Interview at *Guangzhou wenyi* editorial offices, 7 March 1980.
35. Interview at *Zuopin* editorial offices, 4 March 1980.
36. Interview at Guangzhou Municipal Post Office, 30 April 1980.
37. *Zuopin* 1980.1:1–12 (1980).
38. *Shouhuo* 1980.1:116–173 (1980).

39. This and the following discussion of Post Office distribution policies are based on interviews at the Guangzhou Municipal Post Office (30 April 1980) and the Beijing Municipal Post Office (16 October 1979).

40. Interview at the Beijing Post Office, 16 October 1979.

41. In Guangzhou in 1980, I found a hand-copied version of the story "Woman in the Tower" ("Tali de nüren") by Anonymous (Wumingshi), the famous "decadent" writer from the 1940s. In this case, of course, the source for the story could have been a pre-1949 edition in someone's personal collection. In any event, 8 people (to judge from the different handwritings) had pooled their efforts to recopy "Woman in the Tower" during the Cultural Revolution.

42. For example, the controversial filmscript In the Annals of Society (Zai shehui de dang'anli) by Wang Jing (pseud.) was originally published in the unofficial journal called Fertile Earth (Wotu, Beijing) 2:19-59 (1979). It was later published at the official unrestricted level in Cinematic Creations (Dianying chuangzuo, Beijing) 1979.11:22-43 (1979), and in several places at the restricted level, including Guilinshi Shifan "Yuwen Jiaoxue" Bianjishi, ed., Zai shehui de dang'anli: Zhongguo dangdaiwenxue cankao ziliao (Guilin, 1980) I, 204-226 and II, 212-230. Anhui wenxue 1:33-45 (1980) includes a section of "wild grass" from unofficial publications; Guangzhou wenyi (April 1980) published Chen Haiying's "Black Tide" ("Heihaichao") after it had already been published in the student magazines Hongdou (1979.2 [1979]) and Zheyidai (November 1979).

43. A possible exception to the bleak outlook for storytelling was reported in the Shanghai Wenhui bao on 13 July 1980: A bimonthly magazine called Story Gatherings (Gushi hui), which was intended for use in public readings in villages, had been published by the Wenyi Publishing House in Shanghai in 400,000 copies. According to the report, the illiterate masses received these stories enthusiastically, even while "accepting new ideas and points of view" presented in the stories' contents.

44. Interview at the Central People's Broadcasting Station, Beijing, 11 October 1979.

45. Ibid.

46. The 76.5% figure is from China's 1982 census (see The Los Angeles Times, Thursday, 28 October 1982, Pt. I, p. 14); the 95% figure is cited without source under "Pacific Region Statistical Indicators" in Worldview (New York) 24.3:38 (March 1981).

47. Vilma Seeberg, investigating literacy in and around Hefei in Anhui province in 1979-1980, found that about 30% of children do not attend primary school (in the countryside, transportation to schools was an important problem) and that a majority of girl students who do attend school leave in the third grade or earlier to do housework or to care for younger children. Defining literacy as the completion of rural fifth grade, Seeberg estimates China's literacy between 20% and 40%. (Seeberg is a PhD candidate at the University of Heidelberg; her infor-

mation was provided at a seminar at UCLA, 10 February 1981.) A somewhat higher projection of primary-level literacy is suggested by officials of the Ministry of Education. According to Deputy Prime Minister Chen Muhua (*New York Times,* 13 August 1979, p. A4), 6% of Chinese children were not going to primary school in 1979, and, of those who did, 12% dropped out before reaching junior high school. But to assume that a consequent 82.7% of the population had primary education in 1979 would surely be too high. First, it is doubtful that the Ministry of Education's figures adequately account for remote areas of the countryside. Second, the 82.7% figure applies only to 1979, while the rates in earlier years must surely have been lower. For 1966–1976, they would have been much lower, especially if quality of education is considered.

48. Vilma Seeberg found widespread "recurrent illiteracy" in 1979 among people who gained basic literacy in the 1950s, either in schools or in adult literacy campaigns.

49. Rent, water, electricity for a small apartment each cost about 15 yuan in Guangzhou in 1979–1980; a pair of standard blue pants cost 6 to 10 yuan. Among optional expenses, there were, of course, attractive things other than fiction to save for: bicycles (about 150 yuan), sewing machines (about 130 yuan), and electric fans (60–300 yuan), all extremely desirable in a city where buses were crowded, clothes often patched and remade at home, and the summer weather oppressively hot.

50. It is far from contradictory that the price of fiction was a barrier for many people and yet popular items immediately sold out. There were more than 5 million people in Guangzhou in 1979–1980, and *Literary Works,* the only readily available fiction magazine in the city, sold but 25,000 copies at retail, excluding subscriptions. After many would-be purchasers had ruled themselves out on grounds of price, there were still many more purchasers than available copies.

51. Interview with Beijing readers, arranged by the Academy of Social Sciences, 18 October 1979.

52. Interview at Shanghai Municipal Library, 13 June 1980.

53. The slightly higher percentage of men with primary educations seems to be balanced by the fact that young women have a somewhat stronger preference for reading.

54. The other ways include asking the subjective views of publishers at the Guangdong People's Publishing House (who said "1 or 2 million," interview, 4 March 1980) and calculating from the number of primary school graduates. Although primary education was nearly universal in Guangzhou in 1979–1980, it was lower among older groups because of less-than-universal education in earlier years, recent migration from the less literate countryside, and atrophy of reading skills. Assuming that those with functional primary reading skills were about 60–70% of the population, a fiction-reading population of 20% or more would

imply that 1 person read fiction among every 3 who could, and this seems reasonable.

55. "Open Love Letters" ("Gongkai de qingshu") by Jin Fan also originated in hand-copied form and was published in the official press (*Shiyue* [October] 1980.1:4–67 [January 1980]). But this work was not popular entertainment fiction like *The Second Handshake,* and had circulated in hand-copied form among a more elite readership.

56. These two works were cited among the three or four most popular by representatives in Beijing at the Beijing Library (28 October 1979), the Central Broadcasting Station (11 October 1979), and the No. 27 Locomotive Factory and No. 3 Universal Machine Works (18 October 1979); in Shanghai at the Shanghai Municipal Library (13 June 1980) and the Wenyi Publishing House (16 June 1980); in Guangzhou at the editorial board of *Literary Works* and the Guangdong People's Publishing House (4 March 1980); and among readers in all three cities.

57. "Chuban tushu yao kaolü shehui xiaoguo" (Social effects must be considered in book publishing), *Wenhui bao,* 22 April 1980.

58. The Chinese government's message that the Americans were using chemical and biological warfare in Korea appears to have been widely believed at a popular level. *The Second Handshake* includes a similar section about a secret American war-poison research laboratory. Why it is assumed that foreigners would choose to establish such laboratories in China is not clear, but details such as this, which follow popular ideas at the expense of serious reflection on consistency of one's story, are legion in hand-copied volumes.

59. This phrase, from a copy of "The Annihilation of the Underground Stronghold," is the nearest to a political message I have seen in a hand-copied volume.

60. See Perry Link, *Mandarin Ducks and Butterflies: Popular Fiction in Early Twentieth-Century Chinese Cities* (Berkeley, University of California Press, 1981), ch. 2.

61. Guangzhou's evening newspaper *Yangcheng wanbao* reported (30 May 1980) an alarming recent increase in street sales of "hand-copied pornographic fiction" and "nude or semi-nude pornographic drawings and photographs." Miriam London reports the existence in Guangzhou of a hand-copied story called *A Maiden's Heart,* which she describes as "a mediocre first-person tale of a girl's sexual adventures" ("What Are They Reading in China Today?" *Saturday Review,* 30 September 1978.

62. "Kongbu de jiaobusheng" (Terrifying footsteps).

63. The category of youth "waiting for work" was substantial. According to the Guangdong *Handbook for Propaganda and Study* (*Xuanchuan xuexi shouce,* June 1981), there were currently 500,000 youths waiting for work in Guangdong province (p. 31).

64. By comparison, youth in Chengdu, Sichuan, who were just as eager as Guangzhou youth to explore the West during the political relaxation

after Mao, made more of their limited resources. When word of rock 'n' roll arrived in Chengdu in 1978, it became a cause célèbre among rebellious youth; for a time it was *the* way to signal one's emancipation of the mind, one's association with Western culture, and one's solidarity with peers. At the same time, books, films, and television from the West were much harder to get than in Guangzhou, where a dance craze of the same intensity could not have happened. Social scientists might consider the following hypothesis (which clearly can apply to Chinese influences in the West as well): Given approximately equal levels of desire to explore a foreign culture, the less a group knows about it the more flamboyantly it will celebrate what it does know.

65. I am estimating student enrollments as follows: Zhongshan University, 6,000; Jinan University, 3,000; South China Normal College, 4,000; Guangzhou Normal College, 2,000; Guangzhou Engineering College, 5,000; Guangzhou College of Fine Arts and Music Conservatory, 3,000; Zhongshan Medical College, 4,000; Guangzhou College of Chinese Medicine, 2,000; Guangzhou College of Pharmacology, 1,000; South China Agricultural College, 3,000; South Central College of Forestry, 1,000; Guangzhou Army Medical College, 2,000; Guangzhou College of Physical Education, 2,000; Guangzhou Army Physical Education College, 2,000; Guangzhou College of Dance, 500–1,000; Guangzhou College of Industrial Arts, 500–1,000; total, about 41,000–42,000.

66. On a national average, about 5% of college applicants were accepted in 1979–1980 (Chen Muhua, Deputy Prime Minister, quoted in *The New York Times,* 13 August 1979, p. A4). Since unsuccessful applicants usually reapplied in succeeding years, it cannot be assumed that there were 20 would-be students for every student enrolled. Conservatively, there may have been half that many, or about 10 for each active student. In major cities like Guangzhou, the ratio would be still lower for two reasons: first, Guangzhou secondary schools were above the national average in quality and had higher rates of successful applicants; second, the number of college students in Guangzhou represents a concentration of successful applicants not just from Guangzhou itself but from the entire province and beyond. From these considerations it would seem reasonable to estimate a ratio of 3:1 or 5:1 would-be college students to actual college students in Guangzhou.

67. This calculation, based on the answers to questions 1 and 2 in Appendix 2, assumes that the average novel is about 7 times as long as the average short story.

68. Jonathan Culler, "Prolegomena to a Theory of Reading," in Susan R. Suleiman and Inge Crosman, eds., *The Reader in the Text: Essays on Audience and Interpretation* (Princeton, Princeton University Press, 1980), pp. 46–66, especially pp. 49, 66.

GLOSSARY

This list includes Chinese terms, periodicals, and persons (except for major political figures). Place-names and fictional characters are not listed. Nor are literary works unless they are particularly significant or difficult otherwise to identify (e.g. anonymous works, books edited by organizations).

A Ying 阿英
Ai Qing 艾青
Ai Shan 艾珊
Ai Wu 艾蕪
aimei lian'ai 曖昧戀愛
Aiqing xiaoshuo ji
　　愛情小説集
Anhui wenxue 安徽文學
Ao Ao 翱翱

Ba Jin 巴金
Bai Hang 白航

Bai Hua 白樺
Bai Xianyong 白先勇
baihua 白話
Baiyangdian 白洋澱
"Banzhuren" 班主任
bataer 叭塔儿
Bei Dao 北島
bei heiguo 背黑鍋
Beifang wenxue 北方文學
Beifang wenyi 北方文藝
Beijing ribao 北京日報
Beijing wanbao 北京晚報

Beijing wenxue 北京文學
Beijing wenyi 北京文藝
Beijing zhi chun 北京之春
Bi Hua (Kee Fuk Wah) 璧華
（紀馥華）
Bian Zhilin 卞之琳
buteng 扑騰

Cai Kun 蔡焜
Cao Xueqin 曹雪芹
Cao Yu 曹禺
Cao Yumo 曹玉模
Cen Ying 岑螢
Cen Zhijing 岑之京
Chang Jiang 長江
Chen Canyun 陳殘雲
Chen Dunde 陳敦德
Chen Duxiu 陳獨秀
Chen Guokai 陳國凱
Chen Haiying 陳海鷹
Chen Huansheng 陳奐生
Chen Jingrun 陳景閏
Chen Kexiong 陳可雄
Chen Maiping 陳邁平
Chen Muhua 陳慕華
Chen Rong 諶容
Chen Shixu 陳世旭
Chen Suoju 陳所巨
Chen Wangdao 陳望道
Chen Youshi 陳幼石
Cheng Daixi 程代熙
chi butong zhengjian zhe
持不同政見者
Chong fang de xian hua
重放的鮮花
choulaojiu 臭老九
Chow Tse-tsung (Zhou Cezong)
周策縱

chuan men 穿門
Cihai 辭海
Cong Weixi 從維熙
Cui Dezhi 崔德志

Da Li 達理
Dagong bao 大公報
Dai Houying 戴厚英
Dai Wangshu 戴望舒
Dangdai 當代
Dazhong dianying
大眾電影
dazhonghua 大眾化
Dianying chuangzuo
電影創作
dididada 滴滴噠噠
Di'erci woshou 第二次握手
Ding Li 丁力
"Dixia baolei de fumie"
地下保壘的覆滅
Dong Chuncai 董純才
Dong Dingshan 董鼎山
Donghai 東海
Dongshan 東山
Dou E 竇娥
Du Fu 杜甫
Du Jian 杜漸
Du Pengcheng 杜鵬程
Du Yunxie 杜運燮
Dushu 讀書

E Hua 鄂華
ertong 兒童

fan'an 翻案
Fang cao 芳草
Fang Ji 方紀

Fang Xin 方苹
fangsong 放鬆
fante 反特
Fazhi yu renzhi wenti taolun ji 法治與人治問題討論集
Fei Sha 飛沙
feishu 飛書
Feng Deying 馮德英
Feng Menglong 馮夢龍
Fujian wenxue 福建文學
Fujian wenyi 福建文藝
"Fushi" 腐蝕

Gan Tiesheng 甘鐵生
ganyu shenghuo 干預生活
Gao Falin 高伐林
Gao Shan 高山
Gao Shenying 高慎盈
Gao Shiqi 高士其
Gao Xiaosheng 高曉聲
Gao Zhun 高準
Gaoyangshi bucaizi 高陽氏不才子
gaozhuang 告狀
Gong Liu 公劉
Gong Zhi 公質
gongan 公案
Gu Cheng 顧城
Gu Gong 顧工
Gu Junzheng 顧均正
Guan Gengyin 關庚寅
Guangdong wenyi 廣東文藝
Guangming ribao 光明日報
Guangxi wenyi 廣西文藝
Guangzhou ribao 廣州日報
Guangzhou wenyi 廣州文藝

guguai shi 古怪詩
Guilinshi Shifan "Yuwen Jiaoxue" Bianjishi 桂林市師範《語文教學》編輯室
Guo Moruo 郭沫若
Guo Xiaochuan 郭小川
Gushi hui 故事會

Haineiwai 海內外
Haiyun 海韻
Hao Ran 浩然
He Jingzhi 賀敬之
He Qifang 何其芳
He Xilai 何西來
He Zi 禾子
Hong yan 紅岩
Hongdou 紅豆
Hongqi 紅旗
Hu Qiaomu 胡喬木
Hu Shi 胡適
Hu Xieqing 胡絜青
Huacheng 花城
Huang Huoqing 黃火青
Huang Rui 黃銳
Huang Shang 黃裳
Huang Yongyu 黃永玉
huanxiang 幻想
Huaqi 花溪
"Hunan Gongan" Bianweihui 《湖南公安》編委會

Ji Ming 紀明
Ji Si 紀思
Ji Xiaowu 紀曉武
Jiang He 江河
Jiang Jingkuan 姜敬寬
Jiang Zilong 蔣子龍

Jianghu qixia zhuan 江湖奇俠傳

Jiangmen 江門

Jiao Qun 焦群

jiaoxin 交心

Jiefangjun wenyi 解放軍文藝

Jiekai shizong de mimi 揭開失踪的秘密

Jin Fan 靳凡

Jin Hai 金海

Jin He 金河

Jin Jingmai 金敬邁

Jing Fengliang 景奉亮

Jingu qiguan 今古奇觀

jingxian (-xiaoshuo) 驚險 (小説)

jinqu 禁區

Jintian 今天

Jintian Bianjibu 今天編輯部

Jintian Wenxue Yanjiuhui nei-bu cankao ziliao 今天文學研究會內部參考資料

Jiuming qiyuan 九命奇寃

Kaijuan 開卷

Kaiping 開平

Kang Baiqing 康白情

Kang Youwei 康有為

kexue gushi 科學故事

kexue huanxiang xiaoshuo 科學幻想小説

kexue puji (kepu) 科學普及 (科普)

kexue tonghua 科學童話

kexue wenyi 科學文藝

Kexue wenyi 科學文藝

Kexue Wenyi Weiyuanhui 科學文藝委員會

kexue xiaopin 科學小品

kexue xiaoshuo 科學小説

Kong Jiesheng 孔捷生

"Kongbu de jiaobusheng" 恐怖的脚步聲

kongxiang 空想

koutou wenxue 口頭文學

kuaiban shu 快板書

Lan Yangchun 藍陽春

Lao She 老舍

Lee, Leo Ou-fan (Li Oufan) 李歐梵

Li Binkui 李斌奎

Li Bo 李白

Li Boyuan 李伯元

Li Dong 李棟

Li Gang 李鋼

Li Huixin 李惠薪

Li Jian 李劍

Li Jinfa 李金髮

Li Kewei 李克威

Li Qingzhao 李清照

Li Ruqing 黎汝清

Li Shoucheng 李守成

"Li Shunda zaowu" 李順大造屋

Li Tuo 李陀

Li Weishi 李慰飩

Li Yan 李言

Li Yangui 李延桂

Li Yi (Lee Yee) 李怡

Li Ying 李瑛

Li Yinghao 李英豪

Li Yingru 李英儒

Li Yizhe 李一哲
Li Yuanluo 李元洛
Li Zaizhong 李在中
Li Zhaochun 李昭淳
Liang Bin 梁斌
Liang Heng 梁恆
Liang Jianhua 梁劍華
Liang Qichao 梁啟超
Liang Xiaobin 梁小斌
liao tian 聊天
Lin Shu 林紓
Lin Xiao 林嘯
Lin Yaochen 林耀琛
Lin Yutang 林語堂
Ling Bing 凌冰
Liu Bannong 劉半農
Liu Binyan 劉賓雁
Liu Dabai 劉大白
Liu Debin 劉德彬
Liu Fudao 劉富道
Liu Ke 劉克
Liu Liu 劉流
Liu Nianchun 劉念春
Liu Qing (democracy movement) 劉青
Liu Qing (*The Builders*) 柳青

Liu Xinwu 劉心武
Liu Zhanqiu 劉湛秋
Liu Zhaogui 劉肇貴
lixiang xiaoshuo 理想小説
Longtu gongan 龍圖公案
Lou Qi 樓栖
Louie, Kam (Lei Jinqing) 雷金慶
Lu Bing 魯兵
Lu ming 鹿鳴
Lu Wenfu 陸文夫

Lu Xinhua 盧新華
Lu Xun 魯迅
Lu Yanzhou 魯彥周
Lü Chen 呂辰
Luo Guangbin 羅廣斌
Luo Guanzhong 羅貫中
Luo Huajun 羅華俊
Luo Xin 羅辛

Ma Feng 馬烽
Ma Ming 馬鳴
Ma Shitu 馬識途
Mang Ke 芒克
Mao Dun 茅盾
Mei Shaojing 梅紹靜
Meng Weizai 孟偉哉
menglong (-shi) 朦朧(詩)
minban kanwu 民辦刊物
minjian kanwu 民間刊物
Minzhu yu fazhi 民主與法制

minzu xingshi 民族形式
minzuhua 民族化
Mo Lilin 莫里林

nei 內
Ni Ping 倪平

Pan Jie 潘捷
Pan Yuan 潘援
Pang Taixi 龐太熙
pingfan 平反
pingshu dian 評書點
Pu Songling 蒲松齡

Qi Baishi 齊白石

Qian Hai 錢海
Qian Yan 倩燕
Qiao Shi 峭石
qifa 啟發
qigong 氣功
Qin Zhaoyang 秦兆陽
qing 情
Qingchun 青春
qingnian 青年
Qingnian yidai 青年一代
Qingtian; Yang Qingtian
　清天；楊青添
Qishi niandai 七十年代
Qu Bo 曲波
Qu Yuan 屈原
quyi 曲藝

Rao Zhonghua 饒忠華
ren 人
Renmin ribao 人民日報
Renmin wenxue 人民文學
Ru Zhijuan 茹志鵑
Ruan Zhangjing 阮章競

Sanliwan 三里灣
Sanxia wuyi 三俠五義
Sha Yexin 沙葉新
Shandong kuaishu 山東快書

Shanghai wenxue 上海文學
"Shanghen" 傷痕
shanghen wenxue
　傷痕文學
Shao Hua 韶華
Shaonian kexue 少年科學
Shen Congwen 沈從文
Shen Ji 沈寂

Shen Zhiwei 沈志偉
Shenpan qian de jiaoliang
　審判前的較量
Shi Mo 石默
Shi Naian 施耐菴
Shi tansuo 詩探索
Shi Tongxue 師彤雪
Shijie wenxue 世界文學
Shikan 詩刊
Shiyue 十月
Shouhuo 收穫
Shu Ting 舒婷
Sichuan wenxue 四川文學
Sima Chunqiu 司馬春秋
Sima Qian 司馬遷
sixiangxing 思想性
Song Yuexun 宋日勳
Su Ce 蘇策
Su Dezhen 蘇德禎
Su Liwen 蘇立文
Su Ming 素明
Su Shi 蘇軾
Su Yunxiang 蘇雲翔
Sun Shaozhen 孫紹振

Taibai 太白
Tao Xingzhi 陶行知
Tay, William (Zheng Shusen)
　鄭樹森
Tian Jian 田間
Tian Ran 天然
Tong Enzheng 童恩正

wai 外
Waiguo wenxue yanjiu
　外國文學研究
waiwei 外圍

Waiwen Shudian 外文書店

Wan Zhi 萬之

Wang Chuan 王川

Wang Fuchu 王复初

Wang Hejun 王賀軍

Wang Jing 王靖

Wang Meng 王蒙

Wang Ruowang 王若望

Wang Shifu 王實甫

Wang Wei 王偉

Wang Wen-hsing (Wang Wen-xing) 王文興

Wang Wenjin 王文錦

Wang Xiaoda 王曉達

Wang Xiaoni 王小妮

Wang Yaping 王亞平

Wang Ye 王也

Wang Yungao 王雲高

Wang Zangge 王藏格

Wangfujing 王府井

Wanguo gongbao 萬國公報

Wei Jingsheng 魏京生

Wei Yahua 魏雅華

Weilai 未來

Weiminghu 未名湖

Wen Bianjing 温汴京

Wen Yiduo 聞一多

wenhuazhan 文化站

Wenhui bao 文滙報

Wenhui zengkan 文滙增刊

Wenxue bao 文學報

Wenxue pinglun congkan 文學評論叢刊

wenyan 文言

Wenyi bao 文藝報

Wenyi yanjiu 文藝研究

Wotu 沃土

Wu Cheng'en 吳承恩

Wu Jingzi 吳敬梓

Wu Lijun 吳力軍

Wu Qiang 吳強

Wu Woyao 吳沃堯

Wu Xuehe 武學和

Wumingshi 無名氏

Wuxiandian 無綫電

xian 縣

Xian'gang 蜆崗

xiangsheng 相聲

xiangtu 鄉土

Xiao Jianheng 蕭建亨

Xiao Jun 蕭軍

Xiao Qian 蕭乾

xiaoshuo 小說

Xiaoshuo congbao 小說叢報

Xiaoshuo daguan 小說大觀

Xiaoshuo shibao 小說時報

Xiaoshuo xuankan 小說選刊

Xiaoshuo yuebao 小說月報

Xidan 西單

Xie Mian 謝冕

Xie Yicheng 謝頤城

Xin'gang 新港

Xin wenyi 新文藝

Xing xing 星星

Xing Yixun 邢益勳

Xingshi zhencha anli xuanbian 刑事偵察案例選編

Xinhua Shudian 新華書店

Xinhui 新會

Xinyuepai 新月派

xixi suosuo 寋寋窣窣

Xiyingmen 喜盈門
Xu Chi 徐遲
Xu Huaizhong 徐懷中
Xu Jingya 徐敬亞
Xu Shaowu 徐紹武
Xu Xiao 徐曉
Xu Zhimo 徐志摩
xuetonglun 血統論

Yalu Jiang 鴨綠江
Yan Jiaqi 嚴家其
Yang Lian 楊煉
Yang Ling 楊零
Yang Mo 楊沫
Yang Rongfang 楊容方
Yang Shuo 楊朔
Yang Ximin 楊希閔
Yang Yiyan 楊益言
Yangcheng wanbao 羊城晚報
Yao Mingde 姚明德
Yao Xueyin 姚雪垠
Ye Wenfu 葉文福
Ye Yonglie 葉永烈
Yi Shu 伊恕
yinzhang 印張
Yip, Wai-lim (Ye Weilian) 葉維廉
Yiwen 譯文
"Yizhi xiuhua xie" 一隻繡花鞋
yong wu shi 詠物詩
Yongyu 咏喻
You Fengwei 尤鳳偉
You Meng 優孟
You Yi 尤異

Yu Chen 雨辰
Yu Dafu 郁達夫
Yu Guangzhong 余光中
Yu Luojin 遇羅錦
Yu Mei 雨煤
Yu Yimu 余易木
Yu Zhi 于止
Yuan Jing 袁靜
Yuan Kejia 袁可嘉
"Yugong" 愚公
Yuwen jiaoxue tongxun 語文教學通訊

Zang Kejia 臧克家
zawen 雜文
Zeng Zhennan 曾鎮南
Zhang Hanliang 張漢良
Zhang Jie 張潔
Zhang Kangkang 張抗抗
Zhang Ming 章明
Zhang Xian 張弦
Zhang Xuemeng 張學夢
Zhang Xutang 張煦棠
Zhang Yang 張揚
Zhang Yigong 張一弓
Zhanjiang wenyi 湛江文藝
Zhao Guoqing 趙國慶
Zhao Jingshen 趙景深
Zhao Shuli 趙樹理
Zhao Yulan 趙育嵐
Zhao Zhenkai 趙振開
Zheng Wenguang 鄭文光
zhentan xiaoshuo 偵探小說
Zheyidai 這一代
Zhi Xia 知俠
zhisha 咴嘎

zhishi qingnian 知識青年
Zhong Chengxiang 仲呈祥

Zhongbao yuekan
　　中報月刊
Zhongguo funü 中國婦女
Zhongguo Kexue Puji Xiehui
　　中國科學普及協會
Zhongguo qingnian
　　中國青年
Zhongguo qingnianbao
　　中國青年報
Zhongguo Shudian
　　中國書店
Zhongguo xin xieshizhuyi wen-
　　yi zuopin xuan 中國新寫實
　　主義文藝作品選
zhongpian 中篇

Zhongshan 中山
Zhongshan 鍾山
Zhou Erfu 周而復
Zhou Jianren 周建人
Zhou Liangpei 周良沛
Zhou Libo 周立波
Zhou Yang 周楊
Zhu Lin 竹林
Zhu Shucheng 朱樹誠
Zhu Ziqing 朱自清
Zhuang Zi 莊子
zhuti xian xing 主題先行
Zong Fuxian 宗福先
Zong Pu 宗璞
Zu Wei 祖慰
Zuopin 作品
Zuopin yu zhengming
　　作品與爭鳴

Harvard East Asian Monographs

1. Liang Fang-chung, *The Single-Whip Method of Taxation in China*
2. Harold C. Hinton, *The Grain Tribute System of China, 1845–1911*
3. Ellsworth C. Carlson, *The Kaiping Mines, 1877–1912*
4. Chao Kúo-chün, *Agrarian Policies of Mainland China: A Documentary Study, 1949–1956*
5. Edgar Snow, *Random Notes on Red China, 1936–1945*
6. Edwin George Beal, Jr., *The Origin of Likin, 1835–1864*
7. Chao Kuo-chün, *Economic Planning and Organization in Mainland China: A Documentary Study, 1949–1957*
8. John K. Fairbank, *Ch'ing Documents: An Introductory Syllabus*
9. Helen Yin and Yi-chang Yin, *Economic Statistics of Mainland China, 1949–1957*
10. Wolfgang Franke, *The Reform and Abolition of the Traditional Chinese Examination System*
11. Albert Feuerwerker and S. Cheng, *Chinese Communist Studies of Modern Chinese History*
12. C. John Stanley, *Late Ch'ing Finance: Hu Kuang-yung as an Innovator*
13. S. M. Meng, *The Tsungli Yamen: Its Organization and Functions*
14. Ssu-yü Teng, *Historiography of the Taiping Rebellion*
15. Chun-Jo Liu, *Controversies in Modern Chinese Intellectual History: An Analytic Bibliography of Periodical Articles, Mainly of the May Fourth and Post-May Fourth Era*
16. Edward J. M. Rhoads, *The Chinese Red Army, 1927–1963: An Annotated Bibliography*
17. Andrew J. Nathan, *A History of the China International Famine Relief Commission*
18. Frank H. H. King (ed.) and Prescott Clarke, *A Research Guide to China-Coast Newspapers, 1822–1911*
19. Ellis Joffe, *Party and Army: Professionalism and Political Control in the Chinese Officer Corps, 1949–1964*
20. Toshio G. Tsukahira, *Feudal Control in Tokugawa Japan: The Sankin Kōtai System*

46. W. P. J. Hall, *A Bibliographical Guide to Japanese Research on the Chinese Economy, 1958-1970*

47. Jack J. Gerson, *Horatio Nelson Lay and Sino-British Relations, 1854-1864*

48. Paul Richard Bohr, *Famine and the Missionary: Timothy Richard as Relief Administrator and Advocate of National Reform*

49. Endymion Wilkinson, *The History of Imperial China: A Research Guide*

50. Britten Dean, *China and Great Britain: The Diplomacy of Commerical Relations, 1860-1864*

51. Ellsworth C. Carlson, *The Foochow Missionaries, 1847-1880*

52. Yeh-chien Wang, *An Estimate of the Land-Tax Collection in China, 1753 and 1908*

53. Richard M. Pfeffer, *Understanding Business Contracts in China, 1949-1963*

54. Han-sheng Chuan and Richard Kraus, *Mid-Ch'ing Rice Markets and Trade, An Essay in Price History*

55. Ranbir Vohra, *Lao She and the Chinese Revolution*

56. Liang-lin Hsiao, *China's Foreign Trade Statistics, 1864-1949*

57. Lee-hsia Hsu Ting, *Government Control of the Press in Modern China, 1900-1949*

58. Edward W. Wagner, *The Literati Purges: Political Conflict in Early Yi Korea*

59. Joungwon A. Kim, *Divided Korea: The Politics of Development, 1945-1972*

60. Noriko Kamachi, John K. Fairbank, and Chūzō Ichiko, *Japanese Studies of Modern China Since 1953: A Bibliographical Guide to Historical and Social-Science Research on the Nineteenth and Twentieth Centuries, Supplementary Volume for 1953-1969*

61. Donald A. Gibbs and Yun-chen Li, *A Bibliography of Studies and Translations of Modern Chinese Literature, 1918-1942*

62. Robert H. Silin, *Leadership and Values: The Organization of Large-Scale Taiwanese Enterprises*

63. David Pong, *A Critical Guide to the Kwangtung Provincial Archives Deposited at the Public Record Office of London*

64. Fred W. Drake, *China Charts the World: Hsu Chi-yü and His Geography of 1848*

65. William A. Brown and Urgunge Onon, translators and annotators, *History of the Mongolian People's Republic*

66. Edward L. Farmer, *Early Ming Government: The Evolution of Dual Capitals*

67. Ralph C. Croizier, *Koxinga and Chinese Nationalism: History, Myth, and the Hero*

68. William J. Tyler, tr., *The Psychological World of Natsumi Sōseki*, by Doi Takeo

90. Noel F. McGinn, Donald R. Snodgrass, Yung Bong Kim, Shin-Bok Kim, and Quee-Young Kim, *Education and Development in Korea*

91. Leroy P. Jones and Il SaKong, *Government, Business and Entrepreneurship in Economic Development: The Korean Case*

92. Edward S. Mason, Dwight H. Perkins, Kwang Suk Kim, David C. Cole, Mahn Je Kim, et al., *The Economic and Social Modernization of the Republic of Korea*

93. Robert Repetto, Tai Hwan Kwon, Son-Ung Kim, Dae Young Kim, John E. Sloboda, and Peter J. Donaldson, *Economic Development, Population Policy, and Demographic Transition in the Republic of Korea*

106. David C. Cole and Yung Chul Park, *Financial Development in Korea, 1945-1978*

94. Parks M. Coble, *The Shanghai Capitalists and the Nationalist Government, 1927-1937*

95. Noriko Kamachi, *Reform in China: Huang Tsun-hsien and the Japanese Model*

96. Richard Wich, *Sino-Soviet Crisis Politics: A Study of Political Change and Communication*

97. Lillian M. Li, *China's Silk Trade: Traditional Industry in the Modern World, 1842-1937*

98. R. David Arkush, *Fei Xiaotong and Sociology in Revolutionary China*

99. Kenneth Alan Grossberg, *Japan's Renaissance: The Politics of the Muromachi Bakufu*

100. James Reeve Pusey, *China and Charles Darwin*

101. Hoyt Cleveland Tillman, *Utilitarian Confucianism: Ch'en Liang's Challenge to Chu Hsi*

102. Thomas A. Stanley, *Ōsugi Sakae, Anarchist in Taishō Japan: The Creativity of the Ego*

103. Jonathan K. Ocko, *Bureaucratic Reform in Provincial China: Ting Jih-ch'ang in Restoration Kiangsu, 1867-1870*

104. James Reed, *The Missionary Mind and American East Asia Policy, 1911-1915*

105. Neil L. Waters, *Japan's Local Pragmatists: The Transition from Bakumatsu to Meiji in the Kawasaki Region*

108. William D. Wray, *Mitsubishi and the N.Y.K., 1870-1914: Business Strategy in the Japanese Shipping Industry*

109. Ralph William Huenemann, *The Dragon and the Iron Horse: The Economics of Railroads in China, 1876-1937*

110. Benjamin A. Elman, *From Philosophy to Philology: Intellectual and Social Aspects of Change in Late Imperial China*

7 880